Glenn Miller
and His Orchestra

BY GEORGE T. SIMON

THOMAS Y. CROWELL COMPANY

NEW YORK ❧ ESTABLISHED 1834

Copyright © 1974 by Bigbee Productions, Inc.

Designed by Ingrid Beckman

Manufactured in the United States of America

Library of Congress Cataloging in Publication Data

Simon, George Thomas.
    Glenn Miller and his orchestra.

    1. Miller, Glenn.   I. Title.
ML 422.M44S57   785'.092'4 [B]   74-1017
ISBN 0-690-00470-2

1 2 3 4 5 6 7 8 9 10

To Polly Davis Haynes, so deeply loved and admired and respected by all of us who had anything to do with Glenn Miller and his Orchestra, this book is dedicated with abiding affection and appreciation.

Other Books by the Author:

FOREWORD

As the years go by, I'm increasingly grateful that I was a tiny part of the era of the great swing bands. This was the golden age of popular music for me. Not that I contributed anything. I was a listener, a follower, and had been since the days of Isham Jones, Paul Whiteman, Ray Miller and so many others—the days that really preceded the golden age and set the stage for the swing bands to come on with a great surge: Goodman, Herman, the Dorseys, Casa Loma, Artie Shaw, with Glenn Miller in the van.

They were all great, but I have to think the Glenn Miller band was the greatest. Unlike so many of the others, Glenn was not a virtuoso instrumental soloist. And so instead of his horn he did it with great personnel and innovative harmonic experiments producing a sound that was his, and his alone.

I don't suppose there was a single listener in the United States, unless he was tin-eared and tone-deaf, who didn't love and appreciate the music of the Miller band.

You know, it always seemed to me that the musicians and the leaders in those days were a breed apart. Their dialogue was unique, and they spoke in an argot that was unintelligible to the uninitiated, and peculiarly indigenous to the cult.

I really believe the greater part of them were not so much concerned with how much money they earned, or what measure of fame they achieved—although that was a consideration—as they were with the approval, appreciation and esteem of their peers.

They decried and derided any music that was corny or unimaginative. "Commercial" they called it.

They eschewed the route of "note for note," and "play it as it reads." They believed that every piece of popular music was fully susceptible to development and enhancement.

Glenn employed a harmonization that was new and vastly different. If I even attempted a description of what he did, I would be immediately adrift. I think it was the way he voiced his instruments—it was just beautiful. And when you heard the sound, it was recognizable and memorable. It was just Glenn Miller.

And Glenn, as a person, was just as memorable. He was a very good personal friend, from the early days on, ever since he performed on some of the records that I made with the Dorsey Brothers Orchestra during the early stages of my career. During World War II, we were united for the last time—when I sang in London with his great AAF Orchestra.

About the best thing I can remember about Glenn, personally, was his innate taste and class. He loved good things—musically and in his personal life.

Although he came from Colorado, I believe his taste in clothes and life-style was definitely Ivy League. A most attractive man, and, of course, tremendously gifted.

I have no doubt, had he lived, he would have been a tremendous force in the popular music in the years to come—not that he wasn't already.

It is so unfortunate that he isn't still with us here today. But we do have George Simon's book, which tells, as only a man who knew him well can tell, of the man himself. It should be the definitive work on Glenn Miller and his times.

—*Bing Crosby*

INTRODUCTION

I met Glenn Miller for the first time a couple of years before he
organized what was to become the most popular band the world
has ever heard. My initial reaction—that he was an honest,
sensitive, strong-willed, straight-ahead sort of guy—turned out to
be correct. I also figured him for a pretty uncomplex gent. I
couldn't have been more wrong.

We soon became friends, and remained friends throughout his
career. At its height, he even asked me to write his biography, an
invitation I didn't accept at the time, even though I liked and
admired Glenn very much. As I look back, I realize there may
have even been an element of worship in my admiration. Later, I
also learned to resent him.

As I got to know him better, I began to recognize that he was
not only dynamic and dogmatic but also difficult to understand.
His world of all blacks and all whites, but few grays, was encased
in an exasperatingly brittle and hard shell. Though always
deeply dedicated to the public's understanding and appreciation
of his music, he allowed only a few privileged friends the
opportunity to understand and appreciate the man who had
created it.

For some years I remained one of those privileged few. I was
convinced then that I knew quite well just what sort of a man he
really was. But that was before I began my research on this book.
Now, benefitted by many, many months of digging and inter-

viewing, plus thirty years of hindsight, I realize that the Glenn Miller I thought I knew so well was only a part of a very much more complex man whom I now wish I could get to know all over again. And I've learned something else too: No man *truly* is what just one man *thinks* he is.

In my research I interviewed about half a hundred people— his musicians, singers, arrangers, managers and relatives—some close friends of his and mine who had played important roles in his life and career. All agreed that he had made a major contribution to the popular music of his day and that his band, created and magnificently administered by Glenn himself, had emerged as an important style-setter. But there was nothing remotely approaching such unanimity when it came to evaluating Glenn as a person.

Sure, most agreed he was a taskmaster. He was reserved, stubborn, wise and honest. He developed a razor-sharp sense of commercialism. And he wielded it constantly.

But while some faulted him for his emphasis on commercialism, others admired him for his dedication of purpose.

While some deplored an intensity that often spilled over into intolerance, others applauded his cool efficiency and devotion to discipline.

And while some were convinced that he was nothing but a cold fish, the few who knew him well discovered that he could turn into a warm bear.

In my various interviews, I found that those who had pierced that tough emotional hide (maybe I should say "those whom he allowed to pierce that tough emotional hide") reacted most tolerantly to both his good and bad points. For, it seems to me, they were able to put him into broader perspective and to evaluate him and his motives and accomplishments—and they were many, indeed!—as friends who cared as much about him as they did about what he was doing and how he affected their lives. And as the pages that follow reveal, he and his music most certainly did affect very seriously the lives, the careers and the emotions of so many people in so many different ways and in so many different places.

To all those people who, through sharing their observations and feelings with me, helped to establish this broad delineation of Glenn, I offer my deepest thanks. And I thank them, too, for supplying me with so much factual data about the people and situations affecting not only Glenn but also the many others who played such important roles in making his the most popular of all the orchestras of the big-band era. For this book concerns not merely Glenn but also each of those people, or as the billing always read, "Glenn Miller and his Orchestra."

And so I thank Polly Davis Haynes, that wonderfully warm lady who was Glenn's trusted office manager, his wife's dearest friend, and herself married to his personal manager, and who helped me so much in gathering material for this book, constantly encouraging me and even helping in its editing.

And I also thank another of Glenn's cherished compatriots, David Mackay, his close friend and lawyer and now executor of his estate, who tendered me all sorts of cooperation, including complete access to Glenn's personal files, and whose thoughtfulness and faith in me and my project were so valuable and appreciated.

Of course there were the band members—many of them from both his civilian and AAF outfits—who supplied me with words and in many instances with photos: Jimmy Abato, Trigger Alpert, Stanley Aronson, Tex Beneke, Rolly Bundock, Johnny Desmond, Ray Eberle, Bill Finegan, Chuck Goldstein, Jerry Gray, Bobby Hackett, Marion Hutton, Frank Ippolito (especially for those photos he took), Jerry Jerome, Al Klink, Carmen Mastren, Billy May, Ray McKinley, Mickey McMickle, Johnny O'Leary, Jimmy Priddy, Bernie Privin, Moe Purtill, Willie Schwartz, Paul Tanner, Zeke Zarchy.

Then there were those who had worked with Glenn even before he had his own band: the Grand Groaner, Bing Crosby, who has enriched this book with his warm and personalized foreword, plus Smith Ballew, Will Bradley, Benny Goodman, Skeets Herfurt, Roc Hillman, Harry James, Julius Kingdom, Ted Mack, Jimmy McPartland, Gil Rodin, Milt Yaner and the late Gene Krupa and Red Nichols. And those non-musicians later associated with him: Larry Bruff, Bullets Durgom, Cecil Madden, Mike Nidorf, Howie Richmond, Tom Sheils, Joe Shribman, George Voutsas and the late Don Haynes.

Also, I am indebted to those Glenn Miller enthusiasts who cooperated so magnificently, especially Al Timpson with his seemingly endless supply of photos, documents and good cheer; Ed Polic, another splendid source of pictures and encouragement; Warren Reid, who also forwarded a great deal of historical data; and John Flower, whose book, *Moonlight Serenade* (Arlington House), fortified me with so many names, dates and places, and who graciously loaned me many photos from his collection. And on the subject of photos, thanks also to Bob Asen and Milt Lichtenstein for opening their *Metronome* files to me, and to Chuck Suber of *Down Beat* for his contributions. More thanks to radio station WTIC's Arnold Dean and WHO's Ford Roberts, who forwarded tapes of interviews with Miller band members, and WALK's Jack Ellsworth, who sent some photos. And, of course, to Douglas LeVicki and Roland Taylor of the Glenn Miller Society, who directed and escorted me so graciously during my research in England, and Fred Woodruff, the society's Los Angeles–based representative.

For editorial assistance and encouragement, the bow of bows to my eternally empathetic editor, Nicholas Ellison. Thanks also to my noble agents, Marcia Higgins and Don Gold, and to Amy Litt, who caught all my grammatical goofs. And my continuing appreciation to my good friend and literary godfather, Neil McCaffrey, responsible for my two previous books, *The Big Bands* (Macmillan) and *Simon Says: The Sights and Sounds of the Swing Era* (Arlington House), who kept encouraging me all through the writing of this book. And, of course, all sorts of appreciation and newfound admiration to my dear wife, Beverly, who, in addition to her womanly and other warm qualities, turned out to be one helluva interpretive typist.

Finally I should like to extend my deep appreciation to Glenn's relatives—to his sister, Mrs. Irene Miller Wolfe, who told me much about Glenn's early family life and who sent me some rare photos; and to his two children, Steve and Jonnie, with whom I recently spent some delightful hours in their home territory of California. My conversations with them proved to be especially touching. Neither remembered their father—Jonnie had never even seen him—but both were terribly eager to hear all I could tell them about him. How ironic, I thought, that all the others I had interviewed had tried to tell *me* all that *they* knew about Glenn. And now here were the two living people who should have been closest to him and who should have known him best, asking me, "What was he like?"

It was the same question that countless strangers through the years have always been putting to me: "What Was Glenn Miller Really Like?" Before I began writing this book, I would answer with flippant certainty. But now that I have become so immersed in so many aspects of his life, as seen through the eyes and ears and minds and hearts of so many who were so close to him, I realize that not until now am I beginning to comprehend what Glenn Miller was *really* like, what really made him do all the many things—some predictable, others totally not so—that made him such a unique individual: every bit as unique and as beautiful and as volatile and complex as his music itself.

Hopefully, with the help of all those who have contributed to this book, you, too, can decide for yourself, dear reader, what Glenn Miller was really like.

—GEORGE T. SIMON
January 1974

CONTENTS

PART ONE

The Early Years

Chapter 1

Late one cold and wet evening in an attic room of an old house in Bedford, England, fifty miles north of London, Major Glenn Miller was visiting with two of his bandsmen, arranger Jerry Gray and bassist Trigger Alpert. They had been talking about the old days, about Glenn's civilian band, in which these two sergeants had played such important roles. And they were talking about the new days—the "now" days, in which they were playing for the Allied troops in England, and the "to-come" days, when the band would fly over to the Continent and entertain the troops there and then return to America, where Glenn would settle on his West Coast ranch and the band would work hard for six months out of the year and relax for the other six and everybody would make plenty of money and be very happy.

"Glenn liked to drop up to visit us," recalls Alpert, who had always been one of Miller's favorites and for whom Glenn once had "traded" ten soldiers in order to get his civilian bassist back with him. "Maybe it was because he felt at home with us. Anyway, there was none of that G.I. crap. I remember one time when he and David Niven—I think he was a colonel—came by. He'd heard that Jerry had cooked an Italian dinner from some stuff his mother had sent over from the States and he asked, 'How come you didn't invite me?' He said it sort of half-kidding, but I had a feeling he really kind of meant it. He was a pretty homesick guy over there."

Gray also remembers that night very well—when a restless Miller dropped by and asked Jerry if he'd like to fly over with him to Paris on the next day to get everything ready for the rest of the band. "I can still see him, sitting there on the floor, and me lying on the bed. I had a cold and I felt lousy, and so I said, 'No, Glenn, I think I'll go later with the rest of the boys.' Soon after that he got up and left. I can remember him walking down the stairs from the little attic room—and that's the last I ever saw of him."

Major Miller returned later that evening to the Mount Royal Hotel in London, where he was billeted, and where he often met with his executive officer, Lieutenant Don Haynes, a handsome man who looked like a movie star of the thirties, and who had been Glenn's personal manager during their civilian careers. They, too, talked about the future—more specifically about the immediate plans for moving the sixty-two-soldier aggregation to Paris and about who was going to do what. Originally, Haynes had been slated to fly to Paris ahead of the group to find accommodations for the men. But Glenn had been growing so impatient, what with army red tape constantly postponing the move, that he finally told Haynes that he himself would fly over and make the arrangements and Don could come over with the band a few days later.

Wednesday, December 13, 1944, was the day Glenn was supposed to fly to Paris. But the weather was atrocious: rainy, foggy and cold. The shuttle plane, which Glenn would have taken, was grounded. So Glenn waited impatiently around the hotel, and Haynes drove off to Bedford to help the band prepare for its move.

The weather on Thursday, December 14, was just as bad. Glenn remained grounded in London. Nobody was flying. In Bedford, Haynes had lunch with an easygoing, devil-may-care-type fellow-officer, Colonel Norman Baesell, who invited Don to fly with him to Paris, where he was reportedly going, among other reasons, to refill a batch of empty champagne bottles. Haynes told Baesell about the change in plans: that Glenn, not he, was to go. So they phoned Glenn, who welcomed the opportunity, and Haynes drove into London, picked him up, and drove him back to Bedford, where they kept on waiting and waiting for the weather to clear.

On the next day, Friday, December 15, 1944, the weather was still miserable. Again no planes were taking off, and Glenn was growing increasingly restless. He dropped by the band's barracks and talked with his good friend, First Sergeant Reuben "Zeke" Zarchy, another civilian-band alumnus. Suddenly word came through that the trip was on, even though it was still raining and the fog hadn't lifted. "It was typical English weather," reports Zarchy. "They had a saying over there: 'We had a lovely summer this year. Fell on a Wednesday, I believe.' "

Zeke remembers walking Glenn, Colonel Baesell and Haynes in the dreary drizzle out to the jeep that was to take them to the plane. "Glenn called out, 'See you over there, Zeke!' and he drove off into the mist."

The plane was a single-engine, nine-seater C-64 Norseman. Its pilot, Flight Officer Johnny Morgan, had completed his missions and was considered to be an exceptionally able flyer. He had made the same flight many times. There were no German planes in the area and no enemy guns within two hundred miles. What's more, no radio communication was permitted on that day because the Battle of the Bulge was about to begin.

But there was one troublesome factor. The plane had no de-icing equipment. The weather remained not merely wet but also foggy and cold, with temperatures near freezing. Under these conditions, the lightly equipped plane could not fly *above* the weather, where it was too cold, nor could it fly *in* the weather, where the pilot couldn't see. Therefore, if it were to fly at all on this miserable afternoon, it would be forced to fly *below* the weather, close to the English Channel's choppy surface. And this plane was not designed to float!

As Glenn entered the small craft, Haynes called to him, "See you in Paris tomorrow. Happy landing and good luck."

"Thanks, Haynsie, we may need it," Miller called back. Then he looked around the plane. "Hey," he yelled to Baesell, "where the hell are the parachutes?"

"What's the matter, Miller?" retorted the gung-ho, extroverted colonel to the obviously apprehensive major. "Do you want to live forever?"

Those may have been the last words that Major Glenn Miller ever heard.

Chapter 2

The first words I ever heard Glenn Miller utter were:

> "Annie's cousin Fanny is a sweetie of mine,
> She sits and waits at home for me all the time.
> You may know some girls named Annie that are divine,
> But you've never seen a fanny half as pretty as mine."

The place: Nuttings-on-the-Charles, a ballroom in Waltham, Massachusetts. The time: May 1934. The occasion: a one-nighter by the newly organized Dorsey Brothers Orchestra.

Several of us in my thoroughly mediocre Harvard dance band had been thrilled that night by the Dorseys' thoroughly magnificent outfit. Its musicianship was scary, it was so good. It swung as no other band I had ever heard in person. Tommy on trombone and Jimmy on sax and clarinet and Ray McKinley on drums, especially, knocked me clean out. The musicians played with tremendous assurance and professionalism, plus an enthusiasm that permeated even novelties like Glenn's own song, "Annie's Cousin Fanny," climaxed by this serious, schoolteacher-ish-looking trombone player, with the glasses and the big square jaw and the head that somehow seemed too big even for a six-foot-tall body, lumbering down front and, in a nasal, midwestern twang, half talking and half singing those lines about his F(f)anny, followed by an awkward burlesque dancer's bump, a laugh from the dancers who had gathered around the

bandstand, and then Glenn Miller's embarrassed return to his seat in the trombone section.

About a year later I heard two more surprising words come out of that same unsmiling and proper-looking face. They were "Wilbur Schwitchenberg."

This time the setting was much more glamorous: just outside the ultra-swank Rainbow Room, high atop Rockefeller Center in New York, where Glenn was playing trombone and arranging for Ray Noble's band. I'd gone up there, no longer a Harvard undergraduate more interested in his band getting a good beat than in getting an "A" in his ill-chosen field of economics, but now a young dance-band critic, writing for *Metronome*, the country's top popular music magazine, at $25 a month.

The "Wilbur Schwitchenberg" had glumped out when I'd asked Glenn who his favorite trombonist was. I'd expected to hear something like "Tommy Dorsey" or "Jack Teagarden" or "Jack Jenney" or some other trombone great about whom I'd heard. But no, out came this unfamiliar portion of alphabet soup with the explanation that Schwitchenberg, who sat next to Glenn in the Noble band, "can do more things better than any trombone player I've ever heard." Later, as Wilbur became better known, many musicians began to agree with Glenn. Later, too, many musicians found it easier to pronounce and spell his name—after he had changed it to Will Bradley and begun leading one of the best of the swing bands.

The Noble band was the second to which I'd given a straight

The Dorsey Brothers Band: (back row) pianist Bobby Van Eps, bassist Delmar Kaplan, Tommy Dorsey, vocalist Kay Weber, Jimmy Dorsey, Glenn Miller, saxist Jack Stacey; (front row) trumpeter George Thow, guitarist Roc Hillman, trombonist Don Matteson, saxophonist Skeets Herfurt, drummer Ray McKinley.

"A" rating. It had been organized by Glenn for Ray, an Englishman who had been having troubles with the American Federation of Musicians and who welcomed Miller's assistance. The first "A" had gone to Benny Goodman's brand-new band after I'd heard it during its first steady job, a two-weeker at the Roosevelt Grill, where Guy Lombardo usually held forth. In that review I'd made a point of how well the band suited the room, not knowing that on opening night the hotel manager had given it its two weeks' closing notice because he felt his customers wouldn't accept all those loud, brazen, swinging sounds!

Glenn with Ray Noble (center) and Will Bradley (Wilbur Schwitchenberg).

Apparently I was slightly ahead of the times, because it did take a few more months for Swing and Benny Goodman to catch on with the public. Nearby, at the Glen Island Casino in New Rochelle, the Dorseys with their swing band were also trying to attract the kids. But they were having their troubles, too. About the same time that Miller was saying "Wilbur Schwitchenberg," Tommy was yelling "You can take your band and shove it!" at brother Jimmy, as he strode off the bandstand and out of their band.

And the Originals—Duke Ellington, Fletcher Henderson and Jimmie Lunceford—who had created the styles on which others would cash in, were having their troubles because the white world wasn't ready to accept them and let them play the choice spots and receive the same sort of money that the successful sweet bands, like Paul Whiteman, Guy Lombardo and Hal Kemp, were getting.

Then in August it suddenly happened. Nobody has ever been able to explain exactly how and why it did. A Depression-weary world? Kids looking for new kicks? Who really knows. But, for some reason, the dancers at the Palomar Ballroom in Hollywood latched on to the Goodman band as soon as it blew its first notes there. And soon their enthusiasm, plus that of the band's music, inundated homes across the land that tuned in those Goodman broadcasts. A few months later, Tommy Dorsey came up with another band. Artie Shaw and Bunny Berigan and others who, like Goodman and Dorsey and Miller, had been working in radio studios started theirs. And for the next few years, the Swing Race was on.

The black bands began to be recognized: Duke, Fletcher, Jimmie, and up in Harlem's Savoy Ballroom, little Chick Webb with his slim, seventeen-year-old singing discovery, Ella Fitzgerald; and out of Kansas City, Count Basie and his light, supple Swing band. Big bands of all kinds—Paul Whiteman, Guy Lombardo, Glen Gray, Hal Kemp, Kay Kyser, Bob Crosby, Charlie Barnet, Larry Clinton, and many more—began to compete in the emerging big-band sweepstakes, which soon developed into epidemic proportions. Some of the sounds were glorious and lasted for years. Others stank to high heaven and faded away.

Month by month the competition grew. And so did the opportunities. Hotels, ballrooms, and soon theaters opened their doors to the swing bands and their growing hordes of followers, and to the already existing sweet bands that got caught up in the big-band boom. Colleges vied for the best bands for their proms. The radio networks—CBS, Mutual, and NBC's two networks, the Red and the Blue—fought for the rights to broadcast from spots where the bands were playing. And, recognizing their appeal, the cigarette companies—Camel, Chesterfield, Lucky Strike, Old Gold, Philip Morris and Raleigh—competed to sign the top bands for their commercial radio shows, while the three big record companies of the era—Columbia, Decca and Victor—tried to ink the best to long-time contracts.

It was big business. By August 1939, *Variety*, the weekly journal of show business, pointed to dance bands as "one of the most profitable, active and bullish branches of the amusement industry . . . a $90,000,000-to-$100,000,000-a-year business." It noted that bands were employing 30,000 to 40,000 musicians and auxiliary entertainers a year, plus another 8,000 connected with

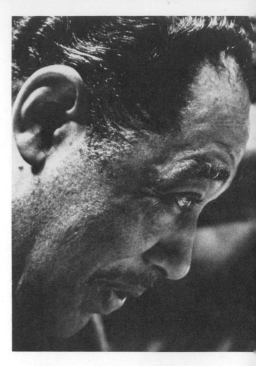

UPPER LEFT: Jimmy and Tommy Dorsey.

UPPER RIGHT: Duke Ellington.

LOWER LEFT: Benny Goodman.

LOWER RIGHT: Paul Whiteman.

UPPER LEFT: Harry James and Frank Sinatra.
BELOW: Kay Kyser.

UPPER RIGHT: Gene Krupa.

the commercial aspects of booking, managing, promoting and transporting the bands.

Though some of the middle-aged public turned out for their older favorites like Guy Lombardo, Paul Whiteman and Ben Bernie, it was the zealous support of the younger generation that established the overall trend and individual popularities among the newer, swingier outfits. Everywhere the bands played, the kids followed. In ballrooms and hotel rooms they'd line up dozens deep in front of bandstands, sometimes dancing but mostly listening and cheering and yelling when their favorites would let loose with a swinging solo. The same sort of responses greeted musicians in theaters, in front of which the kids would line up for hours to make sure of getting choice seats.

Those kids soon developed hero-worshipping relationships with the leaders, the musicians and the sidemen. Like football and baseball fans, they knew who played for whom: that Gene Krupa was Goodman's drummer, Bunny Berigan was Tommy Dorsey's trumpeter, Johnny Hodges was Ellington's alto saxist, Tony Pastor was Shaw's singing saxist, and on and on, often right down to sidemen who never even soloed but whose names they knew as if they'd been printed on scorecards.

Of all those fans, I was the luckiest, because, first as an eager young reporter and eventually as an enthusiastic, slightly older editor-in-chief, I could and did live with the music and its musicians, day and night, loving and cherishing every hour and every minute of that life—and what's more, being paid for it!

During those years I naturally grew close to many of the people who were creating those marvelous sounds. To me they were a fascinating set of individuals: the moody, hard-to-know, introspective, yet sometimes immensely warm Benny Goodman; the volatile, ex⸱⸱able, mercurial, wild and witty Tommy Dorsey, and his broth⸱⸱ Jimmy, less wild but equally witty ⸱⸱ 1 more relaxed and too often self-deprecating. Then there were the extremely intense, very bright, garrulous and self-centered Artie Shaw, and the charming, urbane, self-assured, often fantasizing Duke Ellington. Count Basie and Woody Herman in many ways were alike: relaxed, receptive and exceptionally considerate of those around them. Guy Lombardo and Sammy Kaye weren't dissimilar either; both were dollar-conscious, businesslike, precise and, when it came to swing critics, very thin-skinned. And then there were the eager, direct Gene Krupa; the enthusiastic, baseball-loving Harry James; the wonderfully foggy and always friendly Claude Thornhill, an almost painfully honest man; Stan Kenton, probing, nervous, driving and intensely dedicated to his music and his musicians; and Charlie Barnet, that handsome, independent, balling character who seemed to have more fun than anybody.

And there were the singers too: shy Ella Fitzgerald, ethereal Peggy Lee, cocky Frank Sinatra, self-conscious Dick Haymes, tomboy Doris Day, warmhearted Bob Eberly. And there were so many more—sidemen and arrangers, as well as leaders and singers—who, because of my unique position in their field, I was able to know and often to respect and admire.

But the man I thought I knew best and respected and admired the most in those days was Glenn Miller. I spent a great deal of time with him when he was organizing his band and during its early, struggling period, and I was able to observe at close range how directly and firmly and honestly he acted and reacted toward people and situations, and how consistently he adhered to a strict code of ethics that he applied as much to himself as he did to others.

He seemed, more than any other band leader I'd ever known, to know exactly what he wanted and how to go about getting it. In a totally unconceited way, he exuded self-confidence. He talked softly, firmly and forcefully. He would listen patiently to those he respected, but he was exceedingly strong-willed and sometimes exasperatingly stubborn. Like the exceptional executive that he was, he would make decisions quickly and surely, and he would stick by them. In his professional dealings, and even in some of his personal relationships, he would almost always treat businessmen, musicians and fans in the same way—politely, but curtly and dispassionately.

He was not a tolerant man. There were few grays in his life; there were almost all blacks or whites. But he was willing to stand up for and take full responsibilities for his quick decisions, and he was, it always seemed to me, painstakingly honest.

In many ways, he was the Vince Lombardi of the band leaders—cool, calculating, self-assured and immensely successful. In its comparatively short history, his band broke all sorts of attendance records in theaters, hotel rooms and ballrooms. It captured just about every major popularity poll. Its dozens of hit recordings included the first one-million seller since the mid-twenties. It was starred in two eminently successful movies and held onto the same coast-to-coast radio commercial from the beginning of its popularity until late in 1942, when it disbanded so that Glenn could organize an even greater orchestra in the armed services. In just a few years he had emerged as the most popular band leader of his age and perhaps of all ages. As Dave Garroway once noted, his theme song, "Moonlight Serenade," became America's second national anthem.

As he grew more and more successful, those closest to him noticed an apparent shift in emphasis of values. Once seemingly totally dedicated to music, he later began to waver and to expend as much energy on running his band's business as on making its music. This change hit me forcibly when, at the height of his career, he asked me if I'd like to write his success story. Still as idealistic as he once had been, I immediately thought how great it would be to tell the world about this man who wouldn't compromise his music and who insisted upon living up to his artistic and moral standards. But that wasn't his approach at all. He had some sort of title already in mind—something like *My Band Made Me $756,750 Richer!* or some such figure. We never did get together then.

Perhaps, had I known then what I have since learned about Glenn Miller, about the hardships in his early life, about his puritanical upbringing and its super-emphasis upon success, I might have reacted more sympathetically. And I was to learn later that even though he seemed to exude confidence, he was a man who harbored some serious doubts about himself, doubts that gnawed at him throughout his life.

David Mackay, his long-time business associate and leader, in a recent discussion of Glenn's supposed inner security, noted that "Glenn was a man who had to prove himself, a man who didn't know how long his fame and fortune would last, and who was going to get it while the getting was good."

And Benny Goodman, a close friend for many, many years, after extolling Glenn's honesty and courage and straight-forwardness, began wondering about "his supposed self-confidence. When you get right down to it and analyzing it, what did he really have to make himself sure of himself? He was a pedestrian trombone player and he knew it. He was never that sure of himself. As long as I knew him, from back in the days in the twenties when we were with the Ben Pollack band, Glenn was always concerned about what he was going to be. And you know one thing? I was just as surprised by Glenn's success as he was!"

Chapter 3

"I couldn't stand the name Alton. I can still hear my mother calling for me across the field: 'Al-ton'—it was never 'Awlton,' but 'Al-ton,' with a real short *a*. 'Alton!' she would call, 'Alton, come on home!' I just hated the sound of that name. That's why I've always used 'Glenn' instead."

That's how Alton Glenn Miller, born on March 1, 1904, at 601 South 16th Street in Clarinda, a very small town tucked in the southwest corner of Iowa, would explain why the country's number one band was not Alton Miller's. Apparently young Alton's parents were conservatives, because they named their second son (a girl and another boy were to follow) in honor of Alton B. Parker, who lost to Teddy Roosevelt in the 1904 election.

Probably Glenn's mother picked "Alton"; she made most of the family decisions. Her husband, Lewis Elmer Miller, was a kind but ineffectual man. He worked hard, though never very successfully, as a carpenter, as a school janitor, as a railroad-bridge foreman, and even as a homesteader. According to his daughter, Irene, "There was something in his personality that kept him from putting it all together. Glenn considered Dad a brilliant man who could have done very well if he could just have believed in himself more. Instead he always felt that someone had it in for him, or that someone else was out to get his job."

And so it usually remained for small, energetic, proud, stubborn

Mattie Lou Miller (née Cavender), who looked very much like a Grant Wood painting, to run the show at home.

When Glenn was five years old, the family moved to Tryon, Nebraska (a recent census listed the total population as 198), and lived in a sod hut. Papa Miller worked in nearby North Platte, and, according to a letter from an old neighbor, Mrs. Harry Yost, "Mrs. Miller, Glenn and Deane, well-mannered little boys, held down the claim. Mrs. Miller saw to it that a school was organized and, no other teacher being available, taught it herself for a year or two." Apparently Mattie Lou Miller worked very hard and long hours, because one day she arrived at her neighbor's home, after having picked "cowchips off the range where our cattle had settled . . . took off her dusty gloves and bonnet, looked at her roughened hands and the sand burrs in her shirt and shoes, and wailed, 'Oh, I'm ruined—simply ruined!' "

According to Glenn's older brother, the late Dr. Deane Miller, who later became a successful dentist, the family eased its lonesome existence with music. In their little sod hut Mattie Lou would play the organ, and in their wagon the kids would sing songs as they drove across the prairie. In their little school, which Mattie Lou had organized and which she called "Happy Hollow," the Miller children concentrated on elementary subjects and also had a heavy exposure to religious instruction, with emphasis upon personal ethics.

Those were five rough years, during which the family was almost wiped out by a vicious prairie fire. But everyone pitched in—Glenn milked a neighbor's cow for a dollar a week—and the Millers managed to hang on until they could lay claim to the homestead, which they finally sold. Their next home: a small house in North Platte. There Elmer Miller (like Glenn, he preferred his middle name) worked for a while on the bridges of the Union Pacific Railroad, saving enough money to buy Deane a cornet and Glenn a mandolin. That must have been quite a musical combo: Deane blowing his cornet, Glenn picking his mandolin and Ma Miller pumping the organ, possibly with John Herbert Miller (he later was known as Herbert—naturally), born in 1913, wailing away in his crib! But it was a musical start.

In 1915 the family moved to Grant City, Missouri. Inter-

ABOVE: Glenn's birthplace at 601 South 16 Street, Clarinda, Iowa.

LOWER RIGHT: Glenn with a young mule at the Miller sod hut in Tryon, Nebraska.

UPPER LEFT: Mr. and Mrs. Lewis Elmer Miller.

BELOW: The Miller home on Prospect Street in Fort Morgan, Colorado.

viewed years later by Hambla Bauer of the *New York World-Tele-gram*, Ma Miller recalled that Glenn used to sing in the choir. "But he didn't seem to show much talent when he was young. We gave him a mandolin and one day he came home with an old battered horn. He'd traded it off for the mandolin.

"I didn't know he wanted a horn, though I expected all boys like horns. Glenn never said so, but he never said much anyway.

"Glenn used to work on the beet drys and at lunch hour he'd go yonder down the railroad tracks and play that horn. He just played on that horn all the time. It got to where Pop and I used to wonder if he'd ever amount to anything."

Eventually Glenn got a chance to play "up" the railroad tracks a bit, where others could hear him. Brother Deane, a good trumpeter, had graduated to playing in the town band. Little Glenn would tag along, and he showed such promise and enthusiasm that Jack Mossberger, the band leader, let him into the band and even gave him a shiny new trombone and told him he could pay him back by shining shoes in his store.

Mrs. Ruth Beavers, who, as Ruth Jones, knew Glenn in Grant City, recalls that "he worked before and after school—doing furnace work, sweeping stores, etc. He even had a trap line and came to school one morning smelling of a civet and so the teacher sent him home to change clothes." According to Mrs. Beavers, Glenn was alternately "a bit moody and always telling things that happened and laughing. He loved basketball, and he was popular with all the youngsters."

Glenn also loved baseball and football. His first ambition, according to his replies to his press agent's 1938 questionnaire, was "to become a professional baseball player." His childhood heroes, however, were Horatio Alger and Teddy Roosevelt. By the time he reached high school, he reported, "I excelled in football, but fear of injury to my mouth kept me out of college competition." By then he had become entirely devoted to playing the trombone. "I remember," he wrote, "when I was very young, following a man with a trombone under his arm until he went into a night club and thinking my ambitions would be realized if I were good enough to work in that club."

By 1918 the Millers had moved farther west to Fort Morgan,

Colorado, where Glenn went to high school and worked as a soda jerk and in a sugar factory. The family moved from rented home to rented home—from 508 West Street to 322 Prospect Street to 825 Lake Street. What sort of homes were these? Years later, in 1941, Mattie Lou Miller sold that house on Lake Street, which Glenn eventually had bought for her, for the magnificent sum of $1,800!

Glenn played end on the high school football team, and reportedly made the state's all-star team. He also played the role of "Cruge Blainwood, Mrs. Blainwood's only son," in his high school's production of a play called *Miss Somebody Else.* There is no indication that Glenn overplayed his dramatic role, but, according to brother Herb, he did play so hard in a football game against Sterling High, during which he caught eleven passes, that when he came home he fell flat on his face. He slept for an hour before he got up.

Glenn also played trombone, with very little recognition, in the high school band. Edward Hallstern, who collected the rent at the Millers' Lake Street home, reports that Glenn was not an outstanding musician, "and no one ever dreamed that he would become nationally famous."

Glenn's high school grades were unimpressive: almost all "C's," except for an "A" and some "B's" in math and a failing grade in first-year Latin. He was graduated on May 20, 1921, but by this time he had become so immersed in music that he skipped the ceremonies and traveled out to Laramie, Wyoming, for a band job that failed to materialize. Meanwhile, at home, Mattie Lou Miller accepted her son's diploma from his high school principal, who commented, "Maybe you're the one who should get it anyway; you probably worked harder on it than he did!"

There's no doubt that Mattie Lou Miller did work hard, not just in the fields and not just as a teacher in a one-room school, but as the inspirational head of a family in which she tried hard to establish an exceptionally high code of morality and a really deep-seated and lasting mutual love. And she also expected her children to work hard. The importance of success prevailed in the Miller household. According to Herb Miller, the children

LEFT: Star football end, circa 1920.

Class of 1921

Viola Josephine Aggson
Roxie Lee Artman
Lela Florence Baker
Martha Ovella Beggs
Edwin Curtis Brandt
Pearl Opal Brandt
Leonard E. Brown
Gladyce Irene Casady
Mary Gwendoline Caudle
Marie Gertrude Castner
James Donald Crouch
James Douglas Crouch
Edna Belle Daugherty
Everett Leslie Dennis
Hannah Louise Dickman
Elvin Clifford Drake
Hazel Marie Ely
Verniece Maudie Ewart
Barbara Lucille Farnsworth
Kathryn Louise Farnsworth
Robert Bruce Hayes

Guy Albert Kammerer
Helen Louise Keagy
Opal Amintha Kough
Raymond Kelso Law
Stanley Galwey Layton
Mary Katherine Leonard
Marian Lockwood
Alton Glenn Miller
Vera Annabel Park
Dorothy Adline Parriott
Edythe Verneta Robertson
Alice Louise Spencer
John Hubert Spillane
Marguerite Edna Sutor
John Aldred Talley
Florence Evelyn Trumbo
Anna Kathryne Vannoy
Margaret Louise Warner
Clara Louise Wedlick
Harold DeWitt Wentz
Mary Alda Work

Helen Johnston

Class Officers

President . . . . Donald Crouch
Sec'y-Treas. . . . Edna Daugherty
Class Sponsor . Miss Lucy Hunsaker

were impressed with such slogans as "If you're gonna be good, be doggone good. Don't be a half-way guy!"

Years later, sister Irene, now married to Professor Welby Wolfe of the University of Colorado, confirmed that "the relationship among us was just great. It always was better, I think, than we ever realized then.

"I remember the Christmas of 1927 when Glenn surprised us and just walked into the house unannounced. Mother was washing the clothes over a washboard on the back porch and she had a kettle of hot water on the kitchen stove. 'My God, Mother,' he said, 'is THIS the way you wash clothes?' And the very next day he went into town and bought her a new Maytag washer."

Throughout the years Glenn always remained very close to his mother, always making certain that she was never in need of money or attention. As soon as his band became successful, he brought her east to New York, and from ringside tables at the Glen Island Casino and again at the Hotel Pennsylvania showed her off proudly to all his friends.

Certainly she was a major influence on his life. Her stoical, puritanical ways (she had been head of a W.C.T.U. chapter that railed against the "sins" of alcohol) were reflected in his constant, sometimes unreasonable demands for perfection in himself and in others, and in the emotional inhibitions that seldom let him show his true feelings.

In a letter to me, Irene noted that she and Glenn were "very much alike. We both form quick judgments, are stubborn, and have terribly high standards of perfection, besides being, I'm sure, a little hard to live with."

His unemotionalism was typified by his response to a letter she had written to him in the summer of 1941, right at the height of his career. They hadn't seen one another in a long time, and Irene, full of enthusiasm, wrote that she'd like to join him on the road. His response contained nothing about being glad to see her after all those years. It was simply a cold, curt telegram that read: "Meet me in Lincoln." There was no date, no time of arrival, no place to meet.

Irene figured he would stay at the Cornhusker Hotel, and so she checked in there. "Early Monday morning the phone rang,

ABOVE: Papa Miller with sons Glenn, Deane and Herbert.

UPPER RIGHT: Fastest vest in the West.

RIGHT: Glenn (left) and Deane hold brother Herb.

UPPER LEFT: Herb and Glenn hold the rake; Papa holds Herb.

ABOVE: The baggiest pants in the West.

LEFT: The Prodigal Son returns to Papa.

and here was Glenn. He suggested that I come down and we would have a chat before he went to bed. Needless to say, it was one of my greatest thrills! That whole week, I followed him around the golf course and dogged his every step. I was treated like a queen. It was a time I will never forget." Glenn opened up completely. He just couldn't do enough for his kid sister. The cold, cold fish had a warm, warm heart.

(During her week's visit with her brother, Irene recently wrote me, Glenn had half-jokingly asked, "How come you didn't name your kid after me?" "Because," Irene had replied, "I didn't want you to think I wanted any favors." To which Glenn shot back, "What makes you think I've got any to give?" Later, after Glenn had been lost, Irene and Welby named their second son Glenn Miller Wolfe. By then it was too late for favors.)

Even more involved with Glenn was brother Herb, a professional trumpeter, a music teacher and later a band leader. Herb had none of Glenn's talents, though he did manage to look a lot like him. Glenn often tried to help his kid brother. He gave him a job in the band as road manager, but Herb, perhaps because he was too much in awe of his brother, didn't work out well. Later Glenn got him a job in Charlie Spivak's trumpet section. But Herb couldn't play well enough, and so Charlie let him go. Then Glenn helped Herb start his own band, but that never got very far either. Eventually Herb, a very gentle, down-to-earth, retiring guy, recognized his own musical short-comings. In a warm, appreciative letter to his famous brother, he admitted, "I'll never be much as a trumpet player so have decided to call it quits. . . . I'm just one of those 'arm chair' trumpeters (sound fair at home and worse in public)." He then followed with something even more perceptive. "I certainly appreciate the big help you've given me. It only serves to idolize you more in my mind (which may be one thing that's wrong with me). . . . Thanks again for all you've done. I hope that I can do something some day that will make you as proud of me as I am proud of you."

But Herb did share two personality traits with the brother he idolized. He was stubborn. And he was persistent. As late as 1972 he was again trying to hit the big time with his own band. And, unfortunately, again not making it.

Chapter 4

Glenn graduated from high school in May 1921, but it wasn't
until twenty months later that he matriculated at the University
of Colorado. In between, he traveled to Laramie, Wyoming, for
that job that didn't materialize, and finally wound up with his
first full-time professional engagement as trombonist in the band
of Boyd Senter, an eccentric-sounding saxophonist and clarinetist
about whom musicians have still not turned in a final verdict:
Was he or wasn't he kidding?

When Glenn finally did enter college, he spent a great deal of
his time with a band led by Holly Moyer, a fellow-student, and
somewhat less time attending classes. He completed only three of
sixteen semesters, amassing a total of only 36 out of the 186
credits required to graduate. Again his highest marks were in
math; an 83 in trigonometry was his best grade. His lowest were
in modern European history and freshman gym, in which he
received 40's, and in music—in a first-year harmony course,
which he flunked with a paltry 50!

Still, he kept playing his trombone. And he even began
dabbling in arranging. The Moyer band was a big campus
favorite. Most of its closely knit members belonged to the Sigma
Nu fraternity. As late as 1969 five of them got together for a
reunion at the University. Only Miller and cornetist Joe Baros
were missing. Pianist-leader Moyer was working for a Denver
advertising agency. Drummer Julius "Judy" Kingdom, who

The Holly Moyer Orchestra in Gordon Kerr's Music Store in Boulder: (left to right) Judy Kingdom, Bill Fairchild, Emil (Bill) Christensen, Jack Bunch, Deane Miller, Holly Moyer, Glenn Miller.

remained close to Miller for many years after college, had become a senior bank vice-president in Boulder. Banjoist Bill Christensen was a retired stockbroker, a millionaire. Saxists Bill Fairchild and Jack Bunch had settled down as furniture-store owner and real-estate salesman, respectively.

Bunch, who roomed with Miller and later became a successful Hollywood musician, recalls that the band "didn't like the music as written and we developed a lot of our stuff from listening to phonograph records. One of our favorites was the Cotton Pickers." Ironically, one of that much-recorded group's trombone players, Vincent Grande, was to stand up as Glenn's best man when he was to marry another University of Colorado student a few years later.

The band completed a couple of tours, mostly through Wyoming, once under Moyer and once under its manager, Wally Becker. Early in September 1923 Glenn took a solo trip that could have landed him a job with the outstanding band in the southwest, a band that to this day lives on as one of the legendary outfits of the twenties.

This was Jimmy Joy's band, composed of collegians at the University of Texas. Actually, there was no one in the band by that name. The leader was Jimmy Maloney, and he liked a newspaper cartoon called "Joys and Glooms," so he decided to change his name to "Joy." Simple as all that. The band had a

UNIVERSITY OF COLORADO
OFFICE OF THE REGISTRAR
BOULDER, COLORADO

Official transcript of the record of **Mr. A. Glenn Miller**

I. **Attendance:** Admitted **January 2, 1923** .... to **College of Arts & Sciences**

Attended **no** semesters **three** quarters **no** summer terms

Graduated XXXXXXXXXXXXXXXXXXXXXXXXXXXXXXXXXX Degree XXXXXXXXXXXXXXXXXXXXXXXXXXXXXXXXXXXX

II. **Present Status:** **In good standing.**

Mr. Miller withdrew voluntarily and is hereby granted Honorable Dismissal.

College Credits

Year	Quarter	Descriptive Title	Dep't and No.	Grade	Credit	Grade Points
1922-23 2nd Quarter		Freshman English I		80	3	
		Trigonometry		83	3	
		American Government II		76	3	
		Modern European History		72	3	
		Personal Hygiene		78	1	
	#1	Freshman Gym.	(1)	68	0	
3rd Quarter		Freshman English II		78	3	
		Algebra I		80	3	
		American Government III		70	3	
		Modern European History		71	3	
		Freshman Gym.		90	1	
		Personal Hygiene		83	1	
	#1	Freshman Gym. (Con removed)		Pass	1	
1923-24 1st Quarter		Physiography		71	5	
		American Government I		75	3	
		Modern European History	(3)	40	0	
		1st Year Harmony	(2)	50	0	
		Freshman Gym.	(1)	40	0	

June 22, 1942

Fred E. Aden,
Registrar

ABOVE: A fifty in harmony!

LEFT: Glenn at the University of Colorado in 1923.

OPPOSITE PAGE, ABOVE: The Moyer Band in front of the J. C. Penney Golden Rule Store in Sheridan, Wyoming.

OPPOSITE PAGE, BELOW: Boyd Senter, sax in hand, with his orchestra.

ABOVE: The Tommy Watkins Band in Juarez, Mexico.

motto, painted across the front of the bass drum: "If You Can't Dance, Get on and Run!"

The singer and banjo player in the band, Smith Ballew, was a strikingly handsome man who, during the late twenties and early thirties, became a successful singer and band leader. His girl friend had mentioned to Gretchen Williams, a friend of hers at the University of Colorado, that trombonist Jack Brown planned to leave the Joy band. Gretchen knew Glenn and arranged for him to drive her car to Austin. "I met him when he arrived," Ballew recalls, "and liked him immediately."

Glenn flunked the audition. But Ballew's sympathetic excuse makes sense: "We were playing mostly by ear. Each man had memorized his parts. Practically none were written down. Glenn didn't know what we were doing, naturally. It really wasn't fair.

Anyway, Jack Brown soon changed his mind and came back, so we wouldn't have used Glenn anyway."

So young Miller returned to Boulder, ostensibly to resume his studies. It may have been lack of money, it may have been lack of interest, or it may have been both. At any rate, after failing three out of five courses in the fall of 1923, Glenn dropped out of college and began to concentrate completely on his career as a professional musician.

He stayed on with the Moyer band, and then toured with Tom Watkins and his eleven-piece orchestra, traveling as far south as Mexico. Eventually he landed in Los Angeles, where he went to work with Max Fisher's band at the Forum Theatre on West Pico Boulevard. A schmaltzy, uninspiring outfit, it emphasized melody but very little musical creativity. It also played for acts on the stage. Glenn, who had become a good reader, played his parts well. It was at the Forum that he got the break that was to change his entire musical career—and his entire life, as well. Years later, Glenn, when filling out a questionnaire, listed as "the break of fortune that shaped my career: the interest that Ben Pollack showed in me when he hired me to play and arrange for his band."

Pollack's band, one of the first to play outstanding big-band jazz, was appearing in Los Angeles at the Venice Ballroom. Its leader was an ambitious, driving, dynamic drummer. It boasted a batch of swinging arrangements, written by one of its saxophonists, Fud Livingston. And it was filled with young, jazz-oriented musicians, most of them, like Pollack, out of Chicago, where they had been mesmerized and influenced by Louis Armstrong, Bix Beiderbecke and the other jazz greats who were playing there during the twenties. Though Pollack's musicians probably didn't realize it then, their group was to go down in jazz and big-band histories as one of the most influential and idolized bands of its day.

The band had another saxophonist named Gil Rodin, a close friend of Pollack's, who helped him run the band, who later became president of the Bob Crosby band and subsequently a television producer and recording executive.

Recently Rodin reminisced in his office in posh Universal City, California: "While we were at the Venice Ballroom, Ben received a wire from Chicago that his brother had died. We got permission from the ballroom to return there, and on the train Ben told me how much his folks wanted him to stay in Chicago now that his brother was gone. I was a little homesick, too, and I also wanted to stay home. We thought maybe we'd bring the band back, but we weren't sure that all the guys wanted to return. So we decided to look around for some good musicians in Chicago, break them in on the Coast, and then bring the band back intact.

"When we got home, Ben informed me that he had to sit at home for seven days—for religious reasons—and it would be up to me to look around for new musicians. Well, everybody was talking about this little kid named Benny Goodman who was playing with Art Kassel's band at Midway Gardens. So I went out there to hear him, and he knocked me right on my ear. He used to come to work in short pants, but he kept a pair of long pants in his locker so he'd fit in with the band. At intermission I introduced myself and told him we'd like to have him come to California and join the band. He said, 'O-o-o-h, I'd love to come to California.' Later that night we went out to hear some jazz, and the next day he invited me to come to his home and meet his family.

"Well, while we were at his house, we talked about other musicians, and he recommended a trumpeter named Harry Greenberg and an alto saxist named Lenny Cohen. Pollack and I talked it over, and we decided maybe it would be better not to make all the moves at one time, because it might create friction, and that it might be good to start the changes with Goodman and then replace the others."

The saxophonist Goodman was to replace was a young Colorado musician named Ted Maguiness who, at the time, had as his roommate another young Colorado musician named Glenn Miller. Today Maguiness, better known as Ted Mack, the head man of television's famous *Ted Mack's Amateur Hour*, recalls that "I didn't want to leave California because I was in love with my high school sweetheart who had also moved out there. I would travel down to San Diego from Los Angeles to see her, and I used to gripe to Glenn that if I were going to keep on playing that lousy horn, somebody ought to kick me. But Glenn felt differently. He used to say to me quite proudly, 'Well, Helen is going to marry a trombone player.'

"Glenn was terribly serious about his music. He had a helluva good sense of humor—I can still see that puckish grin—and he was a real gentleman. But, when it came to his music, he never took his eye off the ball. It was nothing for him to stay up half the night teaching himself how to arrange out of Arthur Lange's instruction book.

"I remember he was playing with Georgie Stoll's band and while we were living together he had an attack of appendicitis. We tried to cure it with lots of orange juice and gin, but it didn't work, and finally one night I rushed him to the hospital for an operation. While Glenn was recuperating back in the apartment, we would have some free-for-alls among the musicians who'd come in and try to make Glenn laugh just so his scar would hurt."

Mack's departure from the Pollack band didn't hurt the group too much, because young Goodman's playing was so fantastic. As Mack pointed out: "I just wish I could have played well enough so that it could have been considered an even replacement."

Though Ted Mack self-admittedly was nowhere near the world's greatest saxophonist, Ross Dugat, the band's trombonist, was considered to be about the best West Coast man on his instrument. But Dugat, like Mack, didn't want to leave California for Chicago, and so Ted, who had great faith in Glenn's potential, told Pollack and Rodin about his roommate. As it turned out, never did Ted Mack again—even on his hundreds of *Amateur Hour* shows—uncover a more important artist.

Glenn had left Stoll and was playing with Max Fisher's pit band at the Forum Theatre. According to Rodin, "When Ben got back, we went over to the theater to catch a matinee. But we really couldn't tell much what Glenn could do, because most of what they played was dull, society-band-type stuff. We heard he also arranged, but we had no way of telling which arrangements were his.

"So after the show we went backstage to meet Glenn, and he

The Ben Pollack Band visits Lionel Barrymore (sixth from left) on the MGM lot in Culver City: (left to right) Pollack, saxist Gil Rodin, banjoist Al Gifford, actor Henry Wallthall, Benny Goodman, Barrymore, saxist Bill Sturgess, actor Owen Moore, tuba player Al Lasker, trombonist Al Harris, pianist Wayne Allen, trumpeter Harry Greenberg, Glenn Miller.

really made no special impression on us—a nice, quiet, well-mannered guy, but that was about all. We asked him to come and sit in with our band, and he did. He didn't impress us tremendously, but then Ross Dugat had spoiled us. Anyway, we asked him if he was interested in going to Chicago, and he said very simply, 'I don't care where I play.' He knew our band; he'd been in several times to hear us, and I guess like any other musician he must have been thrilled to be asked to join us.

"But he seemed to be more interested in arranging for the band than playing. That was understandable, because he never had had a chance to write for such good musicians before. We asked him to bring a few of his arrangements to rehearsal, and we liked them. He would copy riffs he heard on records—records by the Wolverines and Ray Miller's band—and then drop them into his own arrangements. He joined the band then, and right after that Benny Goodman came out and joined us, too, and after that came Harry Greenberg, the trumpeter, and a new pianist named Wayne Allen."

The Pollack band soon returned to Chicago with Al Harris,

Greenberg and Miller comprising the brass section and Living-ston, Rodin and young Goodman on saxes. In Chicago they added Benny's older brother, Harry, on tuba, and a banjo player, Lou Kessler, who doubled on violin. These two, plus Allen and the driving Pollack on drums, made up the rhythm section of what was to be one of the really great big-bands of the era.

At first Miller roomed with Allen in the Bryn Mawr Apart-ments at Sheridan and Bryn Mawr on Chicago's North Side. "Barney Glatt, the manager of the apartments, was a good friend of ours," Rodin remembers, "and he would let us rehearse there for free. Glenn couldn't work with the band for a while because he had to wait to get his local union card. He could still rehearse with us, though, and he'd write arrangements for us and for Paul Ash."

Later Glenn and Benny Goodman roomed together in Chi-cago, and, according to Benny, "we often dated together, too. We'd go out to places like the Four Deuces and the Frolics Cafe. Glenn liked to drink. Sometimes, when he became over-loaded, he'd grow pugnacious—but never with me."

Rodin remembers Glenn more as "a social drinker. He was very well liked by the guys. He liked to do what everyone else did. He'd play golf and tennis, and we'd listen to records, and at night, when we weren't working, we'd go out and hear music. All the guys would go to hear Louis and King Oliver, and Glenn would too. But he also liked to hear Roger Wolfe Kahn's Orchestra when it played at the Southmoor. He'd go there every night for a week because he liked that big-band sound and he wanted to see how they used their violins. That's why, when we made our records, we used to add strings to the band, because Glenn was trying to get that sound."

For amusement, Glenn would also like to play practical jokes of the hotfoot variety. Rodin recalls that "when Earl Baker, a trumpet player in the band, got married, Glenn fixed the slats in the bed so that when they got into bed it would collapse. But Glenn was smart: Later, when he got married, he wouldn't let anybody know about it, and he even went far away into Westchester County at some hotel for his wedding night."

When the band opened at the Southmoor, it was, according to Rodin, "a smash! All the musicians came in to hear us. Bix [Beiderbecke, the legendary cornetist] and Tram [Frankie Trumbauer, one of the era's great saxophonists] would come in from Indiana to spend evenings with the band.

"Soon we got an offer to record for Victor. We made several sides. One of them was 'When I First Met Mary,' which Glenn arranged. I remember we added two violins especially for that date. Victor Young [later a famous songwriter and Bing Crosby's musical director] was one of them. We were trying to get that 'Roger Wolfe Kahn' sound that Glenn liked.

"Glenn would write more in the pop vein for us. His idea of jazz was to let the soloist play with some riffs in the background. But Glenn didn't write much jazz for us—mostly the pretty things. Fud Livingston did almost all our jazz arrangements. He was great at writing that ensemble jazz stuff that was so popular in those days."

After the Southmoor, the band went into the Rendezvous Club on the North Side. It was true gangland Chicago, reports Rodin. "The syndicate owned the place and they had their own barber chair and their own barber, and when a guy got a shave or a haircut, he'd be protected by their own guys with machine guns. But they were very good to us musicians."

Close relationships between gangsters and nightclubs abounded during the Prohibition Era days and nights, if for no other reason than that the gangsters were the guys making real money then, and, as so many still do today, they loved to live flamboyantly and to entertain friends, customers and politicians. Many musicians, either directly or indirectly, were their employees, and, in true gangland fashion, the head men took good care of their own.

Ray McKinley, who later was to become one of Glenn's closest friends and who would lead the Miller band after the war, credits Chicago's gangland for letting Miller hear him play drums for the first time.

"The band I was with was playing in some club there—I can't remember which one—and one night there was some shooting going on and I wound up in the hospital with a bullet in me. But those gangsters we were working for paid all my hospital bills and after I got out they put me up at the Palmer House and really treated me like a king.

"One night, while I was recovering, I went over to the Southmoor to hear the Pollack band. I talked with some of the guys, and later, when I went to hear the band again, they asked me to sit in. I guess they liked what I did, because, when it was over, Pollack took me aside and confided he was thinking of packing up the drums and just leading the band. He said he'd send for me when he was ready, but I guess he never got ready—not for me, anyway."

However, some years later, Miller, still impressed by McKinley's drumming, did send for him. But that's another story.

During the summer of 1927 the band returned to the West Coast, playing jobs on the way out. When it got as far as Omaha, Nebraska, Glenn became so ill that they had to call in a substitute. The best trombonist in town, they were told, was a guy who worked in the lunchroom of the local department store. "Everything was going along OK," according to Gil Rodin, "until some people started requesting 'He's the Last Word,' which we'd recorded for Victor. 'I know it; I'll play it,' the trombone player said. 'I got the record.' And you know what? He'd heard it, all right. He'd even memorized Glenn's trombone solo from the record, and when it came time to play it, he played it note for note. But guess what—he played it in the wrong key! His phonograph must have been running fast, but he just kept right on playing anyway—exactly as he had memorized it—a tone higher than the rest of the band was playing. The guys almost fell off the chairs from laughing so hard."

When the band returned to Chicago, it played at the Blackhawk Restaurant, which later became an important spot for many name bands, like Coon-Sanders, Hal Kemp, Bob Crosby, Red Norvo and others. Smith Ballew, who some years before had tried to get Glenn a job with the Jimmy Joy band, fondly recalls Miller's kindness the night he walked into the Blackhawk. By this time, Ballew had formed his own band, had met with some success, then had gotten into a hassle with his booking agency and found himself stranded in Chicago.

"I couldn't work because I had no Chicago union card and I had only a few bucks in my pocket. But I just had to hear that Pollack band in person, and so I went to the Blackhawk, hoping I could get by with just a sandwich and some coffee. I was barely seated when a guy came to my table, stuck out his hand, and gave me a big 'hello.' It was Glenn Miller. He even picked up my check—thank God." Later Glenn introduced Ballew to Pollack, who liked his singing, and "in a few days I was working with Pollack at $125 a week, the most I had ever made at this time, and living in the same hotel with Glenn." Ballew eventually became so popular, via the band's broadcasts on station WGN, that he was offered a big bonus by Ted FioRito to join his band—which he did. "This time Glenn had really gone to bat for me to get me a job." Some years later, Ballew was to return the favor.

As it had been everywhere in Chicago, the band was a big smash at the Blackhawk. It recorded some more for Victor. It added an exquisite jazz trumpeter, Jimmy McPartland, who blew a Bix Beiderbecke-like horn and who in the seventies was still showing many a younger trumpeter what good taste really is. For a while another jazz great, Bud Freeman, who later was starred in the bands of Tommy Dorsey and Benny Goodman, brought his tenor sax into the band that was blazing new jazz trails. With Goodman on clarinet, McPartland on trumpet, and Freeman on sax, the band, spurred on by Pollack's driving drums, had a topflight jazz soloist on every horn—except trombone. But that was going to change.

Chapter 5

 Through its recordings, through its radio broadcasts and through the grapevine, the Pollack band's fame spread to New York. And so the guys were soon invited to come east to the Big Apple and to open early in March 1928 at the Little Club on West Forty-fourth Street between Broadway and Eighth Avenue. Rodin remembers, "It was on the north side of the street, under some theater or other, and they used to charge a three-dollar cover, a lot in those days. But the band was a smash. Every Sunday night the place would be filled with musicians who'd come just to hear us. That used to burn up Lillian Roth, who was the star of the show, and she and the band used to have a lot of fights."

Maybe it was because of the constant hassling with the star—or maybe it was because of something else—but, despite the band's great notices, its engagement at the Little Club was terminated early in May. And for a while thereafter the guys really struggled.

There was even some talk about breaking away from Pollack and perhaps having one of the sidemen front the band. The two most likely candidates seemed to be Glenn Miller and Benny Goodman, and the guys in the band would have arguments as to who would do a better job. Neither one of the nominees, however, was knocked out by the other's potential as a leader.

Goodman claimed that "Glenn was much too stiff to lead a

band." Glenn's reaction was even less kind. "All Benny would do," he prophesied, "would be to stand there and pick his nose."

But they remained good friends, nevertheless, and even became roommates again at the Whitby Apartments on West Forty-fifth Street. Benny recalls, "We spent many a tough day together. We used to 'borrow' empty milk bottles from in front of other apartments and turn them in so we could get enough money to buy some hot dogs for lunch.

"You know, Glenn contributed a lot to the Pollack band. He was basically an idea man, and he certainly was a dedicated musician."

Jimmy McPartland also retains some fond memories, and some less fond, of Glenn during the Pollack days. "He was a very decent man, but he wasn't much of a trombone player. He acted as the band's musical director and he was a real taskmaster. I remember he used to tell me to take home my parts and woodshed them. 'You'll be a better musician for it,' he used to say. It used to get me sore as hell, but it turned out he was right.

"Glenn was terribly competitive. When he played tennis, he'd hit every ball as hard as he could for a winner, but not many of them went in. I soon caught on that if I just kept the ball in play, I could beat him. I did, and he'd get sore as hell. But that was Glenn. He always tried to be the best."

Still, no matter how hard Glenn would drive himself, he could not make himself into what he wanted most of all to be: a first-rate jazz trombonist. He kept trying desperately to emulate the playing of his idol, Miff Mole, but it seldom ever came out that way.

Then one night came the big blow. Gil Rodin admits it was all his fault: "A bunch of musicians invited me to a jam session at the Louisiana Apartments. I remember I was living at the Manger Hotel—that's the Taft now—and Pollack had the room next to mine. That night at the Louisiana Apartments was the first time I'd ever heard Jack Teagarden. He was playing without the bell portion of his horn, just blowing through his slide into a glass and getting that eerie sound—it was the blues—and I was so knocked out, I couldn't see straight. And then he sang, too, and that was just too much! With all due

Jack Teagarden.

respect to Glenn—and he and I were good friends—this was a whole new world to me. When I got back to the hotel, I was so excited about what I'd heard, that I woke up Pollack to tell him about it. He said, yeah, he'd heard the name, and turned over and went back to sleep.

"The next day I asked Jack to come down and sit in. I felt funny about doing that because, as I said, Glenn and I were good friends and I didn't want to show him up. But I just had to have Jack in our band. In the back of my mind I must have figured that maybe we could have two trombones, but that never happened—at least not then.

"Well, you can guess what did happen. Jack knocked out everybody, and, of course, that made Glenn feel pretty uncomfortable. We were scheduled to play in Atlantic City that summer, but before we left, Glenn announced that he wasn't going because he'd had an offer from Paul Ash to do some arranging and he thought he'd take it and stay in town. We all knew, and I felt especially bad, what the real reason was. Glenn must have felt strongly that 'they really want that guy.' And so he made his exit gracefully."

It must have been quite a blow to Glenn, who wanted so much

to be recognized as a great jazz trombonist but who was always coming up against guys who could outblow him. Little wonder that when he was to front his own band some years later, he would, at least for a while, play no trombone at all.

As a further ego-deflater, Glenn had been living in the Pollack band under the shadow of Fud Livingston, whose swinging charts had set the band's style even before Glenn had joined it. And so, most of the time, Glenn, instead of writing the kind of jazz arrangements he really wanted to write, was kept busy arranging corny ballads and trite novelty tunes that the band needed for commercial reasons.

Nor could writing for a big, lush orchestra like Ash's, which played those pseudo-classical bits of nonsense in the pit of New York's Paramount Theatre, have been any more rewarding, creatively. But financially—well, that was an entirely different story. After leaving Pollack, Glenn was able for the first time in his life to settle down somewhere and begin to save some money. But, also for the first time in many years, he had no fellow-musicians with whom he could share his evenings, nights and early mornings. Roommate Goodman and the entire band had departed, and Glenn was left with that feeling of loneliness that eventually envelops so many rudderless bachelors.

And so Glenn began to think more and more of the girl he'd left behind: of Helen Burger, that small, pretty, quiet, well-mannered coed he'd first met in one of their classes and then had courted at the University of Colorado. Through the years he had kept in touch with her—an occasional visit to Boulder, some phone calls, some letters—with the understanding that some day they would get married. But his music was always interfering, and Helen's disappointment and impatience were reflected by the inscription on her picture on his dresser: "To Glenn, the meanest man in the world!"

Eventually Helen began to give up hope, and her parents, opposed to their only child marrying anyone as "unstable" as a jazz musician, must have felt elated when she announced that she was "practically engaged" to someone else.

As soon as Glenn got the news, he went into action. His approach, as always, was practical, unemotional and straight to the point. Convinced that he could now support the girl he loved,

FORMER COLORADO U. STUDENTS MARRIED IN NEW YORK CITY

MRS. GLENN MILLER.
Formerly Helen Burger.

Boulder, Colo., Oct. 9.—Miss Helen Burger, graduate of the University of Colorado and member of the Pi Beta Phi sorority, was married at New York city Saturday to Glenn Miller, also a former university student and now the highest paid trombone player in the United States. They will live in New York.

Miller's parents reside at Fort Morgan. Mrs. Miller is the daughter of County Clerk and Mrs. Fred W. Burger of Boulder county.

ABOVE: Helen and Glenn back home in Colorado.

he sent her a terse wire, summoning her to New York for the purpose of getting married.

Helen Burger arrived at the Forrest Hotel, and on October 6, 1928, with another trombonist, Vincent Grande, and someone named George Dewy as witnesses, Helen and Glenn were married by clergyman Dudley S. Stark. Years later Mike Nidorf, one of Glenn's closest friends, echoed the sentiments of practically everyone who was ever close to the couple: "The greatest thing that ever happened to Glenn Miller was Helen Miller!"

The movie of Glenn's life, *The Glenn Miller Story*, released in 1955, may have presented some inaccuracies and some exaggerations, but nothing in it could have been more true to life than the warmth and love and understanding that June Allyson and Jimmy Stewart portrayed in their roles as Helen and Glenn Miller. During almost two generations I have known many band leaders and musicians and their wives and have seldom been surprised by the tensions that have permeated these marriages— marriages that because of the occupational hazards involved, have needed a great deal of understanding, patience and trust to survive and flourish. Of all those marriages, the one that impressed me as the most endearing and enduring was the one between Helen and Glenn Miller.

But much as I liked and admired Glenn, it was to Helen that I gave most credit for their happiness. In her own quiet way she was an immensely strong person. She would remain discreetly in the background, and yet, whenever Glenn had an important decision to make, he would turn to her, and she would help him. Polly Haynes, their closest friend and confidante, recently described the subtle depth of their relationship: "I've never known any couple that said so little and felt so much!"

One of Helen's greatest abilities was recognizing Glenn's various and varying moods and knowing how to deal with them without ever deflating his ego. She was a master of tact and diplomacy, and especially good at explaining Glenn and his actions to others—but without ever demeaning her husband.

Whereas Glenn was cold and unemotional, Helen was warm and extremely considerate of other people's feelings. Years later Bill Finegan, the Miller band arranger whom Glenn admired so

Newly-weds make such funny faces!

much (though he had difficulty telling him so), was to credit Helen for "making life bearable for me. She was the one who let me know how Glenn really felt. I'd write something I was especially proud of and Glenn would pay me the supreme compliment with a matter-of-fact remark like 'That's a good thing, Finegan.' But then, the next day, Helen would call me aside and say, 'Billy, Glenn came home last night and he was beside himself. He was so excited about what you had written. He thought it was just so beautiful!' That was really a great marriage!"

Helen and Glenn were never able to have children of their own—her serious operation in the late thirties took care of that. So for years they lavished their affections on a little Boston bull terrier named Pops. The best thing Pops did, in the estimation of Finegan, who was obviously less emotionally involved, was to snort and break wind. "And then Helen and Glenn would say, 'Oh, Pops!' in great embarrassment."

But despite his series of emissions that lasted through twelve years of his life, Helen and Glenn loved that little dog. Mike Nidorf remembers when he died. "Glenn actually cried and carried on. He really showed his emotions that time. He wouldn't even think about working, he was so upset."

Just recently, while gathering materials for this biography, I came across a small cardboard box in one of the bottom file drawers in a storage room containing many of Glenn's business papers. The box, turning yellowish, had obviously been there for a long time, tucked away among old bank statements and payroll records. A string was tied around it, and on top of the box appeared just two words in Glenn's own handwriting: "Pops' Ashes."

For that one moment it seemed to me that Tommy Dorsey was not the only Sentimental Gentleman of Swing.

TOP: Pops with Helen and Glenn.

BOTTOM: Pops with Helen and Glenn and Mrs. Burger, Helen's mother.

Chapter 6

"I always felt," said Benny Goodman, "that when Glenn went with Paul Ash, he was just marking time."

Benny was right. Glenn's love remained jazz, and he found little that thrilled him in that huge, stiff, ostentatious orchestra in the pit of the Paramount.

He and Helen took an apartment at 30-60 Twenty-ninth Street in Astoria, just across the Fifty-ninth Street bridge that links Queens and Manhattan boroughs. From there it was a simple subway ride to the recording studios and the theater district where Glenn was to make a living for the next three years as a free-lance trombonist and arranger.

Early in 1929 Glenn cut a dozen sides with a group led by Tommy and Jimmy Dorsey. Some of these featured an up-and-coming singer who loved to hang around jazz musicians. His name: Bing Crosby. Glenn's old friend Smith Ballew, who was to make hundreds of recordings during the next few years, also popped up on several more of those Dorsey Brothers sides.

Throughout almost all of 1929 Glenn too often was paired on records with a better trombonist who made him feel inferior, so that those doubts he had about his jazz-playing prowess kept growing. Tommy Dorsey, of course, was one. The other was Jack Teagarden, who blew with Glenn on many of the records by the era's best white jazz group, Red Nichols and His Five Pennies.

The play on words was obvious—nickels and pennies. Accurate? Hardly. When I first met Glenn in 1935, I questioned him about those recording sessions. "*Five* pennies?" I asked. "Well, yes, I guess so," Glenn replied. "But they usually had another five or so hidden behind the curtains."

Even with Teagarden present, Glenn, who wrote many of the arrangements, did manage to get in a few hot licks here and there. Jazz critic George Frazier, who seldom wrote anything good about Glenn's playing, once recently paid him a huge compliment. Referring to Glenn's obbligato behind Teagarden's vocal on the Pennies' record of "Sally, Won't You Come Back," Frazier wrote, "It is as good as anything that Louis Armstrong ever played behind Bessie Smith."

On one of its dates the group recorded two sides: "I May Be Wrong," which years later was to become the theme song for all stage shows in Harlem's Apollo Theatre, and "The New Yorkers." Both came from an ill-fated Broadway production called *John Murray's Almanac of 1929*, for which Glenn had been hired but for which he was never paid. In a handwritten reply to a request from the Internal Revenue Service for an explanation of deductions he took on his 1929 income-tax return, Glenn listed the show as owing him $493. He also listed as "bad debts" band leaders Freddy Rich, Tommy Dorsey and Ben Pollack! "I have made every effort to collect this amount and to no avail," he wrote. "It is obvious that individual lawsuits would cost more than the bills are worth." Even then, he was exhibiting keen business acumen.

The vocalist on that Nichols date was a former St. Louis jockey named Red McKenzie, an especially warm singer who phrased like the jazz musicians with whom he hung out and by whom he was accepted as a jazz brother. In addition to singing, McKenzie also hummed through tissue paper wrapped around a comb, giving out a sound like a rasping, muted trumpet.

Red was also quite a recording entrepreneur, who used to put together sessions of jazz musicians whom he admired and with whom he'd play his musical comb and sometimes sing. Apparently he liked what he heard of Glenn on that Nichols date because, in November 1929, when he assembled an especially impressive jazz band in Victor's New York recording studios, he invited Glenn as the only trombonist.

The two sides have since gone down in jazz history as two of the music's classics. Not only were "Hello Lola" and "One Hour" magnificent musical items, but they also represented one of the major breakthroughs in blacks and whites playing together. Selected for this session, in addition to Miller, were clarinetist Pee Wee Russell, guitarist Eddie Condon and drummer Gene Krupa, who had just come to New York from Chicago, plus that great tenor saxist, Coleman Hawkins, who was then playing in Fletcher Henderson's band. Several years later, when I was interviewing Glenn for a Hall of Fame article in *Metronome*, I asked him to choose what he thought was the best playing he'd ever done on records. Without a moment's hesitation he replied, "Those two sides I did with the Mound City Blue Blowers, 'One Hour' and 'Hello Lola.'"

During 1930 Glenn divided most of his playing time between the recording studios and the pits of New York's Times Square and Alvin theaters. Red Nichols was his boss in all three places. He was a better-than-average cornet player, who played gentle, loping melodic lines. But his real talent was organizing groups and finding them jobs. Glenn was never especially fond of Nichols, and the feeling was reciprocal. During an interview in the early 1960's Red told me that "there was no questioning Glenn's ability. He was a very 'thoughty' guy. And he was also a very sly one—for Glenn Miller." But Nichols admitted that "George Gershwin gave him [Glenn] recognition for the ride-outs in the original score of *Girl Crazy*," which included such big

Gershwin hits as "I Got Rhythm" and "Embraceable You."

Girl Crazy was one of the two shows that year for which Nichols had assembled the pit band. The other was *Strike Up the Band.* The all-star jazz casts in those pits included Nichols and Glenn and Benny Goodman, among others, as well as young Krupa, who forever credited Miller for having pulled him through. "I couldn't read anything then. But Glenn sat right in front of me and he would cue me in for everything. He was so great to me!" Goodman also still remembers how Glenn helped Gene: "Hildy Elkins was the conductor in *Girl Crazy.* And it was amazing how well Gene followed him—thanks to Glenn, of course."

Glenn continued to make records with the Five (plus) Pennies. In addition to up-tempoed, semi-dixieland numbers, the group also waxed some ballads, including a lovely lazy version of "Tea for Two," arranged by Glenn and featuring Adrian Rollini's languorous low-register sax playing the lead line. It was a unique reed voicing, several octaves lower than, but not dissimilar to, the Miller reed style that a decade later would characterize his own band.

Thanks to Nichols, Glenn and Helen were able to live comfortably in their Astoria apartment throughout 1929 and 1930. Glenn's income-tax return for 1930 lists Nichols as his sole employer, his gross income at $6,239.50, deductions at $1,195.06, and total tax paid, $17.38.

Again he heard from Internal Revenue asking for more information about his deductions. His reply revealed that he was on salary from Nichols at $125 a week during the runs of the shows, even though union scale was only $80 per week, which showed how much Red needed him. During the year he turned in fifty-one arrangements. Copying charges (making individual parts from the original score sheet), which Glenn paid, averaged $10.50 per score: about one-sixth, and even less, of similar charges forty years later. He had his tuxedo pressed once a week for 75¢ and cleaned once a month for $1.50. Obviously, Glenn slurped his spaghetti very carefully.

During 1931 he continued to record with Nichols. He also cut a total of eighteen sides for Goodman, including the now-famous rendition of "Basin Street Blues" by the Charleston Chasers, one

LEFT: (Left to right) Glenn, Helen, and Bobby and Red Nichols ride a horse at New Jersey's Palisades Amusement Park in May 1930.

BELOW: Glenn lends his support to the Washington Monument in a picture taken by Helen.

of Benny's numerous recording units. (Various jazz men, using various names, would assemble various jazz groups for various record companies.) In addition to the arrangement, Glenn also contributed an original verse that began "Won't You Come Along with Me, Down the Mississippi," which has since become as famous as the song itself. The side focused on Jack Teagarden's trombone and voice, and, more than any other recording, helped to establish him as a major jazz star.

Goodman also kept Glenn busy with other work. "Things were going good for me then. I was making as much as $80 a day in the Paramount Studios out on Long Island and I used to recommend Glenn all the time. He was such a dedicated musician and always so thorough."

Glenn worked for radio studio conductors like Victor Young, Carl Fenton, and, on the Camel radio show, Jacques Renard. And he also played for a while under the baton of one John McManus, who conducted the "Ben Goodman Recording Orchestra" for a Broadway musical called *Free for All* during its fifteen performances in the Manhattan Theatre, which later became CBS's Ed Sullivan Playhouse.

Oscar Hammerstein directed the show and wrote some of the music, and Jack Haley was one of its stars. "It was about psychoanalysis," remembers Goodman. He also remembers that the closing notices went up "right after the reviews came out. We renamed the show *Freeze and Melt*."

By 1932 the Depression had become a way of life. The nation still hadn't recovered from the 1929 Wall Street crash, and Franklin Delano Roosevelt was still to come along and lead the country out of its emotional and financial doldrums.

Especially hard hit was the recording field. No longer were all those calls coming in: a nine A.M. date at Brunswick, a two P.M. date at Victor, a six P.M. date for Melotone Records. Radio, too, was yanking at the purse strings, so that the New York scene for a free-lance musician was no longer a happy one. Irving Berlin's lyrics of "All Alone (at the telephone)" became many a musician's theme song.

Glenn, like many others, was beginning to feel the pinch, and so, when Smith Ballew came along and suggested to him that they form a band and return to the road, Glenn accepted the invitation.

Ballew had been leading his own band for many years. He had just changed offices, and his new bookers, the Music Corporation of America (MCA), had set his band for the Palais Royale, a posh nightclub in Valley Stream, Long Island, where it would split the summer season with none other than Guy Lombardo's band. Realizing that this was his biggest chance yet to show the world how good he was, Ballew decided he'd better organize a truly topflight band in place of the run-of-the-mill hotel-type outfit he had been fronting. So he called Glenn. "I asked him if he would play trombone, arrange and rehearse the band for two-fifty a week plus a fifty-fifty split of everything over a thousand dollars a week that I might make. Glenn agreed, and the first musician he contacted was Ray McKinley. I had known him as a kid in Fort Worth back in 1925, and I had even admired him then."

The Depression had cut down employment and the size of dance bands. "It made poor people out of everybody," recently observed McKinley, who had descended to playing with Dave Bernie's (Ben Bernie's brother) six-piece outfit. And so, when Glenn called him, he jumped at the chance to join something bigger and better, especially since Ballew's new band included inspiring musicians like Glenn on trombone, Bunny Berigan on trumpet, Delmar Kaplan on bass and Fulton "Fidgey" McGrath on piano.

"Ballew was a nice, pleasant guy," McKinley recalls, "but he knew nothing about leading and he didn't pretend to. He was extremely handsome. He looked like one of those old Arrow Collar ads. He had perfect symmetry. Somebody once called him a singing Gary Cooper. But he had too easygoing a personality to make a successful leader.

"Glenn, on the other hand, had a lot of energy, and, of course, he knew exactly what he was doing all the time. Glenn was really the main reason I wanted to join the band. I was very much flattered—I guess he hadn't forgotten that night when I sat in with the Pollack band out in Chicago.

"I know Glenn was *supposed* to have arranged for the band, but

Smith Ballew with Frances Langford in *Palm Springs*, a 1936 Walter Wanger production.

I don't remember him bringing in many arrangements that he had actually written. I have a feeling the budget didn't permit it. What he did instead would be to take a printed stock arrangement and make cuts in it for a particular broadcast, and on the next night he'd take the same stock and make a different cut and it would sound like a different arrangement of the same tune. Then sometimes he'd write a short introduction or something, just to give it a little style of its own. But I don't remember his ever coming in with a completely original arrangement."

What McKinley does remember very vividly is that "the band always seemed to be breaking up after each hotel job and then we'd reorganize again when the next job came along. Sometimes we'd have long layoffs between jobs."

The first layoff occurred in August 1932. Ballew had wangled the band a job, with Miller conducting, for a Broadway show called *Chamberlain Brown's Scrap Book*, described as "a potpourri of vaudeville with a non-star cast." Ballew says, "It included everything from comedy to opera and we even got an assistant musical director of the Metropolitan Opera Company to work with Glenn. But our first week's check bounced and the producers said to deposit it again, that it must have been a mistake. But it bounced the second time, too, and I contacted the manager of the theater, who told me the rent hadn't been paid." The show closed after ten performances, but Ballew was stuck for the musicians' salaries. "All the guys refused to accept a nickel from me—all except the string players."

In November the band got a job at the Lowrey Hotel in St. Paul. Jimmy McPartland had replaced Berigan, and Chummy MacGregor, with whom Glenn was to strike up a lifetime friendship, had come in on piano for McGrath.

As he had in his Pollack days, Glenn assumed the taskmaster's role. He insisted the band rehearse every morning before its luncheon sessions, and he soon whipped it into a first-rate-sounding dance orchestra. But, according to Ballew, that wasn't enough to satisfy the hotel manager. "After our first four weeks he said he would only renew us if we added more novelties with things like funny hats, the way Ted Weems' band was doing. I discussed this with Glenn and he was as dubious as I was, but we decided to try it since it would add four weeks to our contract. When we told the band about this, they rose en masse. 'We are musicians,' they said. And so we went ahead and worked on the novelties *without* funny hats."

The experience was, as Ballew noted, "an education for Glenn, when he realized what a big contribution those novelties made to the overall popularity of our band. And he never forgot it.

"Red Nichols and His Five Pennies—all fifteen of them—replaced us and we returned to New York." Came another layoff, followed by a series of engagements, most interspersed with even more layoffs. There was the William Penn Hotel in Pittsburgh, where the band was augmented by The Foursome, who had been in *Girl Crazy* when Glenn was in the pit. Next came the Hotel Lexington in New York; then the Club Forest in New Orleans, where the band featured what Ballew described as "a simply sensational arrangement by Glenn of 'Stormy Weather,' which Harold Arlen had just written and for which he gave me one of the first lead sheets. We were so successful that our four weeks' engagement was extended to six months."

But by late 1933 the road for the Ballew band was running

only downhill. And all those layoffs didn't help build morale, either. McKinley vividly recalls one New Year's Eve at the Muehlebach Hotel in Kansas City. "All kinds of things had been happening. Chummy had been in the lock-up with d.t.'s. And Glenn got juiced—it was the only time I saw him like that. He could be a bad drunk, too. Nobody knows exactly how it started, but I understand Glenn had leaned over and grabbed J. D. Wade's legs [Wade was the lead trumpeter] or maybe it was higher up. Anyway, they got into a real fight, right on the bandstand, and they were rolling on the floor and Frank Simeone, the little sax player, was trying to separate them and he was taking more blows than anyone." According to Ballew, "nobody noticed the battle," a pithy commentary on the state of Kansas City's New Year's Eve celebrants.

Glenn didn't play with the band on its last major engagement, at the Cosmopolitan Hotel in Denver, close to where Glenn's family was living. By then, late 1933, the band had deteriorated, and, according to McKinley, "Glenn didn't want his friends to see him in such a poor setting—the band was beneath his dignity or something. Anyway, he stayed on as manager. He'd rehearse the band for shows, and, of course, he'd show up on payday. He had begun to act more like a tough business executive and less like a musician. He was getting more headstrong than ever, and less easy to get along with."

Ballew agrees. "He was a taskmaster, often to the resentment of men in the band. He was stiff. He had no social amenities and he preferred to remain in the background. He was definitely an introvert. He was hard to know. He never bared his soul to anyone at any time that I know of." Now retired in Fort Worth, Texas, following a successful career as a Hollywood cowboy movie star, Ballew concludes, "I felt I knew him then, but now I have my doubts."

Chapter 7

For Glenn Miller, 1934 was the year of the Dorsey Brothers band. During some of those various 1933 layoffs with Smith Ballew, Glenn had recorded with Tommy and Jimmy's pick-up outfit, composed of New York's more swinging studio musicians, often backing singer Mildred Bailey with Miller arrangements.

Then, during the beginning of 1934, the band waxed some instrumental sides on its own, some issued under the Dorseys' name and some under the names of the group's sidemen.

From time to time Tommy and Jimmy had been threatening to form a permanent band that would go out on the road and work regularly. But according to Roc Hillman, who wound up as the band's new guitarist, it took Glenn to prod them into action.

Hillman was one of several musicians whom Glenn uncovered during Ballew's last stand in Denver. "We were playing with Vic Schilling's band at the Broadhurst Hotel, and Glenn told a drummer-friend of mine that Harry Goodman would be leaving the band and they'd be needing a new bass player. So this friend told me to go over and play for Glenn. I did, and he and Ray McKinley liked me and I got the job on bass. But I also played guitar, and as things turned out, that's where I wound up.

"Later I took Glenn and Ray back to hear our band and they also hired Skeets Herfurt, who played sax, Don Matteson, who played trombone, and Kay Weber, our girl singer. Skeets and Don and I sang as a trio, so that helped.

"Schilling let us go right away—he was very nice about it—because Glenn told us the band had a job at the Roman Pools in Florida and some of their other guys weren't going. So we started back east, but on the way back we heard the place in Florida had gone bankrupt. So we went on to New York instead.

"Glenn was just great to all four of us. He felt responsible and he did everything he could to make life easy for us. On the second night we were there, he took us up to meet Benny Goodman in his hotel room. Then a few nights later he had Tommy Dorsey come up to our room in the Manhattan Towers Hotel, and he had me play my tune, 'Long May We Love,' for Tommy. Tommy liked it and he recorded it. Glenn also took us to the Onyx Club to hear the Six Spirits of Rhythm, and he introduced us to Artie Shaw there."

The Ballew band managed to get a one-week gig at the Hotel Lexington, but Donald Novis, who sang a lot like Ballew, was the featured act, so the booking didn't do the band any good. In fact, the band didn't work at all after that, according to Ray McKinley. "Then one day Glenn phoned me and said that Tommy and Jimmy were getting their band together and he was going with them, and so were the kids from Denver, and would I like to go. I said, 'Sure.'

"The band had a different sound. That was Glenn's idea. Bing Crosby was the big thing then, and Glenn decided to pitch down to his register. So, instead of the usual couple of trumpets and just one trombone, we featured three trombones, Tommy and Glenn and Don, and just one trumpet. Bunny Berigan was there at first. The saxes had a different sound—two tenors and one alto instead of the usual two altos and one tenor; that gave them a lower pitch, too. Skeets and a fellow named Jack Stacey were the tenors and Jimmy played alto and also clarinet. In the rhythm section we had Kaplan on bass, Bobby Van Eps on piano, Roc on guitar, and me. Kay Weber was the girl singer and later on Bob Crosby became the boy singer.

"The band used to rehearse in that little rehearsal room up in the office of Rockwell-O'Keefe [who booked them] in Radio City. Sure enough, the second rehearsal ran true to form—the Dorseys were screaming at each other. I remember Jimmy yelled,

'I suppose you think that means you're the boss,' and Tommy yelled right back, 'You know damn well I'm the boss, because I can talk louder than you!' "

The band started off with a series of one-nighters in New England during the spring of 1934. One of them turned out to be the date at Nuttings-on-the-Charles where I first heard the band and first heard about Glenn Miller—the date on which he ran completely untrue to form by trying to sing those ridiculous lyrics about "Annie's Cousin Fanny."

The band recorded that tune and fifty-eight others for Decca Records during 1934, a year in which Glenn's income dipped to a dismal $3,209.78, his lowest in many years. But, though the pay wasn't great, the experience and the exposure were. Working as musical director and arranger for such a group of outstanding musicians brought him to the attention of many people in the music field, and led him next year into another exciting assignment.

The band settled down during the summer of 1934 in the Sands Point Casino on Long Island, where it had a radio wire. Berigan would show up only half of the time, and so, despite his brilliance, the brothers decided they'd be better off without him and replaced him with a Harvard graduate named George Thow.

Many of the band's most exciting numbers, according to McKinley, were "strictly head arrangements. We'd make them up as we went along—you know—somebody would come up with a riff, and somebody would add something else, and soon we'd have an arrangement all wrapped up.

"Glenn did write a few things for us. I remember one thing called 'Dese, Dem and Dose' that he wrote and we recorded. He used to carry a little organ around with him to work on, but I don't think he did more than four arrangements during the entire summer at Sands Point. Evidently he was a pretty slow arranger—at least in those days. He was all business. No work was too hard for him. But he was also a little standoffish with the guys in the band."

A job as musical director for the battling Dorseys was bound to take its toll. The brothers were constantly squabbling, and the

The Dorsey Brothers Band poses for the calisthenics leader and its press agent beside the swimming pool of the Sands Point Casino on Long Island. Tommy and Jimmy flank Kay Weber in the front row. Don Matteson, Delmar Kaplan, Roc Hillman and Bobby Van Eps are in the second row. George Thow, Jack Stacey, Glenn, Skeets Herfurt and Ray McKinley bring up the rear.

subject was almost always music. Glenn would be caught in the middle, and finally, after an engagement at the Palais Royale on Broadway, he decided he'd had it and handed in his notice.

His decision wasn't purely negative—he knew precisely where he was going. Over in England, Ray Noble had been making some exceptionally fine recordings, and over here in America the public was beginning to buy them. The Dorseys' booking agency, Rockwell-O'Keefe, was looking for new bands so they could compete with the larger Music Corporation of America. They had wanted to bring Noble's band over intact, but when they discovered (1) that the American musicians' union wouldn't stand for it, and (2) Noble didn't have his own band anyway—he had merely assembled top musicians from various English bands for his recordings—they decided it might be a smart idea to get somebody to organize a band of American musicians for him. And, recognizing the fine jobs Glenn had turned in, first for

The Ray Noble Orchestra on the Rainbow Room bandstand: (front row) singer
Al Bowlly, Fritz Prospero, Nick Pisani, Danny D'Andrea, George Van Eps,
Claude Thornhill; (second row) Glenn, Will Bradley, Charlie Spivak, Peewee
Erwin, Jimmy Cannon, Johnny Mince, Milt Yaner, Bud Freeman; (back row)
Bill Harty and Delmar Kaplan. Bradley, Spivak and Thornhill also became
successful band leaders after they left Noble.

Smith Ballew and then for the Dorseys, they contacted him and
he agreed.

And what a band Glenn organized! Charlie Spivak and
Peewee Erwin played trumpets; Glenn and Wilbur Schwitchenberg, who later changed his name to Will Bradley, were on
trombones; the reeds featured Bud Freeman and Johnny Mince,
who later was to star as clarinetist in Tommy Dorsey's band; and
the rhythm section consisted of Claude Thornhill on piano, the
brilliant George Van Eps on guitar, Kaplan on bass, and
Noble's manager, Bill Harty, a not very swinging drummer, who
had arrived with Ray from England. As Bradley once remarked,
"The rhythm section didn't sound as bad as Harty was capable
of playing."

Everything pointed to this becoming one of the great all-
around bands of all time. And, for a while, it proved to be just
that. Noble, suave and sophisticated, arranged ballads with great
musical taste and tenderness. But his English band's jazz efforts
had often bordered on the comical. Now, with the jazz-wise

Miller to take over that department, the band appeared to have all musical bases well covered.

For a while Glenn had his way—completely. Because of union troubles, Ray was not permitted to work for several months. So he went out to Hollywood to write songs for a movie, *The Big Broadcast of 1936*. That gave Glenn the chance to rehearse the band and mold it to his tastes. That was fine, too, with many of the jazz-oriented musicians he had assembled for a leader whose bag was sweet stuff.

When Ray returned from the West Coast, he took over, concentrating on ballads. Both he and Glenn were sticklers for musical details, so the band spent an inordinate amount of time just rehearsing, for which the men were paid—"the first time in history," according to Freeman, "that that ever happened." Merely for rehearsing for nine weeks, Miller got $804, a pretty hefty sum in those days. And he made more money recording on the side. In March he waxed ten tunes with a group of Ben Pollack alumni, who were soon to elect Bob Crosby as their new leader. Glenn composed one of the songs, "When Icky Morgan Plays the Organ, Look Out!"—dedicated to his good friend Dick Morgan, who had played guitar in Pollack's band. Ever hear of the record? Hardly anyone else did, either. Proof: Glenn's royalty check as composer came to $5.38! And he also collected six cents for the sale of three pieces of sheet music!

Then, on April 25, 1935, Glenn Miller recorded for the first time under his own name. Utilizing six horns, a rhythm section and a string quartet, he waxed two sides for Columbia Records, "Moonlight on the Ganges" and "A Blues Serenade," that featured his old boss Smith Ballew, plus an instrumental of "In a Little Spanish Town." For a finale he dispensed with the strings and recorded an out-and-out jazz variation on "Pagan Love Song," which he titled "Solo Hop." It featured some great trumpeting by Bunny Berigan, the tenor sax of Eddie Miller and the clarinet of Johnny Mince. But on neither of the two jazz sides was there a single note of solo trombone. Was it modesty, or did Glenn have such little respect for himself as a jazz musician? No one will ever know. His second try at making money as a composer through records about equaled the success of his first.

According to his first royalty statement, Glenn's record of "Solo Hop" sold less than eight hundred copies!

Meanwhile, the Noble band had continued its rehearsals. Late in April it played its first dances, and early in May it began recording for Victor. On the first date, in addition to a couple of ballads, it waxed two of Glenn's jazz arrangements: "Way Down Yonder in New Orleans," complete with the repeated rhythmic riffs Glenn always liked to feature, and a racing rendition of "Chinatown, My Chinatown."

Throughout Glenn's stay with the band, its music remained distinctly divided between Noble's pretty ballads and Miller's semi-dixieland jazz attempts. It was almost as if there were two different bands, Noble's and Miller's. In musical tastes and backgrounds Glenn and Ray may have seemed far apart, and yet they found a common meeting ground in their fetishistic dedication to details and precision and in their constant awareness and appreciation of the importance of a commercial approach.

They were alike in other ways, too. Both were very strongwilled. Both were very articulate, though rather reticent about talking. Each believed very strongly in his particular approach to music, and neither one was especially good at compromise. For a while their approaches and their personalities meshed nicely. But only for a while.

The first year was a good one. The band packed the swank Rainbow Room, atop the RCA Building in Radio City, "sixty-five stories nearer the stars," as the announcers used to say on those remote broadcasts. The guys enjoyed the job, even though they had a three A.M. closing, seven nights a week. But the good pay made it all quite bearable. In 1935, working almost exclusively for Noble, Glenn grossed $7,573.70, up to then an all-time high for him.

But, in addition to the money, the guys enjoyed themselves. They had pride in the band as a whole and in several of its jazz soloists, especially Bud Freeman, whose wildly inventive solos created all sorts of excitement. According to Bradley, "Glenn and I would bet on whether Bud would come out of his augmented spins. Glenn would say, 'Two drinks he doesn't make it,' and I'd say, 'Two drinks he does.' I used to win a lot of drinks that way."

Claude Thornhill emerged as the band's "character." One night, when business had been slow, the manager of the room told the band at two A.M. that they could go home—there weren't any customers left. So down to the sixty-fourth floor they went to change from their tuxes into their street clothes. Most of them were about to leave when Bill Harty, the band manager, came rushing in and announced that some of the Rockefellers—who only owned the joint—had come in with a big party, and they wanted to dance. Disgusted, the guys changed back into their work clothes and trudged back into the room, all except Thornhill, who seemed to have disappeared. But that didn't matter too much, because Noble also played the piano. And so they started to play again. Can you picture that sight, and the reactions of the Rockefellers, when, in the middle of the first number, into the swank Rainbow Room walked Claude Thornhill, impeccably dressed, except for one variation: He'd purposely neglected to put on his pants!

Long before I joined *Metronome,* when I was still in college, I had been enthralled by Ray Noble's English records, and so, almost as soon as I had joined the magazine in 1935, I used to gravitate toward the new Noble band. I didn't have enough money to go into the Rainbow Room as a paying customer, but I did discover that between sets the guys in the band would come out of a side door and sit in a lounge close by. So I would hang around there and talk with them, doing some interviews but generally just discussing music.

One of the nicest gents I ever met was Al Bowlly, Noble's South African singer, whose warm and tender phrasing was a true reflection of his personality. As I began to become accepted by the guys, their dressing room on the sixty-fourth floor became in-bounds for me. One of my fondest memories is of Bowlly taking me aside and telling me he'd like to sing me a song that Glenn had just written. Actually, only the melody was Glenn's; the lyrics were by Eddie Heyman, best known as the lyricist of "Body and Soul."

Al was a very sentimental guy who had no trouble showing his emotions, and I thought he was actually going to cry as he sang,

Al Bowlly.

without any accompaniment, the new song he had just learned and which obviously had affected him very much.

Later the song was given a new set of lyrics when it was retitled "Moonlight Serenade," but who remembers the words? Yet, ever since I first heard them, I've been unable to forget the original lyrics of "Now I Lay Me Down to Weep," as Al Bowlly crooned them just for me that early morning in the band's dressing room:

Weep for the moon, for the moon has no reason to glow now;
Weep for the rose, for the rose has no reason to grow now;
The river won't flow now,
As I lay me down to weep.

You went away, and the break in my heart isn't mending;
You went away, and I know there is no happy ending,
There's no use pretending,
As I lay me down to weep.

When you were mine, the world was mine,
And fate constantly smiled.
Now in its place, I have to face
A pillow of tears, all through the years.

Though you are gone, I still pray that the sun shines above you;
Time marches on, yet I know that I always will love you;

The first four bars of the original manuscript of what later became Glenn's theme song, "Moonlight Serenade," then titled "Now I Lay Me Down to Weep." This copy in Glenn's own hand was given to author Simon so he could come up with new lyrics. He did, but his "Gone with the Dawn" set wasn't used either!

> I'll keep dreaming of you,
> As I lay me down to weep.*

Gil Rodin recalls that one night Glenn came into the Hotel New Yorker where the Bob Crosby band, composed of many fellow Ben Pollack alumni, was playing. He said, "I've written a song and made an arrangement of it." The band ran it down, but, according to Gil, "it was full of unison clarinets and flutes and not in our style. I told him I thought it was a great melody and asked him to arrange it for our band. But he said, 'Let's wait until I get it published.' " It never was published until it became "Moonlight Serenade," and was never recorded by any band—even Noble's—until Glenn's own band did it four years later.

Of course, Noble could easily have recorded it, and chances are he might have, if he and Glenn had become better friends. But it didn't pan out that way, as it so seldom does when two creative and talented, but hard-nosed, individuals try working together over an extended period of time.

Certainly Ray did nobly, financially speaking, for Glenn. He gave him a base pay that rose as high as $175 a week and paid him extra for recording dates and one-nighters and for working on *The Big Broadcast of 1936,* so that Glenn's total weekly pay ranged from a one-week low of $130 to a one-week high of $356.

* TRO © 1967, Essex Music, Inc. Used by permission.

Considering the wage level, the price levels, and the 4 percent income tax then prevalent, Glenn made a lot of money out of his Noble association.

But, despite the good money, Glenn was beginning to feel restless in the band. I sensed this during several talks backstage at the Rainbow Room. At first we discussed the past and he told me about his days with Red Nichols, and I listened wide-eared as I got the inside dirt on what it was really like within that great group whose records I had played so often. And we talked about the present, too, and about the Noble band and some of its outstanding musicians, like Bud Freeman, Johnny Mince and Peewee Erwin, all three of whom would soon join Tommy Dorsey; and lead saxist Milt Yaner, who would be going with Jimmy Dorsey; and Thornhill and Will Bradley and Charlie Spivak, who would later be leading their own bands.

And there were other musicians and other bands we'd talk about. Glenn was a big Benny Goodman admirer, and we'd also share our enthusiasm for Jimmie Lunceford, and, of course, for Duke Ellington.

I always had the feeling—even then—that Glenn wanted so very much to be included among these elite of the jazz world. He was honest enough to recognize and admit his limits as a jazz trombonist. But he as yet had no way of knowing how he would fare competitively as a swing band leader, and the thought of showing the world—and that included his fellow-musicians, of course—that he could be a stand-out, if not as a jazz soloist, then as a leader in a field that included so many of the men he admired, certainly must have entered his very shrewd and analytical mind.

His candor, coupled with his close involvement with the sort of music we both loved, and, of course, his receptiveness to my eager overtures led me to believe that I was developing a really good friendship in my new and exciting world of jazz. And, as it turned out, I was right.

In those days I was still living with my family in a brownstone house on West Eighty-ninth Street off Central Park West. We were a closely knit, slightly snobbish and somewhat intolerant upper-middle-class Jewish clan, filling much of our five-story house with music. On the second floor we had a living room with two phonographs. On the parlor floor we had a large music room with two pianos and a Mason and Hamlin organ. There my oldest brother, Dick, would practice his piano concertos, or Henry would play with his string quartets, or Alfred and a friend would play show tunes on the two pianos.

Down in the basement I had my own type of music room, a pad devoted to jazz, complete with my phonograph, record collection, and set of drums, on which I tried, with total lack of success, to emulate Gene Krupa, Chick Webb, Ray McKinley, Ray Bauduc, and others, as I drummed to their records. Sometimes I'd play extra loud and purposely leave a window slightly open, just in case some band leader might pass by and discover my genius.

Naturally, I was considered the family lowbrow, and I guess I was. Nobody else in the house had any appreciation whatsoever of jazz. Dick, who in 1924, at the age of twenty-four, had founded the publishing firm of Simon and Schuster, often brought home to dinner some of his intellectual compatriots, ranging all the way from authors like Will Durant to musicians like George Gershwin. Henry was a professor of English at Columbia, and he'd invite some of his fellow-intellectuals to the house.

Faced with such competition, I hesitated bringing any "lowbrow jazz musicians" home to dinner. Few, if any, I figured, would receive the far-too-important seal of family approval.

But then one night, for some reason or other—maybe it was because he always seemed so bright and was always so polite—I got up enough courage to display Glenn to my family. And I was overjoyed when I saw how he charmed them all. Not that his conversation was especially scintillating or his humor especially titillating. I think it was more that they never expected a jazz musician to be so down to earth, to talk so directly and so clearly, and just to talk so much good, common sense. For me, it turned out to be an evening of beautiful, reflected glory. I had brought home a winner!

Later that evening Glenn and I went downstairs to the basement to listen to our kind of records, and it was then that he let me in on his big secret: He was going to start his own band.

The author, hoping to be discovered!

He didn't know yet exactly when or where or even what kind of a band he was going to have. But it would be a musical one and it would play some jazz, that was certain. He still had a lot of planning to do and decisions to make, including the finding and hiring of the musicians who would fit into his scheme of things. And that was one of the reasons he was taking me into his confidence. In my adventures as a *Metronome* reporter and critic, I heard an enormous number of musicians. How about my letting him know where some of the better prospects were located? He'd appreciate that. Maybe I could, in fact, help him get his band started.

Would I?

Damn right, I would.

PART TWO

The Band That Failed

Chapter 8

During 1936 the Noble band's popularity began to ebb. In the previous year it had latched on to well-paying jobs, including a radio commercial. It had looked as if the following year would be just as good, and so, before leaving for a vacation in England, Noble and manager Bill Harty had assured the men that there would be big things happening during the next season.

Well, the band went back into the Rainbow Room all right, and the steady flow of recording sessions continued, but the radio commercial didn't materialize, and when, during the first theater tour after the Rainbow Room engagement, the guys were asked to take a cut in salary, several of them said "No, thanks." Most vehement was Glenn, who never could tolerate broken promises and who hadn't been getting along too well with Noble and Harty anyway. It was he who led an angry walkout that included many of the band's top musicians, and from which the band never recovered.

While marking time until he could get his own band started, Glenn played radio dates, most of them with Freddy Rich's orchestra, and even worked for a while with Vincent Lopez's band. He also sat in on a recording date with the new band of his old boss Ben Pollack, which sported an exciting and completely unknown young trumpeter named Harry James, whom Benny Goodman was soon to grab (I raved about him in *Metronome* and called him "Henry James!"), and a marvelous clarinetist named

Irving "Fazola" Prestopnik, whom Glenn would eventually hire.

Glenn and Helen were living very comfortably in their apartment at 37-60 Eighty-eighth Street in Jackson Heights, and Glenn could have settled, as many of his compatriots did, for the life of a studio musician. That meant playing the "vanilla" sort of music called for by the various sponsors—music that would never offend anyone, or excite anyone, including the musicians themselves. Some of his friends had been able to compromise; they had learned how to stomach such a bland and, for a creative musician, gigolo-like existence without throwing up. But for others, Miller included, it proved to be almost too much of an effort. A few, like Goodman, Shaw and the Dorseys, were now leading their own bands. And many more had signed up as sidemen in the new wave of swing bands. But Glenn had already paid his dues as a traveling sideman. For him there was only one way out. He would start his own band.

He talked it over with Helen. Obviously, it would mean a change in their life-style. No more relaxed evenings at home. No more regular paychecks. No more security.

Of course, it would be a gamble. But Glenn had made up his mind, and there have been few minds harder to change than his. He was sure he could make out. After all, he had, in one way or another, acted as co-leader in the bands of Smith Ballew, the Dorsey Brothers and Ray Noble. Certainly he'd gained enough experience there—he had learned what to do and what not to do, and, perhaps most important of all, how to handle musicians and how to balance his creative daydreams with the commercial facts of life. His credentials were impeccable.

I realized this as we discussed what kind of a band he was going to have. He talked about Jimmie Lunceford and about his showmanship. He emphasized that he wanted a good combination of Swing and ballads. For a while we talked about some of the pretty arrangements he had written for Red Nichols, with the low, mournful sax lead, but Glenn discarded the idea of this style because he thought it might sound too melancholy.

And we'd talk about Glenn himself, and from these talks and some we held later on, I learned more about the man, including some of his likes and dislikes. His favorite author was Damon

Runyon. His favorite book was the Bible. Spencer Tracy and Olivia de Havilland were his favorite movie actor and actress.

His big loves were trout fishing, playing baseball, listening to good music, sleep and money. His pet hates were bad swing music, early-morning telephone calls (he liked to sleep from 4 A.M. until noon) and the phrase "good-bye now." His favorite quotation, he once stated, was not from the Bible, nor from Runyon, but from Duke Ellington: "It Don't Mean a Thing If It Ain't Got That Swing!"

Of course, we'd talk a lot about what his band was going to be like. I liked the way he played trombone, and I wondered how he would feature himself. When he told me that he wasn't even going to play trombone, I was shocked. But his explanation made sense. "I can't play as well as Tommy Dorsey, so why should I come out second best?" I hadn't realized how little he thought of his own playing, or how much he needed to be *the* best. Had I idolized him less, I might have begun to suspect right then and there that maybe this wasn't such a superbly self-confident guy after all.

Late in 1936 we started looking for musicians. Benny Goodman had already given Glenn a good lead. While driving through New Britain, Connecticut, he'd heard a band on a local radio station that sounded somewhat like his own—maybe not as slick or as accomplished but with a fine spirit and a very good jazz clarinetist. Benny and his friend John Hammond investigated and found that the leader was a local lad named Hal McIntyre, who also played the jazz clarinet and who had copied some of the Goodman arrangements off records.

So one day Benny put in a call to Hal at his home. "Hello," he said, "this is Benny Goodman." McIntyre, who'd always been kidded about his worship of Goodman, thought it was a gag and said, "That's great—well, this is Jesus Christ," and hung up. Finally Benny's secretary put in another call and explained to Hal that it really *was* Benny calling. Goodman then invited Hal to come down to New York, and, so a couple of his friends claim, Hal even played with the band for a few days. ("I'm not sure. I don't remember. He may have," Benny recently recalled with his most charming vagueness.) McIntyre's widow, June, then his girl friend, believes that Benny introduced them to Glenn at a rehearsal, though I always thought that Glenn had never met Hal until one very cold, wintry night when we drove up to Cromwell, Connecticut, to hear him play.

I remember we met him at his home and we liked him immediately. He was warm and friendly and direct—typical of the all-American type of boy with whom Glenn hoped to stock his band. He had lined up some other local musicians, all members of his own band, for an audition in the New Britain radio studio. So we followed him over there, he leading the way in an old model-A Ford convertible with the top thrown back on that frightfully frigid night. We thought the guy was some sort of a nut. But we were wrong. He just liked fresh air.

As it turned out, the only musician in the band whom Glenn wanted right then and there was Hal himself, who I thought played a pretty good jazz clarinet—an instrument on which he was seldom heard thereafter. Hal tried to talk Glenn into hiring some more of his guys, but, except for the bass player, who had to leave early to make another gig, Glenn wasn't interested. Later, bassist Rolly Bundock reports, "He did send for me. He sent me a telegram and asked me to join the band on just two days' notice." Bundock, who stayed for three years and three months, recalls that "Glenn was very warm to begin with. He was just modulating from being a sideman."

Meanwhile, back in late 1936, the search for musicians continued. Part of my job at *Metronome* was to go around town and review bands. In the November issue I had written about the band of Harry Reser, who had become famous on radio as head of his Cliquot Club Eskimos. He had lost his commercial radio series and was now leading a new and rather swinging outfit composed of some of New York's younger musicians. They were playing at the Arcadia Ballroom on Broadway at Fifty-third Street. Two of the young sax players had impressed me especially: George Siravo, the lead altoist, and Jerry Jerome, who played the hot tenor. I took Glenn over to hear them and he offered them both jobs. They accepted.

Some time later I took Glenn over to the Holland Hotel, far west on Forty-second Street, to hear a clarinetist. He didn't impress us too much, but the tenor man in the band did, and so we stayed around to listen. We had ordered sandwiches and coffee, after which our waiter disappeared, only to show up a bit later as the master of ceremonies for some third-rate floor show. Later he came back to our table and asked us what we'd like to drink. When we told him more coffee, he told us that wouldn't do—we'd have to order some booze if we expected to stay around. When we told him we didn't want any, he conferred with the head waiter, then returned and asked us to get out. And so we left, after making sure that the tenor man, Johnny Harrell, would show up the next day for rehearsal.

The episode amused Glenn. "That was the first time," he told me, "that I've ever been thrown out of a joint for *not* drinking."

In the past, Glenn had had his drinking bouts, and they hadn't always been pleasant ones. Various people who have seen him in his cups have proclaimed him "a mean drunk" and "a monster when he drinks," and one person described him as "a drunk right out of central casting. He used foul language."

David Mackay, for years his attorney, reports that once, in the early days of his marriage, Glenn went out on a toot that lasted a couple of days. It cost him more than he had on him, and, to pay off, he had withdrawn a bundle from a checking account which he and Helen shared. This infuriated Helen, who apparently had had to put up with such a routine before, and so she decided to go on a binge of her own. According to Mackay, "She went to the bank and drew out all the rest of the money from the account. And then she went into Manhattan and bought all the clothes she'd always wanted to buy. It taught Glenn a lesson."

Glenn, whose father apparently had also lost some bouts to the bottle, was acutely aware of his own problem and what it might lead to. He had told me that as long as he would remain a leader he intended to stay strictly on the wagon; that he couldn't afford to take any chances, because, he intimated, after a few drinks he could easily turn into a pretty rough and unattractive character. I must say that until he went into the army, I never saw him touch a drop, though various band members have reported that every once in a while when the band was traveling by train, Glenn would bust loose with a few—sometimes even more—and depending upon his mood, he might have a great time with a few friends. More often, though, he'd be apt to lash out angrily at somebody or some situation that had been bugging him.

In the early part of 1937 the band rehearsed regularly in the Haven Studio on West Fifty-fourth Street between Sixth and Seventh avenues, approximately on the same spot that the Half Note, one of the city's leading jazz clubs, now stands. It was a dingy walkup floor-through of what might once have been a swank town house. Its décor was strictly god-awful-oriental. Mr. Haven was a gentle, very particular elderly man who always reminded me of a retired actor or scenic designer who'd never quite made it. In fact, the whole atmosphere reminded me of a Clubhouse for Retired Veterans of the Gay World.

It was up there that we used to trudge to rehearse. By this time I had become thoroughly immersed in the band's career. I had attended most of the rehearsals, sometimes as an observer, at other times as the band's drummer. For quite a while Glenn and I could find no drummer who satisfied us, and since I had played drums sort of professionally and knew the arrangements and was available anyway, Glenn would ask me to play along.

For me, it was a beautiful education. I have, during my many years in the music field, attended many rehearsals and have noticed how various leaders work. But I can't remember ever watching anyone who knew so exactly what he wanted and who knew so well how to get it. Though a perfectionist, Glenn mixed his demands with patience. He must have been acutely aware that these young musicians needed more help than the veterans with whom he had been playing, and he gave it to them unstintingly. Sometimes some of his friends, top musicians like trumpeter Charlie Spivak and saxist Toots Mondello, would drop by and sit in to help out. But generally Glenn was all on his own with these comparative youngsters. He kept helping them in every way that he possibly could. I can remember, for example, when the saxes were having difficulty with a certain passage, and Glenn, instead of trying to describe in words the kind of phrasing he was looking for, would step right into the midst of the section with his trombone and say, "Listen, fellows, follow me. I'll show

THE COUNTRY'S NEWEST COMING BAND?!

Last month there was a little news item in this magazine to the effect that Glenn Miller was organizing his own band. That item inspired this writer to search the rehearsal halls for the Miller embryo. He found it, and what he heard was even more inspiring than the short article that inspired the search. In the first place there are some arrangements in that new Miller library that are (to coin a counterfeit phrase) really out of this world. And Miller, besides great talents as an arranger, possesses other attributes which should help him nicely in what already looks like a pretty easy climb to the top for him. He's a thorough, as well as a thoroughly hep, musician; knows what he wants, and, judging from the qualities of his embryo, knows how to get what he wants. And there are a couple of non-personal attributes which should make the Miller stock soar, so far as the swing fan market goes: No. 1 is clarinet-man Hal McIntyre whom Miller uncovered in the wilds of Connecticut; No. 2 is tenor-man Johnny Harrell, a Texan, whom Glenn stumbled across in one of those weird and commercial 42nd Street joints here in town; No. 3 is fine hot trumpeter Sterling Bose of New Orleans, Pollack, Dorsey, and Noble vintage, who's decided to cast his lot with the Merry Miller Men. All of you swing men out there can expect plenty. Your first chance to hear a sample should be six sides of Decca records Glenn is making the first of this month. Listen!

Success Prediction #1—from the March 1937 issue of *Metronome* magazine.

you how I want it played." And he'd instruct the trumpets and the trombones the same way.

While helping out Glenn, whom I began to admire more and more each day, I continued to write for *Metronome*. In the February 1937 issue I announced that his band was in rehearsal, and then next month I went out on a limb and predicted, after hearing it, that one of these days this would be the country's number one band. It must have seemed like a ridiculous prophecy to just about everybody, because just about nobody, except those of us who had been attending rehearsals, had ever heard the band. And most of the rest probably hadn't even heard of its existence. But that's the way I felt—and, I thought, with good reasons.

By March, Rockwell-O'Keefe, who was booking the band, had worked out a deal for a single recording session with Decca. I was in Chicago on a reviewing trip when I received a wire from Glenn announcing the date and wanting to know if I'd come back to play it. Of course, I did. It was the first and only commercial record session I ever played.

And it was a session I'll never forget. I was so nervous that I couldn't control my hands, and they trembled so that I found it almost impossible not to play triplets instead of single strokes. And Glenn didn't help, either. Faced with time limitations, he drove his musicians—me, especially, it seemed—incredibly hard. It was the custom on recording dates to make four sides. However, in those days the union placed no limit on the number of sides a band could record, provided they didn't work for more than three hours. So Glenn, the shrewd businessman that he was, aimed for six sides in three hours—and he got them, too.

Most of us had become pretty familiar with the arrangements, having played several of them at rehearsals. But to make sure that he had some proven pros who could hold the young group together, Glenn hired some of his studio friends for that date. Spivak, New York's best lead trumpeter, Mannie Klein, the town's best all-around trumpeter, and Sterling Bose, a good jazz player, comprised the trumpet section. Howard Smith, who played piano for Tommy Dorsey, and Dick McDonough, one of the all-time guitar greats, performed in the rhythm section that included young Ted Kotsoftis on bass and that young *Metronome* writer on drums. Glenn was still refusing to play, so the trombones consisted of newcomers Jesse Ralph and Harry Rodgers. Carl Biesecker, a tenor man with a lovely tone, joined Siravo, Jerome and McIntyre in the sax section. Hal also contributed an arrangement of "I'm Sittin' on Top of the World," the sixth side we did on the date, on which he played jazz clarinet à la Goodman. The other arrangements were all Glenn's.

Of Glenn's five scores, only one, "Peg o' My Heart," was strictly instrumental. The others all featured vocals, an obvious attempt to be commercial. The entire band sang on "Moonlight Bay." Trumpeter Bose sang "Anytime, Any Day, Anywhere," backed by a vocal trio, the Tune Twisters, one of whom, Jack Lathrop, three years later joined the band as guitarist and occasional vocalist. On the other two sides—"How Am I to Know," a song associated with Smith Ballew, and "Wistful and Blue"—Glenn used a totally unknown singer named Doris Kerr. Nobody could figure out quite how she rated the date until word got out that she was the daughter of an important NBC executive. Glenn was attending to business even then.

Shortly after the recording session, he started attending to business with me, too. I remember well the night he put it to me. We were driving around, still looking for musicians, and he turned and said, "Look, I think you'd better decide what you want to do. Do you want to go with the band or do you want to stick to writing for that magazine of yours?"

Naturally, I'd given some thought to leaving *Metronome* and seeing whether I could make it as a jazz drummer. But, after having heard the records, and also after having relived the emotional trauma of those torturous three hours during which Glenn pressured me as I'd never been pressured before, I'd begun to realize that I'd be happier and hopefully more successful as a writer.

And then there was one other important determinant: my whole life-style. I'd been brought up in a comfortable home, perhaps too well protected in my younger years, and, I must admit now, probably scared to go out completely on my own, away from all the security I had always known, into a world where I'd have to rough it.

By then I'd learned enough about the life of a traveling band musician so that I couldn't be snowed under by any delusions of glamour. I knew how the average guy lived—hours and hours of traveling by bus in cramped quarters, eating in crummy diners, sleeping, not in one's own comfortable bed, but in some cheap hotel room, limited changes of clothes, getting soaked in the rain and having no home to dry out in—and it didn't intrigue me. I was at least a semi-spoiled young man and, as I look back at me now, also probably at least a semi-snob. What's more, there was no drinking in our family, and the possibility of being trapped among heavy drinkers, as some musicians were, I guess probably frightened me. I was, as you can see, a rather slow maturer. Maybe, had I grown up sooner, I might have left *Metronome* for Miller. But I didn't, and, quite frankly, I'm not sorry.

Six weeks after the record date, on May 7, the band played its first engagement, a one-nighter in the Terrace Room of the

Hotel New Yorker as a substitute for Gus Arnheim's band, which in those days sported a young piano player named Stan Kenton. I was there that night, but not as drummer, having already made the decision to stick to writing. Glenn had hired Eak Kenyon on drums, and Chummy MacGregor had come in on piano. The rhythm section didn't impress me at all (professional jealousy, perhaps?), but the rest of the band did. And the entire band so impressed Ralph Hitz, president of the hotel chain, that he arranged with his friend Seymour Weiss, head of the famed Roosevelt Hotel in New Orleans, for the band to open there in mid-June.

For the New Yorker engagement, the band received union scale, which amounted to a total of $397.50, of which $48 went to Glenn. That spring it cut four more sides, this time for Brunswick and all instrumentals: "I Got Rhythm," which Glenn had played hundreds of times in the pit of *Girl Crazy*; "Time on My Hands"; "Sleepy Time Gal"; and a Miller original called "Community Swing." The personnel had changed considerably, with only the saxes lining up as they had on the first record date. Spivak sat in again to bolster the trumpets. Bose, who played with the band when he was able to, was apparently drying out somewhere, and so he didn't make the date. Tweet Peterson and Ralph Capelli were the other two trumpeters. Jesse Ralph was still on trombone, flanked this time by Bud Smith, lately of the Noble band. The rhythm section was completely different: MacGregor was on piano, Bill Peyser played guitar, Rolly Bundock played bass, and Kenyon was the drummer. The records turned out to be just fair, not as good as the Decca batch, as Glenn agreed.

Then, for its first steady engagement, the band played for two weeks at the Raymor Ballroom in Boston. The lineup was basically the same. Vi Mele, a musical singer who was also a good pianist, had joined as the girl vocalist, and Jimmy Troutman, an exceptionally good all-around player, had taken over the lead trumpet chair.

The Raymor, on Huntington Avenue, close to Symphony Hall, was to become the band's resting place. Once probably considered elegant, it had aged into a typical mid-city ballroom. Heavily draped and dimly lit, it offered about as much glamour

Boston, June 1937.

Kathleen Lane, best of all Miller singers.

as a men's locker room. But it had a loyal clientele and a very gentle and understanding manager in Hughie Galvin, who liked Glenn and the band, and who took them back after they returned from their first road trip.

The band's personnel remained intact for a while. Bose behaved and returned with his booting horn. Kathleen Lane, a gorgeously proportioned girl who, for my dough, sang better than any girl singer Glenn ever had, replaced Vi Mele. The band played a few one-nighters, including one at the Playland Casino in Rye, New York, and another at the Chagrin Valley Hunt Club in Gates Mill, Ohio. For each of these it received the munificent sum of two hundred dollars!

The band opened at the Roosevelt in New Orleans on June 17. The hours were rough: 6:30 P.M. to 2:00 A.M. on weekdays and to 3:00 A.M. on Saturdays, plus afternoon sessions from 2:30 to 5:30 on Saturdays and Sundays. The men received scale of $73.30 a week, which wasn't bad for those days. But, after deducting their salaries, commissions, and union and social security payments from the total of $1,250 he was receiving weekly for the band, Glenn wound up with a grand total of $5.75 per week for himself. Out of this came his living expenses and money for arrangements and various other incidentals.

But, even though he was operating at a loss, Glenn was benefitting from the engagement. If nothing else, it boosted his morale. The band was a huge success, breaking all records for longevity at the hotel. In fact, Glenn's confidence apparently had received such a boost that he finally decided to take his trombone out of its case and blow it in front of his band—for all the world to hear—and to hell with Tommy Dorsey! He admitted in an interview that he was "susceptible to stage fright, a drying of the mouth, shaking of the knees, and blankness of the mind." But he went on to say, "I have practically overcome it by developing confidence in myself and my band. Deep abdominal breathing is helpful, too."

His optimism was further reflected in a letter which Helen wrote to me—pinch-hitting, as she explained—on August 8, 1937, shortly before the band closed at the Roosevelt:

Dear George,

Glenn is always saying that he wished you knew this or that and still the monkey just never seems to find time to even eat properly let alone sit down and write, so I will try to tell you of a few of the things he has mentioned.

In the first place, he got a great kick out of your telegram from Boston. When his gang [the Pollack alumni, by then the Bob Crosby band] get together, he surely gets lonesome to see them and he did wish that he could have been with you and Gil [Rodin]. Then there was your last letter you wrote about the Brunswick releases. It was funny about that. He had been fussing about those records and saying exactly the same things you said in your letter. Most of the boys felt the same too, although once in a while you find a few that like the last batch. Glenn is so in hopes that the next ones will turn out much better.

About his men. He says to you very confidentially that the drum and cornet situation is his best worry. This seems to ruin his disposition no end. The boy from Denver that took Jimmy Troutman's place has been a terrific disappointment in every way and will have to go just as soon as Glenn can find a replacement. The guitar was of no particular use so Glenn is going to try five saxes. The boy they call Faz from Arnheim's band is joining here as soon as his two weeks notice is up and Glenn is going to try five in the sax section and no guitar, for a while anyway. The band has improved so much everyone says and Glenn surely wishes you could hear it. He has no complaint at the way things have gone for us here. Five weeks was the record length any band ever stayed and when we finish here, which is August 25, the boys will have been here ten weeks. That's something, isn't it? We go directly to Dallas from here and open the Adolphus Hotel on Friday noon, August 27th. Glenn only hopes he may have a little good luck there with the band, inasmuch as that is his first chance at a Hitz Hotel. Well, it won't take long to see, will it, George?

The boys in the band have all been swell and have worked so hard. They are really the grandest bunch you could ever wish for.

Before I mail this to you, I will see if Glenn can't just scribble

ABOVE: The Roosevelt marquee.

LOWER LEFT: Glenn helps Kathleen Lane onto the Roosevelt bandstand.

LOWER RIGHT: Sterling Bose doing the "Touli Touli" dance.

ABOVE: (Left to right) trombonist Bud Smith, saxist Jerry Jerome, Glenn, bassist Rollie Bundock, trumpeter Tweet Peterson, guitarist Bill Peyser.

LOWER LEFT: The Swinging Mr. Miller.

LOWER RIGHT: Hal McIntyre in the newly opened New Orleans Sugar Bowl.

a note too. I probably have forgotten to tell you the most important things, but since I am pinch-hitting you will forgive me I know.

> Best regards to you, George,
> Helen and Glenn

[In Glenn's handwriting] Simon, Simon, you louse. I thot you were coming down for your vacation. Hows to make Dallas?

Not everyone showed as much enthusiasm for the band. Though the customers were obviously pleased, not all the critics liked it. Several years later Glenn received a letter of apology from one who was to emerge as a leader in the United States House of Representatives. Regarding the Roosevelt engagement, F. Edward Hebert wrote Glenn on March 6, 1942:

Dear Glenn:
It's a long time since I penned a piece for the New Orleans States the night you opened in the Blue Room of The Roosevelt and said that your band had too much brass in it. Remember?
Times have changed plenty since then. Today you are the Nation's No. 1 band leader. And Me?
From newspaper columnist and critic (?) I am just another Congressman. One of 435—count 'em.
I'm glad I was wrong in what I wrote when I reviewed your opening and I want you to know that like many of my colleagues who only so recently changed their minds when the subject of "pensions" was brought up—I agree you are tops!

> Kindest personal regards,
> F. Edw. Hebert

From all indications, the band hated to leave New Orleans, where many of the guys were having a ball. Glenn had arranged for them to receive membership in the New Orleans Athletic Club, which meant that those who wanted to use the athletic facilities could do so, while those who were more interested in bending a few elbows could work out at the bar.

On the subject of bars, the owner of a string of them came into the Blue Room one night, was introduced to Glenn, and gave him a copy of a song he had written. Presumably aware of the owner's contacts and influence, Glenn proceeded to make an arrangement of his song for the band to play, and, sure enough, the neophyte songwriter brought in hordes of friends regularly—just to hear his song.

Glenn was learning fast.

Chapter 9

 That first Glenn Miller band never again had it so good as it did during its first important engagement, a happy wedding for the band and its public. After New Orleans the honeymoon was over, and life was never the same.

Shortly before the band had closed at the Roosevelt, Irving "Fazola" Prestopnik, the clarinet player whom Helen had mentioned in her letter and whom Glenn had first heard on that 1936 Ben Pollack recording session, joined, and the week after the band opened at the Adolphus, Bob Price replaced Ralph Capelli on lead trumpet. Musically, both proved to be great additions. Fazola, who really wasn't much of a saxophonist, was featured on clarinet, and it was his presence that indirectly led to the clarinet-with-saxes sound that was to set the band's style. Price blew a powerful horn, and in time he gave the brass section a solidity it had never enjoyed since the days when Charlie Spivak had been sitting in.

But both Fazola, a round-faced, round-bellied portion of lard, and Price, only slightly more sylph-like, were potent boozers, and the effect they were to have on some of the other guys in the band, who looked up to them, and eventually upon the band's morale, was devastating.

The engagement at the Adolphus, like that at the Roosevelt, was a seven-day-a-week affair with luncheon sessions included.

Fazola.

Again Glenn received only union scale, which meant another financial loss for him. But this time there was no compensating encouragement from hotel manager and patrons. Glenn's old pal Benny Goodman saw the picture.

One evening the King of Swing, whose band was also working in Dallas, dropped into the gloomy setting. "Glenn seemed very discouraged and I kept telling him not to quit, to keep at it and just stay in there. I told him, 'One morning you'll wake up and you'll suddenly say, "Hey, the band sounds great!"'

"I knew how he felt, because I had had some experiences like that when my band was playing at Billy Rose's Music Hall. Things were so rough for us then, that I couldn't ever be sure which musicians would be there on any given night!"

Glenn had some interesting comments to make about Benny and Fazola, about whom he could grow pretty emotional—for Glenn. "I sincerely believe," he wrote to me, "that Faz is the only clarinet player with a chance these days. Shaw, Mince and all of them play like Benny and they will not live long enough to cut him. Faz, like Ol' Man River, jes' keeps rollin' along and he doesn't want to know from anyone. I doubt if he has ever heard more than just a few Goodman records and up until Dallas he never met or heard Benny personally. Benny listened very closely when Faz was playing.

"While on Benny, he was his usual swell self to us in Dallas, and that band, George, is without doubt the greatest thing in the history of jazz. I thought they were good at the Pennsylvania, but they have improved one hundred percent since then. That cornet section is the Marvel of the Age, and Krupa is more of a genius than ever to me. He drums with his head which is a real rarity."

Drummers were still very much on Glenn's mind these days. Kenyon proved to be a nice, gentle soul, but he played like one, too. So during the Dallas stay Glenn took on a new drummer, a youngster named Buddy Schutz, whom I had been raving about and who later wound up as a mainstay in Jimmy Dorsey's band. But this time Glenn and I disagreed drastically.

The Hotel Nicollet engagement in Minneapolis that followed Dallas offered no more encouragement. The schedule was a backbreaker: from 12:30 to 2:00 every afternoon, and then from 7:00 to 9:00 P.M. and 10:00 P.M. to 1:30 A.M. every night. For this the band was paid a total of $1,300 per week. But Glenn's weekly expenses, not including arrangements, living expenses and other incidentals—in other words, just salaries and commissions—came to $1,319.02. So, before he even started living, he was out $19.02 per week.

Again, it might have been worth it if the band had scored a hit, as it had in New Orleans. This contract also called for a four weeks' engagement with options. But this time no options were exercised.

On October 12, 1937, Glenn contacted me from the Nicollet. I had written to him in Dallas, suggesting that Zeke Zarchy, who had left the Bob Crosby band, might be a good bet to stabilize the still-floundering trumpet section. Dopey me had failed to realize that, because of his financial condition, Glenn couldn't afford major leaguers. "Don't faint—take it cool—relax a minute and we'll start," his letter began. "I phoned Gil [Rodin] as you suggested and he told me that he paid Zeke a figure I cannot possibly match, so I gave the matter up. We have two pretty fair cornet players now [Note: Glenn would often refer to trumpet players as cornet players, probably because of his close association with Red Nichols and Jimmy McPartland, both of whom played cornet rather than trumpet.], Peterson and a fellow by the name of Bob Price. I believe in time that he will work out fine. Also a third guy by the name of Ardel Garretson that may develop into something—we'll see.

"The front line of the band would gladden the heart of anyone. The saxes are beautiful and for my dough there is only one Faz.

"We are getting a new drummer (thank God) in a couple of weeks, Doc Kearney [Note: also known as Carney] of Detroit, about two hundred and fifty pounds of solid rhythm, I hope. The boy we have is pretty bad and MacGregor says outside of being a bad drummer he has a quarter-beat rest between each tooth which doesn't enhance the romantic assets of the band. . . .

"George, I wish that I could see you and thank you for the interest you have taken in us. You surely have been a wonderful help and I hope you will continue to be on the lookout for men that might improve our combo."

Then the Miller financial frustration crept in. The Crosby band, through its president, Gil Rodin, had fallen upon a benefactor named Celeste LeBrosi, an extremely wealthy lady, who followed the band wherever it played. "Think you could try," Glenn continued, "and get Mrs. LeBrosi, or whatever her name is, to detour a little to the North, and maybe we can slip a knife in Rodin's back and steal one of his fans.

"I don't know just where we are going from here—I guess no one else does either. We are hoping for some sort of a radio set-up that will let more than three people hear us at one time. If this drummer only works out, there will be nothing to stop us from now on, barring mishaps, of course. . . .

"This is about all for now, George. I am practically exhausted from all this, so it looks like a nap and so to work. . . . Your friend, Glenn."

Doc Carney did give the band a solidity it had lacked at all previous times, including that first Decca record date. He also gave the band a distinction that very few knew about and that it was never to achieve again. As Jerry Jerome, the band's tenor saxist who was very close to Glenn, recently revealed: "Doc Carney, whose real name was Cenardo, had reddish hair and freckles, and he was Spanish-looking. He was part-Negro. But he passed because nobody ever pointed it out." Without realizing it, the Miller band had broken the color line, a distinction about which nobody seemed aware or to care.

The band's jazz improved, thanks to Doc's strong beat, Fazola's gorgeous solos, Price's biting lead horn, and, of course, Glenn's arranging tricks, like the repetition of riffs, the "ooh-wah" sound, created by the brass waving metal derby hats in front of the bells of their horns, and those sly diminuendos broken by bursting, blasting brass barrages that built up to rousing climaxes—tricks he was to keep for the rest of the band's history.

Glenn liked to experiment with the sound of the reed section. Sometimes on up-tempoed tunes, to create more excitement, he'd have all five men playing high up on their clarinets. Then, to create a warmer sound on ballads, he would voice the reeds lower, using the tenor sax instead of the usual higher-pitched alto sax as the lead horn.

Great as he was on clarinet, Fazola did present one problem. He was not a very good saxophonist, and sometimes on ballads he'd just be sitting there while the four other reed men blew their saxes. One night, according to Rolly Bundock, Glenn had an idea. Rather than having Faz do nothing, he suggested that he double the tenor-sax lead on his clarinet. It sounded rather nice, and Glenn used the voicing sparingly, if for no other reason than to give Faz something to do. He even included it in a few bars of his recorded arrangement of "Humoresque." But he really didn't give it too much attention at the time. But later on . . . !!

As the band began providing him with more kicks, Glenn decided to join in the musical fun. He began to play more and more solos and to get his lip back into shape. But, hard as he tried, he could not rid himself of certain inhibitions. The specter of Tommy Dorsey and his gorgeous tone and astounding technique kept haunting him.

Had there been no TD before him, GM might have tried to establish his trombone as his band's distinguishing musical trademark. All the other successful big bands had theirs: Tommy

and his trombone, Goodman and Shaw with their clarinets, Guy Lombardo with his wheezing saxes, Kay Kyser with his College of Musical Knowledge, Sammy Kaye with his Swing and Sway, Shep Fields with his Rippling Rhythm. More and more, Glenn became obsessed with the necessity of finding his own distinctive and distinguishing sound. Obviously, neither his own trombone nor his jazz arrangements supplied the answer.

Following the Minneapolis engagement, where the band's music surpassed its reception, Miller and Company returned to the Raymor in Boston for more lean pickings: a six-days-a-week stint for $1,000 and two five-days-a-week runs for $770 each. In November it recorded four more Brunswick sides, including "Humoresque" and one of Glenn's originals called "Doin' the Jive," which created no furor at all. Then in December, when the band's morale had hit an all-time low, it labored for five hours but managed to record only two tunes, one of which,

"Sweet Stranger," featured an exquisite Mildred Bailey–like vocal by Kitty Lane, the best ever on any of Glenn's civilian band's recordings. But just two sides in five hours—when any band in normally good shape could complete at least four in three hours!

Everything seemed to be going wrong, even little things. Typical was the band's first theater date. I remember that initial show at the Adams in Newark. Glenn had prepared very carefully. One of his big mood numbers was his arrangement of "Danny Boy," also known as "Londonderry Air." To heighten the effect, Glenn had decided to precede the number with a completely dark stage. Then, as the brass section, gathered around one mike, would start the tune, a tight pin-spotlight would pick them up. And what happened on that first show? The second the brass blew those opening notes, the pin spot came on—directly on the five reeds, waiting with their horns at their sides at another mike for their entrance sixteen bars later!

And then there were the bigger things that went wrong, too, like one of the better boozers wrecking one of the two cars that the band needed for transportation, while another smashed up the truck.

But the most lasting blow of all was Helen, who hadn't been feeling well for weeks, being rushed to the hospital for a major operation that would forevermore make it impossible for her and Glenn to have children of their own.

As 1937 was drawing to a close, loneliness, frustration, and discouragement, battling for first place in Glenn's life, seemed to be headed for a three-way tie.

Of course, if the band had been in good shape, Glenn might not have felt so low. But it wasn't. Various personnel changes, caused by guys quitting or being fired, made it impossible for Glenn to achieve the precision that meant so much to him. And the weather grew so cold that some of the boozers began buying extra fifths for warmth and to see them through the boring, non-playing hours in what must have been some of New England's chilliest and most dismal towns.

Glenn wasn't too unhappy when Garretson left, because his replacement, Tommy DiCarlo, was a powerhouse trumpeter, though a "character." But when Tony Viola replaced George Siravo, one of the few remaining original musicians, the band lost not only a good saxist but also a fine arranger and a warm, enthusiastic person whom Glenn respected as a musician and as a friend.

Glenn respected even more Siravo's sidekick from the Harry Reser band, Jerry Jerome, an especially bright person who had completed three years of medical school before bowing to the Depression. One of the few thoroughly responsible sidemen, he had, as he put it, "become Glenn's trusted lieutenant. One of my assignments was to room with Fazola and Bob Price, both heavy drinkers, to make sure they got on the bandstand on time. I remember, they used to drink until four or five in the morning. It was always a contest to see who could outlast whom.

"They looked for other kicks, too. One night Faz tried to get high on marijuana. But he never smoked cigarettes and so he didn't know how to inhale. So Price and I put a wastebasket over his head and packed towels around his neck so the air couldn't get in, and then we gave him some marijuana to smoke. He almost suffocated to death. But he got high."

But booze still topped the kick list. And sometimes it became a necessity. "I remember one bitter-cold night we were on our way to play in the Armory in Oneida, New York. I was sitting in the back of the car between Price and Faz. We had no heaters, and we were freezing, so Faz said, 'Let's get some juice,' and we stopped and they picked up two fifths of Gordon's gin and I bought a pair of baseball socks to keep my feet warm. But they got so cold anyway that I finally decided that I needed some of the gin to keep from freezing to death. At first I felt nothing, but when I stepped out of the car, I fell flat on my face. And then when we got into the Armory and all that heat suddenly hit me, I just passed out cold. And *I* was the guy Glenn had sent to make sure that Faz and Price would get there all right!"

Glenn's love or appreciation of Fazola got him to break one of his own strongest vows. According to Jerome, "It was Faz's birthday [December 10, 1937] and he decided to celebrate and toss a party for the guys up in his hotel room at the Copley Square. So he bought a few bottles, and we were going pretty good when Glenn walked in. Of course, Faz asked him to have a drink. Now, as you know, Glenn hadn't had a drink since the band first got started, so he told Faz, 'No, thanks.' But Faz began to pout, so Glenn finally broke down and had a couple of quick ones with the guys. I'm sure the only reason he gave in was to make Faz feel good."

Glenn himself must have felt really good a few days later—on December 15, to be precise—when his band got its first coast-to-coast radio broadcast via Boston's WBZ and the NBC network, an opportunity Glenn had been looking forward to for many months. Nothing much happened as a result, but two days later Glenn got another boost when Les Biegel, a trumpeter whose playing he greatly admired, replaced Peterson to give the band another vital jazz voice.

Biegel arrived just in time to play the band's last night at the Raymor. Then back to those icy roads again and more one-nighters, including a fraternity dance at Bowdoin College way up in Brunswick, Maine, for which Glenn received exactly $125 for the entire band—its all-time low.

The last week of 1937 began high and ended low. Doc Carney had played well enough, but Glenn had been spoiled playing with drummers like Krupa, McKinley, and Pollack. One of his favorites among drummers he might possibly afford was Maurice Purtill, who had been working with Tommy Dorsey while Davey Tough, the band's regular drummer, had been drying out in a sanitarium. But Davey was returning, and Purtill would be at liberty, Tommy told his good friend Glenn, who then decided to replace Carney with Purtill. And so on Christmas night, at the Brookline Country Club in Brookline, Pennsylvania, Purtill made his debut with the Miller band. His playing fired up the band, and it swung that night as it had never swung before.

Glenn was ecstatic. But his ecstasy lasted less than twenty-four hours. Early the next day came a desperate S.O.S. from Dorsey. Davey had fallen off the wagon again, Tommy had a lot of important dates to play, including a commercial broadcast— and, please, Glenn, old pal, would you rush Purtill back.

Glenn was heartbroken. The night before, the band, thanks to Purtill, had swung as Glenn had always felt it could and should.

It had finally happened, and it could happen again and again. But Tommy was his friend, and his friend was in big trouble, and that was that. So back went Purtill, and in his stead came the veteran Vic Angle, experienced but totally uninspiring, whose dixieland combo brand of drumming fit the Miller style like a size-34 suit would have fit Fazola. The band's music had finally joined the band's finances in Disasterville!

Successive dates in Reading, Pennsylvania; Auburn, New York; Easton, Maryland; and, finally, on New Year's Eve of 1937, in York, Pennsylvania, seemed absolutely meaningless. For Glenn, his once-promising career had deteriorated into a barrage of backbreaking one-nighters through snow and over icy roads; never sure about arriving at any of them; wondering which guys would show up sober and which guys might not show up at all; worried about a wife who had just undergone a major operation; growing more and more frantic about where the next money was coming from; faced with a future with no engagements that might bring some semblances of recognition, all encompassed by an ever-gnawing awareness that, musically and commercially, his band was going absolutely nowhere.

And so, on New Year's Eve, at the Valencia Ballroom in York, Pennsylvania, Glenn Miller gave his men their final notice. They played one more date, on January 2, at the Ritz Ballroom in Bridgeport, Connecticut, and that was it. Glenn had worked terribly hard, driving himself into a state of complete nervous exhaustion and a feeling of almost uncontrollable desperation. But all his expertise, experience, patience, musical knowledge, and commercial sense still hadn't been able to add up to anything except failure.

He returned to New York, broke and depressed, not knowing what he was going to do, where he was going to go, or if he'd ever again lead a band.

Chapter 10

 His musicians were sure the band was finished. His booking office insisted to the press that he was merely taking a vacation before making some personnel changes. As for Glenn himself, he was certain about nothing, except that he was dead broke.

In their Jackson Heights home, he and Helen talked long into the strangely empty evenings. They realized that, as an arranger and a sideman, Glenn could again make a comfortable, if unexciting, living. But they had contributed so much, emotionally and financially, to the band that they couldn't reconcile themselves to giving it up completely. Besides, Helen, like those of us who had been close to Glenn, still felt strongly that he could succeed. And, after a while, again so would he.

But planning and dreaming didn't take care of immediate business. So Glenn began calling up his old friends for work.

Benny Goodman suggested that Glenn write a couple of arrangements for his band. Rolly Bundock, who was then doing all of Glenn's copying work (copying the notes from the scores to the musicians' individual parts), recalls that the suggestion didn't pan out too well. "Glenn wrote an arrangement for Benny of Hoagy Carmichael's tune 'One Morning in May,' but Benny threw it out. He said it was too pretty and too much was going on."

Glenn's musical relationship with another old friend, Tommy Dorsey, proved to be more fruitful. For many years the two trombonists had been close, in a way that resembled brotherly open warfare—in a way, come to think of it, not much different from the way Tommy and Jimmy Dorsey related to one another. Both Glenn and Tommy liked to run their shows, and both were good at it. Both played trombone, though one was better than the other. They had competed in the past for the same jobs, and competition of almost any kind—sports, financial, or leading a band—appealed to both. And yet, beneath a superficially friendly relationship, in which each called the other an endearing "Harve," lay the potential for a fierce personal rivalry that, given the proper setting, was bound to erupt.

Glenn didn't join Tommy as a regular member of his band. He didn't want that and Tommy respected his position. But Tommy was able to find a spot for him on his Raleigh cigarette radio commercial. At least that paid the rent.

It was at the rehearsal of one of those Raleigh shows that I finally cornered Glenn. Since the breakup of the band he had been giving me the frigidaire treatment. We'd see each other at openings or some other places, but there was absolutely no indication of any warmth. And when Glenn wanted to cut someone, that someone would get cut! He'd give you that steely stare through those rimless glasses, with no expression at all on his face, and once he was sure you felt the freeze, he'd turn away and ignore you completely.

I couldn't, for the life of me, understand why he had suddenly zeroed in on me. We had remained friendly throughout the past year, right up to the band's bust-up, and he had called me after he had come back to town. And then all of a sudden, for no apparent reason whatsoever, I found myself in the Miller deep-freeze.

To say that the treatment didn't bother me would be a damned lie. Of course it did. I was still young and sensitive and immature. Feeling in awe of people, especially those who were making more money than I was (I knew few who weren't), or who had achieved other kinds of success, was not too difficult for me. In those early years it was easy for me to look up to Glenn, whom I admired so much, as a father figure or at least as an older-brother figure.

So it took a lot of courage, after those rebuffs, for me to take the initiative. But I did, one afternoon at the Raleigh rehearsal. I asked him point-blank what the hell was on his mind and why was he acting this way. He suggested I stick around until later, when we could talk more. Then it came out, and I suddenly discovered a part of Glenn Miller that I had never known before.

"Look," he began, "I thought you were a friend of mine." When I told him I thought so, too, and that was precisely why I couldn't understand his attitude, he came back with, "Well, if you're a friend of *mine,* what the hell's the idea of getting Jerry Jerome a job with *another* band?"

Jerry, a warm, bright, and observant guy—"Remember," he reminded me years later, "how Glenn would always tap his cigarette a couple of times before lighting it, and how his jaws used to twitch whenever he was annoyed?"—had been one of Glenn's favorites. But, I pointed out to Glenn, that didn't mean he owned him, especially since he no longer had a band for him to belong to. I also reminded Glenn that I had uncovered Jerry for him, that he was a friend of mine, too, and that after Glenn had broken up the band, neither Jerry nor anybody else—me included—had any assurance that he'd ever break it in again. And so when another good friend, Red Norvo, had told me he needed a tenor man, I told him about Jerry and Red hired him. What, I wanted to know, was so horribly deceitful or disloyal about that?

Begrudgingly Glenn admitted that maybe I wasn't a traitor after all, and that Jerry had a right to earn a living where and when he could. But the incident showed me a part of Glenn's character I'd never known before: a petulant possessiveness toward those whom he wanted to but couldn't always control. On the surface, our relationship returned to what it had been. But deep down inside I began for the first time to question the idolatry about him that I had, perhaps quite foolishly, created. And so, in their own way, the freeze and the subsequent thaw turned out to be profitable experiences for me. And they also gave me the first clue that Glenn was planning to reorganize after all.

The Jerome incident drew out another of Glenn's traits: his

stubbornness. He still wanted to get Jerry back in the band. Years later Jerry told me that "a few months after Glenn had disbanded, and Red's band was in New York, Glenn called me and asked me to meet him at the Rialto Bar on West Forty-ninth Street near the Van Cortlandt Hotel. He said he wasn't a Tommy Dorsey or a Jack Teagarden or a Kay Kyser—yet, but he was very optimistic because he had come up with a new sound that he thought was both musical and commercial. And you know what he did? He offered me a three-way split if I would come back. It would be Chummy [MacGregor], Glenn and me, and each of us would put up a car and split the profits. And he told me we'd have a drawing account, too.

"But I wasn't interested, because I didn't feel like returning to that rigid, routine discipline. I was much too free-blowing a jazz player, and I needed more freedom. But, after he did start his band again, I'd go up to the Haven Studio and help him rehearse the saxes."

Jerome, who later became a successful producer of commercial jingles, still wonders whether he made a mistake by not accepting Glenn's offer. But since MacGregor, who was even closer to Glenn personally, never wound up with a piece of the action, it looks as if Jerry made the right non-move.

The MacGregor-Miller relationship lasted for a long time, though it wasn't nearly as long or as two-sided as the movie *The Glenn Miller Story*, for which Chummy was a consultant, would lead you to believe. The film depicted them as close pals all through Glenn's career, even back to the pre-Pollack days, years before they'd ever even met! And in the movie Chummy came through as the strong character, while Glenn, thanks to Jimmy Stewart's persistence in acting like Jimmy Stewart, came across as the wide-eyed but headstrong adolescent. It's difficult to decide which portrayal was more inaccurate.

In real life Chummy was super-dependent upon Glenn, who liked him personally and admired him for his honesty, decency and loyalty, and also because he was always good to his mother. Only an average pianist, whose dragging of tempos used to drive some of the others in the rhythm section up the wall ("We tried our best to tune him out," one of the quartet once told me),

Chummy and Glenn.

Chummy was devoted to the band and willing to do just about anything his friend Glenn asked him to do, which made him a valuable personal, if not musical, asset. During the early days he did some of the music copying, kept the financial records and drove one of the cars—all without any extra pay. He occasionally wrote his own arrangements, none of which thrilled his fellow-musicians. Yet, in his own quiet way, he fulfilled many of Glenn's needs, and though the two of them would sometimes argue vehemently, each managed to retain great personal respect for the other.

Unfortunately, after Glenn died, Chummy, unlike others in the band, seemed unable to function as a musician without the help of his boss. So he gave up playing piano and turned to music publishing, and for a time represented the Miller Estate on the West Coast in a minor capacity. He remained close to Helen, who trusted him personally, and sometimes sat for her two adopted children, who became very fond of the man they used to call "Grandpa Mac." But then one night at the Miller home, when he was feeling no pain, Chummy excoriated Glenn so bitterly over a matter concerning just a few dollars that Helen asked him to leave, and from then on their once warm friendship lingered in the low forties. During the years before his death by cancer in March 1973, Chummy MacGregor led a quiet and at times distressingly lonely life.

Of all the musicians in the band, MacGregor and Hal McIntyre remained closest to Glenn over the longest period. While all the other band members would travel in the bus, either Chummy or Hal would often wind up beside Glenn in the front seat of his Cadillac. So close were they to Miller that some of the less enchanted musicians liked to refer to the two of them, rather unfairly, I thought, as "the Gestapo."

McIntyre, who died in a tragic bedroom fire in the late fifties, and Glenn spent much of their non-bandstand time together. On the road they shared the same room, and during the band's more scuffling times they shared the job of driving the band's truck. So it was only natural for the guys to feel that Hal was "Glenn's boy," and, even though he was generally well liked by everyone, some of the guys couldn't relax completely with him for fear that anything they did or said might be reported to the discipline-conscious boss.

I always found Hal to be a very pleasant and direct guy. He smiled a lot (Glenn called him "the Beaver"), but it was a genuine, happy smile from a genuine, happy guy. He was a great

Lense-louse McIntyre, plus an admiring
Willie Schwartz.

public relations man for the band because, in addition to his
good nature, he had a brilliant memory for names of employers
and patrons. Until he left to start his own outfit, with Glenn's
blessings and backing, he remained Glenn's major contact with
music publishers and was primarily responsible for programming
the various sustaining radio broadcasts that emanated from the
hotels and ballrooms where the band was playing.

So close was Hal's relationship with Glenn that in the early
spring of 1938, when Glenn decided to form another edition of
his band (with financial aid from Helen's folks, the Burgers, who
took out a second mortgage on their home), it was McIntyre
whom he first contacted.

Hal spoke about the start of the second edition on a radio show
over station WAAT in May 1945: "After the first band broke up,
I took all the equipment up to our farm in Cromwell, Connecticut, and got a job in a factory and played with my own band at
night. I used to call up Glenn every Sunday afternoon at one and
try to argue him into starting the band again. But he'd always
say 'Nothing doing,' and that he had gone through $18,000 too
fast to want to go back into the band business.

"Well, one afternoon he was driving through Cromwell and he
called me from a diner. I went over to see him, and we talked for
a while and I brought up the subject of starting the band again.

At first he said 'No,' but I sort of detected a lessening of resistance, and I kept working and working and working on him until he finally said, 'OK, we start rehearsals at the Haven Studio next week.' "

PART THREE

The Band That Made It

Chapter 11

The Haven Studio hadn't changed much. There was still the dimly lit combination waiting-room and parlor with the dilapidated, overstuffed furniture and the kooky oriental décor, and there was still the barren studio in back, with its old piano, its rickety folding chairs and its two dusty windows.

The setting hadn't changed, but the personnel of the Glenn Miller band most certainly had. "One thing I definitely won't have this time," Glenn assured me, "is some of those prima donnas." What he meant, of course, was that he was going to look for young, eager musicians, whom he could control and who'd be more interested in living for the band than for personal kicks.

He'd also definitely decided that he really wasn't going anywhere by trying to outswing the Goodmans and the Shaws and the Dorseys. A basically sweet band with a unique, identifiable sound but which still could play the Swing the kids wanted would, he was convinced, stand a much better chance.

He never could remember precisely the moment when he decided to emphasize his new reed-section sound. He had been experimenting with it in his first band—but only a few bars at a time. But during his self-imposed band-leading sabbatical, he began to realize that perhaps *this* was the unique, easily recognizable style that could set his band apart from all the rest.

It was a sound he had uncovered purely by accident during his

Ray Noble days and had later revived briefly to give Fazola something to do. "Peewee Erwin, now playing trumpet for Tommy Dorsey, was with us in the Noble band," Glenn once told me during a *Metronome* interview. "At the time, Peewee had a mania for playing high parts; he always asked me to give him stuff written way up on his horn. Sometimes I'd write things for him with the saxes playing underneath.

"There came a day when Peewee left and a trumpeter who couldn't hit those high notes replaced him. In desperation, we assigned those B-flat trumpet parts to Johnny Mince, now also with Tommy Dorsey, on B-flat clarinet and doubled the clarinet lead with Danny D'Andrea [a violinist who doubled on reeds] an octave lower on tenor sax. That's how the clarinet-lead sound, which people call 'our style,' started."

The new style depended not only on Miller's writing but also on the way it was played. It required a very broad, seemingly breathless way of phrasing, a sweeping legato style that no other dance band was then using. It could turn out to be something truly unique in a field that for many years hadn't deviated much from the routine musical voicings.

During the "vacation" some of Glenn's favorites had taken jobs with other band leaders. Jerome had gone with Norvo. Fazola, whose clarinet Glenn also hated to lose, found a perfect spot for himself in the dixieland-blues-playing band of Bob Crosby. Kitty Lane first went with Isham Jones, then with Bunny Berigan for a while before getting married and settling down as a wife. Les Biegel returned to Minneapolis to front his own small jazz band.

There were only four others whom Glenn wanted to keep. His old friend MacGregor was back on piano—he had a lifetime hold on that chair. Rolly Bundock, the dependable bassist, was also invited to return. And so were the two important section leaders: first trumpeter Bob Price, who played so well that Glenn was willing to overlook his boozing, and first saxist McIntyre.

In addition to McIntyre, the new sax section included Sol Kane and Bernie "Josh" Billings, who didn't stay with the band very long, and Willie Schwartz and Gordon "Tex" Beneke, who were to remain with it throughout the rest of Miller's civilian career as two of its most important voices.

The new brass section was more temporary. Price was flanked by a very exciting Philadelphia jazz trumpeter named Johnny Austin, a former drummer, who unfortunately was a better soloist than a section man, and by Gasparre Rebito, a quiet journeyman section player. For trombone, Glenn turned to two younger brothers of already established big-band musicians: Bob "Brad" Jenney, whose brother, Jack, played the sexiest-sounding trombone of all time, and Al Mastren, whose brother, Carmen, was Tommy Dorsey's guitarist for years, and who, himself, wound up five years later in Glenn's AAF band.

The only new musician in the rhythm section with MacGregor and Bundock was Bob Spangler, a friend of Austin's, who played driving, though sometimes plodding, drums. Glenn also extended the junior fraternal pattern into the singers, taking on Bob Eberly's younger brother, Ray, who had never worked with a band before, as his first boy vocalist. The girl, pretty and vivacious Gail Reese, who sang adequately, was more shopworn. She had worked for Charlie Barnet and Bunny Berigan.

My role in assembling these men was less significant than it had been with the first group. Perhaps, because of the Jerome incident, my enthusiasm for working with Glenn had abated a bit, though I did continue to support the band regularly in *Metronome* and eventually I recommended some other musicians whom he did hire.

Besides, there were so many other exciting things in the big-band world during the beginning of 1938 for me to focus on: Benny Goodman's famed Carnegie Hall concert; Count Basie besting Chick Webb in one of the great Battles of the Bands; Gene Krupa breaking away from Goodman and debuting with his own band; Goodman and Tommy Dorsey swapping slews of musicians à la big-league baseball teams, and the beginning of a whole bunch of *Metronome* columns by Harry James, Tommy Dorsey, Jimmy Dorsey, Gene Krupa, and others, on most of which I assumed the role of a ghost.

I did discover one new musician for Glenn, a young saxist and clarinetist working with Julie Wintz's band at the Top Hat

Young Willie Schwartz.

nightclub across the Hudson River in Union City, New Jersey. The band wasn't much, but Willie Schwartz was. I had raved about his saxophone playing, but Glenn's unusually keen commercial ear detected in his clarinet the semblance of the sound he wanted to lead his new reed style. It turned out to be a masterful bit of recruiting, because Willie's tone and way of playing provided a fullness and richness so distinctive that none of the later Miller imitators could ever accurately reproduce the Miller reed sound.

Schwartz, now an extremely successful musician in Hollywood's studios, recently explained to me how he mastered his unique approach to playing the clarinet. "It's different from both the legitimate and the jazz techniques. It's louder and stronger, and it requires an entirely different way of thinking about playing the horn. You have to think of it more like a lead saxophone, and it took me a long time to develop that approach. It wasn't until I'd been doing it for about six months that I realized that I was playing entirely differently than I had been taught. It turned out to be a different instrument for me.

"Glenn first heard me when the Wintz band was at Roseland —that was after you'd reviewed us at the Top Hat, and I remember I was thrilled to death when a big-name studio musician asked me to join his band."

Like most of the members of that new group, Schwartz became completely dedicated to Miller. "He was a father figure to me. He had already been where I wanted to be. I felt our future was in his hands. I remember how hard he worked with us. The blend of the saxes wasn't good at all for quite a long time, maybe for five or six months, but he would keep encouraging us. I always respected Glenn. He treated us—all of us in the band—as a team. Every bit of success we had he was responsible for.

"Just being a member of that band gave you such confidence. I remember later when we were at the Cafe Rouge and that feeling of '*being* somebody' as I walked across the floor up to the bandstand. Six months earlier I would have walked around the perimeter of a ballroom to get to the stand.

"Glenn never changed. He was always the same. As the band became more successful, he relaxed more. He began to have much more confidence in us and often he would not be there at the start of an evening. For a long time it remained exciting for me, maybe because I was young and exuberant.

"The only drag was that the band didn't really swing. Glenn always had trouble with the rhythm section. He'd keep exhorting the guys. 'Let's get a beat going,' he'd say. And then, after hearing Basie, he'd ask, 'Why can't we play like that?' and he would chew us out for not being exuberant. I remember he would get on us for not watching Purtill during his drum solos. 'Watch the drummer,' he'd say, and then he'd remind us, 'People want to be entertained.' He expected us to be entertainers as well as musicians.

"The band certainly was commercial. I'd call it the Lawrence Welk of its day. It had the same dedication to precision and showmanship. It was like a well-oiled machine. But towards the end it became a bore."

The most commercial cylinder in that machine was a musician-singer who joined up just a few days after Willie did. Schwartz remembers the entrance well: "I can still see Tex walking in that day with his sax wrapped in a towel!"

Gordon "Tex" Beneke had been recommended to Glenn by his old friend Gene Krupa, who'd heard about him through one of his own tenor saxists, Sam Donahue, but who had no room for him in his own new band.

"Glenn called me in Detroit. I was playing with Ben Young's band," reports Beneke, who now lives in St. Louis but still tours all over the country with semi-pickup bands, some of which play the Miller music fairly well and some of which play it fairly badly. "When I asked him what the job paid, he told me all the guys were making the same—fifty bucks a week. But I insisted that I get two dollars and fifty cents a week more than anybody else and finally Glenn agreed.

"I drove for twenty-four hours through the snow to make that first rehearsal. When I got there I was going to ask Glenn to let me get some sleep, but he said, 'No, get out your sax.' So I went downstairs to my 1936 Plymouth and got the horn and started playing. I remember I was playing Jerry Jerome's book, and everything was fine until we got into the vocal part of the arrangement. Jerry had been singing some part of it—I think the tune was 'Doin' the Jive'—and Glenn would sing 'Hi, there, Buck, what'cha say?' But when it came to me, he sang, 'Hi, there, Tex, what'cha say?' That's when the whole business of calling me Tex began."

Beneke turned out to be one of Glenn's favorites—if not *the* favorite in the band. A very easygoing, likeable guy, he maintained a low-key, unperturbable charm which he wafted toward everyone. As for his playing, his ballad solos turned out to be lovely bits of innovations, but his up-tempoed jazz attempts were much less impressive, sometimes even approaching corn. Most of the musicians, both in and out of the band, felt that Al Klink, who later on played the other tenor sax in the section, could easily outblow Tex as a swinging jazz musician. But here again Glenn's commercial sense and stubbornness prevailed. He considered Tex not merely a musician but also a commercial personality, and so he never missed a chance to feature him. And so while Klink smoldered in the background, Glenn kept thrusting Tex into the spotlight.

Glenn glances at
"favorite" Tex Beneke.

Tex always appreciated and admired Glenn. Back when the band was going through its most scuffling days, Gene Krupa offered Beneke a job at better pay. The Miller future looked bleak, but Tex refused the bait—he had that much faith in Glenn. And that faith has never wavered. Just recently he told me: "Glenn would have done so much that we would never have had such a lull in music. He would have continued to hold the kids in his hand. He knew where the bread would be."

Glenn always appreciated Tex—except perhaps early one morning when the band assembled in Victor's recording studio for a 9 A.M. session. "We were playing at Meadowbrook over in New Jersey at the time and all the guys were supposed to bring their music along to the date. But I forgot mine, and Glenn had to call off the entire session just because of me." Other bandsmen have reported that Glenn didn't talk to Tex for two whole weeks.

"Glenn would also get mad at me sometimes because I just couldn't learn lyrics. I still can't. But I can learn anything on the sax if I hear it just once.

"Glenn was strict. Everybody knows that. He was tough on musicians, all right. He used to insist on proper haircuts, proper

A nine-year-old Texas saxist
with his very first horn.

shines, both feet on the floor, and the same amount of white
showing in every man's breast-pocket handkerchief. And he also
used to insist upon proper enunciation. We had to sing 'Don't Sit
Under the Apple Tree,' not 'Don't Sit Under the *Yapple* Tree.'

"I loved the man. He taught me so much about playing my
own sax. And I knew he liked me. I could tell by the way he'd
stare at me while I was playing a solo. He'd look at me and I'd
look right back at him. It didn't bother me the way it bothered
some of the others. I know Johnny Best used to say, 'When he
gives me the fish eye, I can't blow.' But it wasn't that way with
me at all."

Glenn made Tex into a star, mostly by featuring him as a
vocalist, often with the Modernaires and sometimes with Marion
Hutton, on such tunes as "Don't Sit Under the Apple Tree,"
"I've Got a Gal in Kalamazoo," and "Chattanooga Choo Choo."
But Tex, always friendly, warm, relaxed, and extremely considerate of other people's feelings, never acted like a star. According
to drummer Maurice Purtill, "Tex's big ambition was to go back

Tex blows high; Al Klink knows why.

to Texas, eat some chili, and play some blues. He didn't mix with
too many of the guys."

Tex was an inveterate tinker and he spent much of his time
operating a ham radio. He and his wife, Marguerite, who was
constantly pushing his career harder than he seemed to want to
have it pushed, stayed together much of the time.

Al Klink, Beneke's supposed rival on the other tenor sax chair,
recalls that "Tex, or Cuz, as some of us called him, and I had
many common interests, like model airplanes and little one-cyl-
inder engines which we used to run in the dressing room on
theater dates. There'd be grease all over the place and people
would get carbon monoxide headaches from the fumes and
sometimes they would even filter into the theater. Glenn would
stop us if the noise interfered with the movie they were showing,
but I don't recall that he ever stopped us because of the smell.

"I will say this about Tex: There is not a finer gentleman on
earth than Tex Beneke. All the guys in the band, and even Tex,
would say, 'Klink, you ought to play more solos.' The arrangers

would write things for me, but Glenn would cut them out." During a recent interview Tex stated unequivocally, "Klink should have been featured more."

One thing that Beneke may not know until he reads this: Marion Hutton, during a 1971 interview, told me, "I was madly in love with Tex, but I could never show it. I hated it when we gave up driving the cars because I always rode with Glenn and Tex."

And Tex might even feel a bit embarrassed when he reads what Johnny O'Leary, the band's road manager, now retired, had to say late in 1972: "Tex Beneke has always been wonderful to me. Once he invited me out to St. Louis to visit him in his home, with all expenses paid. And every Christmas I get a card from him and there is always a fifty-dollar check in it."

In addition to his musical contributions, Beneke added warmth and wholesomeness to the band. To some, he may also have added romance, though by far the most romantic voice in the band belonged to another youngster who joined when Schwartz and Beneke did. This was Ray Eberle.

I remember Ray when he came with the band. He was a small, lighter, less impressive version of his older brother, Bob—Jimmy Dorsey's singer, who, along with Tommy Dorsey's Jack Leonard and Casa Loma's Kenny Sargent, were then the most popular of all boy band-vocalists. I remember how Bob, in his own quiet way, exuded confidence and how Ray, in his own quiet way, exuded trepidation.

For me there never was nor would be any argument as to who was the better singer, and my preference for Bob was shared by just about everybody I knew—except Glenn. Here again his loyalty and his stubbornness superseded his music appreciation, and even though he had liked Bob's singing when both were in the Dorsey Brothers orchestra, he kept on insisting to me that Ray was a better vocalist "because he doesn't sing so far behind the beat, the way Bob does."

Ray claims his similarity in looks to Bob made Glenn conscious of him in the first place. "One night I was visiting Bob when he was singing with Jimmy Dorsey's band at the New

The Eberle Brothers: (left to right) Walter, who never sang with a name band; Bob, who sang with Jimmy Dorsey's, and Ray, who sang with Glenn's. (Bob later changed the spelling of the family name to "Eberly.")

Yorker Hotel. As I walked past Glenn's table, I could see him do a double-take. So he asked Billy Burton, the band's manager, who I was, and when Billy told him, Glenn invited me over to the table. The next thing I knew he offered me a job.

"The next day I went over to the Haven Studio to rehearsal, and I was terribly scared. I had never sung with a band before. But Glenn was very patient with me. He was like an older brother, only he wouldn't call me by my right name. He used to call me Jim, and when I asked him why, he said, 'because you look more like a Jim than a Ray to me.' He even had 'To Jim' inscribed on a wrist watch he once gave me for Christmas."

I always felt that Glenn had Ray's keys pitched so high that he couldn't help sounding strained and thin. Sometimes, when Glenn let him relax into his lower register, Ray's voice would sound richer and less tense. But those times were too infrequent for me. Therefore, I seldom praised any of his vocals, and naturally he resented my constant criticisms. Eventually a strain developed between us, so I never got to know him as well as I did others in the band.

Recently, when I expounded my theory to Ray, he didn't quite agree with me—par for our course. Something else bothered him more, he said. "Some of those tempos were just too fast." At least we agreed on something!

Ray, Tex, Willie and all the rest rehearsed with the new group for several weeks, and Glenn's optimism kept mounting as the band began to sound better and better and as he realized that he now had himself a far less bottle-conscious, cleaner-cut crew that would give the all-American appearance which he considered so important.

But the optimism suffered a sudden setback when he learned where his new group would be opening—back again at the same old depressive Raymor Ballroom in Boston.

Chapter 12

"Note, for example, his unique style of scoring for one clarinet and four saxes, and then some of the moving background figures he writes for the brass to play into hats, and you'll get a pretty good idea of the swell, set style upon which he and his men are working."

The quote comes from a June 1938 review I wrote for *Metronome,* after the band had opened on April 16 at the Raymor, with Artie Shaw at Roseland-State and Chick Webb at Levaggi's its major competition. There, for the first time, it began to feature that new reed sound that was to set it apart from all the others in the Big-Band Sweepstakes. But everything else was by no means set. The personnel had already undergone one change: Stan Aronson, a very likeable and very good musician from Connecticut, replaced Josh Billings on tenor sax. And more changes were to come.

Aronson, now a member of the Hartford Symphony and the University of Hartford faculty, credits bassist Rolly Bundock, with whom he had played in Connecticut, with getting him into the band. "I was playing at Child's Restaurant at 105th Street and Broadway and making thirty-five bucks a week, plus two meals. That was good pay in those days, so when Rolly talked to me about joining the band I wasn't too interested. But when I went down to the Haven Studio and heard that gorgeous reed sound, I was hooked."

Stan remembers Miller with fondness. "He saved my life when I was in the army. He really went to bat for me and got me out of an infantry unit and into the orchestra of *Winged Victory*. He didn't have to do that. But you know with Glenn; if he liked somebody, he'd go all out for him."

Like others, Aronson was impressed with Glenn's emphasis upon discipline. Ditto with his candor. "The night before we opened at the Raymor, he called a meeting of the band and he told us, 'Look, I know some of you have heard stories about how much trouble I used to give some of the leaders in town. Well, I want you to know that I'm not going to stand for anything like that in *my* band. Anybody gets out of line, and out he goes!' And he meant it, too. When Sol Kane started griping about not getting enough jazz clarinet solos, that was the beginning of the end for him. And later, when Bob Price's drinking began to interfere with his playing, he was on the way out, too."

The new, younger musicians may have given the band more of an all-American-boy look, and the new reed-voicing may have provoked more of a romantic sound, but for the band the job still remained the same old Raymor grind. And Glenn's own problems continued. His financial condition remained horrendous. Just how hard he pinched pennies was reflected in the daily expense sheets on which he listed every single cash payment that could possibly be charged to running a band: a five-cent telephone call; ten cents for a daily flower, presumably for his buttonhole; ten cents for coffee; ten cents for stamps; fifteen cents for cigarettes (remember those days?); fifty cents for having his tuxedo pressed. Beneke reports that Glenn paid off the guys separately in cash in the bathroom at the Copley Square Hotel so that nobody could see what the others were making. Thus Tex's $2.50 bonus remained a secret.

The Raymor grind began to take its toll. The griping increased. Willie Schwartz reports that Sol Kane was growing so dissatisfied that when he heard that Red Norvo was in town, he decided to phone him to see if he had an opening in the band. He called Red's room, and when a voice answered, Sol identified himself, explained how unhappy he was with Glenn, and asked if Red could use him. Unfortunately, he'd neglected to find out whom he was talking to, and he certainly never expected that Glenn would be in Red's room and would pick up the phone while Red was in the shower! Shortly thereafter Bill Stegmeyer, an experienced saxist who also arranged, replaced Kane.

Rolly Bundock, as part-time arranger and copyist, saw more of Glenn in those days than most of the musicians did. "I used to go up to his room to talk things over. It was almost always about some particular tune. But Glenn sensed things weren't going too well in the band, and one night, after some of our guys and some of the guys in Woody Herman's band had had a party, he began to do a little digging. 'Hey, that was quite a party you had last night,' he said. 'I hear there was lots of bitching.' There was, but I wasn't going to tell him anything, so I said, 'I didn't hear anything.' And then I asked him, 'Hey, are you paying me too much money? I thought I came on the band just to play bass.' And he knew right away he shouldn't have put me on the spot like that and so he said, 'You're right,' and he never asked me a question like that again." Bundock's description of the discipline-dedicated Miller: "He was the General MacArthur of the music business."

In May the band recorded four more fateless Brunswick sides, including a Miller original, "Sold American," based on the Lucky Strike cigarette chant constantly heard on radio. Glenn must have hoped that the company might use either the tune or his band—or maybe both—but nothing of the sort ever happened.

Finally, in mid-June, Glenn did get something he'd been waiting for ever since he first started his band: a steady New York engagement. The Paradise Restaurant on the west side of Broadway just above Forty-ninth Street (years later it was turned into Bop City) wasn't the ideal place, and Glenn knew it. But it would give the band a chance to be seen and heard, and the job also included several coast-to-coast broadcasts a week.

But, whereas the band had been playing strictly for dancing at the Raymor, the Paradise job called for music for a floor show filled with dizzy show girls in sleazy production numbers, leered at by a bunch of visiting salesmen who couldn't care less for the finer points of good music. To lower Glenn's ego even further, his

134 / GLENN MILLER AND HIS ORCHESTRA

band received second billing to the starred musical (?) group called Freddie Fisher and his Schnickelfritzers, six good musicians who bastardized music by purposely playing as cornily as possible.

Dressed in its brand-new gabardine uniforms ($35 apiece from Brisk Brothers Tailors), the band was forced to play two or three shows a night—tough ones, too, with lots of tempo changes and loud, high blowing to fit the semi-carnival mood of the shows. So loud did the band play that Milton Berle (or his press agent) quipped that "the chorus girls can't even hear the propositions!"

What made it even worse, though, was that the shows took so much out of the musicians, especially the brassmen, whose lips were almost bleeding, that the band sounded pretty sloppy on many of those broadcasts that were supposed to beam its great sounds throughout the land. It appeared to be a bonehead booking, but eventually it was to pay off in a way that Glenn could then never suspect.

Right after the Paradise Restaurant, according to Howard Richmond, who had just become the band's press agent (today he is one of the world's most successful music publishers and talent managers), Glenn hit what "must have been his all-time low. The band was playing in New Jersey, at Reed's Casino in Asbury Park, and Glenn was especially proud of the way it played ballads. On this particular evening, all the kids who came in got little plastic bags filled with cotton snowballs. The band was playing some beautiful number when a bell rang and all of a sudden these kids began throwing those cotton snowballs at the band. Glenn just stood there and let them hit him. Some of the balls even went into the bell of his horn. He didn't think it was at all funny."

Nobody seemed to be very interested in the band. That included record-company executives. The last Brunswick date had been a bomb, and Glenn knew he could do better, if he could just get the chance. The importance of records in winning over the kids hit him especially hard one night at a fraternity party following a dance at Cornell. "Those kids," he told Richmond, "had Tommy Dorsey records stacked this high! If I have to play for them, one by one, across the country, I'll never make it."

One of the band's radio shows from the Paradise first drew it to Richmond's attention. "I'd never heard of Glenn Miller, but I went right in to the club that same night. I remember the band was playing 'Pavanne,' and it was *so* beautiful. When the band got off the stand, I introduced myself to Glenn at the bar and I told him I wanted to be his press agent. I was already handling Larry Clinton's band at the time. He said, 'I can't afford a press agent. I can't even afford a band!' " But Richmond wouldn't give up and finally agreed to work for Miller for fifty dollars a month.

Howie was attracted to Miller by more than his music. "I idolized him from the first moment I saw him. He was a commanding guy, youthful but mature. He looked like security, like all the things I'd never found in a band leader. Of course, all Mickey Mouse band leaders looked like security. I'm talking about jazz leaders. To me they always looked like they didn't know where they were going to sleep the next night.

"I discovered that Glenn was the greatest disciplinarian in the music business. He was a stickler for perfection. He was very demanding, but he never demanded anything from anybody that he couldn't perform himself.

"The only thing I found—and this was later on—that he lacked was the ability to inspire musicians and singers to be creative on their own. He could never have created a Sinatra, for example. He always listened for the correct blend of a section instead of for any special individual feeling from a performer. And that's why, after a while, the band developed into a group of toy soldiers."

Meanwhile, the band's struggle for existence continued. Gail Reese left, to be replaced by Virginia Vonne, to be replaced by the statuesque Linda Keene, none of whom appealed to Glenn as singers. But from time to time little things did happen that would raise his spirits, like the trombonist he discovered during the week in August when the band was playing in Atlantic City at Hamid's Million Dollar Pier and again losing money (total take

On Hamid's Million Dollar Pier in Atlantic City, August 1938: (left to right) trombonist Brad Jenney, saxists Bill Stegmeyer and Hal McIntyre, pianist Chummy MacGregor, saxists Tex Beneke and Stan Aronson, trombonist Al Mastren, vocalist Linda Keene, Glenn, Ray Eberle, trumpeters Johnny Austin and Bob Price, drummer Bob Spangler, clarinetist Willie Schwartz, bassist Rolly Bundock, trumpeter Louis Mucci.

for the week was $1,200) just so that it could get the air-time from the place.

One evening, after work, Helen and Glenn went into a nightclub that turned out to be a strip joint. But there they found the trombone player who turned out to be one of the band's mainstays and who, with his wife, became one of the Millers' dearest friends.

Paul Tanner, now a professor of music at UCLA, where he teaches a course in the History of Jazz to six hundred students, was then a shy, gangling musician out of Skunk Hollow, Kentucky, and was sitting in semi-permanently with Marty Caruso's band. "The guys in the band liked my playing, so they chipped in and hired me at $15 a week. I was ambitious, but I was also pretty scared in those days and I stammered like mad. Finally I got up enough courage to go over to Glenn's table and I said, 'Can you say you like my playing because I want to make trombone my living and I'd sure like to get a recommendation from you.' But Glenn had other ideas. He said, 'How soon can you pack and go with me?' and I said, 'This is all I've got. I'm ready right now.' And so I went with the band.

"When I joined, I had a great upper register, but Glenn wouldn't give me any top parts. I asked him why and he said, 'I want to help you become an all-around trombone player.' So at first he gave me only the bottom parts."

Glenn's theory eventually paid off handsomely for Tanner. He developed into such an outstanding trombonist that now, as Paul Tanner, Ph.D., he is invited to appear as a jazz and classical trombonist and lecturer the world over—even in Japan, Hungary, Poland and New Guinea.

I first remember him as about the slowest-moving gent I'd ever seen. Glenn called him "Lightnin'." But he had no trouble at all getting around his horn. When he first joined the band, he impressed a bunch of us with his loosely phrased, blues-tinged solos. Still, Glenn seldom featured him. Could have been, perhaps, that he didn't want to create one more nemesis for himself, à la Jack Teagarden. Maybe that's why Tanner never did emerge as a Miller star, the way Tex Beneke, Ray Eberle and Marion Hutton did.

Like Paul, Marion also blossomed after leaving the Miller band, in her case not so much career-wise, but more as a human being. All the guys loved her like a sister. Chuck Goldstein of the Modernaires, who worked regularly with her, has stated simply that "Marion Hutton was the nicest girl you could ever meet." And drummer Maurice Purtill has noted that "everybody respected her. Sometimes we'd have those crap games on the bus and there'd be some pretty bad language, but she'd just sit there up front and not say a thing. She was a gem."

Like just about every band's girl singer, Marion took a lot of ribbing. She had all sorts of nicknames—Goldie-locks, The Brat, The Whack, Tootsie-Roll, Rosebud, Snow White, Sissy, and even The Dopey Duchess. In those days she wasn't exactly an intellectual heavyweight, or even middleweight, and she didn't pretend to be. Therefore, I was all the more delightfully shocked, upon visiting her recently at her home on Laguna Beach in

California, where she is now married to arranger-conductor Vic Schoen, to discover how beautifully she had matured. She was no longer singing professionally. Instead, she was deeply involved in several cultural and social projects while at the same time working toward her B.A. and M.A. degrees in psychology. A wonderfully sensitive and thoughtful woman—and prettier, by the way, than she had ever been before—she was able to look at herself and her days in the Miller band with a remarkable degree of honesty and objectivity. And she talked about it all very freely.

Her Miller saga began when she was a vocalist in the Vincent Lopez band. "Betty, my sister, was a part of the show. We were playing at the Ritz-Carlton Hotel in Boston and there was a fiddle player in the band named Nick Pisani, who had worked with Glenn in the Ray Noble band. Glenn had made a special trip to Boston to hear us, and Nick introduced Betty and me to Glenn, and Betty immediately started to do a good selling job on me. Finally Glenn said, 'Come to New York. I'll pay your expenses.' So I went to New York and auditioned with the band. Glenn was kind, but he was clipped and not very warm. Still, I got the job all right.

"I started with the band on a southern tour. I remember I learned the tunes on the way down in the car. I was scared to death. Betty was already so firmly entrenched and I kept apologizing for not being as good. But Glenn kept encouraging me."

Glenn had invited me to ride with him on that trip. I remember Marion very well. She was scared all right. Tex and Paul Tanner were also in the car—Marion up front and the three of us in the back—and I remember our trying to play "ghost," the game when somebody calls out a letter and the next person has to add another one, with the object being to avoid completing a word. Marion didn't play very well, and, as I recall it, Tex and Paul had trouble figuring out how the game worked, so after a while we gave up.

I do remember how kind Glenn was to Marion and how much he impressed upon her that he wanted her to appear as the all-American girl and that she really shouldn't worry too much right off about her singing. But he carried that all-American stuff a bit too far. On the first couple of dates he introduced her as "Sissy Jones," a name he thought went with apple pie, ice cream and hot dogs better than Marion Hutton did. But by the end of the trip he had reconsidered, and Marion got her name back.

"I was only seventeen then," she recalls, "and so Glenn and Helen became my legal guardians. He was like a father because I never had a father that I remembered. I grew terribly dependent on him. He represented a source of strength. After all, isn't a little girl always in search of her father? He fulfilled the image of what a father ought to be. If he had told me to walk up Broadway naked, I would have. Of course, I was a people-pleaser to begin with. But I was terribly afraid of incurring his wrath."

Marion's childlike attitude automatically created a sibling-rivalry situation between her and Ray Eberle. "I was terribly jealous of Ray. Glenn had me sing all those crap songs. I couldn't understand all of what seemed to me to be a lot of favoritism toward him."

Marion has admitted that she wasn't a good singer. She felt she was more of an entertainer. Glenn concurred. "We'll cover up her singing," he once told a friend, "with good arrangements." Tenor saxist Al Klink's observation about Marion's off-key singing was a little more subtle. "The mike is out of tune tonight," he'd explain.

In order to try to please Glenn and to win more of his affection, Marion tried various tactics. "Once I went ahead on my own and took some singing lessons from Mimi Spier [an exceptionally good vocal coach, to whom many singers went with their troubles], basically because I wanted to surprise and please Glenn. I remember working on the tune 'Ding, Dong, the Witch Is Dead.' I hated it. On the record date I did it the way I had learned to do it with Mimi, and Glenn gave me a look that would have melted an icecap. He said, 'What in the world are you doing?' I said, 'I'm taking lessons,' and he merely said, 'Knock off the goddamn lessons. I want you to sing like Marion Hutton.' I was crushed. I realized then there was nothing in the universe except what *he* wanted. It was 'The Doctrine According to Glenn.'

"The big trouble, I realize now, was that Glenn would squeeze

ABOVE: Marion and Tex, her crush. BELOW: Marion and Ray, object of her jealousy. OPPOSITE PAGE, ABOVE: Marion and Glenn, her father figure. OPPOSITE PAGE, BELOW: Marion the "People Pleaser."

anyone who loved him absolutely dry. You had to be prepared to know that you wouldn't get much back. He really owned me, lock, stock and barrel; musically, emotionally and financially."

Marion's sense of frustration must have been almost unbearable. The father figure just wouldn't respond the way she expected it to. For a long time she took it as a personal affront. "With the band I felt I was just a thing, that's all." But years later she began to realize that the problem was not hers alone. "Glenn just wouldn't allow himself to show much compassion or feeling. He was full of guilts and he overcompensated. He was, I feel, an angry, hostile person. And the rage that went on inside of him was his inadequacy. He always felt inferior as a trombonist to Tommy Dorsey and Will Bradley. It was sort of like a little boy's 'I'll show them' attitude and he would take it out on others.

"You'd never guess it from watching him, but I'm beginning to realize that Glenn, like so many of us, had his share of fears. The whole outside world may have loved him, just as much as I did, but I wonder now whether down deep inside he *really* liked *himself.*"

Chapter 13

September 1938 turned out to be a good month for Glenn Miller. His band made its first records on RCA Victor's Bluebird label. And Glenn finally got a manager who was really going to help the band.

The band hadn't been doing very well for Brunswick Records and vice versa. As a matter of fact, Brunswick wasn't doing very well for any bands during that era. Decca, on the other hand, was blossoming with Chick Webb's "A-Tisket, A-Tasket," featuring Ella Fitzgerald; Bob Crosby's "Big Noise from Winnetka"; and other sides by Jimmy Dorsey, Casa Loma, Jimmie Lunceford and several more bands.

But the company with most of the truly big hits was RCA Victor, where an astute and highly controversial director of recordings named Eli Oberstein, who was accused of having a financial interest in some of the label's bands, held sway. In 1938 the Victor label produced some huge big-band hits: Benny Goodman's "Don't Be That Way," Artie Shaw's "Begin the Beguine," Tommy Dorsey's "Boogie Woogie" and Larry Clinton's "My Reverie."

By then, recordings had become increasingly important for the bands. Disc jockeys had emerged not merely as record spinners but as important and influential personalities. The kids listened regularly to such shows as Martin Block's *Make Believe Ballroom* in New York and Al Jarvis' similarly titled show in Los Angeles, and when they heard them play certain records over and over again, they'd be very likely to go out and buy their own copies. And the more those jockeys played a band's records, the greater the number of kids who would show up in person when it appeared at a local dance or theater.

But, because of the dismal reception of his previous Brunswick recordings, Glenn had been unable to land another recording deal. It took the success of another band's record, Larry Clinton's "My Reverie," to open up a whole new Miller recording future.

Howie Richmond, still working for Glenn, really believed in the band—even more than in Clinton, his major band client, who was riding high at that time with several big records, a radio commercial and a summer season's engagement at the prestigious Glen Island Casino.

Larry had also emerged as a successful "composer" by turning classical themes into popular songs. As one wag commented, "It goes in Larry's ear and comes out his pen." After Clinton's recording of "My Reverie," originally a Debussy theme, had become such a huge hit on Victor, Oberstein asked Larry which band he thought should record his song on RCA's cheaper Bluebird label. Oberstein was leaning toward Artie Shaw, but Richmond, who was in on the conversation and who carried some weight with Clinton, spoke out against Artie: "I resented some of the things he had been saying against Benny Goodman. Besides, I had just spent the weekend with Glenn and the band and I'd heard his gorgeous arrangement of 'My Reverie.' It was different from Larry's, because Glenn treated it strictly as an instrumental. And when Glenn saw how much I liked his arrangement, he said, 'Why don't you tell your friend Larry Clinton you liked it.' And so I told Larry and Eli, and the next thing Eli called Glenn. Now this is something I could never figure out: The instrumental arrangement was just great, but on the record date, Eli, who liked to run things his way, changed it all around." The result: a road-company Tommy Dorsey approach, with Glenn blowing a pedestrian trombone for sixteen bars and Ray Eberle singing a chorus, but with the unique reed sound relegated to a secondary role. As Richmond noted, "The whole thing became a real hodgepodge. It just didn't come off at all."

I remember Oberstein well. A very headstrong character, he had an overbite that made him look as pugnacious as he really was. He liked to tell Les Brown and Bunny Berigan and Clinton and others with whom he was associated exactly what they should do. And they almost always did it. But what a comeuppance he would have had if he had tried that sort of stuff with Glenn, once the Miller band had become firmly entrenched!

Ballads with vocals and swinging instrumentals were Oberstein's forte, and so, on the rest of the band's first Bluebird date, it recorded some big-band jazz. "King Porter Stomp" and the two-sided version of "By the Waters of Minnetonka" may have some historical significance, but as big-band jazz they are hardly spellbinders.

Aside from some dedicated people like Richmond and a few good friends, Glenn was getting very little help from others. For a while Arthur Michaud, who was managing Tommy Dorsey, had also been taking care of Glenn's affairs, but that didn't work out and even before the first edition had busted up, Michaud had disappeared from the picture. Jack Philbin, then a song plugger in Boston and more recently Jackie Gleason's executive producer, helped out for a while, at $20 a week, though no one was ever quite sure whether he was more interested in the band or in Marion Hutton, whom he later married.

Actually Glenn's staunchest supporter and even sometime-savior during those struggling days was his old friend—but soon to become a bitter rival—Tommy Dorsey. Richmond recalls: "One night after the band had played at Playland in Rye, just outside New York City, I drove Glenn and Helen down to Fifty-second Street to one of those clubs which Glenn hated to go into because he wasn't drinking. But he had to meet Tommy there because Tommy was going to give him some money to meet his payroll. When he came out, he looked very relieved. Tommy must have loaned him a lot of money—something like $2,500, I think, because the next day Glenn told me that his financial troubles had been solved for a while."

Only recently I was talking with Benny Goodman about the

Miller-Dorsey relationship. "Glenn used to be very subservient toward Tommy," Goodman pointed out. "But they got along very well until they got into some sort of financial tangle. Money always louses up a friendship."

What Tommy and Glenn soon got into wasn't so much a financial tangle as a financial *tri*angle, with Cy Shribman as the third side. Cy was a big, gruff, warm, virile gent out of Boston, just the opposite of the cringing, weak character who appeared under his name in *The Glenn Miller Story*. Few men in the music field have ever been as thoroughly respected for their honesty, shrewdness and farsightedness as was Cy Shribman.

Cy and his brother, Charlie, had started in the music business in the twenties as ballroom operators. Both loved good music and respected good musicianship. And so, when they'd find bands in which they believed, they'd encourage them. Sometimes this meant booking them into their own ballrooms so that they would have enough work to keep them going. At other times it meant actually investing time and money in them. Mal Hallett was their first such success in the days when his band sported young, upcoming sidemen like Gene Krupa, Jack Teagarden, Frankie Carle and Jack Jenney. Later they had helped Tommy Dorsey for a while, but they had figured even more prominently in the successes of Artie Shaw and Woody Herman before they started supporting Glenn.

Today Cy has emerged as a legendary character among ballroom operators. His business acumen, his courage and his memory all figured in his nightly transactions, when he would travel alone between the various bands and ballrooms with which he was involved, his pockets stuffed with thousands of dollars, some of which he would collect in one place, after which he'd ride to another to pay off one of his bands, collect more money from the box office and continue to another spot where he would repeat the process. How he managed it nobody ever really knew. All his pockets bulged with rolls of bills of apparently undetermined amounts. But Cy knew exactly how much there was in each, and when he'd arrive to pay off a band, he'd merely put his hand into a pocket, finger one of the rolls and out would come the precise number of dollars to which the band was entitled. Then, when he'd return to his office, he'd enter all his transactions in the daily ledger. It was all strictly from memory, and yet the Shribman books remained in perfect order.

According to Cy and Charlie's nephew, Joe Shribman, now a successful personal manager on the West Coast, it was Mike Nidorf, one of the heads of the Rockwell-O'Keefe booking office, which later became even more famous as General Artists Corporation, who talked Cy into financing the Miller band. Mike, a brilliant salesman, had great faith in Glenn and obviously wanted to help him. Setting him up with Shribman was a masterful stroke, so far as Glenn was concerned. But for Mike it eventually boomeranged.

Richmond recalls Glenn's ecstasy after the Shribman deal had been set. "He called me on the phone to tell me about it. 'Cy is going to pick up all our bills, including all the money I owe Tommy, and give us some work besides,' he said. By then those bills must have mounted to around ten or twelve thousand dollars. In exchange, Cy was to get twenty-five percent of the band's profits. A day or two later Glenn gave me all my retroactive pay, about twelve hundred and fifty dollars. It was the biggest paycheck I'd ever gotten, by far. And he told me I had a lifetime deal with him if I wanted it."

Glenn may have been ecstatic. But Tommy Dorsey was positively furious. Apparently he had believed that, because he had been advancing Glenn all that money, he automatically had a piece of the band. Like Shribman, Dorsey was a shrewd purveyor of talent, and he, too, had tremendous faith in Glenn's ultimate success. Glenn offered to return all the money he had borrowed immediately, but that didn't satisfy Tommy. He turned Glenn off completely. And he went even further. He had his manager, Arthur Michaud, build a brand-new band around Bob Chester, a tenor saxist, friend, and son of an extraordinarily wealthy Detroit lady. The band copied the Miller style, complete with the clarinet-led reeds and the ooh-wah brass punctuations. And, because of his close ties with Victor Records and Eli Oberstein, Tommy succeeded in placing the new Chester band as direct competition on Glenn's Bluebird label! Greater fury had no band leader than Tommy Dorsey.

With Shribman's support, the band found steady work. Every Tuesday and Saturday it played at Boston's Roseland-State Ballroom, owned by the Shribmans, and for most of the other nights there'd be dates at colleges and at various other New England ballrooms which the brothers controlled.

But the struggle wasn't over. Recognition was still slow in coming. For quite a while the band seldom pulled as many as three hundred customers a night into Roseland-State. On the other hand, a group called Joe Mack and his Old Timers, which played old-fashioned music in the square-dance tradition, regularly attracted well over a thousand fans. The corn was still hard to cut.

Nevertheless, the regular Tuesday-and-Saturday-night nationwide CBS broadcasts from Roseland-State were helping. The buildup was slow, and, just as today the young underground is the first to latch on to embryonic stars, so some of the college kids around Boston discovered that the "in" thing to do was to "go dance to that new Glenn Miller band over at Roseland."

Except for one trumpet chair, the personnel remained refreshingly steady. Louis Mucci, who had taken over for trumpeter Gasparre Rebito, left to be replaced by Bob Peck, who was replaced by Jack Kimble, who was replaced by Claude Bowen, who eventually gave way to Legh Knowles. And in mid-December Cody Sandifer took over for drummer Bob Spangler.

Each musician received $50 a week, Beneke included. So did Marion Hutton. But Ray Eberle was paid only $35, presumably because he didn't have as many dresses to buy and keep clean. Band boy Warren Jordan got a paltry $20 a week, the same amount that part-time manager Jack Philbin received.

During the 1938 fall season the band, still financially strapped, saved a few bucks by making out their weekly income and expense reports on payroll forms that had "Mal Hallett Orchestra" printed across the top. Glenn's total take was always entered next to Mal's name. For the eleven weeks ending December 17, Glenn's total income was $1,128.89. It wasn't much, but still it was the first time in almost two years that the band had finished out of the red.

Shribman and Miller both recognized the need to get out of the Boston area and down to New York where the action was. But the only spot in New York interested in booking the band was the Paradise Restaurant, and even they weren't too enthused. To prove it, they offered Glenn $75 a week less than they had paid him in June. He accepted.

The poor money, the same old floor shows leered at by the same old traveling salesmen, the management's failure to pick up the two weeks' option, and the almost total lack of recognition had to be depressants. But Cy kept encouraging Glenn, and so did those of us in New York who had become so attached to the band. And, as it turned out, the Paradise proved to be the band's most important showcase.

Apparently the collegiate underground had reached Iona Prep in New Rochelle, New York, because an undergraduate there in charge of booking a band for a Christmas dance had reserved Glenn's group for the night of December 26. Because of this previous commitment, the management of the Paradise released the band for the night. The astute young booker was Tom Sheils, who later would go to work for Glenn, and whose father held the very influential post of Supreme Court Justice for Westchester County.

The band turned in such a fine job at Iona that young Sheils went over to Glen Island Casino to tell Michael DeZutter, who managed the room, about it and to suggest he consider it for next summer. DeZutter had already been approached by Mike Nidorf, but when the son of one of the county's most prestigious and influential citizens also pitched the band, DeZutter figured maybe he ought to give it a listen, at least.

In order to please the bawdy customers at the Paradise, Glenn often concentrated upon loud, blaring music that would fit their mood. So on the night that DeZutter decided to audition the band, Nidorf warned Glenn: "When you see me come in with him, play soft and send Marion over to the table." To this day, Mike still can't figure out what Glenn was or wasn't thinking that night. "As soon as we walk in, what does Glenn do but play louder than ever! Marion proceeded to charm DeZutter, but not enough, because finally he said, 'This is not for us. Find me somebody else.' But I wouldn't find anyone else for him. I didn't want to.''

At about the time that Tom Sheils was discovering the Glenn Miller band, Glenn himself was discovering a young arranger who was to create some great musical and commercial contributions both for his band and, later on, for others. This was young Bill Finegan, who during the fifties became famous as co-leader and co-arranger of the wonderful Sauter-Finegan orchestra. To many musicians who passed through the Miller band, Bill's unique, colorful and adventurous arrangements were the most musical and the most exciting in the band's large library.

Bill, a shy, quiet, low-keyed guy, who looked more like a chemistry student than a musician, recently reminisced with me in his Rumson, New Jersey, home, which he was then busy painting for his new wife and their two young children.

"I remember just when I joined Glenn. I'd written an arrangement of 'Lonesome Road' for Tommy Dorsey. I was one of a whole staff of Tommy's arrangers. Glenn came into the New Yorker Hotel one night and Tommy played the arrangement. Later Glenn called me over to his table and started asking me some questions. It was like an inquisition: 'What bands do you like?' I told him Duke and Lunceford. He asked, 'How about Basie?' and I said, 'Of course.' He asked some more questions and then he asked me to send him an arrangement. So I sent him something on 'Blue Room.' It was a tour de force; I had to show him my whole bag of tricks. A couple of weeks later he called me and told me he wanted me to work for the band. 'We could use a dozen of these in our book,' he said. So I started arranging for him. I remember the first tunes I did were 'Cuckoo in the Clock' and 'Romance Runs in the Family.' He paid me forty bucks a week for as many arrangements as I could write. At the end, he was paying me a hundred and fifty a week for just two arrangements.''

Finegan's arrangements invariably created emotions. His rhythmic scores projected spontaneous excitement; his richly textured ballads evoked melancholia and sentimentality. One of his contributions, a finger-snapping arrangement of "Little

Brown Jug," turned out to be the band's first swing hit, a bit of realism ignored by the producers of *The Glenn Miller Story,* who placed it as the last arrangement Glenn ever wrote.

As the band's first regularly employed arranger, Finegan represented a new challenge to the competitive Miller. Heretofore Glenn had written almost all the arrangements himself, and so he had maintained complete control over everything the band played. But Bill began writing "some wild things. I was experimenting and discovering." Glenn obviously wasn't pleased. He wanted more conformity. So he began to try to exercise a great deal of control over young Finegan. "I used to complain about his continual editing of my arrangements. It was OK at first, when we had to cut down to fit the tune onto one side of a record. But after a while Glenn would start editing just about everything, and it soon became a battle of wits between us. [Herb Miller once said that Glenn used to admonish Bill to "bring it *down* to *our* level!"] I would try to anticipate what he was going to do by black-penciling my own arrangements before he could. Finally he plain told me, 'You keep writing. I'll handle the black pencil.' Today, when people ask me what I think was the best arrangement I ever wrote for the band, I really don't know, because everything I wrote went through that meat-grinder."

Finegan's plight later received sympathy from some fellow-bandsmen, like arranger-trumpeter Billy May, who told me, "My heart used to bleed for Billy Finegan because Glenn's ideas were really not that good. And to make it worse, Chummy MacGregor was always adding some crap, like three clinks."

Throughout his career, Bill was plagued by emotional hangups. Extremely sensitive and introverted, his continuing self-doubts were nourished by the combination of a controlling boss and a dominating wife. Little wonder then that many times he lacked the courage to complete an arrangement. Fellow-arranger Jerry Gray, like Miller a lover of routine, apparently resented such unreliability. "Bill Finegan gave the impression of being a genius because he fluffed his job," he recently told me. And Miller also seemed to have little sympathy for Finegan's hangups. According to drummer Moe Purtill, "Sometimes Finegan would hole up for a few weeks and just write and never show up. Then he'd return with his arrangements and Glenn would be very sarcastic and introduce him to the band."

And how did Finegan react? "I reacted to his ice-cold personality in a cocky sort of way. He always had the barb out and he would bring it out in me."

One way Bill could dig back at Glenn was through his trombone playing. "Tommy Dorsey played loud, so Glenn felt he had to play loud also. Sometimes he'd play so loud that I'd have to find ways for him not to demolish the brass section. He wasn't a great trombonist, but he was better than his records show him to be. He felt secure within the brass section, rather than as a soloist. There he would belt out his parts so much that the section would be out of balance. So I began writing bass trombone parts for him because I loved to hear them belted out the way he could. 'What are you doing, Finegan?' he'd ask me, and I'd tell him he was the only one who played so loud that I could hear those parts. I don't know whether Glenn appreciated not playing lead trombone. But I know I did. It was a pleasure, really, hearing him play way down low." And it was also Finegan's way of finally asserting himself.

Glenn's bass trombone playing may have impressed Finegan some—but not as much as his executive ability. "He functioned like the head of a well-organized corporation. Once he sent me to Cincinnati to listen to a jazz trumpeter in Red Norvo's band. He wasn't any good. But I heard Gozzo playing lead [Conrad Gozzo later emerged as the greatest lead trumpeter in the country. He was Al Hirt's idol for years.] and I thought he was great. So I told Glenn about him. But he wasn't one bit interested. He had sent me to hear a *jazz* trumpeter, and that's all he wanted to hear about."

Finegan found that Miller's organized, corporate-executive approach also pervaded music itself. "He liked to work out things mathematically, especially his harmonic sequences. I'd figure out my own without using math, and then he couldn't wait to get to a piano to see how my sequences worked out mathematically. He always kept touting the Schillinger method of arranging, which used the mathematical approach, and I always kept rejecting it. I felt math should not be the instigator of music. But this organized method suited him perfectly. It was a practical rather than an idealistic approach to music, which is exactly what his band was all about, too." And which could also explain why Glenn in college wound up with high marks in algebra while flunking music.

"And still there were times when he could be very emotional. On more than one occasion I moved him to tears. He'd break down, but he wouldn't want anyone to see he was affected, so he'd go over in a corner. I remember he did that when he first heard my arrangement of 'A Handful of Stars.'

"Glenn loved Delius and Ravel, especially Delius' 'On Hearing the First Cuckoo in Spring,' and Ravel's 'Introduction and Allegro' and String Quartet in F. Once, when we were at Meadowbrook and I was down in the dumps, he and Helen brought me back to their hotel room in Paterson and Glenn played Ravel for me. He liked to play everything in thirds. I'd imitate Glenn for Jerry Gray. Finally I got so brazen, I imitated Glenn for Glenn, and he laughed.

"All in all, Glenn was very patient with me. He'd explain to me that I was not the only one who could get stuck writing under pressure and he admitted that he'd sometimes gotten stuck too and that he had called Claude Thornhill to bail him out. And there were times when I would even call Glenn in the middle of the night and say, 'Hey, I'm stuck on an ending.' And he would talk with me and get me off the hook—even if I'd woken him up at four in the morning. He was very good to me that way.

"You know, as I look back at it all now, I realize that there was probably one thing that Glenn wanted more than anything else. It may be hard to believe it, but I think what Glenn wanted most of all was to be needed."

Chapter 14

The frustrating and often humiliating engagement at the Paradise proved to be the perfect topper for 1938: a rancid icing on a mildewed cake. Nineteen thirty-nine couldn't be any worse, and as it turned out, it wasn't—not by a long shot!

But even before the Paradise, doubt and despondency kept nagging Glenn. I remember how utterly down he had been during another discouraging southern tour. The band had really been bugging him. Those sloppy trumpets and that slovenly rhythm section, which was about as spry and swinging as a nineteenth-century porcelain bathtub, made the band he wanted so much to be proud of sound like just another pickup group.

And so, once again, Glenn had told me that he was about ready to call it quits—and for good this time. But then along had come the encouraging Cy Shribman, and then that first Bluebird recording session, and Glenn began reconsidering, and decided maybe he'd hang on a little longer after all.

Soon 1939 did begin to offer some encouragement. Mike Nidorf kept talking more and more about the possibility of going into Glen Island Casino for the summer. We all knew Mike was a great optimist as well as a great salesman, and so nobody took him more than fifty percent seriously. And yet, who knew? Maybe Michael DeZutter would change his mind.

And then, too, there was Glenn's showing in the latest *Metronome* All-Star Musicians poll, in which he had never before

RCA Victor's Frank Walker hands Glenn his new contract to sign. Watching are Victor's A&R director Leonard Joy, Miller manager Mike Nidorf and newly appointed Miller attorney David Mackay.

placed in the running. But the magazine's January 1939 issue announced that the readers had voted him fourth among all lead trombonists, and second, topped only by Jack Teagarden, among jazz trombonists! It was at least one sign that musicians and fans alike were becoming Glenn Miller–conscious.

And so were some of the disc jockeys, especially the highly influential Martin Block, whose *Make Believe Ballroom* often served as a barometer of a band's popularity. Block liked the sound, and he liked Glenn, and so the new records began to get some important air-time.

RCA Victor must have noticed this, because they offered Glenn another recording date. On the previous one, they had paid him $150 per side (the musicians, of course, were paid the usual union scale of $30 per session) with no provisions for royalties. This time they raised the ante to $175 a side. What's more, they offered him a one-year contract with a guaranteed number of releases. It sounded good, though not as good as what the bigger names, with their 5 percent royalty deals, were getting. But Glenn, not yet big enough to barter for more, signed the one-year non-royalty deal.

Glenn was a shrewd businessman. So were Nidorf and Shribman. But none had any legal training, and, with more contract negotiations likely to come along, Mike and Cy suggested it was time for Glenn to get himself an attorney. Glenn mentioned this to RCA Victor's head man, Frank Walker, a homespun straight-shooter whom he greatly respected. The timing was perfect. One of the company's top lawyers had just returned to private practice. Walker thought he would be ideal.

Shortly before the close of the Paradise Restaurant date, they met in Walker's office—Walker, Miller and David Mackay. "The first time I ever met Glenn," observed Mackay recently, "he didn't impress me as the band-leader type. I thought of him as a schoolteacher or minister type. And I still think of him that way."

What Miller thought of Mackay is obvious: He considered him to be one damned good lawyer. And so he turned over all his legal matters and eventually most of his business affairs to him. After Glenn was lost, Helen Miller continued the relationship, and now the soft-spoken, rimless-spectacled, conservative Mackay, as executor of the Glenn Miller Estate, makes every decision on every important matter concerning Glenn Miller. The move to Mackay turned out to be one of the smartest Glenn ever made.

During the Paradise engagement Glenn made another good catch. Taking the advice of trumpeter Legh Knowles, with whom he was driving back from New England from a one-night stand (occasionally the Paradise let the band off to fulfill some previously booked dates), he stopped off in Danbury, Connecticut, to ask Al Klink if he'd like to join the sax section.

"It was quite a shock," recalls Klink. "The doorbell rang at four o'clock in the morning on a cold winter night and woke up the whole family. It was Legh—we'd often played together—and with him was Glenn with a red scarf wrapped around his head. I remember they came into my room and I stayed there in bed while Glenn and Legh talked to me about joining the band. Glenn said he wanted me to play alto sax, but I told him I didn't want to, that tenor was my horn. But he promised that as soon as there would be an opening on tenor, he'd let me switch over, and he kept his word."

Klink accepted the offer, thinking he was there for more or less of a trial period. It was a feeling he never quite lost throughout the entire three and a half years he stayed in the band, always in the shadow of Tex Beneke and his tenor sax.

"All the time I was with the band, I had the feeling I could very easily be replaced. Glenn just never gave me any indication that he liked me or my playing. For example, when we were at Glen Island Casino, I'd just gotten a mouthpiece that I loved and I played it for Glenn in the dressing room, all excited, and asked him how he liked it. But he just turned and said, 'Well, I can take it or leave it.' And that's about all he ever said about my playing. He used to make me feel about an inch high, but it was not deliberate on his part. It was more my problem, because I was always in-going and I always wanted to avoid leaders and their wives. As I look back now, I realize that Glenn never really put me down; he just never really put me up!"

Others kept trying to build up Klink, but Glenn had ears only for Beneke. Bill Finegan claims he used "every trick in the book to get solos for Klink. If I wrote in a solo for him on an arrangement, the first time we'd run it down, Glenn would switch parts and give the one with a solo in it to Tex. He just kept Al blowing the lead along with the clarinet. On some arrangements I'd even write throwaway solos for Tex and big fat ones for Al, but Glenn would switch even those around."

Once in a great while Klink was rewarded with a solo, as in "Boulder Buff" and "Sun Valley Jump," neither of which he thinks were any good. And Al dismisses his famed sax challenge with Beneke on "In the Mood" as "a piece of crap, as everybody knows."

Klink thinks that his inability to establish any sort of personal relationship with his boss may have resulted from an innocent misunderstanding concerning trust that took place right after he joined the band. "It had to do with the very first paycheck. I noticed it had the words 'Glenn Miller Special' printed across the top and I was looking at it, wondering what that meant, when Glenn looked at me, his eyes flashing with fire. 'Is something wrong with it?' he asked. He must have thought I considered it inadequate, or that I was questioning the amount. But that wasn't the case at all. In fact, to me, it was a large sum for a

Glenn and Klink.

one-nighter, something like forty dollars. I was just innocently trying to figure out what that 'Glenn Miller Special' stood for."

In the Miller band Klink seldom realized his full potential. But later, with Benny Goodman, Tommy Dorsey, and the Sauter-Finegan and *Tonight Show* bands, he blossomed into one of the country's truly great tenor saxists, an opinion shared by almost everyone with whom he has played. All he needed was a little of the encouragement that Glenn seemed unable to give him. "I used to think all bands were like Miller's. Then I joined Benny a week after Glenn's band broke up. Now, in the Miller band, if I walked down the street, Glenn would ignore me. So when I joined Benny and I was passing through the diner on the train and I saw Benny sitting there, I ignored him, because 'I thought that's the way things are. But Benny called out, 'Hello kid, come on and sit down.' I found it very easy to communicate with Benny, much easier than with Glenn."

Once, Klink recalls, the communication with Miller was good, but it required an emergency as a catalyst. "We were somewhere in the Midwest when I got word that my mother was in an automobile accident and was in the hospital. Glenn heard about it and asked me if I wanted to go see my mother. When I told him I did, he made all arrangements for me to go. He took care of everything. He was very kind."

Bill Finegan was right: Glenn certainly wanted to be needed. In a way, it was too bad that there weren't more personal emergencies to help other members of the band who couldn't break through Glenn's ridiculous stoicism and confounded inhibitions. For then they also might have discovered a beautiful part of Glenn Miller—the part that too few of us were privileged to have known.

Chapter 15

The band departed the depressing Paradise late in January and one-nighted its way through a series of college proms and ballroom dates. After the non-reaction of the corn lovers on New York's Great White Way, the response of the college kids to the romantic ballads and the joyous jazz proved to be especially refreshing. The series of broadcasts from the Paradise obviously had been well received, and Shribman and Nidorf, often working as a team, had little difficulty booking the band into such schools as Vassar, Massachusetts State, Middlebury, the University of Vermont, Mount Holyoke, LaSalle and the University of Buffalo. Even at the ballrooms, many of which the band had previously played before small crowds, the dancers began to respond more, both in numbers and in enthusiasm.

And there had been that second Bluebird recording session, on which the band waxed four tunes, none of which, unfortunately, created much of a stir. Three of them, including Bill Finegan's first arrangements, featured Marion Hutton, and it could have been after hearing these that Glenn decided that he should feature Ray Eberle more. Marion was doing a helluva selling job in person. But on records all that enthusiasm and that cute smile didn't come through enough to compensate for all those out-of-tune notes. But at least Glenn had produced four more sides for the kids to buy and the disc jockeys to play.

Early in February came the announcement that the band had

been booked for
Frank Dailey's
received some ev

It was Wedne
day. Helen and
those rehearsals
in with a huge
announced triun
Island for the s
Michael DeZutter.

It was electrifying news. Every new band wanted to play Glen Island because it attracted more college kids than any place in the country, because it offered a whole slew of coast-to-coast radio wires and because that job was just about the most prestigious engagement any band that wanted to get to the kids could play. Casa Loma, Ozzie Nelson, the Dorsey Brothers, Charlie Barnet and Larry Clinton had all made their initial impact there. I'd never seen Glenn so happy and so optimistic.

But first came the Meadowbrook, which also catered to the kids. Located on "Route 23, the Newark-Pompton Turnpike, in Cedar Grove, New Jersey," as the announcers used to say, it played most of the big swing bands for a few weeks at a time. Larry Clinton, who was riding high on his big recordings of "Deep Purple" and "My Reverie," preceded Glenn, who wasn't nearly as well known to the kids as Clinton, Tommy Dorsey, Jimmy Dorsey, Gene Krupa and other big names that played there. In fact, when Clinton announced that Glenn Miller would be following him into the spot, some of the kids called out, "Who's Glenn Miller?"

One of the callers was George "Bullets" Durgom, a young, short, prematurely balding dynamo who bore the unofficial title of "Frank Dailey's Goodwill Ambassador." He was a character, a fantastic dancer, a member of several high school and fraternal organizations, and the hub of Meadowbrook's activities.

After Durgom—who later worked for Glenn before graduating into top personal-management ranks (Jackie Gleason was his client)—called out, "Who's Glenn Miller?" Clinton called him over and said, "Bullets, if you don't know, come with me." And he led Durgom to Glenn's table. Bullets still remembers that night. "Naturally, I was embarrassed and nervous, especially when Larry said to Glenn, 'If this guy doesn't like your band, you're in trouble.' But Glenn and Helen were both very nice to me and Glenn asked, 'Will you be here for my opening?' I said 'Sure,' and I was there every night."

The Meadowbrook was a big, barnlike place. It had a large dance floor with a bandstand at one end and a balcony running around the three other sides. The acoustics were excellent, so that the band's six broadcasts per week let the country hear some superb samplings of what this new style of dance music sounded like—better by far than its recordings, which were made in one of the worst-sounding studios ever to intimidate any band.

The kids at Meadowbrook loved the band, and Frank Dailey and his brothers, Vince and Cliff, picked up its option even before the end of the first week, extending the four weeks' engagement to seven.

RCA Victor, aware of the band's growing potential, offered it more dates. During April it recorded a dozen sides, including five all-time Miller hits: "Little Brown Jug," "Pavanne," "Runnin' Wild," "Sunrise Serenade" and the famous Miller theme, "Moonlight Serenade," which still gives me goose-pimples every time I hear it. Much as he liked the original lyrics of "Now I Lay Me Down to Weep," Glenn had discarded them because he felt they were too melancholy for a theme song. He felt the same way about a set titled "Gone with the Dawn," which I had submitted. Robbins Music bought the melody and assigned Mitchell Parrish, who had written the words for "Stardust," to come up with something as good. Mitch's first effort was called "Wind in the Trees," and the song might have eventually come out that way. But Abe Olman, professional manager at Robbins, had learned that Glenn was going to record Frankie Carle's "Sunrise Serenade." So why not back it with something called "Moonlight Serenade?" He mentioned the idea to Mitch and Glenn. They liked it, and so "Wind in the Trees" became "Moonlight Serenade"—with the possible exception of Tommy Dorsey's "I'm Getting Sentimental Over You," the most poignantly evocative of all big-band theme songs.

Presented with the first steady engagement in which it could focus entirely on dance music for kids, the band's performances at Meadowbrook improved greatly. And the tentative-sounding trumpet section took on a solidity and crispness it had never known before when Glenn hired Mickey McMickle, a lean, sharp-visaged, serious trumpeter—in some ways a junior edition of Glenn, himself—who had been the mainstay of Mal Hallett's brass section as far back as the early thirties, when he had played alongside Gene Krupa, Jack Teagarden and Jack Jenney.

Glenn had been after McMickle for over a year. "He first asked me to come with the band in 1937. He'd heard me play at some jam sessions we used to hold at the old Avery Hotel in Boston. When he asked me to join, I had a nerve ailment called Bell's palsy. That meant I had to play with the sole of a shoe next to my cheek, and I wasn't in any condition to join then. But in 1939, when I was working in Philadelphia at the Walton Roof, Glenn saw me again and told me he was going into Meadowbrook and invited me to hear the band. I heard it and I knew it was for me. I replaced Lee Castle, who was filling in on the jazz chair. The two other trumpets were Bob Price and Legh Knowles. Eventually I replaced Price on lead."

McMickle anchored the trumpet section continuously from the day he joined until the band broke up, with only three weeks' leave when he had a cyst on his lip. Bobby Hackett, who joined later on, recently told me, "Whenever the trumpets sounded really good, it was because McMickle was playing the lead. He was an unsung hero and a helluva guy, too. He was the only trumpeter who ever tried to help me. In those days I was just guessing and doing about everything wrong. But he straightened me out on a lot of things."

During his first weeks with the band, Mickey played almost all the jazz solos, as Price continued to hold down the lead chair. Thus he appeared as the featured soloist on the recordings of "Runnin' Wild" and "Little Brown Jug," which I had once credited to Clyde Hurley, an error that was picked up by too many other writers. But he soon switched to the lead chair and never again recorded a jazz solo with the band.

McMickle certainly sparked the band. But the man who, for my dough, made an even more noticeable difference was drummer Maurice "Moe" Purtill, Glenn's 1937 one-day Christmas gift from Tommy Dorsey.

I first discovered the improvement in the rhythm section before I even knew that Moe had joined the band. Andy Picard, a nice guy but not a very inspiring drummer who had been working at Nick's with the dixielanders there, had replaced Cody Sandifer at Meadowbrook, and the heretofore weak rhythm section began to sag even more. Then one evening, while listening to Glenn's broadcasts, I was flabbergasted by what I thought was the reincarnation of Picard. I called Glenn the next day to tell him so. "Hell," he told me, "that wasn't Andy. That was Moe Purtill. He joined us last night."

Purtill was an old friend of mine. He's still a friend. The first time I heard him was back in 1936 when he was a young unknown playing with Bob Sylvester's only slightly less unknown band at the Arcadia Ballroom. I flipped, I raved about him in my review of the band, and immediately went after Red Norvo to add Purtill to his drummerless sextet. Red did, and Moe's soft, swinging brushwork fit the unit admirably.

With Glenn, Moe was something else again. Glenn's conception of Swing was very different from Red's, as I found out during many arguments he and I had about Red's soft, subtle, swinging band. Glenn thought it was gutless and emasculated. He preferred more muscle, and it was precisely because of Glenn's constant insistence on a hard, driving, flashy attack, that, for me at least, Moe never played as effectively for Glenn as he had for Red. By comparison with all who had preceded him, me

Purtill and Alpert.

included, he was a giant. But Glenn never let him relax enough to allow him to settle into that easy, swinging groove he had found in the Norvo band.

Several other Miller alumni have agreed with me on that point. Willie Schwartz noted, "As Glenn put the pressure on Moe, he'd drink more and wave his hair more. But he wouldn't swing more." Chuck Goldstein, one of the Modernaires, observed, "When Glenn would leave the stand to sign autographs, Moe and the band would swing more." I myself, when I first played with the band, and later when I occasionally filled in with the AAF outfit in New Haven, found it terribly difficult to relax with Glenn looking at me. I had the feeling he was trying to control all of my movements, which, when one takes into consideration the caliber of my drumming, might not have been too bad an idea at that.

Trigger Alpert, who played bass next to Purtill, liked the way Moe played but adds the qualification "with *that* band. He had a unique sound. He tried to copy Davey Tough. He was also a big fan of Sonny Greer's. He played more or less the same way on everything because Glenn wanted him to. I enjoyed playing with him."

Recently Moe, now living with his attractive new wife in

Liberty, New York, where he teaches and plays in a local club, dropped by to see me. As friend to friend, and drummer to drummer, we discussed the Miller situation. He didn't entirely agree that his playing had changed as much from the Norvo days as I thought it had, but he did agree completely that the Miller rhythm section was by no means a good one. "Ours was the only big band in the world that had only a two-man rhythm section. MacGregor was shaking all the time, and Glenn didn't like Dick Fisher, our guitarist, so he never really got to play. You hardly ever got to hear him on our records." Chuck Goldstein of the Modernaires, who later joined the band, recently told me, "That rhythm section was really something. Everybody was in business for himself!"

Purtill was a great admirer of Miller, though he still doesn't put his band on a par with Norvo's. "That was the greatest musical band there ever was. I cry when I think of it and that it didn't make it. It was the only band I ever heard of where, after work, the guys would ask to rehearse."

With Miller, such requests weren't necessary. Glenn would rehearse and rehearse and rehearse the band. "The trouble was," says Purtill, "it was too well rehearsed. It never made any mistakes. We did practically every record on one take. It was the greatest studio band that ever went on the road!"

Some of those who believed the band would have swung more with a different drummer recognize that Purtill may have kept the job because Glenn liked him so much personally. Moe doesn't deny that he got along with the boss much better than many others did. "We had an understanding right from the start. When I joined, I came out of Tommy Dorsey's band and that was anything but a Boy Scout troop. You had to have a drink the first thing in the morning or you'd be ostracized. You remember, I joined Glenn at Meadowbrook, and so after the first few sets I asked Rudy, the bartender, for a drink at the bar. He told me he wasn't allowed to serve the musicians—Glenn's orders. Just then Glenn walked over and saw what was happening, and I still don't know why, but he told Rudy to give me a drink."

Glenn seldom drank when he had his civilian band, though occasionally he'd lift a few, and then Purtill most likely would be

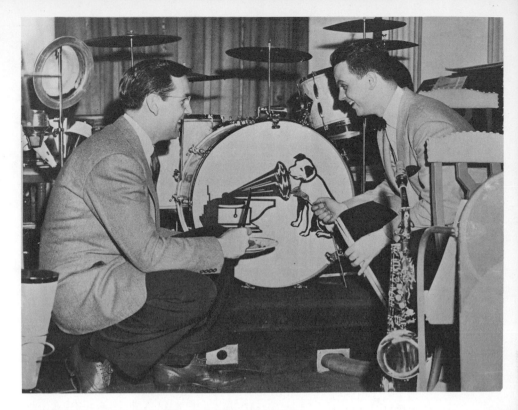

Glenn and Moe feed the dog that continued to feed them.

there to join him. "I remember one time when we were doing a split week at a theater in Providence, and Glenn and I were drinking in the bar at the hotel. He loved to shoot crap, and so finally he invited me up to his room to shoot a few and have a couple of more drinks. We got pretty looped and he started to unburden himself about some things to me. He was sitting there in his shorts and after a while he got up and went into the bathroom, talking all the while. But I'd had enough by then, so I walked out and went to my room and to bed.

"The next day at the theater, Johnny O'Leary, the road manager, was shaking. He came to me and said, 'Mr. Miller told me to give you your two weeks' notice.' And I said, 'You go tell him I'm leaving now.' I didn't know what it was all about, but I wasn't about to have anybody fire me without telling me why.

"But I did play the first show. We used to play 'Bugle Call Rag' way up, real fast, and I'd have a short drum solo. But this morning, Glenn really put me on. He kept me playing and playing. I was so hung over I thought I would faint. Finally I got off the stand. I was soaked clear through. I went over to Glenn and I yelled, 'What the hell are you doing to me, anyway?' And he just looked at me with that hard look he can give people he doesn't like, and he said, 'You son of a bitch! You walked out on me last night, and there I was, an idiot, sitting on the can and talking to myself!' " Ten minutes later Glenn withdrew the two weeks' notice.

Glenn had a thing about the guys and booze. Purtill remembers that "he liked to test us, especially if he thought some of us had been drinking. We used to have all sorts of cuts in our arrangements, but he usually gave us plenty of warning before we had to make them. One night at the Sherman Hotel in Chicago, when he thought some of the guys had been drinking, he started to call out all sorts of cuts at the very last second, just to test the guys to see if they could play all right. But they all came through."

Purtill is convinced that "never in the music business was there a smarter cat. He had it all covered. And not everybody knows how generous he was. Several times he gave us one hundred–dollar bonuses, especially on theater dates when things were going especially good for him.

"You know, when you look back now, you realize that Glenn was a lot like Sinatra—shrewd and generous, and, if he liked you, that was it—he couldn't do enough for you. I think Glenn's one big failing was that he tended to prejudge people. A sax player would come into the band and Glenn would look at the way he walked and he wouldn't like him."

Like Sinatra, Glenn respected musicians. What's more, as Purtill noted, he demanded respect for them. "When we played at hotels, he insisted that they be allowed to sit at tables with the customers. 'They are guests here,' he used to say."

Glenn would reveal his tenderness to those he trusted. Purtill was one of the few. "He tried to be rough, but that was just a pose. And, you know, he loved kids, and I think it really killed him that he couldn't have any of his own. I remember one time when he said he wanted to adopt my son, John. We were staying at the Wardham Park Hotel in Washington, and John was

publishers and other well-wishers augmented the usual collection of college kids, so that the large room was well filled. Excitement and enthusiasm pervaded Glen Island that evening, and by the time it was over, you felt you may have been a part of one of those "A Star Is Born" affairs.

My date for the opening was a very young singer who'd recently arrived in town and was performing regularly, without pay, on station WNEW simply to get exposure and experience. Just as I had prophesied success at the start of 1937 for Glenn, long before his band was known, so had I gone out on the limb early in 1939 for unknown Dinah Shore. I even tried to get her a job with Miller and with several even more important bands. But Dinah, like Glenn, didn't have too many other believers at first.

One thing I'll always remember about her, in addition to her brightness and great sense of humor, was her refusal ever to say anything bad about anyone, a policy which neither Glenn nor I followed. As we danced up to the front of the bandstand on opening night, Glenn leaned over to talk to us. I mentioned that Nick Kenny, the *New York Mirror* radio columnist, who wrote songs which he hoped bands he praised would play over the air, had just come in. Glenn, no Kenny fan, gave us one of those "so-who-the-hell-cares" looks, whereupon Dinah, trying to find something nice to say about Nick, retorted, "Yes, but you've got to admit he has a good sense of humor, don't you?" "Sure," came back Glenn, "he's got to have, to be able to write songs like that!"

In addition to playing good, stylized dance music, Glenn introduced some commercial innovations that evening. Recognizing the importance of Glen Island, he had prepared a special medley of songs associated with each of the big bands that had gotten their starts there. Later in the evening he introduced one of his first "Something Old, Something New, Something Borrowed, Something Blue" medleys, a song grouping that later became an integral part of all his broadcasts.

The numerous coast-to-coast air shots, punctuated by the enthusiastic reactions of the dancers, gave the same impetus to Glenn's career that the broadcasts from the Palomar Ballroom had given Benny Goodman's four summers earlier. But there was one drawback: The pay was lousy. With so many bidding for the job with all its coast-to-coast broadcasts, Glen Island could get away with offering only local union scale—$35 per musician and a little more for the leader. This meant that Glenn had to dig into his own pockets, or into Cy Shribman's, to cover necessities such as publicity, photographs, entertaining critics and reviewers, and simple, personal living expenses.

In addition, his payroll had grown. He had hired a road manager, Tommy Mack, a bright college graduate who had been working in Shribman's Boston office and who relieved Glenn of many of the day-to-day administrative details. And, like so many others, he had been so captivated by Bullets Durgom's enthusiasm that he talked him into leaving his job at the Stock Exchange and becoming his band boy. This meant taking care of the instruments, setting up bandstands and doing other flunky work. But Bullets immediately contributed much more, mingling with the kids at the Casino on their own level and adding a lightness to the band that helped loosen up some of the guys, Glenn included.

The financial drain might have bugged Glenn if he hadn't seen for himself that the band was finally catching on and that as soon as the Casino engagement was finished, he'd finally begin to make real money in theaters and one-nighters. Nevertheless, he wasn't going to run any risk of getting burned again. Cash was still tight, and Glenn was going to hold onto all that he could. Sometimes people would try taking advantage of him, whereupon Glenn, with his blunt, no-nonsense manner, would set them straight.

This happened one evening when a reviewer came in, not just with his date but with a party of six. They remained for the entire evening, with cocktails before dinner and rounds of drinks later on. When the waiter brought their check over to Glenn for his OK, Glenn balked. Most of us freebees always had the decency to order lightly, especially when we were covering a new band. But this character's check had come up to around $75, which was a lot in those days, and Glenn wasn't about to be sucked in. It was a gutsy thing for him to do, but he did take the check, walk over with it to the critic's table, and, handing it to

"Seventy-five bucks!!??"

him, say, "I'm sorry, but if this is what it's going to cost me to get a write-up, I can't afford it."

Proof of how much the band had caught on appeared in the results of two midsummer polls: Martin Block's on WNEW, where Glenn, unplaced the year before, finished fourth, behind Benny Goodman, Artie Shaw and Tommy Dorsey, and ahead of Jimmy Dorsey, Harry James, Count Basie, Sammy Kaye, Gene Krupa, Jimmie Lunceford, Larry Clinton, Charlie Barnet, Richard Himber, Glen Gray and Kay Kyser; and *Metronome*'s poll, where his band placed fourth in the sweet division and fifth in the swing and the Favorite of All listings, after having finished 26th, 18th and 37th respectively in 1938.

During the engagement, Glenn strengthened the band even more. He added a guitarist, Dick Fisher, a quiet, handsome lad who, like some other sidemen who were never given much of a chance to shine, plodded along inconspicuously throughout his career with Miller.

I got back on the scouting trail again. While reviewing some records by Ben Pollack's band, I'd been knocked out by a tremendously hard-driving, mammoth-toned trumpet solo on a tune appropriately titled "So Unexpectedly." I checked to see who had played it, found out his name was Clyde Hurley, then presented my discovery to Glenn. He was just as thrilled as I had been, put in a call to his old boss Pollack, and soon Hurley was sitting in McMickle's jazz trumpet chair, with Mickey replacing Bob Price on lead trumpet.

Unfortunately, Clyde never played as well for Miller as he had for Pollack. When he first joined the band, he tried hard to impress everyone by going for a lot of high notes. Finally one day I asked him why he was pressing so hard instead of blowing that wonderful mid-range, booting style I'd heard on the records. He told me point-blank that the band didn't inspire him one damn bit, that he couldn't stand Purtill's drumming, and so he was trying as best he could to create his own excitement.

During the summer I also came up with a couple of jazz clarinetists. Gabe Gelinas, who'd replaced Stanley Aronson, who had left for what he thought would be a better job with Will Osborne's band and whose rear end was still sore twenty-five years later because of self-inflicted boots, was a fine section man but not enough of a jazz clarinetist to suit Glenn, who began looking around for a replacement. I don't remember where I did find Hal Tennyson—I think it might have been in a small nightclub on West Forty-ninth Street—but Glenn liked him enough to keep him with the band for a couple of months. But then one night early in August I told Glenn about a brilliant clarinetist named Jerry Yelverton whom I'd found in Barry Wood's basically sweet band playing at the Claremont Inn, right in the shadow of Grant's Tomb on New York's Riverside Drive. "You got your car here, don't you," said Glenn, "so why don't you drive down and pick him up and bring him back for rehearsal." I did, Jerry sat in, and Glenn hired him.

For me, Jerry, an Auburn College graduate, was one of the best jazz clarinetists I'd ever heard. But he was colorless, very bashful, with a look of a high school physics major who'd work the lights at a prom to avoid having to ask some girls to dance. He had all the polite manners of a well-reared southern young man. He didn't smoke, he didn't drink, and when he'd get really mad he'd mutter his most bawdy swearwords, "Christmas turkey!" Jerry sat on the stand between Hal McIntyre and Tex Beneke, and Hal once told me that he and Tex had a ball muttering the filthiest swearwords they could think of, just loud enough for Jerry to hear, and then watching him cringe. Poor Jerry, a real gentle soul, never had a chance, and, although Glenn did let him play a solo now and then, he never received the recognition that I thought his talents deserved.

During the Glen Island stint Glenn also lost one of his top attractions, but fortunately only for little over a week. Late in July Marion Hutton collapsed on the stand, apparently from exhaustion, and was rushed to a hospital. During her absence Glenn used a comparative unknown whom he had flown in from Memphis, Tennessee. A scared but very vibrant and exciting singer she was, too. Her name: Kay Starr. She appeared on two Miller recordings, "Baby Me" and "I'm in Love with a Capital You," and then departed, later to join Charlie Barnet's band and finally to emerge in the late forties as one of the country's top singers. ("I remember I was very young then and had come to New York with my mother—we used to do things like visit the Automat," Kay recently told Miller historian John Flower. "I don't recall just how Glenn did find me, but I do remember I had trouble being heard because they couldn't bring the mike down low enough for me!")

As the band's popularity grew, so did its recording output. At RCA Victor, Leonard Joy, a very gentle soul, a former musical conductor and an appreciator of what was good in music, had replaced the admittedly strictly commercial Eli Oberstein. He became so enthused with the band that he wanted to record just about everything in its library. As it was, he settled for a total of thirty-six sides during the fourteen weeks that the band played at Glen Island. Most successful were either instrumental standards, like "Pagan Love Song" and "Isle of Golden Dreams," or original instrumentals such as Glenn's own "Sold American," a chanting bit of jazz based on the cry of the tobacco auctioneer in the then-current Lucky Strike radio commercials (Was Glenn crying for a sponsor? He had already recorded the piece a few months earlier on Brunswick); "Glen Island Special"; and the most famous of all the band's instrumentals, "In the Mood."

No Glenn Miller recording illustrates more dramatically Glenn's remarkable ability to take an arrangement, cut out all the extraneous parts, and reduce it to a beautifully constructed, workable gem. Joe Garland, the composer of "In the Mood," had originally given the arrangement to Artie Shaw, but Artie could never record it because it ran much longer than the three minutes and twenty seconds' maximum time for one 78-rpm side. However, years later, Artie's version of the piece, taken from a radio broadcast and running six and a half minutes long, did appear on a Shaw long-playing record.

Like the Miller recording, the Shaw version starts off with the familiar twelve-bar sax riff, played twice. Then follows the next theme, which in the Miller version consists of two similar eight-bar phrases repeated, which then serve as the chord progression for the soloists that follow. But in the Shaw version those sixteen bars comprise only the first half of a full thirty-two-bar chorus, which, following those sixteen bars (i.e., the eight-bar theme played twice), goes into another eight-bar theme as a release and then returns to the original eight bars. What Glenn did was to cut out the eight-bar release and the final eight bars, reducing that thirty-two-bar chorus to a series of simple sixteen-bar phrases. And then, having recognized the catchiness of that opening twelve-bar riff, Glenn scrapped Garland's closing thirty-two-bar ensemble choruses and focused on the saxes, who repeat that opening riff over and over again, then die down slowly as he baits his listeners with repeated fadeouts, until finally the band bursts into the familiar rousing, explosive, full-ensemble, screaming finale.

Though "In the Mood" became one of Glenn's all-time hit records, he was never able to collect anything from the proceeds of its sales. How come? Because he was still bound by his no-royalty contract, so all he ever received for "In the Mood" was the original $175! No wonder Victor released the recording so many times! However, late in 1972 David Mackay, as executor for the Miller Estate, was able to engineer a deal, partially retroactive, whereby the company began to pay royalties on every single record that Glenn recorded for Victor, including "In the Mood." Too bad Glenn couldn't have been around to luxuriate in such a coup!

How those kids loved to jitterbug to "In the Mood"! Contrasted with some of the band's earlier, way-up-tempoed "killer-dillers," the new favorite hit just the right medium tempo for dancing—"not too slow, not too fast, just half-fast," as Louis Armstrong used to announce with a lecherous grin.

Glenn and I often disagreed about his tempos. Too many of them, I would complain, were unnecessarily fast. "You don't need to ram it down their throats to prove that it swings," I'd complain. And so, when the kids lapped up the groovier-tempoed

Famous sax-battlers Klink and Beneke "In the Mood."

"In the Mood," I felt as though I'd scored at least a point-after-touchdown.

We would also argue about his penchant for insisting that the rhythm section always emphasize four beats to the bar. I contended that, especially on ballads, if the bass played just two beats, it would make dancing that much easier. But I couldn't win. Finally, for his clincher, Glenn muttered, "The trouble with you is you dance just like Smith Ballew." Since I'd never seen Ballew dance, I could have taken this for a compliment. But I didn't.

One of the nice things about Glen Island was that it had a spacious dance floor. It gave plenty of room to the kids who wanted to jitterbug or to hold each other closely, as well as to those who wanted to crowd around the bandstand and just watch. I don't remember any more enthusiastic audiences than Glenn used to draw there, night after night.

The band closed at the Casino on Wednesday, August 23, before 1,200 appreciative fans. And that night, when the guys had finished playing, the kids tossed a special party for them.

Never in the history of Glen Island Casino had any band or any leader won over its fans the way Glenn and his musicians and singers had, and never again was any band ever to do so. Glenn Miller had most certainly arrived!

Chapter 17

The only drawback at Glen Island had been the money. Glenn had been willing to go even further into the financial hole because he knew that as soon as he got out on the road, he'd start recouping. But none of us really expected that he would recoup so much so quickly.

The band's first weekly gross proved an excellent barometer: the biggest business in three years, $22,500 worth, at Loew's Capitol Theatre in Washington, D.C. "Glenn Miller, starting its first big-time vaude tour," reported *Variety*, "stops its own show four times, boots three other acts into sock position, and sends its audience home convinced."

The band had grown both in stature and in numbers because Glenn at last had begun to make enough money to afford a move he'd been wanting to make for months—to increase his brass section from six to eight men. "Three-part harmony sounds too thin," he explained. "Now with four trumpets and four trombones I'll have two more full-sounding sections."

The new trumpeter, Johnny Best, turned out to be one of the finest the band ever had. An experienced and expert musician, who, according to Zeke Zarchy, the great lead trumpeter who played next to him for a while, "never played a bad note in his life," Johnny brought taste, authority, and true jazz feeling into the band. His Louis Armstrong–like phrasing was a joy not just

The new "Economy" Brass Octet: trombonists Paul Tanner, Tommy Mack, Glenn and Frank D'Annolfo; trumpeters Legh Knowles, Johnny Best, Mickey McMickle and Clyde Hurley. Rolly Bundock is the bassist.

to his fellow musicians but to the many fans with whom he became a favorite. He seemed to be a shy, retiring guy, but Johnny would, on occasion, speak out, as he recently did to a researcher for Time-Life Records.

Once one of Artie Shaw's swingingest trumpeters, and most recently a successful California avocado rancher, Johnny never fully appreciated Glenn's emphasis upon commercialism. "I enjoyed the Shaw band much more," he confessed. "The difference was that Glenn was a little colder and the music was a little stiffer. The Shaw band was freer and looser. With Glenn, we had to toe the line on practically everything, from shoes to haircuts to how we played.

"Glenn looked up to Artie. When I joined him after leaving Shaw, he told me, 'I want you to play like you played with Artie.' I tried, but the band had a set way of phrasing. Everything was set, and that was how it was played."

Glenn, with his usual eye for economy, had Tommy Mack, his

road manager, double on the fourth trombone chair, a temporary move until he finally settled a bit later upon a much more
experienced musician, Frankie D'Annolfo, who performed ex-
pertly forever after in the section, and who also played all of
Glenn's parts when he wasn't on the stand.

Another new member joined in Baltimore, where, during the
first week of September, the band attracted a record 19,000
customers to the Hippodrome Theatre. Some weeks before, while
driving through the city, I had heard on my car radio a
clarinetist with a gorgeous, big, round sound. I checked the
station, WBAL, and found that he was an eighteen-year-old kid
named Jimmy Abato, and when I returned to New York I raved
to Glenn about him. Soon thereafter the band played Baltimore
and Glenn sent for Jimmy.

I doubt if throughout the history of the Glenn Miller band
there was ever a more unpleasant relationship than the one
between Jimmy and Glenn. I recently talked with Jimmy, who,
under his given name of Vincent Abato, has since emerged as
one of the most respected clarinet and alto saxophone guest
soloists in the world of classical music. But, according to the
emotional and sometimes volatile Abato, respect is something he
felt he never even remotely received from Glenn, who, in his
unfortunate snap-judgment style, must have decided the minute
he met him that he didn't like him.

A still bitter-sounding Abato recently reported on their first
meeting in Glenn's room in the Lord Baltimore Hotel: "Tommy
Mack, Glenn's road manager, called me to come over to
audition. When I got there, Dick Fisher was in the room to
accompany me on guitar. I played one tune, 'Tea for Two,' but
Glenn didn't react. All he said was, 'Come see me at the theater
tomorrow.' "

The next day Abato went to Glenn's dressing room in the
theater. "He came in and didn't say a thing and I just kept
sitting there like a dummy." Finally, Abato alleges, "Glenn said,
'Kid'—he always called me 'Kid,' never anything else—'Kid, I
like your playing but I don't know whether to hire you because I
don't like to hire Italians and Jews. They're troublemakers.' "
Abato claims he was so taken aback that "I didn't know what to

The saxes double as dancers to bring more entertainment into the band: (left to right) Jimmy Abato, Willie Schwartz, Tex Beneke, Al Klink and Hal McIntyre.

say. Nobody had ever talked to me like that before. Later on that night I talked to my pop, a man who couldn't read or write English but who had a great feeling for people, and he told me I'd never be happy in that band. And he was right."

Jimmy was a great technician. And he had a beautiful tone. But he admits he was never a natural jazz player and so he could understand why Glenn seldom featured him. "I was a good pirate. I could copy the great jazz players. But Glenn was Benny Goodman crazy, and nobody could play that good!"

Rolly Bundock recalls Jimmy the new clarinetist as a cocky kid in those days. "Once when Glenn was explaining a sax passage, Jimmy started listing all the chord changes. And Glenn didn't like it. 'OK, Genius,' he told Jimmy, 'I'll do the talking.' And Jimmy looked up at him and answered sarcastically, 'OK, God!' "

The Abato-Miller relationship continued to deteriorate during his six months with the band. "When I got married and brought my wife into the Cafe Rouge," Jimmy recounted bitterly, "Glenn wouldn't even come over and congratulate her the way the kids in the band did. And just a little while before, when Paul Tanner had gotten married, Glenn had given him and his wife a hell of a gift." Finally, word got around that Glenn was considering Ernie Caceres as a replacement. "Moe Purtill, who I think liked me, warned me to look around for another job. So I contacted Paul Whiteman, who was playing at the Strand Theatre, and I got the job right away. I was never featured on a single Miller record, but Whiteman had me play a solo on our first date."

Apparently Whiteman was not as "Benny Goodman crazy."

The unfortunate relationship with Abato served as a classic example of Glenn's stubbornness and his penchant for dividing his world into blacks and whites with no grays. Nothing Jimmy could do seemed to satisfy Glenn, and the feeling soon became reciprocal. As Purtill recently remarked, "It was typical of Glenn's biggest failing: the way he would prejudge people. Probably he didn't like the way Jimmy acted when he was auditioning and so the guy never really had a chance."

The same sort of snap judgment could have prompted Glenn's alleged remark about Italians and Jews being troublemakers. Certainly the bigotry that infected some midwestern Protestants during the first quarter of the century must have touched him, so that, under strain, he could have fallen back on such clichés. I do know he was conscious of racial and ethnic characteristics. I remember he would even create his own generalities. "Italian trumpeters," he once told me, "seldom play good jazz. But they do make great lead men." And he liked to quote Ben Pollack's remark that "you can't have a good band without at least one Jew in it."

But, despite thoughtless clichés, like the one he tossed at Abato, to me and to others who knew him well Glenn Miller was not, as some who didn't like him have insinuated, a bigot. Certainly, by today's standards, his racial generalizations appear unenlightened and naive. But I'm inclined to agree with what others who were close to him feel—that even though he may have judged some people too quickly and sometimes unjustly, he always judged them strictly for themselves. For example, he didn't relate especially well to such white Anglo-Saxon Protestants as Johnny Best, Al Klink, or Dick Fisher, and yet he got

Glenn strikes a mood on stage.

along wonderfully well with Jews like Trigger Alpert, Zeke Zarchy, Stan Aronson and Willie Schwartz; with Italian-Americans Frank D'Annolfo and Jerry Gray; and, outside the band, with Cy Shribman, Charlie Spivak (his closest friend for years), Benny Goodman, Gil Rodin and many other non-WASP's, none of whom has ever indicated that he felt even an inkling of prejudice.

Thoughtless sometimes, sure! Bigoted forever, no!

After Baltimore the band set out on a series of record-breaking one-nighters.

At the New York State Fair in Syracuse it attracted the largest dancing crowd in the city's history.

On the next night it topped Guy Lombardo's all-time record at the Hershey Park Ballroom in Hershey, Pennsylvania.

The night after that, it bettered Kay Kyser's all-time gross at Lake Compounce in Bristol, Connecticut.

Less than six months earlier the band would have considered itself lucky to have drawn 25 percent of the gate of either of those two big-band giants.

Glenn's one-nighter agreements with most promoters consisted of a guarantee of $1,250 against either 50 or 60 percent of the total receipts, with occasionally lower fees for those few who had befriended him in his early days. During his first week of post–Glen Island one-nighters he exceeded his guarantee on every engagement. His week's take of a little under $12,000 about equaled his total income from personal appearances for the entire year of 1938!

In mid-September the band returned to the theater circuit. At the State Theatre in Hartford, Connecticut, it again broke all records. And then came its biggest theater booking of them all—the New York Paramount, which never had wanted Glenn before. The three-week stand, shared with the Ink Spots, pulled in a whopping gross of more than $150,000, with Glenn averaging a weekly $5,400 for himself. He even outdrew Artie Shaw, who was appearing at the neighboring Strand Theatre, and so impressed the Paramount management that it immediately booked him in for another date for the following year with a guaranteed minimum of $6,500 per week.

In those days, bands had replaced films as the big draws in many of the country's largest movie houses. Often they received billing above the movies, with the competition among the houses for top bands at least as keen as for the biggest movies. The kids may never have lined up in the early-morning hours to get choice seats for a movie, but they sure did just to get good looks at Miller and Goodman and Shaw and the Dorseys and various other top bands.

The band was getting so hot that it even pulled kids into theaters despite movies that they didn't want to see. For example, early in November it played the Stanley Theatre in Pittsburgh along with a picture titled *They Shall Have Music,* which starred, of all people, Jascha Heifetz, hardly a jitterbug favorite.

Joe Cohen, reviewing the bill in *Variety,* wrote in part:

> They [the kids] whistled and stomped through a neat Brahms; they yelled for Miller through the crystal purity of the Heifetz tones, and by the time "The End" was flashed on the screen, the Stanley was a shambles of ecstatic and expectant excite-

ment. Much of the dialog in the film went by the boards; the symphony music got the ha-ha, and the kids would have nothing of anything but Miller. . . .

Incidentally, it's not hard to understand the current enthusiasm for Miller. He has a corking outfit, equally at home in swing or sweet and excelling in both. Current Cinderella Man of the band biz is a modest, self-effacing fellow with a shy, engaging manner and a trombone that speaks volumes for him.

The money was coming in from stage shows. The money was coming in from one-nighters. But, except for the measly $175 per side, nothing was coming in from records. Glenn was very dissatisfied, and Frank Walker, smart businessman that he was, wanted to keep one of his top attractions happy. So he tore up the non-royalty contract and wrote a new one. It called for double the payment for each side—a jump from $175 to $350—but more importantly, that payment was merely an advance against a 5 percent royalty, the same rate that Dorsey, Goodman and Shaw were getting. In addition, the new contract guaranteed a minimum of fifty sides per year.

Evidence of the band's impact upon the music business itself was its selection by ASCAP (the American Society of Composers, Authors, and Publishers) for a huge October 6 Carnegie Hall concert along with three all-time-great bands. In its first informal battle of music, the Miller band created even more of a sensation than his rivals that evening: Paul Whiteman, Fred Waring and Benny Goodman.

Further indication of the impact of the new Miller style on the 1939 music scene was its use on the ultraconservative Lucky Strike Hit Parade radio series. Mark Warnow, a pretty creative conductor and arranger in his own right, openly admitted he was copying Glenn's clarinet-lead reed sound. Why? "Because," he said, "if something's good, why not use it?"

After the Paramount came more one-nighters and more record-breaking theater engagements. At the Earle in Philadelphia the band topped Goodman's opening-day and Kay Kyser's Saturday-night records, and in a predominantly black theater in Camden, New Jersey, it topped Cab Calloway's all-time attendance figures. And yet the band did lay some eggs. It drew terribly at a poorly publicized concert at the County Center in White Plains, only a few miles from Glen Island Casino; and at the Coliseum in Greensburg, Pennsylvania, for no apparent reason it drew little more than half the customers Hal Kemp had pulled in.

And not all of its recordings turned out well either. Harry James had a big instrumental hit with "Ciribiribin." Glenn's version with a Ray Eberle vocal was a flop.

Dick Jurgens, with Eddy Howard singing, scored a smash with "Careless." Glenn's and Ray's version didn't cause a ripple.

The Orrin Tucker–Wee Bonnie Baker recording of "Oh, Johnny, Oh, Johnny!" was a huge seller. Glenn's version with a Marion Hutton vocal lay on dealers' shelves.

A few months later Tommy Dorsey with Frank Sinatra and the Pied Pipers made a tremendous hit out of "I'll Never Smile Again," which Glenn had recorded several months before Tommy did. Few of even the most devoted Miller fans ever heard of Glenn's version.

In mid-November the band returned to Meadowbrook for one of its most triumphant engagements. The kids turned out in droves. And the band's success was beginning to be reflected in its members' weekly salaries. No more $35 paychecks, à la Glen Island. Instead, Purtill and three of the trumpets were getting $100 each. Beneke was getting $85. The four other saxes, the three trombones, one trumpeter, bass, piano, guitar and each of the singers were getting $75 each and Finegan's arranging salary had risen to $62.50.

In addition to Finegan, some free lancers occasionally wrote for the band. It was becoming obvious that Glenn needed more regular arranging help, and so when Artie Shaw suddenly deserted his band in mid-November and darted off to Mexico, Glenn made a pitch for Jerry Gray, his chief arranger. It was one of his smartest moves.

I'd known Jerry for many years, as far back as 1933 when he was playing hot fiddle and jazz accordion in a Boston dive under his real name of Jerry Graziano. A few years later I had seen him again when he played violin in Artie Shaw's very first band. Later we were to room together as members of Glenn's AAF band, and many years after that, during the early seventies, we were to meet again when I flew down to Dallas, Texas, where he was working steadily as a successful leader of the band at the city's most posh hotel. He remembered very well when Glenn made his pitch:

"The day after Artie broke up, Glenn called me. I was still in shock. I thought that band was the greatest band of all, and I thought Glenn's was corny. To me, Glenn's band didn't swing like Artie's. It never did, though later on it had more depth. I joined Glenn, but my heart still wasn't in it. The band was at Meadowbrook, and Glenn paid me a hundred and fifty a week for three arrangements. I had been doing five a week for Artie. But I was still moaning for Artie's band. But after I made up my

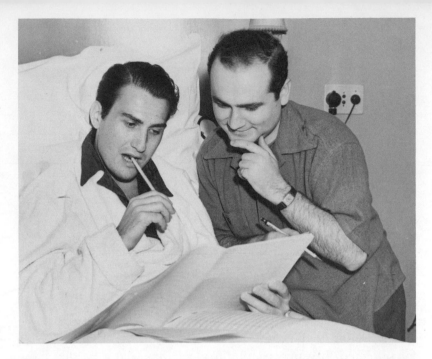

Jerry Gray visits an ailing Artie Shaw with whom he was "happier musically."

mind to accept things as they were, things started to click. I may have been happier musically with Artie, but I was happier personally with Glenn."

Glenn and Jerry became very close, closer than Glenn had ever grown with Finegan. For one thing, Jerry was much more pliable. Whereas Bill would fight for every idea in which he believed, Jerry was perfectly willing to go along with what Glenn thought was more effective commercially. Like Glenn, he leaned toward simple rhythmic riffs instead of far-out harmonies. And Jerry, as I found out even more surely during our roommate days, was an able politician, smart enough to take suggestions from others and, if need be, to let others take credit for ideas that might have been his own.

Some connected with the band have claimed that Gray followed the Miller patterns religiously. It was for this reason, according to arranger Billy May, that "Jerry fit the band perfectly." But Gray insists his contributions were strictly his own. "All Glenn would do would be to give me a tune and say, 'Make an arrangement of this.' He never sketched out anything ahead of time. He hired me because he had stacks and stacks of my Artie Shaw records in his room at the Pennsylvania.

"What Glenn did do for me that was so great was that he kept encouraging me to write original things. If it weren't for him, I might never have composed anything on my own. Remember 'Pennsylvania 6-5000'? Well, you know how that came about? I'd written an arrangement of 'Dipsy Doodle' for the band and it had a little sax background riff. Glenn heard it and said, 'Why don't you make a tune out of that?' So I did. Glenn, as you know, was a great idea man."

Jerry proceeded to write a batch of originals for the band: "Caribbean Clipper," "Sun Valley Jump," "Here We Go Again," "The Spirit Is Willing," "The Man in the Moon," and the most famous of all his tunes, "A String of Pearls." Jerry recalls that "Glenn suggested putting his name on that one as co-composer. But he listened to reason."

Glenn's willingness to give full credit to Gray offers another example of how much he would do for someone he really liked personally. Most band leaders, in return for plugging their arrangers' originals, would insist upon coauthorship, which meant 50 percent less royalties for the actual composers. But Glenn let Jerry keep all the money. On the other hand, Bill Finegan reports that he wasn't that fortunate. "Glenn would put his name on my originals," he claims. "To me, that was a swindle."

Finegan was never as commercial as Gray. Jerry's list of hit arrangements is astounding: "Elmer's Tune," "Moonlight Cocktails," "Adios," "American Patrol," "Anvil Chorus," "Chattanooga Choo Choo," "I've Got a Gal in Kalamazoo," and the final version of the AAF band's biggest hit, "St. Louis Blues March." Jerry Gray most certainly did a lot for the Glenn Miller band.

On the other hand, Jerry quickly admits that Glenn contributed much to his success as an arranger and as a person. "He made me feel secure. I liked him because he was a businessman who appreciated music. I remember one thing he taught me was how to be on time. Once, when I was late, he took me aside and very gently said to me, 'Do you realize you kept all those people waiting and how much you cost everyone?' I was never late again. You know, it's funny, but he never did those little petty things, like fines, with me. He didn't even make me march in the army band! Maybe that was because he was sympathetic with arrangers."

Jerry recalls only one major disagreement he had with Glenn. "I told him I didn't like all that waving of the derbies and the horns that the brass used to do. And you know what he said to me? He said, 'Jerry, now I know for sure that I'll never have you stage a show for me.' "

Chapter 18

The addition of Jerry Gray was only one of Glenn's moves to keep up with his changing fortunes. He knew that by the end of the year, activity could easily reach the frantic stage. In addition to its intensive schedule of personal appearances the band would soon start a thrice-weekly commercial radio series for Chesterfield cigarettes. And so Glenn hired Mike Nidorf, who'd been representing him at GAC, as his personal manager, and took on David Mackay on a regular retainer basis to handle the increased legal traffic.

There was a lot of other work to be done, too, like answering the mammoth amount of fan mail that kept pouring in. So Glenn decided to open his own office. Helen had been trying to help out, but she was not a secretary, nor could one person any longer handle all those details.

Helen's closest friend in those days, and forever after, for that matter, was a delightful young lady named Polly Davis. She had been married to Claude Thornhill, also a close friend of the Millers', and after an amicable divorce had taken a job on the West Coast. But when the Millers contacted her about opening the office, back she rushed, even though it meant taking a salary cut from $175 to $50 a week. "It was a tiny office at first," Polly recalls, "but less than a year later we had a huge office with eight girls and I was making much more than $175."

The importance of Polly Davis to the success and security of

Polly.

Helen and Glenn Miller was tremendous. Not only was she absolutely magnificent at running the office, but her handling of people, Glenn included, was masterful. Of all the people connected with the band, I know of no one who was more loved and more respected by performers, by businessmen, and by both the Millers than Polly.

Her attitude toward Glenn combined reverence, tolerance and understanding. She was privy to everything that went on—to dealings with musicians, with singers, with managers, with bookers, with sponsors and with fans, as well as with many who were involved in Glenn's personal life. Glenn had complete faith in her tact and in her talent. As the correspondence piled in, Glenn would merely make brief notations on specific portions he wanted answered, leaving it to Polly to make his curt remarks sound polite and human. In her unique position, as friend, confidante and secretary, Polly, who later married Don Haynes, could evaluate everything that went on, and she did this with amazing clarity and objectivity. She admired Glenn for his directness, for his honesty, for his talent as a businessman and as a musician, and for his deep devotion to Helen and loyalty to his friends. But she also recognized how the increasing pressures had changed his life-style. Though he had achieved much of what he had been working for, Polly began to discern an increasing impatience, plus an even greater inability to bend and to relax. But she never changed in her devotion and her admiration of his basic decency. "He was all business, and some people hated him for that. But he had had so many hard knocks, so when the money finally started coming in, he watched it very carefully—so carefully, in fact, that I don't think he ever truly enjoyed having it. It was too bad, because I remember the fun we used to have, Glenn and Helen, and Claude and I, during those days with Ray Noble. But when you're such a success, financially, sometimes something happens."

Glenn and Helen loved Polly. He called her "Perkins," after a comic-strip character named Polly Perkins. To Helen she was, and remained for the rest of Helen's life, her closest, dearest and most trusted friend. And no one ever more deserved the Millers' love and trust and friendship than Polly Davis Haynes, who during the later sixties and early seventies was pursuing her own career as manager of a leading West Coast bookstore.

Few understood Glenn as well as Polly did. In fact, many people didn't understand him at all. Consequently, opinions of what he was really like varied, even within the band, all the way from dependent Chummy MacGregor's deep affection to rebellious Jimmy Abato's utter hatred.

It was Chummy's idea for the band to give Glenn a big Christmas present that year. He and Hal McIntyre worked out a deal to buy a brand-new Buick in exchange for Glenn's old car plus fifty bucks apiece from each of the guys in the band. At a meeting of the musicians, Chummy and Hal asked the guys to vote. There was no secret ballot, just a hand vote, so, as one of Glenn's lesser admirers noted, "We couldn't very easily refuse."

Earlier that Christmas Eve the band played at the famous Savoy Ballroom up in Harlem, where it broke the all-time record held by, of all bands, Guy Lombardo! Later in the evening the guys herded Glenn into the lobby of the Pennsylvania, and there, wrapped in cellophane with a special license plate of "GM-1" and a special horn that played the first four notes of "Moonlight

The plaque for the Buick, with all the guys' signatures. "Lightnin' " is Paul Tanner; "Eb" is Ray Eberle; "Mose" is Stan Aronson; "Chingers" is Ernie Caceres; "Daisy May" is Billy May; "Luke" and "Mr. Hill" are mysteries. The plaque was signed months after Christmas; thus personnel reflects a later date.

Serenade," and with a Christmas card that read "To Glenn from the Boys" stuck in the windshield, was Glenn's new Buick. It was the only time that most of the guys had ever seen the man, whom Tommy Dorsey used to call "Old Klondike," come even close to tears.

Chapter 19

"Do you smoke the cigarette that satisfies?" That's how the voice
of Paul Douglas began the broadcasts of Glenn Miller's *Moonlight
Serenade* radio series for Chesterfield cigarettes on Tuesdays,
Wednesdays and Thursdays over the entire Columbia Broadcasting System. Emanating first from a CBS Playhouse at Broadway
and Fifty-third Street and later from another on West Forty-fifth
Street, the series climaxed the band's meteoric rise that had
begun just a little over half a year ago.

Larry Bruff, who represented the advertising agency, Newell-
Emmett, on the show and who often did the announcing when
the program went on the road, remembers the series from the
beginning. "It was back in October 1939. I had just joined the
agency and Don Langan, head of our radio department, called
me from Chesterfield's office and asked me who I thought would
sell more cigarettes, Glenn or Shep Fields. I told him Glenn, and
when he came back to the office he said, 'It's going to be Glenn
Miller.'

"Nobody was too sure just how strong Glenn would be. So to
play it safe, we added the Andrews Sisters to the show. Now that
was a lot of music for just fifteen minutes, so I went down to the
Pennsylvania to see Glenn in his room (I remember it wasn't
nearly as glamorous as I thought it would be), and we met with
McIntyre and MacGregor to lay out the first three shows.
Counting commercials and things, we had only twelve minutes of

The Chesterfield Show. ABOVE: The Andrews sisters with Glenn. OPPOSITE PAGE, ABOVE: Glenn with agency-rep and part-time announcer Larry Bruff (left) and producer Jean Hight. OPPOSITE PAGE, BELOW: The maestro delivers his message.

music and three of those had to go to the Sisters. That meant only nine for the band, and so, to get more tunes into each program, Glenn decided to feature those 'Something Old, Something New, Something Borrowed and Something Blue' medleys."

To get in as much music as possible, Glenn kept insisting that the scripts be cut to a bare minimum. To save time, he often would go from one tune directly into the next, with identifications of songs and vocalists coming in over softer passages. "The only scripts he really worked on," Bruff recalls, "are the ones when we'd salute the various armed services camps."

Glenn worked well with Bruff and his producer, Jean Haight. But friction soon developed on the show, not so much between Glenn and the Andrews Sisters, who were natural rivals for as many minutes of air-time as each could get, as between the Sisters themselves. According to Bruff, "After a few weeks the girls weren't even talking to each other—they'd gotten into a fight or something—and so we were having a helluva time trying to figure out what they wanted to sing." But the Andrews' internecine warfare soon mattered not at all to the show, because after thirteen weeks the agency had become convinced that Glenn could carry it alone. So battling Patti, Maxene and LaVerne departed.

From then on, the show ran very smoothly. Bruff found Miller very easy to work with. "Oh, sure, he was stubborn about his music. But he always had a good reason. He was a well-organized businessman, one of the finest and nicest men I've ever known.

"For one thing, he was terribly honest. I remember he kept insisting that his press agent stick only with the facts. And only if a guy didn't do his job right, would Glenn complain.

"In Chicago we had a terrible engineer who kept insisting that he was giving us what he called 'The Chicago Sound.' Whatever it was, it was awful. So Glenn insisted they get rid of him. When the network told him the guy was the best they had, Glenn told them, 'If *he's* your best, then give us your worst.' So we got a guy named Ray Noreen. Glenn taught him how to get what he wanted and he turned out to be the best engineer in Chicago.

"Another thing I liked about Glenn was his modesty. He never made an entrance on the show. Instead, he was always with the band as it appeared. Also, he would cut out his own trombone solo before he'd cut anyone else's.

"You hear things about Glenn having no sense of humor. That's not true. I remember once when we were pre-empted at the last minute on one of our broadcasts from Detroit and Glenn decided not to tell the guys in the band. So we went right ahead as though we were doing a regular show. But right in the middle of it, Glenn yelled out, 'I don't want to play "Tuxedo Junction"!' The guys thought he had flipped. Then, for a closer, I announced that 'this is the Solumbia Crawbasting Piston.' That's when the guys caught on to Glenn's gag."

Though Glenn kept recording regularly in Victor's studios, the off-the-air recordings of those Chesterfield shows later provided just as much material for the host of Miller LP's still available today. Bruff reports that Glenn insisted upon the off-the-air-checks being made—and at the sponsor's expense, too. "But we never played them," Bruff notes, "which is why those acetates stayed in such good shape."

The Chesterfield shows and a three months' engagement at the Cafe Rouge of the Hotel Pennsylvania, beginning January 4, kept Glenn and the band exceptionally busy during the first quarter of 1940. But the guys liked it, because for the first time they were able to settle down for a long stay near home. For Glenn it afforded opportunities to consolidate his various activities: musical, promotional and personal.

He worked hard with Howie Richmond, still his press agent, who got Glenn to send "somewhat personal letters of thanks" to 2,300 juke-box operators. He bought the front cover of *Orchestra World* magazine for a cool $150. Either he or I (I don't remember who) wrote a Glenn Miller arranging column for *Metronome*, in which he gave more advice about showmanship than he did about arranging.

With help from Polly Davis, he began to catch up on his correspondence with disc jockeys, many of whom were running special Glenn Miller promotions and some of whom were reporting how he was running away with their contests.

Detroit's Jack the Bell Boy, one of the nation's top disc jockeys, wrote Glenn in February, "It may interest you to know that you are leading my request list by such a wide margin that all the other artists' records put together do not pull the number of requests that you do. Of fifteen hundred telephone requests, one hundred and twenty-five telegrams and fifty letters daily, you pull an average of over sixty percent."

But the biggest disc-jockey boost of all came from the band's winning the influential Martin Block *Make Believe Ballroom* poll on New York's top radio show on station WNEW. New York was then far and away the most important spot for big bands, and Glenn had run away with the town's highest honor.

For his newfound success, Glenn even received a congratulatory letter from Dale Carnegie, the era's # 1 success adviser, whose *How to Win Friends and Influence People* had headed the best-seller list for months. Carnegie had discovered that he and Glenn had been born in the same area of Iowa. "We still have a souvenir plate with a picture of the Clarinda Insane Asylum," he

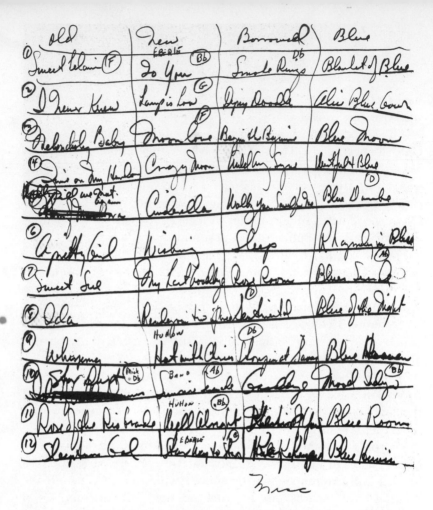

Glenn's own projections for those "Something Old, Something New, Something Borrowed, Something Blue," medleys. At bottom of "Borrowed" tunes he couldn't decide between Hal Kemp and Kay Kyser.

wrote, to which Glenn replied, "Glad to know you are also a Clarinda, Iowa product. Hardly know how to interpret your crack regarding the picture of the Clarinda Insane Asylum."

The band's three months' stay at the Cafe Rouge also gave it plenty of time to build up its library. All-night rehearsals, starting at three o'clock in the morning, were commonplace. Despite his success, Glenn refused to relinquish the pressure—on himself or on any of the others whose lives seemed more and more under the control of his continuous quest for perfection.

In addition to Jerry Gray's and Bill Finegan's regular

A proud Mr. Miller in the Cafe Rouge—on the stand with his famous reed section; at the table entertaining his visiting mother.

contributions, music publishers would contribute arrangements of tunes they wanted to have plugged. These included some jazz instrumentals as well as the usual and predominantly dreary pop songs. Finegan recalls that Lou Levy, a very hip and energetic publisher, would bring in batches of scores written by Harlem arrangers. "Glenn would invariably pick out those that had some sort of riff in them. I'd redo some of them, but I won't tell you which, because I don't want to be associated with them."

By far the most successful of those simple riff recordings was "Tuxedo Junction," which sold 115,000 copies in the first week. The band had heard Erskine Hawkins play the tune on the night the two bands had played at the Savoy Ballroom, and Glenn had noted the crowd's reaction. The Hawkins band had recorded the tune the previous summer, but only the most hip had dug the record, and apparently none of the influential Millerians were among them. According to Chummy MacGregor, Hal McIntyre had obtained a lead sheet from one of the saxists in Erskine's band and Jerry Gray had brought in a simple sketch of the tune to one of those early-morning rehearsals. The guys liked playing it and they began contributing their own ideas, so what eventually emerged was a conglomerate creation, known in musicians' parlance as a "head arrangement."

The band kept sounding even better. I was especially impressed with the way it played at the early dinner sessions and said so in my February 1940 *Metronome* review, pointing out that Glenn was trying less hard to impress the folks with the outlandish tempos he used on killer-dillers like "Runnin' Wild" and "Bugle Call Rag." Instead, he was settling into more relaxed grooves, with numbers like "Tuxedo Junction" and "In the Mood," and I wondered if both he and the times hadn't outlived those over-obvious screamers to which nobody could dance. I imagine Glenn read the review, but it made no difference. Later every evening, and during every stage show, he kept playing those racers just the same and the kids kept screaming just as loud.

In February Glenn strengthened his personnel. Trombonist Al Mastren had developed some trouble with his arm. Howard Gibeling, a good arranger, replaced him for a while, and then when Gibeling left, Tommy Mack returned to fill in until Glenn could find a permanent replacement.

The search ended one night at Murray's in Tuckahoe, New York, a few miles from Glen Island, where Tommy Tucker's band was playing. "It was quite a job," Jimmy Priddy recalls. "We were doing something like ten broadcasts a week. I was the only trombone player in the band. One night Helen Miller and Polly and Don Haynes came up to look me over. They asked me to come down to the Cafe Rouge for a 3 A.M. rehearsal. When I got there, Glenn took me over in the corner and said, 'Get your horn out.' It was like a short-arm inspection. Then he said, 'Play for me.' I did and he said, 'You're short of breath. You don't hold your notes out long enough.' I thought I was the greatest in the world, but that audition shook my confidence. I didn't know if I should take the job or not. I realized later that was just Glenn's way of establishing discipline at the start."

Priddy did take the job, and for many months Glenn continued to intimidate him. "Discipline was Glenn's whole bag in that band—musically and in every other way. And he was smart enough to know it. He could be especially rough on trombone players. If he could hear a slur while you were changing the position of your slide, he would say, 'Get the Lassus out of it' [a reference to a slurping, sliding, novelty instrumental called 'Lassus Trombone']."

After a while Jim grew closer to Glenn. "He and I used to play tennis and I would beat his ass off. He wanted to win, and the guys used to tell me that was one good way of getting fired." But like McMickle and Purtill and a few others who stood up to Glenn, Priddy stayed around until the civilian band's last engagement. And soon thereafter he wound up as lead trombonist in Glenn's AAF outfit. "I remember when I joined the army band. He told me I was going to be the first trombone player, and he gave me nothing but encouragement. He would go out of his way to say something sounded good. He would never do that in the civilian band. You know, I really admire the guy now. He helped me when I needed him."

Another Miller admirer joined a few days later. Ernie Caceres had been playing lead alto and jazz clarinet in Jack Teagarden's band when Glenn sent for him to replace Jimmy Abato. Ernie was a cute, fiery little Mexican, and Glenn saw in him commercial as well as musical possibilities. Maurice Purtill recalls the first Chesterfield show on which Caceres played. "He squeaked on clarinet on the last number. That was something Glenn couldn't stand, and so after the show he let Ernie have it. But Ernie screamed right back at him, telling Glenn that he'd been playing baritone sax all night and his clarinet reed had dried out because he hadn't had a chance to touch it. The excuse made so much sense that Glenn accepted it."

Shortly before he died, Ernie wrote to Leonard White, a Miller buff and historian, about his days with the band. He explained that he got along fine with Glenn, "maybe because I never bothered him for anything except concerning our work, and at the right time.

"I did have a disagreement with him around 1941 and it resulted that, instead of leaving the band, he gave me a bigger raise and we were a lot more friendly afterwards because he admired anyone that could take care of himself in business and also musically.

"He was also the type of guy that would get some talent out of

Ernie Caceres singing with Marion Hutton and the Modernaires.

you that you yourself didn't even know you had. I was just fooling around on a train trip, and the next rehearsal he had me singing with the Modernaires."

Priddy and Caceres arrived just in time for the band's busiest schedule: fifty-four performances per week, including the usual twelve sessions at the Pennsylvania (six dinner and six supper sets), three.Chesterfield rehearsals plus three Chesterfield broadcasts, and thirty-six shows during the first week of another Paramount Theatre engagement.

Maybe it was the mounting pressure. Maybe it was simply that he was driving himself too hard. And maybe it was just a bug. Whatever it was, the night before the Paramount opening, Glenn wound up flat on his back in Mount Sinai Hospital, a victim of a bad case of grippe, plus a sinus infection and complete exhaustion. It was the first time he missed any part of any of his band's performances.

To Glenn's rescue, and to the rescue of Paramount Theatre manager Bob Weitman, who was extremely well liked by all band leaders, came Glenn's past friends to lead the band. Tommy Dorsey, who was playing at Meadowbrook, subbed for most of the daytime shows. Gene Krupa, playing at the Fiesta

ABOVE: Tommy Dorsey leads the band on the Paramount Theatre stage.

BELOW: Glenn thanks Charlie Barnet, Gene Krupa, Dorsey and Dick Stabile for pinch-hitting for him during his stay in the hospital.

Danceteria one block away, filled in too. Charlie Barnet came over from the Hotel Lincoln and Dick Stabile came down from the Essex House to help out. Even announcer-actor Paul Douglas pinch-hit for a couple of shows.

Jerry Gray conducted the band on the lone Chesterfield show that Glenn missed. Down at the Pennsylvania, Charlie Spivak and his brand-new band filled in while the Miller men were doubling at the Paramount and doing their Chesterfield broadcasts.

Glenn and Cy Shribman were backing Charlie's band, the first of several in which they were to invest. Spivak played a brilliant trumpet. "The Sweetest Trumpet in the World" was his billing, but it always seemed a shame to me that he would so often hide his gorgeous, full-bodied tone inside a mute. Later I found out that the mute was strictly Glenn's idea, that he wanted Charlie to project the same kind of romantic intimacy that Tommy Dorsey did on trombone. After one particular broadcast, when Charlie had dared to blow his wonderful open horn, Glenn sent him a telegram with the word "mute" repeated fifty times.

I knew Charlie quite well in those days, and we would argue about his emphasis on using the mute. I felt there was an opportunity for some leader with a big, thrilling, open trumpet to take over, and, sure enough, while Charlie kept muting his sound, along came Harry James with his open trumpet to make a big name and lots of money for himself—although his sound was not nearly as beautiful as Spivak's. In the late sixties, in an interview with John S. Wilson in *The New York Times*, Charlie reminisced about the tug-of-war that was going on between Glenn and me, and guessed that maybe I had been right after all. Credit me with one more point-after-touchdown.

Glenn stayed away for only a few days. His legs were wobbly, but he was obsessed with fulfilling his responsibilities. He returned sooner than his doctors wanted him to, managing to lead the band for a bit more than half of its two weeks' stay at the Paramount, as well as on his radio commercial and at the Pennsylvania, without collapsing.

On April 4 the band closed its three months' stay at the Cafe

Rouge, after having set some exciting attendance figures. Glenn had been guaranteed a minimum of $2,000 per week, against a percentage of the gross take. In every one of the thirteen weeks, he exceeded his guarantee, pulling in for himself anywhere from $2,030 to $3,054 weekly. With all the money coming in from his various activities—the Chesterfield series, the Paramount and other theater dates, and the numerous one-nighters—Glenn had paid off all the debts that had been haunting him through the past three years, and, in addition, had bought himself a $75,000 annuity!

David Mackay still recalls the day when Glenn bought that annuity: "We were sitting in the office. The annuity represented the first bit of financial security Glenn had ever known, and it was affecting him. I could see that he was trying hard to hold back his tears—tears of gratitude, I assume. Then, as he signed the check for the annuity, he looked up at me and said, 'Just think, David—a year ago I couldn't have signed a check with the decimal point three spaces farther over to the left!' "

Chapter 20

The torrent of income created a brand-new problem for Glenn: what to do about income taxes. For ten years, from 1929 through 1938, his taxes had averaged less than six dollars a year. For 1939 they had skyrocketed to a little over two hundred. Undoubtedly they would soar much higher, and so David Mackay began looking for tax-saving devices.

Late in March, Mackay reports, "I made Glenn move to New Jersey, which, unlike New York, had no state income tax. But Glenn didn't relish moving away from the sidewalks of New York. He loved the city. When I told him he *had* to move, he asked, 'When?' and I said, 'Tonight.' And he looked at me in amazement and said, 'Who the hell wants to move to Siberia?'

"Well, we finally compromised on his moving in a week. As a starter, he and Helen stayed at the Plaza Hotel in Jersey City for four weeks. Finally they found a place they loved over in Tenafly—the Cotswold on Byrne Lane. It was an old French castle–type building that had been made over into apartments. Glenn's was on the first floor, overlooking the golf course. He could get to and from work in twenty minutes.

"After a while he learned to love 'Siberia.' One day I walked into their apartment and I saw a lovely painting. I asked him where he'd gotten it and he told me that it was a present from the state of New Jersey. What he meant, of course, was that he used the money he would have paid out on New York State taxes to pay for the painting."

Mackay found other ways to save money. He made sure that some of the income went to Helen, who continued to help out Glenn—"a move," he proudly admits, "that was defended successfully by us with the Treasury Department." And to help clarify the financial picture, he imposed a schizophrenic financial existence on Glenn, opening different bank accounts in the names of A. Glenn Miller, Alton Glenn Miller, Alton G. Miller and just plain Glenn Miller.

Mackay also worked out a series of stiff employment agreements between Glenn and his singers and arrangers. For example, Ray Eberle's fifteen-year exclusive management contract called for Glenn to receive a healthy percentage of Ray's income, except for those services performed in connection with the Miller orchestra. An insight into Glenn's keen business tactics, farsightedness, and suspicious nature: He insisted upon guarantees and damages from Ray should he—Ray, not Glenn —fail to live up to the agreement.

Ever the businessman, Glenn devoted a lot of his time, energy and talent to maintaining an A-1 relationship with his cigarette sponsor. Polly Haynes has pointed out that many of the things he did, some of which may have annoyed band members and other associates, were predicated solely upon keeping the Chesterfield people happy.

"Glenn always made sure that everybody was smoking Chesterfields," recalls Johnny O'Leary. "When we were in Holly-

Glenn tries to convince Charlie Spivak to switch to Chesterfields.

wood, making a movie, some of the guys would play cards when they had nothing else to do on the set and they'd have their cigarettes out—all different brands—and Glenn had me go over and cover every pack that wasn't Chesterfields with a piece of paper. And I remember that the band boy always had to have a pack of Chesterfields ready for Glenn at all times."

Like road manager O'Leary, Raul Hidalgo, the band boy, was both liked and admired by the musicians. Sturdily built and tremendously strong, he took care of the music, the music stands and the heavier instruments, loading them on and off the bus or train, setting them up before the job and then tearing them down afterward. In addition, he ran errands, served as Glenn's valet and in general made himself extremely useful.

A good band boy was an absolute necessity to the big bands. In addition to his muscle, he also needed tact and patience, plus an ability to adjust himself to the various personalities within each band. Few did their jobs as thoroughly, as gracefully and as graciously as the broad-shouldered, bull-necked Hidalgo.

After its closing at the Pennsylvania, the band began another one-nighter tour, again setting numerous attendance records. But it left every Tuesday, Wednesday and Thursday open for its Chesterfield shows. Since the majority of the band's dates during this period were in the South, the broadcasts emanated from a small theater in its Washington headquarters, the Wardman Park Hotel. Of course recordings remained important, too, and periodically the band migrated to New York to wax more sides.

Late in April it recorded one of its most successful and also one of its most notorious sides. The successful one was "Pennsylvania 6-5000," a Gray original that immortalized the hotel's telephone number and sold 40,000 copies in the first week. The other side was called "W.P.A." It sold no copies; in fact, it became the only Glenn Miller recording never to have been released. John Hammond—then, as today, a fighter for minority rights—waged a campaign against the song. He insisted that the lyrics degraded blacks, who, he was convinced, predominated in President Roosevelt's Works Progress Administration program. Through his efforts the song was condemned by musicians' Local 802, whose president and secretary shared Hammond's views. In essence, this created a boycott for the song, the only one that I know of which the musicians' union ever imposed, and which was extended to network radio programming.

How offensive were the lyrics? Judge for yourself. Here are some of them:

> "W.P.A. W.P.A.,
> Sleep while you work, while you rest, while you play.
> Lean on your shovel to pass the time away.
> Don't mind the boss if he's cross while you're gay.
> Three little letters that make life okay." *

In the midst of all the Chesterfield shows, the one-nighters and the recordings, Glenn made several personnel changes. For quite some time he had had a yen to rehire Jack Lathrop, once a member of a vocal group known as the Tune Twisters which had recorded with the band on its first Decca session. Jack was a cute, impish sort of guy, not as virile or as handsome or as good a

---

* Copyright 1940 by Shapiro, Bernstein and Co. Used by permission.

guitarist as Dick Fisher, whom he was replacing, but a classic prototype of the all-American-boy-next-door-who'd-never-dream-of-kissing-the-girl image that Glenn seemed to think enhanced the band's appeal. And since Glenn tended to underplay the importance of the guitar (it was often barely audible on recordings), cute Jack, with his pleasant, lightweight style of singing seemed like a stronger commercial asset.

The other replacement was more important. A cyst on Mickey McMickle's lip forced him to quit playing for several weeks. Like many other leaders, Glenn had always admired the trumpeting of Reuben "Zeke" Zarchy, who had led the brass sections of the Benny Goodman, Artie Shaw, Bob Crosby, and Tommy Dorsey bands. With by far his strongest lead man sidelined, Glenn decided to go for who he thought was the best.

"Actually," recalls Zarchy, who now teaches trumpet and still plays in Los Angeles, "Glenn had wanted me to join to replace Legh Knowles, but when Mickey got that cyst, he really went after me. He offered me a hundred and seventy-five a week, plus extra for recordings, which was very good money in those days. So I took the job."

Zarchy, an intelligent, outspoken gent, who later was to become Glenn's first sergeant in the army, figured he'd better find out exactly what was what in the Miller band. He'd heard all sorts of reports about Glenn's strictness, so he asked him about them right away. Miller's explanation: "Everybody's making more money than they ever made in their lives. We pay more money than any other band in the business. I don't think it's unfair of me to be strict or unreasonable of me to ask the band to look presentable." Adds Zarchy, "Glenn sure gave a lot of weight to the cosmetic aspects of the band!"

Zeke fit well with Glenn musically and personally. Both loved to play golf. "What a bug he was! No matter where we were or what time we'd get to bed, if there was a golf course available he'd call me at eleven and say, 'Let's go out and play. You ready?' Willie Schwartz, Ernie Caceres, McMickle and I were the golfers in the band. Even when it was raining, Glenn would want to go out on the course. He'd arrange to have the caddies hold umbrellas over our heads."

A swinging Miller tees off. Background kibitzers are Chummy MacGregor, host Max Kerner, owner of Detroit's Eastwood Gardens where the band was playing, and Hal McIntyre.

Don Haynes, who later managed the band and lived with Glenn, remembered that sometimes Glenn would arrive in a town at 11:00 A.M. and be on the course by 11:45. The only four-day holiday Glenn ever took he spent on the golf course in Pinehurst, North Carolina. That's where he shot his hole-in-one. As he did all through life, he pushed himself hard, even while on vacation. He played 102 holes in three and a half days. On one day he played thirty-six holes. Golf was not a game of relaxation for him. It served, instead, as a marvelous outlet for his competitiveness as well as for the tension and anger and frustration that he kept trying for so long and so hard to repress. "He often shot in the seventies," Haynes recalled. "But he wanted to hit the ball so hard that he used a driver that weighed twice what it should have. With it he could drive over three hundred yards. [And in any direction. But he did use regular irons—Wilson Top Notch, to be exact.—G.T.S.] He always walked fast and he was always serious about his game. No, I won't say that golf was a social game for Glenn."

Glenn's competitiveness erupted in other ways. For instance, playing the horses intrigued him. But his constant traveling made it difficult for him to place bets. So, as a game, he and Helen and Chummy put up $5,000 between them and turned the money over to a fellow named Ray Johnson to compete against the bookies for them. After many months they decided to close the account. Ray had lost $1,335.09. But Glenn had gotten his kicks.

Johnny Desmond, who sang with the Miller AAF band, remembers Glenn as one of the most competitive characters he had ever come across. "One time when we were playing touch football over in England, Glenn had the ball and I was chasing him, and just as I was about to touch him, I tripped and really banged into him, and we both went sprawling on the ground. I apologized and asked him if he was all right, and he said 'Sure.' But a couple of plays later, Glenn comes barreling clear across the field and knocks me down. And I didn't even have the ball! He just wanted to prove himself to me, I guess."

But of all the sports, golf remained by far Glenn's favorite. Zarchy enjoyed playing out on the course with him even more than playing on the bandstand. And so, with summer coming along, he decided to stay with the band, even after McMickle returned. So Glenn lopped off Knowles, a good all-around trumpeter who, unfortunately for his sake, didn't play golf. A few weeks later, he decided to get rid of another trumpeter, the powerful Clyde Hurley, who shared the jazz with Best and who also played some of the lead. But golf had nothing to do with it.

Hurley was never one of Glenn's favorites, and vice versa. According to McMickle, Clyde got into a crap game one night, had a few belts, and made some derogatory remarks about Glenn, not knowing that Glenn, in the next room, could hear everything that was going on. A couple of nights later, after the job, Glenn got in his cups and decided to confront Hurley. "So you think I'm a jerk, am I!" he sneered, and he gave Hurley his notice. "I will say this, though," reports McMickle, "he went ahead and got Clyde a job with Tommy Dorsey." Charlie Frankhauser, a fat-toned, Gene Krupa alumnus, took over Hurley's chair.

During May, Glenn took on another trumpeter—but only as

road manager. This was his younger brother Herb, whose burning desire was to become a first-rate musician but who knew he wasn't good enough for Glenn's band. So when Tommy Mack left, Herb accepted his older brother's offer to join as a non-player. Inwardly, though, Herb must have kept on hoping that maybe someday he could make it. Sometimes, when the band's train would stop somewhere for a while, Herb reportedly would get off and stand at the side of the train and blow into his mouthpiece—apparently just to keep his lip in shape until the emergency might arise when Glenn would have to call upon him. Eventually, when Glenn realized how much playing his horn meant to Herb, he arranged for him to get a job in Charlie Spivak's trumpet section, and Eak Kenyon, who'd played drums in the first band, came in as the new road manager.

In June, the base of operations shifted to Chicago. From the Civic Theatre came the thrice-weekly Chesterfield broadcasts, while on the other days the band played one-nighters in the Midwest, breaking records in several more ballrooms before settling for two weeks in the famous Panther Room of the Hotel Sherman, where it did the best business in the hotel's history, bigger even than that of two big Chicago favorites, Ben Bernie and Buddy Rogers.

The band's overall popularity was reflected in the midsummer Martin Block poll. Previously the contest had been confined to the local New York station, but Block had arranged for twenty more stations throughout the country to have their listeners vote also, so that now the poll reflected the tastes of the entire country. According to *Variety*, the top ten finalists with their total votes were:

Glenn Miller	44,446
Tommy Dorsey	23,645
Benny Goodman	16,321
Sammy Kaye	13,854
Kay Kyser	11,619
Gene Krupa	10,104
Charlie Barnet	8,469
Jimmy Dorsey	7,537
Artie Shaw	5,532
Jan Savitt	4,377

The band continued to set new attendance records: 5,000 at the Municipal Auditorium in St. Louis; 11,300 in Kansas City; 3,500 at Buckeye Lake in Ohio; 4,000 to break Lombardo's all-time record at Fernbrook Pavilion in Wilkes Barre, Pennsylvania. Swing bands in general and Miller's in particular had become so popular with the kids that they wouldn't take any substitutes. When WPA officials in Boston suddenly decided, without notice, to cancel an outdoor swing band concert on the Boston Common and present a stodgy brass band playing stuff like the "William Tell Overture" instead, the kids grew so angry that one thousand of them marched to the stage door of the RKO Theatre, where the Miller band was playing, and wouldn't be placated until Glenn came out to meet them and sign autographs.

Successful as the band was in those days, some of us kept denigrating its swing. For some reason or other, it just couldn't seem to loosen up sufficiently. Everything was played with superb accuracy, but as Jimmy Priddy once mentioned, "If you're not going to be a little bit sloppy, you're bound to be stiff. And that band sure was stiff!"

Purtill had helped. MacGregor and Lathrop would have been just as effective in a society band. As for Rolly Bundock, he was an excellent bassist, who in later years in the West Coast studios developed into quite a driving player. But with the Miller band, Rolly, a very nice and gentle soul, appeared nervous and unsure. Like many of us who had played under Glenn, he probably never felt completely at ease or confident, and no musician under such a handicap can possibly swing. Finally Rolly decided that he wanted out, so he told Glenn that he planned to enter the Juilliard School of Music to study symphonic bass. Glenn then hired Tony Carlson, the younger brother of Woody Herman's famed drummer Frankie Carlson, who stayed with the band for only a couple of weeks until Glenn discovered Herman "Trigger" Alpert.

"When Trigger joined the band, he made the difference between night and day," Jerry Gray recently told me. "And I don't mean to put Rolly Bundock down. I've used him many times since on dates. But Trigger had a light swing; he played so loose, and he didn't ever bog down."

The band had returned to New York for another series of Chesterfield broadcasts and Trigger was in town, too, a fresh young bassist out of Indianapolis, playing with Alvino Rey's band on the Hotel Biltmore Roof.

"It must have been Benny Goodman who told Glenn about me," surmises Alpert, who reigned as one of the country's foremost bassists until he retired a few years ago to pursue an even more fruitful career as a color-portrait photographer. "We had a fine rhythm section—Buddy Cole on piano and, can you imagine, Davey Tough on drums! Benny came in on a Friday night to hear the band and I guess he told Glenn about me because on the next Monday night Glenn came up. Right after that I went home for my folks' twenty-fifth wedding anniversary. The job was over and we had nothing cooking, so I took my time about returning to New York.

"In those days, I kept a room at the Hotel Astor, and when I got back, there must have been seven to ten slips in my mailbox all telling me to 'call Bullets.' When I called him he asked me, 'Where you been?' and I asked him, '*Who* are you?' I'd never heard of him. He explained he was working for Glenn and that they'd been trying to contact me for a week. They wanted me to go to Boston to see Glenn, but I told them I was broke, so they sent a car, of all things, around to the hotel with the money I needed to get there, plus a plane ticket.

"Well, when I got there I went directly to the hotel and Glenn was there with Cy Shribman. They asked me if I wanted a drink and I said 'No, thanks.' That impressed them, I guess. Then Glenn started asking me all sorts of questions, like, Did I drink? Was I married? Did I have any commitments? Who was my favorite bass player? I told him Jimmy Blanton, which probably impressed him, too. Then he asked me what sort of salary I wanted and I told him I'd leave it up to him. Now that really impressed him no end. So I got the job, went back to New York to get my bass and then joined the band on a theater date. I remember I had to memorize the bass part of 'Danny Boy' first because we played it in the dark."

A Miller-autographed photo to Ma Alpert.

Trigger scored an instant hit with Glenn and with the rest of the musicians. Not only was he a fine bassist, but he also exuded an infectious enthusiasm and joy. Billy May has described him as "one of the unsung heroes. He was really pushing that band. He always kept trying, but, you know, he still remained apprehensive about how Glenn would like it."

Glenn loved Trigger. Everybody could sense that. If Glenn could have adopted one guy in the band as the son he so much longed to have, Trigger Alpert would have been the one. And yet, those damned emotional hangups would never quite let him show how much he loved him.

Trigger loved Glenn, too, though, like others, he felt the frustrations of never quite knowing where he stood. "I remember one night in St. Louis on closing night, I was playing real loud. I thought I was, quote, getting with it, unquote. But Glenn shhh-d me with one of those 'Cool it, kid!' looks. So I proceeded to get loaded, and when we got on the train I told Glenn I wanted to quit. He just looked at me and said, 'Who do you think you are, you cocky kid?' And the next day he took me aside and he said, 'Your job is to be the best damn bass player in the world. What you should be thinking is what Artie Shaw is thinking about when he plays: I'm going to be better than Benny Goodman.'

"It was hard to figure out how Glenn would take things. Once when we were playing 'Tuxedo Junction,' I inserted a little break all on my own in an empty spot. I wasn't supposed to do it; it was just one of those spontaneous things. Glenn said nothing, so the next night I did the same thing. And I kept it in from then on. But still Glenn never said a word. He didn't even look at me. I had no way of knowing whether he liked it or not. Then, after I went into the army, I heard one of the band's broadcasts, and you know what? He had my break orchestrated for four trombones—that's how much he must have liked it. And yet he never told me once that he did."

How typical of Glenn Miller! He would find it almost impossible to *tell* people with words that he liked something that they did. And yet, when crises arose, he could always *show* through some sort of *act* just how much he really cared—like what he did for Trigger and his marriage. "You remember, George," Alpert was recently saying, "when we were in the Air Force band in New Haven. You were with us—in fact, you were the guy who gave her away—when Connie and I were going to be married and Glenn was going to be best man and we went into that dingy office of the Justice of the Peace and Glenn insisted that this was no atmosphere for us to get married in. And so he arranged for us to go over to the Justice's house, and that's where we first got married. And then a few days later, when our folks heard about it, he arranged for another ceremony, that one in the Yale Chapel, and he again was our best man and he had the entire string section there to play 'Serenade in Blue' and Tony Martin sang 'Dearly Beloved.' And afterward he gave us that party and a war bond for a wedding gift."

How come introverted, stoical, typically WASP-ish Glenn Miller loved this extroverted joy-filled lad so much? Marion Hutton recently offered this poignant explanation: "It struck me that Trigger represented what Glenn would have liked to have been. He would have liked to have been as open and as gregarious and as uninhibited and as loving as Trigger was."

Chapter 21

Much was happening during the fall of 1940 throughout the world and within the big-band arena as well.

Japan, which had just officially banned all jazz, joined the German-Italian axis. A pretty, young singer named Doris Day joined Les Brown's band.

Germany fired bombs on Britain. Tommy Dorsey fired a bombed Bunny Berigan.

Congress started the draft. Lionel Hampton started a new band and Benny Goodman reorganized his old one.

The outside world was in turmoil. But within the Miller band, life was relatively serene, and, at times, rather romantic.

One afternoon Helen Miller, Polly Davis, and I were drinking coffee in the drugstore on the ground floor of the RKO Building in which Glenn had his office. They seemed ready to burst. "George, we're going to tell you something, but you've got to promise not to tell a soul, yet," they gushed like two high school girls about to reveal who had asked them to the prom. "Polly," Helen said, "is going to marry Don. You're the only one outside the four of us who knows about it."

Don was Don Haynes, a strikingly handsome man with a great deal of charm, who, after graduation from Ohio State University, had sold bands so successfully in the Midwest that GAC had enticed him away from one of its competitors and brought him into New York. Glenn liked him immediately, and soon Don became the liaison between the band and the GAC office.

The marriage turned out to be a beautiful one, and it brought Helen and Polly and Glenn and Don closer together than ever. Later Don became Glenn's personal manager, then his executive officer in the air force. After the war he became associated with the Miller enterprises, but, after some misunderstanding with Helen and David Mackay, he went out on his own. For a time he sold insurance; later he entered the postal service, rising to an important executive spot before a massive heart attack ended his life on June 4, 1971.

Through it all, those good times and those hard times, Polly and Don stuck together. Their relationship reminded me very much of Helen's and Glenn's. Neither couple could have wished for anything more.

The other marriage, that of Marion Hutton to Jack Philbin in 1940, must have seemed like another happy happening. Jack had been devoted to Marion since the band's early days in Boston, where he had been a song-plugger, and then later when he had assumed his semi-managerial role. A relaxed, soft-spoken Irish-American, he never hid his feelings about Marion, and so their marriage wasn't unexpected. But its suddenness was.

Glenn knew about, but didn't entirely approve of, Jack's attentions to Marion. According to Marion, he warned Jack, "If you're going to fool around with my girl singer, you're going to wind up where the Sears Roebuck catalog goes." [Indigent midwesterners often found extra duty for these catalogs in outhouses.] But Glenn's threats didn't dampen the romance. "Besides," Marion insists, "what I wanted most of all was to be a wife and a mother. I had no drive for a career. But I was afraid to speak out because I felt there must be something wrong with somebody who didn't want this fabulous career."

Suddenly one day in Washington, Marion and Jack announced they were getting married. "With the band, I always felt I was just a thing," says Marion, "and that's how Glenn treated me when he found out." His reaction, Marion feels, contained more suspicion than joy. "He came right out with it

Don and Polly Haynes (at right) with others close to Glenn during a
get-together in the Cafe Rouge: (left to right) manager Cy Shribman, publicist
George B. Evans, Helen and Glenn, and emerging bandleader Charlie Spivak.

and asked me why I was getting married. It was not a happy
thing for me. I even had to buy my own wedding ring."

But at least Marion had her wish. She had a husband, and
soon she would have a son.

There was further wifely action within the band that fall.
Glenn started his own music-publishing company called the
Mutual Music Society, and one of its highest-paid employees,
drawing $600 a month, turned out to be Mrs. Glenn Miller.

The idea of a band leader forming his own music-publishing
company was nothing new. Years previously, Fred Waring and
Guy Lombardo had started theirs and had made scads of money.
Later Tommy Dorsey formed his company and Benny Goodman
financed and shared in the profits of one run by his brothers.

Music publishing could be a profitable venture for band
leaders. Whenever a song was played on the air, its publisher
would receive a credit from ASCAP (the American Society of
Composers, Authors, and Publishers), the publishers' and songwriters' collection agency, which received payments from the
radio networks for use of the songs. At the end of each quarterly
period, the society would make proportionate payments to
publishers and writers, based on the number of times each
particular song had been broadcast.

In addition, recording companies paid royalties to publishers of songs they recorded. These usually came to two cents per side, which the publisher and the writer(s) of each song split, fifty-fifty. Often leaders would discover some song they wanted to record, and, if the composer didn't have a publisher, as many neophytes didn't, the leader would send him to some publisher friend who would then split the profits with the writer.

But why, some leaders began to reason, should these publishers, who contributed nothing, share in 50 percent of the income? Since the band was actually giving the songwriter his big break, why shouldn't the leader share the profits instead? And so the more astute leaders began forming their own publishing companies, to which they would "urge" the composers to assign their songs.

Some leaders took unfair advantage of the songwriters, who needed their recordings and air plugs and were in no position to bargain. These vultures not only assigned the songs to their own companies, but they also listed themselves as co-composers. Thus, the leader, who had contributed nothing at all to the composing of the song, but only to its exploitation, would rake in 75 percent of all profits (50 percent as publisher and one-half of the remaining 50 percent as "co-writer"), while the poor composer had to settle for 25 percent! And this pertained not just to the leader's recording (for which he was paid additionally as the performer) but also to recordings of the tune by all other artists!

The potential profits from music publishing obviously intrigued Glenn. He began to devote more and more time and energy to his new venture. Though Leo Talent, an old friend from the struggling times in Boston, was hired to run the company, it was Glenn who called most of the shots. At times he would even assume the role of a song-plugger. Note, for example, the contents of this letter, written on November 11, 1941, to Bing Crosby:

> Dear Bing:
> Since your recent visit to New York, Leo Talent, head of our music firm, Mutual Music Society, has been pestering the 'jesus' out of me to send you a copy of Papa Niccolini.
> If you like it fine—if you don't—what with the defense

situation as it is, you might be able to use it in lieu of the Sears Roebuck Catalogue. . . .

Sincerely,
Glenn Miller

Aside from Glenn's preoccupation with that Sears Roebuck Catalogue, the letter reveals how thoroughly he had become immersed in business, and surprisingly and maybe even distressingly, how much he sounded like so many song-pluggers who wouldn't come out directly with a "please play my song" approach. Instead, they would hide behind some flimsy excuse, as Glenn did with his reference to Leo Talent's pestering.

In those days the song-pluggers' selling approach reminded me of a press agent's. They'd talk to you about something that they figured would please you, and then, when you thought they had just about talked themselves out, they'd turn to you and start with the magic word "Incidentally." Of course, the "incidental" words that followed invariably turned out to be non-incidental pitches for the plugs or favors for which they hoped they had already softened you up. Sad to state, during the past thirty years, too few song-pluggers or press agents have deviated very much from this routine.

Song-plugging did contain some very honorable and often helpful and genuinely concerned gents. But it also contained some whining leeches. Unfortunately, the very nature of the job made it terribly demeaning, because, when you got right down to it, the basic aim was to try to get someone to do you a favor by playing your tune, and so you had to find some way—any way—to show your appreciation, and, above all, to retain your patron's good will.

To make matters worse, some band leaders used song-pluggers for everything they could get out of them: theater tickets, booze, women, and not too seldom outright cash gifts. Because of my close friendships with so many leaders, I was offered several song-plugging jobs. But I turned them all down—even though it would have meant much more money than I was making at *Metronome*—primarily, I guess, because to say what I wanted to

Glenn (center) at the Cafe Rouge flanked by (left to right) Tommy Dorsey's band manager Bobby Burns, Tommy, songwriter Rube Bloom and a favorite music publisher, Jack Bregman of Bregman, Vocco and Conn.

say and to do what I really believed in meant even more to me.

And yet, despite the one-sided setup, some relationships between band leaders and song-pluggers, or "contact men" as they later preferred to be called, were warm and cordial and even evolved into strong friendships. Glenn, a man of strong likes and dislikes, and thus accused of playing favorites, became very friendly with veterans like Jack Robbins of Robbins Music, Jack Bregman of Bregman, Rocco, and Conn, and Norman Foley of Feist Music, who had been hanging out with musicians for years and who knew how to deal with leaders like Glenn and the Dorseys. But the favor-seeking whiners who didn't know how to approach Glenn sometimes got treated roughly. Fortunately for both them and Glenn, he had set up enough buffers in MacGregor and McIntyre and later in Chuck Goldstein of the Modernaires and Johnny O'Leary, the new road manager, so that he could be spared some of their pressures, and the poor pluggers could be spared some of Glenn's impatience and sarcasm.

Chapter 22

The song-pluggers' brigade worked full time that fall after the band opened at the Cafe Rouge for its second engagement there. The schedule became hectic: six nights a week plus three Chesterfield shows, including three rehearsals—plus plenty of rehearsals to go over the many new arrangements that were coming in, including some exciting ones written by one of the new trumpeters, Billy May, who joined the band soon after its opening.

Glenn hadn't been happy with his trumpet section. Frankhauser hadn't worked out as well as expected, and Zarchy, who'd only planned to stay a short time anyway, had been replaced by Phil Rommel, who, in turn, had given way to the veteran Maxie Kaminsky, filling in until Glenn could find a permanent replacement.

Bullets Durgom found Maxie's replacement, a kid trumpeter named Ray Anthony, who was playing in Brooklyn with Al Donahue's band. He told Glenn about him; Glenn told Bullets to bring the kid in and have him sit in with the band, which Bullets did, and, according to him, "Ray tore up the joint."

Anthony's involvement with the band was never particularly happy. He had a big fat tone in his lower register, but like so many youngsters whose musical development preceded their emotional growing-up, he could be unbearably cocky. Few in the band grew close to him, and certainly he was no favorite of

ABOVE: The new Miller bandstand in the Cafe Rouge is christened by Tommy Dorsey's Bobby Burns and bandleaders Charlie Spivak, Les Brown, Larry Clinton, Woody Herman and Sammy Kaye at the January 1941 opening night.

Glenn's, nor of trumpeter Mickey McMickle, who assumed most of the lead parts and all of the high endings after Zarchy left. To Mickey, Ray, who after the war was to lead his own successful band, was at that time "a lousy trumpet player and a precocious

Ray Anthony.

little brat. I remember he once said to me, 'Christ, if I had a shallow mouthpiece like yours, I could hit those high notes too!' So I gave him my mouthpiece and took his and played all my parts just the same."

Billy May played a much more important part in the band's musical development. When he joined early in November, it was sounding so stiff and stylized that some of the musicians were growing restless and bored. But Billy changed that.

Through his arrangements, and also in part through his wonderfully effervescent and carefree attitude, May injected a much-needed looseness and joie de vivre into the band. The jazz-loving musicians immediately gravitated toward him. A big, whalelike man, full of enthusiasm, he was even able to win over the reserved boss, who, for some reason or other, didn't object to Billy's kooky wildness the way he did to the free-swinging behavior of some of the others. Billy was a boozer, all right, but a happy one who had absorbed splendidly the basic training—musical, social, and alcoholic—available to all who matriculated into the high-swinging Charlie Barnet band.

"I was with Charlie in the spring of 1939 at Playland Casino in Rye. Business was terrible. Glenn was getting all of it down at Glen Island Casino. I remember Charlie used to say, half-kiddingly, 'Let's run Glenn Miller out of business!' And so we did crazy musical things like playing 'Sunrise Serenade,' one of

Glenn's big numbers, and Charlie would blow the melody and the rest of the band would be playing Duke Ellington's 'Azure' against it.

"By the time the band got to the Palomar in Los Angeles in August, it was jumping. That was the most enjoyable band I ever played with. I'd arrange just the beginning of a tune, maybe one chorus, and then the band would work out the rest of the arrangement. Everybody seemed to contribute something. It was all so free and easy.

"But it wasn't at all like that with Glenn. The difference between working with his band and Charlie's was that with Miller you had to have everything just right—uniform, neckties, socks, handkerchiefs, and so on—or else you'd be fined. But Charlie's band was much looser. I remember one night the bass player came in wearing the wrong-colored jacket. So, instead of fining him, Charlie made a joke out of it and had the guy play a whole bunch of solos down front as sort of a guest artist."

According to Billy, Glenn never had the ability to make a band swing the way Charlie could. "He would hit on a formula and then he would try to fit everything into it. There was no room for inventiveness. Even the hot choruses were supposed to be the same. Jerry Gray was perfect for the band. He followed the patterns exactly.

"Glenn was basically a businessman. The only man I ever knew him to be envious of was Kay Kyser, because he was the only band leader making more money than Glenn was."

Even before he played or wrote a note for the band, Billy discovered Glenn's keen business mind. "In October of 1940 Myles Rinker, Mildred Bailey's brother, came to hire a trumpet player for Glenn out of Charlie's band. He took Bernie Privin, but Glenn didn't want him. He was so shrewd. He wanted me instead, because he knew I could also arrange.

"When I went in to talk to Glenn about money, I tried to use the old squeeze play—you know—Barnet vs. Miller. But Glenn was too smart for that. He made me an offer and said, 'Say yes or no, right here.' He wouldn't give me the chance to run back to Charlie and try to play one guy against the other." So May

Billy May blows toward an exhibitionistic Miller on the Cafe Rouge bandstand.

accepted the offer: $150 a week or union scale (whichever was higher), plus $25 (later raised to $50) for each score.

Billy joined the band on Election Night. "I remember the date, because Glenn was mad that night: There wasn't any business in the room because they weren't permitted to serve liquor." Shortly thereafter May wrote his first arrangement for the band, the old standard "Ida," featuring a vocal by Tex Beneke. Billy knew how much Glenn liked the Lunceford band, so he wrote it in that style. "I even patterned the vocal after Trummy Young with the band answering. But Tex didn't want to sing it that way." So a fine Billy May idea never got off the score sheet.

Billy's approach was often offbeat. He arranged a lovely ballad version of "I Got Rhythm" which band alumni still rave about, and he tried a few more "unusual" ideas. But generally he followed Glenn's orders to "write a thing like . . . ." Once on his own he arranged a tune called "Summer Shadows" that Hal Dickenson of the Modernaires had written. "But Glenn wouldn't play it because he was mad at Hal." He also wrote a few originals for the band. "Long, Tall Momma" was one. "That was Glenn's title. And there was 'Daisy Mae' and 'Measure for Measure.' And I used to arrange a lot of those patriotic things."

Billy's compositions carried his last name, but not his first one. He had already signed a writer's contract with Barnet, so for the originals he wrote for Glenn he used his wife's name, Arletta May. "Later," Billy recalls sadly, "I gave all the tunes to Arletta as part of our divorce settlement. Then along came the movie *The Glenn Miller Story* and she wound up making around twelve thousand dollars on my tunes. I got nothing."

As a good businessman would, Glenn kept trying to get Billy to assign his original compositions to Mutual Music. "In September, just before the band broke up, Leo Talent was trying to get me to sign. We were talking in a dark studio at the Chesterfield rehearsal. Leo mentioned that Charlie Spivak and Hal McIntyre were 4-F and they were Glenn's bands and they'd be around and they could record and broadcast my tunes, and he really put on the pressure. But I refused. Then the lights went on and I looked and saw Glenn was sitting just two seats away. It was never quite the same thereafter. He gave me the freeze."

For a number of years after the band broke up, Billy remained bitter about Glenn. After the war he even wrote a letter to Al Klink, in which he sarcastically noted that he had heard that "Adolph Hitler is alive and playing Fender bass with Glenn

Miller in Argentina." But success as a band leader and as an arranger-conductor in the West Coast studios (he was Frank Sinatra's favorite arranger for a while), plus an active interest in solving certain problems of fellow-musicians, helped Billy to mellow and mature.

Now he is able to look at Glenn more objectively and to understand some of the pressures that beset his old boss. "Glenn wasn't a bad guy. He was just very uptight. Toward the end, he drank a little more and the band loosened up more, too. He had a lot to offer. I sometimes wonder what he would have been like if he had come back. Would he have been as corny as Welk or as exciting as Stan or Woody? We'll never know, will we."

Chapter 23

 One night in October, as I walked into the Cafe Rouge, Glenn came over and said, "I want you to go and talk with Johnny O'Leary, our new road manager. Listen to him and see if you don't agree that he's the only man you ever met who speaks with no punctuation!"

After a couple of minutes of listening to O'Leary ramble, I agreed completely with Glenn. A moon-faced, enthusiastic Boston Irishman, he would prattle on from one subject to another without ever giving you even the slightest hint of when he was about to switch. It was like trying to follow a game of verbal, three-cushion billiards.

But nonstop rambler/prattler O'Leary turned out to be a godsend for Glenn. He was a stickler for details and a master at following routines. A graduate of the Shribman office, he knew all the tricks promoters played, and he'd catch all of them at each and every one of them. He was a genius at clocking the gate, with his hidden clicker in hand, counting every paying customer and every freebee who walked in, and then at the end of the evening coming up with the correct total paid attendance, on the basis of which the band would be paid. With O'Leary on the job, Glenn never again had to worry about any promoter shortchanging him.

But Johnny had more to offer than clicking customers and checking promoters. As road manager, it was also his job to check

"The greatest guy in the whole organization," Johnny O'Leary, poses as a drink-buyer as Willie Schwartz plays bartender. Others (left to right): Hal McIntyre, Paula Kelly, Paul Tanner, Ernie Caceres, Jack Lathrop, Al Klink, Billy May, Trigger Alpert, Mickey McMickle, Jimmy Priddy and Tex Beneke.

on the musicians, on what uniforms they were to wear, when the bus left, what hotel they'd be staying at, whether they'd arrived on time, whether they'd left on time and all sorts of other routine details. He performed these rites with such amazing grace and charm and patience that, instead of being offended by his scoutmastering, the musicians loved him. "The greatest guy in the whole organization was Johnny O'Leary," Maurice Purtill recently proclaimed. "With all those things he had to do, he never got hacked at anyone. He was a saint!"

Johnny attributes some of his success to his never having been a musician. "The band had several musicians as road managers before I came in, and they sometimes had a tendency to get too lax. Glenn told me that once when the band was supposed to go to York, Pennsylvania, and sleep there before the one-nighter, the guys talked Tommy Mack into letting them disobey Glenn and stay over in Washington, and so a little while after that he hired me as the band's new road manager."

Glenn's sharply disciplined routines bugged many of the musicians. But from the business-minded O'Leary they drew only supreme admiration. "Glenn always did everything right on time and he would always start the band promptly at nine P.M. on the nose, and when he said 'twenty-minute intermission,' he meant twenty, and not twenty-five, and during those intermissions Glenn would usually stay on stage and sign autographs. After the date Glenn would give the guys one hour in which to eat. One time, when we were playing in Omaha, some of the guys weren't ready to leave on time, so Glenn said, 'O'Leary, it's five past two. Let's go!' And off we went, leaving five guys—Purtill and Caceres were two of them, I remember—and they had to fly to the next town at their own expense."

Glenn's action merely invoked Rule 14 on a list of regulations which he had prepared for his managers: "Establish importance of everyone being ready to leave when bus is supposed to leave, and fine those who are not ready to leave on time."

In addition to numerous directions regarding contracts, transportation, sound systems, local union regulations, baggage, etc., the list contained these additional specifics:

> "Give members of the band a complete schedule nite of job—for complete set-up of job following day—such as time of leaving—time of arrival—place of engagement—hours—where hotel reservations are made, if any—where you [manager] can be reached—where Miller can be reached.

> "Be sure all members of band know what uniforms to wear.

> "Discuss with leader as to how far you can go concerning the conduct of the band personnel riding in bus and on stand—this pertains to smoking on stand, talking, drinking, etc."

According to O'Leary, Glenn's insistence upon observing details also covered the distances the band could jump between dates. He set a strict limit of 300 miles. "Once Glenn got real mad at Joe Shribman because he had booked him on a date that ran 304 miles. Glenn had clocked them on his Cadillac."

Miller also set limits on admission prices. He resented the kids being gouged. "Once when we played Lakeside Park in Dayton, Ohio," O'Leary recalls, "the promoter charged $2.50 admission. Glenn didn't like that. The promoter told him the band was so big, it could get away with charging that much. And it did. But Glenn always wanted to watch out for the kids, and so, after that, he had a clause written into all future one-night contracts that called for no more than a one-dollar admission, plus tax, unless the promoter had written permission from Glenn to charge more."

Taking care of business, for Glenn, also included taking care of the kids. Johnny remembers the night they jammed 7,200 customers into Sunnybrook Ballroom in Pottstown, Pennsylvania. "If a kid wanted to go to the bathroom, the others would have to lift him over their heads—that's how jammed tight they were. And do you know what Glenn's reaction was? 'Suppose the floor caved in with all those kids there!' "

Glenn developed a keen sense of responsibility toward those kids. They were his bread and butter. At times the steady diet may have caused him some emotional nausea, but most of the time, unlike some other band leaders, he treated them with an amazing amount of patience and courtesy. O'Leary reports that "Glenn would never duck out of a theater the way some other leaders did. He always went right out to the stage door and met the kids. I remember once there was a big, big crowd outside the Paramount in New York and the backstage doorman said to Glenn, 'You're not going to go out *there*, to all those kids, are you?' And Glenn said, 'When they're *not* out there, *that's* when I'll be sorry!' "

Glenn's continuing concern for the commercial paid off. According to *Variety*, Miller, during 1940, grossed more than any other leader except for Kay Kyser—an estimated $700,000, topped only by Kyser's cool one million. And where did all that money go? The sum of $26,750 was listed as Glenn's personal income, with another $9,000 going to Helen. Commissions to GAC amounted to around $50,000. In addition, Michael DeZutter, with whom Glenn and Cy Shribman had entered into a losing promotional deal, keeping Glen Island Casino open for the

"When they're *not* there, *that's* when I'll be sorry!"

winter, reportedly received $30,000. Shribman himself came in for $17,500, and Mike Nidorf, Glenn's other manager, got $12,500. And then, of course, there was the band's payroll for the year—$232,442 worth—not to mention all sorts of other items such as bus and train fares, hotel rooms, publicity, running the office and many more expenses connected with running a big-time organization.

Obviously, somebody out there loved the band. Sometimes that even included some jazz-oriented musicians and critics, especially when Glenn would let the guys really blow, as he did one night late in 1940 during a mammouth battle of the bands in New York's Manhattan Center. Only one of the assembled twenty-eight, Jimmie Lunceford's, topped Miller's that memorable night. And, since no band was ever known to have topped Jimmie's, the second spot was nothing to be ashamed of—especially since the rest of the competition included Benny Goodman, Count Basie, Les Brown, Lucky Millinder, Will Bradley, Erskine Hawkins and almost two dozen more.

I was there that night, and I don't think I ever heard the band sound as inspired. Certainly the swinging competition helped. So did the recent addition of Billy May's trumpet, arrangements and freewheeling spirit. Critic Amy Lee, reviewing one of the band's Cafe Rouge broadcasts two nights later, also singled out Billy for those contributions. But then, just like several other jazz-oriented critics, whose opinions never seemed to worry or influence Glenn, she began longing for less inhibited playing from the entire band. Commenting that its music constituted "an appeal to the head rather than to the heart of the listeners," she continued, "as an aggregation that has been rehearsed until every bar of every tune is letter-perfect, the Miller men probably have no rivals. For precision, attack, shading and blend, the band cannot be topped.

"But," she concluded, "is letter-perfect playing worth the inevitable sacrifice of natural feeling?"

It was a question that as long as three decades later, many listeners, including even some of the musicians playing in the band at that time, would still be arguing about.

Chapter 24

The war kept building in January of 1941 as Franklin Delano Roosevelt was inaugurated for an unprecedented third term. And the music field was waging a war of its own, too. ASCAP and the radio networks had been unable to agree on rates for the use of songs copyrighted by the society's publishers. And so the networks had banned all ASCAP songs from their broadcasts and had set up their own collection agency, Broadcast Music, Inc. To supply new tunes, new BMI publishing firms were created. In addition, a few of the ASCAP firms, including Miller's Mutual Music Society, switched their affiliations to BMI.

But the net effect was pretty lousy music. ASCAP had the best songwriters and just about all the songs that everyone knew and liked. By comparison, BMI, until it could produce its own hit tunes, had little to offer. And so, to give listeners more recognizable melodies, many of the bands made swing arrangements of very old songs whose copyrights had expired and so were no longer controlled by ASCAP. The air fare began to grow pretty thin. Broadcasts grew monotonously alike. At one point, "I Dream of Jeannie With the Light Brown Hair" had been played so many times by so many bands that Eddie Sauter wrote a protest melody called "I Dream of Jeannie With a Dark Brown Taste in My Mouth."

Glenn couldn't play many of his big ASCAP hits, like "In the

Mood," "Tuxedo Junction," "Pennsylvania 6-5000" and "Sunrise Serenade." He couldn't even play his own theme, "Moonlight Serenade." So he used a new one, "Slumber Song," written by Chummy MacGregor and assigned to Glenn's own BMI publishing firm.

Good and bad news broke for the band early in January. The good news: *Down Beat* magazine announced that Miller had topped all other bands in its Sweet Band Poll. The bad news: Following a gossip columnist's item that she was going to have a baby, an embarrassed, pregnant Marion Hutton announced that she was retiring for the duration.

It was a shock to Glenn. He immediately started looking around for a replacement. The ideal choice seemed to be Dorothy Claire, a pert, vivacious, extroverted blonde, who had been singing with some of Glenn's friends in the Bob Crosby band before joining Bobby Byrne's new outfit. Glenn made her an offer and Byrne burned. Dorothy accepted, and a few weeks later Bobby started a suit against Glenn.

Actually, all the ensuing legal bother to hold onto Dorothy may not have been worth it. With both Crosby and Byrne, Dorothy's cute, gay, carefree approach had been very effective. But for some inexplicable reason, not so with Glenn's band. And, girl-to-man, she and her new boss never hit it off too well. Perhaps Glenn expected too much: another attractive entertainer like Marion, but who could also sing well. However, having raided Bobby's band, he couldn't easily admit he was wrong.

But the guys weren't too impressed, either. Possibly they'd been spoiled by Marion, whom they all loved the way they would love a sister. As a person, Dorothy was somewhat sharper and a bit hipper than Marion—all in all, an attractive, warm, and, I always felt, very decent young lady, who'd been much appreciated in the Crosby and Byrne bands. I could never quite understand why she didn't fit into Miller's better than she did. But she just didn't. Later she blossomed into a leading lady in Broadway musicals. She starred in *Finian's Rainbow*. But in Glenn's book, she never seemed to rate much higher than a bit player.

Dorothy Claire with the full band at the Cafe Rouge. Top row (left to right): Johnny Best, Ray Anthony, Mickey McMickle, Billy May, Maurice Purtill, Trigger Alpert, Jack Lathrop, Chummy MacGregor. Second row: Paul Tanner, Jimmy Priddy, Frankie D'Annolfo, Glenn, Willie Schwartz, Al Klink, Hal McIntyre, Ernie Caceres, Tex Beneke. Front row: Ray Eberle, Dorothy, Modernaires Bill Conway, Hal Dickenson, Ralph Brewster, Chuck Goldstein.

More in the Miller groove were the Modernaires, four young men from Buffalo, who joined the band a few days after Dorothy did. Glenn had been wanting a vocal group for quite some time, if for no other reason, as he once told me, "than to bring people up around the stand to notice the band." During the struggling days, he had even tried forming a group with Tex, Ray, Gail Reese and Paul Tanner, but it had never worked out. Then he had hired Jack Lathrop, hoping he would organize a quartet. But that never happened, either.

Now, with Marion gone, Glenn decided he definitely needed another attraction. Chuck Goldstein, the group's chubby, for-ever-grimacing extrovert, now one of the country's most success-ful jingle producers, credits disc jockey Martin Block for the group's joining the band. "We had recorded 'Make Believe Ballroom' with Charlie Barnet's band. That was Martin's theme. Then we went with Paul Whiteman's band. But by 1941 Martin wanted a new theme, and Glenn was going to record it for him. He needed a group and Martin suggested us. We went to rehearsal and I guess Glenn liked us because we recorded 'Make Believe Ballroom Time' with him.

"By then, Whiteman was about ready to give up his band, and when Glenn asked us if we'd like to join the band and go to Hollywood and make a movie, we asked Pops to let us out of our contract. Well, you know what a sweetheart Whiteman was. Of course he let us go.

"The Mods consisted of one Presbyterian, Hal Dickenson; one Catholic, Bill Conway, who also played guitar; one Christian Scientist, Ralph Brewster, who played trumpet; and one Jew, me. We never read music. We heard everything in our heads. Bill would sit at the guitar or at the piano and we'd learn our songs that way. Hal Dickenson was the lead singer because he could only sing the melody. Sometimes I'd sing the harmony at the bottom, and sometimes I'd sing it way high up on top. Remember? Some people thought we had a girl with us.

"We made a hundred and twenty-five apiece on the road and a hundred when we were in New York—and that included everything: records, radio shows, even movies. At Christmas Glenn gave us each a hundred-dollar bonus and we were glad to get it. You've got to remember that times were different then. Out of that hundred and a quarter, I was able to send home eighty-five each week."

Glenn signed the group to a ten-year management deal guaranteeing them their salaries, but also giving his publishing company first right of refusal on all songs they wrote, with no royalty payments to them for any performances of their songs by the Miller band.

But if Glenn was a tough businessman, he was also a patient teacher. He worked hard with the Mods. "For one thing," Goldstein points out, "he taught us to emphasize the melody. With Whiteman, we always wanted to knock out musicians. But Glenn kept saying, 'Always establish the melody. Then you can do your special material. But always come back to the melody.' It was something like what Whiteman had told us: 'Start good and end good.' "

Whiteman had been fairly easygoing. Glenn was something different. "He was always the General," Goldstein recently

Modernaires Conway, Dickenson, Goldstein and Brewster.

emphasized. "Everybody knows what a disciplinarian he was. But that could boomerang. Glenn had a rule that we could never take off our jackets. Well, after one of our first jobs with the band, we packed our uniforms in a trunk, to be taken to the next town. They were those heavy corduroy things. Next day, when we opened that trunk, you could have called a recess because of the smell. After that, we always carried our own clothes!"

The ebullient, outgoing Goldstein was one of the fortunate few able to break through to Glenn on a personal level. But it took a personal crisis for it to happen.

"We were doing one of the Chesterfield shows when Paul Douglas met me at the stage door and said Glenn wanted to see me right away. I went over to him, and Glenn took me aside and told me that they'd gotten word that my dad had had a stroke, and he had already made arrangements for me to go back to Buffalo to see him. But because of the weather the planes were grounded, and so Glenn got me on the next train instead. I got to Buffalo at eleven-thirty, but my dad had died at ten.

"After the funeral I flew to Washington, because the band was playing a theater date there. Glenn met me at the stage door and asked me if I wanted to work. I said 'Sure.' Then he told me he and I were going out together after the last show.

"Late that night he took me to the Variety Club, and he

ordered a bottle of bourbon and a bottle of rye. Then he said to the waiter, 'Put them on the table and don't bother us unless we call you.' He was like a father to me that night. He kept telling me to take it in stride. He was absolutely marvelous to me. He talked as if the thing had happened to *him!*

"Afterwards, we went downstairs. By this time I was stoned. I got into a cab and directed the driver to take me back to my hotel. He started to laugh. I couldn't figure out why. I soon found out, because all he did was take a U-turn and deposit me across the street, right in front of my hotel!

"I'll never forget that night. Nobody could have been kinder or more thoughtful than Glenn was then."

Chapter 25

Glenn looked out for those he liked, and once in a while he'd even go so far as to unzip his discipline—provided, of course, nobody knew.

Take the time Tex Beneke had won the *Metronome* All-Star Poll as the Number One Sweet Tenor Saxist. We scheduled the annual recording of the available winners for midnight of January 16. Glenn, by the way, had finished second to Jack Teagarden in the Hot Trombone division, but Jack was out of town, and so I had invited both Glenn and Tex to play on the session. Glenn refused. Why, I was never sure. Could have been that he felt he shouldn't leave the Cafe Rouge bandstand that early. Could have been, too, that he still had little confidence in his playing among the Jazz Greats whom I assembled in Victor's studio that night: Benny Goodman on clarinet, Count Basie on piano, Tommy Dorsey on lead trombone, Coleman Hawkins on tenor and Benny Carter on alto sax, Charlie Christian on guitar, Buddy Rich on drums and a trumpet section of Ziggy Elman, Harry James and Cootie Williams.

In Glenn's place, I got J. C. Higginbotham. As for Tex's spot, I wasn't too sure whether or not he'd be able to make it. Not that it bothered me that much, because, frankly, I didn't think he belonged in the same league with all those established stars. But he did make it, entering the studio at the very last minute.

Years later Tex laughed about what happened that night at

the Cafe Rouge before he left for the studio. "Glenn wanted me to play the date, all right. But you know what a disciplinarian he was. We were all part of the team, and we were all supposed to stay on the stand till the last note was played. There was no way he could give me permission to take off without setting a precedent he didn't want to set.

"Then he had an idea. When the last set started, I was to start griping and keep on griping, and finally he would get so teed off—or at least seem to—that he'd tell me to get off the stand and get out of there.

"I did just what he told me to. After he called off the first tune, I grumbled. He just looked at me but said nothing. Ernie Caceres, who was sitting next to me, told me to take it easy. On the next tune I griped even more, and Ernie kept nudging me to cool it. Finally, on the third tune, I let go with something about how ridiculous it was to play that kind of a tune then. Ernie was really upset by now. Glenn looked at me and asked, 'What did you say, Tex?' I said, 'I didn't say anything.' But he kept after me. 'I heard you say something.' And I said, 'All right, Glenn, I said I couldn't see why you want to play that tune now.'

"Well, that was all Glenn needed. 'Look,' he said as seriously as he could, I guess, 'if you don't like it, why don't you leave?' And I said, 'All right, I will.' And with that I picked up my sax and my clarinet and started to walk off the stand.

"But guess what happened then! Ernie, who was a good friend of mine, got so upset that he got up and said, 'If Tex goes, then I go, too!' And he picked up his horns and started to leave also. Glenn got him to come back, but I don't think he quite ever forgave Ernie for that."

Glenn never quite forgave me for the way I treated Tex on the date. During the more than six minutes of great jazz that the band recorded, I gave him only one solo—and that was just a fast and fairly meaningless two-and-a-half-second break near the start of "Bugle Call Rag." As any dedicated, jazz-respecting jazz producer would have, I gave the extended tenor sax solos to Hawkins. Years later Tex, who, like almost every sax player, revered Hawkins, told me I was absolutely right. But not Glenn. Tex was his boy, and I had sloughed him off.

The 1941 *Metronome* All-Star Band led by Benny Goodman (far right) in front of
drummer Buddy Rich. Saxists are Tex Beneke, Benny Carter, Toots Mondello
and Coleman Hawkins. Trombones are J. C. Higginbotham and Tommy
Dorsey, and trumpets are Harry James, Ziggy Elman and Cootie Williams.
Pianist Count Basie and guitarist Charlie Christian also played on the date.

Two nights after the *Metronome* All-Star date, the Miller band
closed its long run at the Cafe Rouge. Again it had turned in
some impressive weekly attendance figures, breaking even its own
previous record. Ten days later it opened at the Paramount and
drew more huge crowds, then made some more recordings and
headed west.

In February it won the Martin Block WNEW poll once more
and had its commercial radio series option picked up by
Chesterfield. Under the new agreement the band could broadcast its shows directly from theaters. Previously, the cigarette
company had taken the band away from the theaters in which it

was playing and into large auditoriums, where it broadcast before nonpaying, invited guests. Many theater managers considered those free concerts unfair competition with the stage shows for which the kids were required to pay admission. They had objected strenuously, and, since the free broadcasts also cut in on Glenn's own weekly gross, he went to bat for them with Chesterfield and won.

After the Paramount date, Glenn gave Ray Anthony his two weeks' notice. The Modernaires' Ralph Brewster had been getting his lip into shape and Glenn, forever economy-minded, planned to use him on the fourth trumpet chair. Naturally, young Anthony was heartbroken. According to Johnny O'Leary, when the band arrived in Ray's home town of Cleveland and Anthony didn't appear with it on the stage of the Palace Theatre, his father dropped by and asked Johnny, "What's the matter? Did Ray do something wrong?" Tactful Johnny tried to explain that Miller was merely trying to save some money. "But I told Glenn about Ray's father anyway. By then, he had heard Ralph play and he knew it wouldn't work out, so he told me, 'OK, get the kid!' And he hired him back. I was so glad for his father's sake. And one thing I will say for Ray: He was a good kid when it came to taking care of his folks."

Anthony stayed on. But Dorothy Claire didn't. Bobby Byrne's lawyers had kept putting on the pressure, and soon Glenn felt the fight wasn't worth it. One night he ran into Bobby in a Columbus, Ohio, hotel and he agreed to Dorothy's return if Bobby would withdraw his charges. In her place, he hired Hal Dickenson's pretty young wife, Paula Kelly, who had been singing in Al Donahue's band. She joined Glenn and her husband just in time for a long train ride from St. Louis to Hollywood, where on March 24 they all began work on the band's first movie, *Sun Valley Serenade.*

For several years, the movie moguls had noticed how the big bands' personal appearances could pull kids into theaters, even when the movies were lousy. So, they figured, why not hire the bands for their lousy movies and draw the kids into all their theaters, including those without stage shows. And so, in true Hollywood fashion, they began presenting them—with a maximum of glitter and a minimum of authenticity—in all sorts of stupid films, like Benny Goodman and *Hollywood Hotel,* Artie Shaw and *Dancing Co-Ed,* and Tommy Dorsey and *Las Vegas Nights.*

During the summer of 1941, when the big-band craze probably reached its dizziest heights, a big batch of bands were toiling on the Hollywood lots. Charlie Barnet, Count Basie, Xavier Cugat, both the Dorseys, Goodman, Glen Gray, Woody Herman, Harry James, Sammy Kaye, Gene Krupa, Kay Kyser, Guy Lombardo, Jimmie Lunceford, Freddy Martin, Alvino Rey, Jack Teagarden and others were making movies, just about every one of them forgettable.

Not so, though, for Glenn and *Sun Valley Serenade.* A stickler for the truth, he insisted upon a thoroughly believable script before he'd go before the Twentieth Century-Fox cameras. And keen businessman that he was, he demanded that the band become an integral part of the story and not just be thrown into some inconsequential scene, the way so many other bands had been. He had achieved star status and he was now demanding and getting star treatment.

Sonja Henie and John Payne played the romantic leads, and Milton Berle, Lynn Bari, Dorothy Dandridge, Joan Davis and the Nicholas Brothers were also featured in the film. As for Glenn, he played the part of band leader Phil Corey, and he played it so well that ultra-pro-jazz critic Barry Ulanov, no lover of the Miller band, praised him in *Metronome* as

> a convincing band leader, and, even more important, a convincing human being in this film. He's on mostly for music, but most of the film is music and the dozen or so reels are a better showcase for the Glenn Miller band than they are for the Sonja Henie torso and limbs, with and without skates.
>
> Never has a movie made more of a popular band, and never has a movie featuring such an organization presented its music so tastefully. From the shadowed figures of the bandsmen which serve as background to the credit titles of the picture to the easy presentation of the rehearsal scene that features "Chattanooga Choo Choo," the band is really brilliantly directed, lighted, photographed.
>
> The first appearance of the men of Miller is at an audition.

ABOVE: Paula and the Mods.

BELOW: Waiting to see and hear the Miller band.

The Tommy Dorsey Band in *Las Vegas Nights*. In the back row are the four Pied Pipers with Jo Stafford, singers Connie Haines and Frank Sinatra standing together and drummer Buddy Rich. The pianist is Joe Bushkin.

After a few bars of their theme, "Moonlight Serenade," with a happily grinning Miller directing, and the audiences in the film houses going mad as they recognize the band and the music, the boys go into a pleasant tune that features Lynn Bari singing. . . . Though the band has never played with Lynn before, they back her with smooth perfection and the Modernaires harmonize her without a hitch. . . .

Pictorially, Trigger Alpert and Maurice Purtill take the honors. Trigger hops around like mad, and Maurice looks like the movies' idea of a swing drummer, all right. They stay within the bounds of good taste, however, and the rest of the band just looks happy and as if they play for a living rather than chew scenery. The story is believable, and happily centers around the band, so that the whole thing is a triumph for Glenn Miller and the band.

The band made quite an impression on the folks at the studio. "When we recorded the sound track," recalls Chuck Goldstein, "Daryl Zanuck and the entire brass came in to listen. It was a great thrill working on that sound stage. The band never sounded as good on records." Recordings taken from the sound track and released many years later by Twentieth Century-Fox Records prove that Chuck is absolutely right.

Chuck recently revealed that the Modernaires heard on the sound track weren't just the Modernaires. "We needed a bigger sound for 'It Happened in Sun Valley.' All of us had always dug the singing of Six Hits and a Miss—especially Pauline Byrne, who was the 'Miss.' In fact, we had a mutual admiration society thing going with them. So, to get that bigger sound, we invited them to sing with us. What a ball! And what a sound!"

But for Glenn, the picture's most important sound was the sound of its biggest recording hit, "Chattanooga Choo Choo." Written for the film by Mack Gordon and Harry Warren, it was performed in the picture not only by Tex Beneke and Paula Kelly and the Modernaires, who made the famed recording, but also in a long, brilliantly danced, but, by today's standards, Uncle Tommish sequence by the superb Nicholas Brothers, and by the very beautiful Miss Dandridge.

As they have always done with musical pictures, the movie moguls insisted that the band record its music first and then play-act to the sound track. Most bands in movies, responding to square directors' exhortations to "get hot," overacted outrageously. The Miller band exhibited a bit more restraint, though some of their pyrotechnics still seemed pretty unbelievable to those of us who knew how musicians really performed in person.

Trigger Alpert insists that in the eyes of at least one person the picture made him a star. "Sometime after the movie came out, our train had a stopover in my home town, Indianapolis. So I called my mom ahead of time, and when we get there, I get off our private car and Mom is standing there with an *overcoat* box dripping with fried chicken, fried cookies, and all sorts of cooking. She gave me a big kiss and a hug and then she looked at the porter and said, 'Did you see *Sun Valley Serenade?*' He said 'Yes,' and then she points to me and says, 'That's *him!*' Ten seconds of mugging and I'm a star to her. That's a *real* Jewish mother for you. She used to say things like, 'Try this cake; it's light as a fender'!"

The band had a good time in Hollywood. The pay was so good that Trigger and Maurice Purtill rented Ben Bernie's sumptuous Beverly Hills home—just the two of them. They even hired a maid and bought a car, a Model T Ford, for $75. "But," says

Scenes from *Sun Valley Serenade*: (Above) romantic lead John Payne makes a
point to Glenn and Milton Berle as band members try to look interested;
(below) the superb Nicholas Brothers in the "Chattanooga Choo Choo"
sequence.

Alpert, "it never ran. So we'd take cabs to work. It was a convertible."

Purtill doesn't quite remember it the same way. "It really wasn't a convertible. It was a sedan. But we had the top cut off to make it a convertible."

Glenn and Helen also lived royally in Beverly Hills, first on Roxbury Drive and then at 517 North Foothill Road, where they often entertained their friends.

The day before the band completed the picture, it began a three weeks' engagement at the famed Palladium Ballroom in Hollywood. A tremendous crowd, filled with movie celebrities, attended one of the biggest big-band openings of all time. But, contrary to custom, *everybody* who walked into the place had to pay—even critics, reporters, influential disc jockeys, and all the orchestra wives, including Helen Miller herself.

The move was strictly Glenn's. Beginning long before the band's engagement, the Palladium had issued many complimentary passes in exchange for plugs, and many people had been saving them for the Miller opening. But Glenn, whose take depended on the total gross, insisted that all the "free-bees" become "pay-bees." And, despite a lot of hard feelings, he got his way.

The move paid off handsomely in dollars. During the first week, the band set a new Palladium record. But even that couldn't erase the ill will between Glenn and the Palladium management, and so, when the band returned to California the following year to make another movie, Glenn bypassed a return to the Palladium.

Johnny O'Leary once explained Glenn's financial philosophy. "He didn't want any penny that *wasn't* coming to him, but he did insist on getting every penny that *was* coming to him. After we left the Palladium we played one-nighters and one of them was in Oakland where there was a promoter who Lou Levy, the manager of the Andrews Sisters, warned us had robbed him. So Glenn hired six guys to watch all the six doors leading into the place and to check all tickets.

"Some promoters would try some fast tricks on us. The way we would count the number of tickets sold would be to take the

An example of Glenn's insistence on "getting every penny that was coming to him." Note his refusal to pay for his trombone unless the company would absorb the $3.82 express charge.

number of the first ticket on the first roll of tickets and the number of the last ticket on the last roll sold, and then subtract one from the other. If the promoter was honest, that would work out all right. But one night I noticed that the tickets weren't arriving in sequence, and so we began to check around and we found out that the promoter had taken the last hundred or so tickets off the roll and taped them into the middle somewhere so that the last number we'd see would not be the highest number. Well, we knew something was up, so Glenn had the guys take out every ticket that was dropped into the admission box and count them all up, and then we got paid on the basis of the total number of tickets."

On the basis of such experiences, Glenn wasn't too happy with West Coast one-nighters. Maurice Purtill recalls the unpleasantness of the very first job the band played the night after closing the Palladium. "It was up in Fresno, and it turned out they were having some big festival somewhere else in town on the same night. Naturally that hurt our attendance, and at intermission the guy who was promoting us on all those West Coast gigs came crying to Glenn. So Glenn said, 'I tell you what I'll do. I'll split the loss tonight with you and we'll draw up a new deal.' And for the rest of the dates on the tour he asked the guy for a lower guarantee but a higher percentage of all admissions above the guarantee—a jump from the usual 60 percent to 70. The guy took the deal. So then what does Glenn do but start to really promote himself in every town we were playing—all sorts of radio and personal appearances—and so naturally he made out great. So then the promoter asked him to go back to the original deal, but Glenn, who was a tough businessman, wouldn't do it. In fact, after that he wouldn't do any more one-nighters on the West Coast."

Glenn was tough. But he was also fair, especially to promoters who treated him well. O'Leary remembers the promoter who frankly told Glenn his problem ahead of time. "We sold a lot of advance tickets to middle-aged people," he said. "Will you play some soft music and maybe some waltzes for them?" This was a promoter who had always been on the up-and-up with Glenn, and so Glenn, realizing he had a real problem, cooperated and deviated from the norm—an unusual concession—for the sake of the old-timers and the promoter.

While the band on the West Coast was having its series of one-nighters, back on the East Coast, Marion Hutton, who had departed so suddenly, was having her very special night. On May 26 she gave birth to the baby she had almost lost five weeks earlier. Polly Haynes, who had visited her in the hospital then, had been deeply touched by Marion's attachment to the band. In a letter to Helen Miller, Polly had written, "All Marion wanted to do was talk about you, Glenn and the band. She loves you all so much. She will never get over not being with the band."

In a classic example of cool noncommunication, Glenn had never convinced Marion he wanted her back, and, moreover, wasn't sure she wanted to return. A month after the baby was born, Polly wrote again, suggesting that in case Glenn were not interested in Marion, he might consider hiring Alice O'Connell, a superb singer, even better than her sister Helen, who was starring with Jimmy Dorsey's band. Ten days later came another

letter from Polly: "Marion wants to come back all right," she reported, "but didn't think you were interested. She said she didn't want any more kids for a long time, anyway." Six weeks later, with Marion assured that Glenn wanted her back and Glenn assured that she wanted to return, Marion rejoined the Miller band.

Polly Haynes had closed the communications gap.

Chapter 26

 By the spring of 1941, the military draft had been making inroads into the dance bands. Tommy Dorsey had lost two of his stars, singer Jack Leonard and clarinetist Johnny Mince. Benny Goodman had given up his brother Irving, a trumpeter; Larry Clinton's Tony Zimmers, a fine tenor saxist, had been drafted, as had many musicians from other bands.

In the Miller band, only Glenn and Chummy MacGregor were protected by the thirty-five-year maximum age. And only Mickey McMickle, whom Glenn had nicknamed "GOMOTS" for "Grand Old Man of the Trumpet Section," seemed safe. But the draft even caught up with him.

The rest were obvious draft-fodder. Ray Anthony at 19 had recently passed the minimum age. Ray Eberle and Jimmy Priddy were 22. Willie Schwartz and Paul Tanner were 23. Trigger Alpert, Billy May and Maurice Purtill were 24. Al Klink was 25. Tex Beneke, Johnny Best and Hal McIntyre were 27. Ernie Caceres was 29, and Frank D'Annolfo had reached the ripe old age of 30. As Alpert, in reviewing the guys' ages, recently noted: "No wonder we acted the way we did. We were just kids!"

First to go was Trigger, the ebullient bassist, for whom Glenn held the most paternal affection, and for whom he had previously maneuvered a six months' deferment from his local draft board.
"But that shouldn't reflect on Glenn's patriotism," Alpert

recently noted, "because in those days we weren't even in the war."

Before Trigger left, he contacted another bassist, Doc Goldberg, to replace him. "Chummy MacGregor asked for him especially," Alpert recalls, "because he'd heard him playing that boogie-woogie stuff in Will Bradley's band and Chummy liked to play that style."

However, Goldberg couldn't join the band immediately, so for two weeks Glenn hired Meyer "Mike" Rubin, little remembered by Miller followers but now one of the best-known bassists in the West Coast studios. "Glenn made a big mistake when he didn't keep Mike," says Chuck Goldstein, "because he was a really great bass player. And he was a ballsy guy, too. He liked to put Glenn on. I remember Glenn made him go out and buy a pair of those black and white Florsheim shoes we had to wear and then told him to make sure they always looked good. So Mike told everyone, 'I have to pay more for shoetrees now than I used to pay for a pair of shoes.' And when they put the spotlight on him for his bass solo, he said they ought to put it on his shoes instead because they cost so much!"

According to Goldstein, Rubin also wasn't afraid to talk back to Miller. "Trigger had left the bass book a mess, and when Mike couldn't find one of the parts and Glenn kept bugging him to hurry 'because this is costing money,' Mike yelled back at him, 'OK, then *you* find the part!' " Such courage came easily to musicians who knew they weren't going to stay with the band.

Goldberg, however, remained with the band until the very end. Not as driving or as colorful as Alpert, his deft touch and fine tone nevertheless stood out in the often-maligned rhythm section.

Three days after Alpert's exit co-manager Mike Nidorf, engaged in a power struggle with Cy Shribman, also left. The continuous rivalry between the two had finally forced Glenn to make a choice, and so he went with Shribman, his benefactor and business partner in the Glen Island Casino winter venture and in the bands of Charlie Spivak and Claude Thornhill. But Mike didn't suffer. He began his own immensely successful

The soon-to-be-departing Mike Nidorf flanked by Glenn, band leader Tony Pastor and Helen Miller.

career and wound up a tremendously wealthy and highly respected member of the worldwide corporate business community.

The Glen Island winter season venture was a financial flop. Too many kids were away at school, and dancing by the water's edge on cold winter nights didn't especially intrigue their parents. But the news on the two Miller-Shribman bands was more encouraging. Spivak's, well established by now, was doing well, and Thornhill's was catching on.

Glenn's relationships with the two leaders, both of them close personal friends, were quite different. He was constantly giving advice and making suggestions to Charlie, and retaining as much control as he could over the band. The more dependent Spivak seemed to like Glenn's active interest, sometimes contacting Glenn for advice even before he had decided to offer it.

But with the more confident Thornhill, it was quite the opposite. Glenn respected his impeccable taste, his ability as an arranger, and his all-around musicianship so much that he never interfered with his creativity. And justifiably so, for Claude's

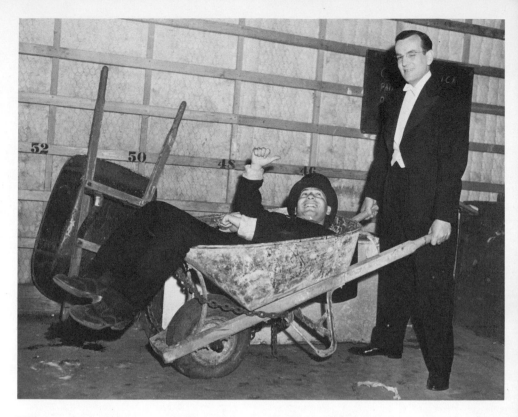

Things-to-Come-Department: Bullets Durgom on the Twentieth Century-Fox movie lot in a gag shot. Was the wheelbarrow facing toward Tommy Dorsey?

turned out to be just about the most musical outfit in the entire history of dance bands. Thornhill was just as vague as Miller was dogmatic, just as gentle as Glenn was forceful. And yet each knew exactly what he wanted from his musicians and how to get it out of them. Few people in the world related as well to Glenn as Claude did, and few enjoyed as great rapport based on mutual respect.

Glenn's relationship with another old friend, Tommy Dorsey, reverted in June to one of its "off-again" stages. Bullets Durgom, then working for Glenn as a record-promotion man and doing an outstanding job, figures that their smoldering rivalry caused Tommy to offer double what Glenn was paying him to switch over. When Bullets told Glenn he'd stay if Glenn wanted him to, Miller replied, "No, you go with Tommy, but you must never discuss my name with him. And, if you don't like it there, you can come back here." Durgom insists that he never did discuss

Alec Fila, "the most inspiring musician the band ever had," second from left, with Johnny Best, Mickey McMickle, Billy May and Moe Purtill.

Miller with Dorsey, but he did find out one thing: "Glenn was the best teacher I had as a businessman. But Tommy was the best teacher as a musician."

Early in July, Ray Anthony left the band again, but this time for good. He was replaced by another young trumpeter, Alec Fila, who had been playing lead in the Bob Chester band, which had been imitating Miller's, and also in Benny Goodman's. For me, Alec was one of the greatest lead trumpeters of all time, a powerful musician with a brilliant, piercing tone that would lift you right off your feet. I was constantly getting him jobs, none of which he held too long. Willie Schwartz recently tabbed him "the most inspiring musician the band ever had. When he played the opening of 'A String of Pearls' it would scare the hell out of everybody." Unfortunately, the young and talented Fila could be just as cocky as the man he replaced, so he and Glenn never hit it off too well, either. Come to think of it, I was getting pretty proficient at recommending good musicians with whom Glenn couldn't get along—Jimmy Abato, Jerry Yelverton, Clyde Hurley, Fila.

Two days after Alec joined, along came another trumpeter who not only thrilled the guys in the Miller band, but who set standards of melodic beauty and exquisite taste that still persist to this day. Bobby Hackett joined on July 10, 1941, replacing Bill Conway (who had previously replaced Jack Lathrop) on, of all instruments, the guitar!

Jazz lovers became incensed when they heard that Glenn had hired Bobby to strum in the rhythm section instead of to blow his gorgeous cornet solos. But Glenn admired Hackett's horn just as much as anyone did. "In fact, later on," Bobby recalls, "he seemed to get his biggest kicks late at night on the last sets when he and I would play duets. He'd play the melody on trombone and I'd play little cornet fill-ins behind him. He used to call us 'the Happiness Boys.'

"But when Glenn hired me, I wasn't playing cornet. I'd just had some dental surgery, so I couldn't blow my horn. Cy Shribman—one of the greatest guys who ever lived—called me one day. It seems that Ernie Caceres had been prodding Glenn to take me, and so Glenn had called Cy. Now Cy knew about my trouble with my teeth, so after he asked me if I wanted to join and I told him sure, he said, 'By the way, you gotta bring your banjo!' 'Banjo?!' I said. 'Well, bring it, whatever it is,' he told me. So I went to New York and borrowed a guitar and joined the band.

"Now, Glenn really didn't need me. He had four good trumpets, and I was just a luxury to him. But Glenn wanted to help me out. To me he was a very wonderful guy, and I always considered it a great honor to have played for him.

"Glenn cared about people and their problems. When I joined the band, I still owed MCA twenty-three hundred dollars and I didn't see how I was ever going to pay it back. So one day Glenn called Billy Goodheart at MCA for me and he said, 'Look, you want to hold him to the twenty-three hundred? If so, you'll probably get nothing. So why not settle for a thousand?' They did, and I paid them eventually. But that's the way Glenn would go to bat for you."

As a guitarist, Hackett figures he contributed very little to the band. "Every note was wasted. You never heard it. On

Guitarist and cornetist Bobby Hackett.

recordings they had a mike in front of me, but it was never open!" Bobby doesn't think too much of himself as a guitarist, though for the Miller rhythm section he was more than

the opening show, Jack O'Brian, who was then a critic, showed up, and he was a big jazz buff and he asked Glenn to have me play a cornet solo. I was just about ready to sneak on the stage with just my guitar when Glenn called out 'Rockin' Chair.' Now, that had a five-minute cornet solo for me in it, and Glenn knew it. And he also knew the condition I was in. But that was his way of making a guy straighten up. It was really rough. I remember I had to lean against the riser on the bandstand just so I wouldn't fall down. I shook all the way through it.

"Talking about Fats Waller, when we were in Boston and he was playing at the Tic Toc Club, I'd meet him at eleven-thirty every night after we finished at the theater and sometimes we'd stay out until five or six in the morning. At the end of the week, Glenn looked at me and said, 'Junior, I didn't think you were going to make it.' "

Glenn's empathy for Bobby's drinking problem was doubtless bolstered by his respect for his unique musicianship. He seldom cracked down hard on Hackett, who, drunk or sober, managed always to retain his gentleness. On the other hand, according to Bobby, "When Glenn drank, which he didn't do very often, he went berserk. One night on stage he was in his cups, and I was laughing. He asked me what I was laughing at. I told him I wasn't laughing *at* him, I was laughing *with* him. Then he snapped at me, 'Do you wanna go back to work at Nick's down in Greenwich Village again?' And I snapped right back at him and I said, 'Why? You wanna go back with me?' "

Who knows, maybe Glenn would have liked just that. More than almost anything else, believes Hackett, "Glenn was a frustrated jazz player. I think he would have given all his money if he could have played trombone like Jack Teagarden.

"I don't believe too many guys realized what a sensitive man he really was beneath that exterior. Some musicians, I know, have put him down, but they do that with so many leaders. Sometimes they're just jealous of financial success.

"When I joined the band and I was making good money at last, some of the same people put me down, too. They accused me of selling out. Hell, I wasn't selling out; I was selling *in!* It's funny, isn't it, how you go right into the wastebasket with some critics the minute you become successful."

Chapter 27

❧❧ The pace had been grueling. For more than two years the band
❧❧ had been working steadily. The only days Glenn had taken off
had been those few at the beginning of March in 1940, which he
had spent in the hospital.

The band's first vacation was due to start following a two-day
engagement on July 25 and 26 at the Surf Beach Club in
Virginia Beach. It would last for nineteen days, and during that
time, in addition to playing some golf, Glenn had planned to
enter Johns Hopkins to try to get rid of a skin infection that was
so severe he wore gloves to protect—and to hide—his badly
irritated hands.

But the vacation never materialized. A July 27 letter from Don
Langan, the Newell-Emmett advertising agency's account execu-
tive, to Benjamin Few, vice-president in charge of advertising for
Chesterfields, tells why.

> Dear Mr. Few:
>
> I hope you get this note before Miller sees you Monday, as I
> feel the young man is due an explanation. When he got here
> Friday afternoon, I went to see him and found him terribly
> upset and worried over a message he'd received from New York.
> It was clear that an unfortunate misunderstanding had oc-
> curred, and when he was told that if he didn't do the
> Chesterfield programs from N.Y. "he would do no more," he
> got a bad case of shocked feelings.

The actual state of things was that he had made a *tentative* reservation at Johns Hopkins, upon advice of doctor, pending a talk with me here. Naturally, I knew about his illness but felt that everything would turn out all right as I guessed a bit of panic had been stirred up in him by the doctor and it wouldn't be too hard to persuade him to go to N.Y. on schedule and think things over a little further before taking action that would upset the routine.

His trouble is a skin infection that starts with a rash and develops into a form of a small blister that's dangerous to exposure. The stuff is all over his body, but much worse on his lower legs and feet, and when I saw him Friday his hands were swollen quite badly and his face in a "peel-y" state. You couldn't help feeling a bit sorry for him, with the physical discomfort and the injured feelings over the N.Y. message. Naturally, by the time I saw him, he was prepared to return to N.Y. immediately after this engagement, and, as he put it, do the program if he had to use stilts. He said that, because it is hard to stand on his feet, wear shoes, etc. . . . I think he felt that way because he works so hard to win Chesterfield friends on these personal trips, and he said, "You know yourself nothing means more to me than my radio programs."

And so, because of Chesterfield's pressures, Glenn canceled the big nineteen-day vacation. Instead, during the next three weeks the band took off four days at a time, working only the Tuesday, Wednesday, and Thursday broadcasts from New York. As Paul Tanner recently commented, "Even that much vacation was really a big deal for us."

When the band resumed its full-time work schedule on August 15, Glenn's rashes, eventually attributed to nothing more than a bad case of nerves, had disappeared, and something much prettier—Marion Hutton, back from her own, much longer vacation—had reappeared. But there was sad news, too. Pops, the Miller's cute Boston terrier, who for the last ten years had helped to fill their childless void, died. Both Glenn and Helen were devastated, and for once the usually taciturn and stoical "Klondike" didn't even try to hide his feelings. Amazing, but also sad, that a little pup could produce more of an overt emotional reaction from Glenn than almost anyone or anything else!

Always on Glenn's mind: the Chesterfield show. Jack Benny's Don Wilson announced some of the West Coast programs; the Modernaires, Marion Hutton, Tex Beneke and Ray Eberle were featured no matter where the show originated.

Glenn's depression wasn't helped by conditions outside the band world. His career continued to flourish. But his country's impending involvement in another World War depressed this patriotic American, born and raised in the country's isolationist heartland. President Roosevelt had already held what appeared to be an emergency meeting with Winston Churchill. Japan had been making threatening gestures. Congress had passed the draft extension bill, which meant that more and more young men, including many of Glenn's friends, would soon be going into service.

Bill Finegan pointed out that as the war clouds grew darker, Glenn grew more morose. "He had an honest concern about his country. I thought of him as The Sentimental Patriot." And he also had an honest concern for the welfare of his band. His keen business nose smelled the coming shortage of plastic materials. "So you know what he did," Tom Sheils, then working in the Miller office, recently related with admiration. "He sent me to Chicago to buy 250 Shastock mutes for the brass section, and then he stored them in a warehouse and sent for them as he needed them."

Clearly a man of patriotism and action, Glenn also began looking toward the needs of the men in our training camps. He inaugurated a radio series called *Sunset Serenade*, dedicated to those in service. For each program he selected five camps, which were asked to conduct polls for their favorite songs. The five (less, if there was duplication) would be played on the air; listeners would be asked to vote for their favorites, and the camp that had proposed the winning song would be awarded a combination radio-phonograph. In addition, each camp would receive fifty recordings—and they wouldn't all be by the Miller band, either.

The first of these programs emanated from the Steel Pier in Atlantic City, where Glenn, apparently unbeknownst to him, had been booked for the weekend preceding Labor Day—an engagement that bewildered George Hamid, owner of the competing Million Dollar Pier, who had hired the band regularly, even before it had become fashionable to do so.

Hamid's son, George, Jr., who later took over the enterprises, told me recently about that weird weekend:

Marion, Glenn, Willie, Al, Moe, Tex, Ernie, Bobby, Ray and Billy check the Men of Lowry Field's selection—for the publicity man, of course.

"We were terribly hurt that Glenn had decided to play the bigger Steel Pier. We knew they could pay him more than we could, but we figured he would be loyal to us because we had hired him even before he was well known, and Glenn was always known to be loyal to his friends.

"We lived in a house on the side of our pier, and who should show up late in the afternoon of the day Glenn was to play the Steel Pier but Glenn himself. He had been at our house before, whenever he played our pier. He walked in and said 'Hello' to us all and sat down. He told us he was terribly tired and just wanted to rest a bit.

"Well, Dad didn't know quite how to take this. Here is Glenn, playing for the opposition, but coming to us first just to rest and relax. Finally, Dad asked him why he had gone over to the other side. Glenn was flabbergasted. He had taken it for granted that he was playing our pier again and had just dropped by, as he always had done, to visit. When he realized that Mike Nidorf had booked him into the Steel Pier, he was furious. Of course he had to go through with the date, but to show you the kind of a man Glenn was, he told my father, 'Look, I'm going to make this

up to you. Next year, instead of just one, I'll give you two dates!'
And he kept his word, too. In the summer of 1942 the Glenn
Miller band played our pier twice, and I don't think he ever did
that for any other promoter. In our books, Glenn Miller was a
very decent and honorable man.''

In the fall of 1941, band business was booming. The New York
area alone looked like the Hollywood studios of a few months
ago. When Glenn opened for the third time in the Cafe Rouge of
the Hotel Pennsylvania on October 6, he was competing with at
least twenty top bands within the metropolitan area. Just look at
this lineup:

> Mitchell Ayres—Blue Gardens
> Blue Barron—Hotel Edison
> Count Basie—Cafe Society Uptown
> Tommy Dorsey—Meadowbrook
> Eddy Duchin—Hotel Waldorf-Astoria
> Benny Goodman—Hotel New Yorker
> Harry James—Hotel Lincoln
> Art Jarrett—Hotel Biltmore
> Sammy Kaye—Essex House
> Ray Kinney—Hotel Lexington
> Andy Kirk—Famous Door
> Little Jack Little—Pelham Heath Inn
> Guy Lombardo—Hotel Roosevelt
> Vincent Lopez—Hotel Taft
> Johnny Messner—Hotel McAlpin
> Vaughn Monroe—Hotel Commodore
> Teddy Powell—Rustic Cabin
> Muggsy Spanier—Arcadia Ballroom
> Claude Thornhill—Glen Island Casino
> Tommy Tucker—Colonial Inn

In addition, name bands were playing in theaters like the
Paramount, Strand, Loew's State, Apollo and Capitol, and
ballrooms like Roseland, the Savoy and the Golden Gate. And
throughout the country, hundreds more, all well known to the
millions of kids who idolized them, were filling ballrooms, hotel
rooms, theaters and college gyms. And of all those hundreds, the
one leader the kids idolized most of all was Glenn Miller.

Such fame brought intense pressures. In addition to his

backbreaking schedule, he was constantly being harried to appear here and there, to do this very special thing for that very old friend, and to grant personal interviews to everyone from *Time* magazine to the editor of *P.S. 162 News*. And unlike other leaders who couldn't or wouldn't take their careers and public as seriously, Glenn remained dedicated to what he recognized as his responsibilities to his friends and his public.

He unburdened himself to me one evening: "I really don't know quite how to handle all this. Sometimes I feel like I'm acting like a real phony. But I can't help it. So many people are asking me to do so many things—and I really want to do some of them—but I just literally don't have the time. It's murder. I find myself doing things I'm ashamed of doing, like making up stories just so I won't hurt people's feelings. *You* know I don't like to do that. But *I* know that most people wouldn't understand if I told them just the plain, simple truth! I just don't have the time. I guess in my position I can no longer be the kind of a guy I really want to be."

To relieve the burden somewhat, Glenn decided to take on a full-time manager, someone who could take care not only of his own band's business, but also that of the two he had already launched and the third which he was about to launch. And so he turned to the handsome young man who had been doing such a good job for him at GAC as a booker and for Polly Haynes as a husband.

"I joined at the Pennsylvania," Don Haynes recalled. "And I think the reason Glenn liked me was because I never interfered with the band."

Don was a bit too modest. Glenn liked him because he knew his job and did it well, and because he knew how to treat people, including Glenn. A natural salesman, with years of experience in the band field, he could be counted upon to anticipate and then take care of details. And he was shrewd enough never to push Glenn, but to glide along with him in a strong, supportive role. Probably no one, including Cy Shribman and Mike Nidorf, ever worked so closely and so well with Glenn as Don did.

Of course, there were other ties. There was his wife, Polly, Glenn's secretary and Helen's closest friend. The Hayneses and the Millers often spent what little leisure time they had together.

Don and Glenn at Pinehurst's ninth hole, immortalized by Glenn's shot.

And then, too, Don was a good golfer. He was there the day that Glenn shot his hole-in-one in Pinehurst, North Carolina. Such occasions somehow sharpen friendships.

With a full-time associate to watch over the business, Glenn expanded his outside activities even more. He had already become involved with the new bands of two other close friends, Charlie Spivak and Claude Thornhill. Now he was about to launch a third, and Don would be a big help.

Hal McIntyre's wife, June, says that Glenn had been promising Hal his own band for quite some time. One night he broke the news quite dramatically. "Mac," he said, "you're fired. You're on your own. You're going to have your band, and I want you to be ready in two weeks."

According to June, Hal didn't sleep for two weeks. "I had to massage his back every night, he was so nervous." Apparently the massages worked, because Hal organized his band quickly and went out on the road—up to New England to work the same Shribman circuit that the Miller band had played three years earlier.

Hal's band was a good one—though, like Glenn's, it suffered from a weak rhythm section. But it did have some interesting arrangements by Howard Gibeling and later by Dave Matthews, who wrote in an Ellington vein. And Glenn presented Hal with about forty of his own band's arrangements which he seldom played because they didn't fit neatly enough into the Miller mold. Included were a few of Billy May's charming originals, most notably his delightfully swinging "Daisy Mae," which McIntyre later recorded for RCA Victor.

The Miller-McIntyre band relationship, though stemming from friendship, was strictly business. Glenn had signed the band with the William Morris Agency, which at the time, trying to wean Glenn away from GAC, agreed to give him one-third of the agency's 10 percent booking commission. In addition, the Miller office also collected a managerial fee for Glenn's and Don's and Polly's and very possibly Helen's (on paper, at least) services. It turned out to be quite an incestuous investment.

The day after Hal left, another Miller alumnus started his band. Ray Anthony had returned to Al Donahue, then had dug

Glenn speeds the departing Hal McIntyre.

up enough financial support to form his own group. Both bands, thanks in part to their leaders' apprenticeships with Glenn, turned out to be very good musically. Each reflected the personality of its leader. Ray's was more intense and eventually became more commercial. Hal's was loose and easygoing and musically more inventive. But Hal never had Ray's drive, and though he worked many of the top spots, thanks to Don's connections, he was never more than moderately successful.

McIntyre's lead sax chair in the Miller band was filled briefly by Ben Feman, a wonderfully free-phrasing lead saxist whom I'd always admired in Larry Clinton's band but whom Glenn obviously didn't like as much.

Ben lasted a little over a month, and then Glenn made an interesting move. He switched his favorite hot tenor man, Tex Beneke, to the lead chair, where he played alto instead of tenor sax, and brought in an old pal with whom he had played way back in the Red Nichols days, Babe Russin, to blow Beneke's book. Babe had been leading his own band, with very little success, after stints with Tommy Dorsey and Benny Goodman, and he proceeded to contribute some great jazz excitement to Miller's. However, his stay was even shorter-lived than Feman's. Nobody ever did find out whether it was because Babe was unhappy with the band or Tex was unhappy playing alto, but, in any case, Russin left to start yet another group. And so Glenn engineered a swap with his old pal Goodman. In return for lead saxist Skip Martin, who also arranged and whose gutsy tone gave the sax team a virility it had never known before, Glenn gave his old roomie lead trumpeter Alec Fila, who reported to Goodman with a bad lip. "Swap a flop for Benny," reported *Metronome*. With Fila gone, Bobby Hackett left the rhythm section and joined the trumpets, while Bill Conway moved from the midst of the Modernaires to play guitar. The band was becoming more and more involved in its own game of musical chairs.

And shortly after the start of its third engagement at the Cafe Rouge it also became involved in a squabble with the management of the Hotel Pennsylvania.

On October 4 Glenn had inaugurated a series of Saturday afternoon *Sunset Serenade* broadcasts from the Cafe Rouge, admission to which was paid by the kids in U.S. savings stamps, which Glenn, in another move to aid the morale of our troops, donated to the USO. In addition, he kept sending records and radio-phonograph combinations to the various service camps.

The sessions became such huge successes that complications soon set in. As *Variety* pointed out:

> Glenn Miller and executives of the Pennsylvania are to huddle this week to set a limit on the number of admissions to Miller's Saturday afternoon USO benefit concerts. Hotel is objecting to the increasing mobs the sessions are drawing, pointing out that furniture and other appointments in the room are being mishandled and the returns to the hotel itself don't square up. . . .
>
> Past week for instance Miller played to 1,340 people in a room that normally seats up to about 400 patrons but can close up tables' ranks to handle 625. This meant that guards had to be stationed around the bandstand to keep crowd at safe distance.

Saturday, October 4

AM

A.M.	WEAF	WOR 710k	WJZ 770k	WABC
8:00	(faded)	News; P. Robinson	European News	The World Today
8:15	Richard Leibert	Songs; Danny Dee	Rendezvous	Music; beauty
8:30	"	Talk; music; talk	Texas Jim	Missus Goes Shopping
8:45	News	Talks	String Ensemble; news	Adelaide Hawley
9:00	Deep River Boys	'Dear Imogene'	Breakfast Club:	George Bryan, news
9:15	Isabel M. Hewson	Medical Talk	Don McNeill, orch.	Melodic Moments
9:30	Lawson's Knights	News; music	"	'Old Dirt Dobber,'
9:45	"	News; Ed Fitzgerald	"	Tom Williams
10:00	Don Carper Quartet	Rainbow House,	Andrini Trio	'Jones and I,'
10:15	Happy Jack Turner	with Bob Emery	Cadets Quartet	Sammie Hill
10:30	'America, the Free':	"	Four Polka Dots	'Gold It You Find It,'
10:45	"	"	Rose Lee, songs	Treasure Hunt
11:00	'Lincoln Highway,'	News, P. Robinson	Rex Maupin's Orch.	News; Burl Ives
11:15	guest	Jimmy Shields, tenor	"	Coffee Club
11:30	Vaudeville Theater:	U.S. Army Band	Children's 'Our Barn':	Dorothy Kilgallen
11:45	Jim Ameche	"	Madge Tucker	Hillbilly Champions

AFTERNOON PROGRAMS

Time	WEAF	WOR	WJZ	WABC
Noon	News, Don Goddard	'Man on the Farm'	Indiana Indigo	'Theater of Today':
12:15	Consumer Time	"	Howard Ropa, songs	Elissa Landi
12:30	Dr. Alfred G. Walton	News, Alois Havrilla	Farm and Homes	Stars Over Hollywood:
12:45	Matinee in Rhythm	Happy Jim Parsons	4-H Club	Drama
1:00	"	Music	"	Nila Mack's 'Let's Pre-
1:15	From New England	World Series	"	tend,' for children
1:30	to You	Baseball Game	Vincent Lopez's Orch.	Buffalo Serenade
1:45	News; Defense Bonds	"	Football Game:	Football Game
2:00	Campus Capers	"	Pittsburgh vs.	"
2:15	Football Game:	"	Purdue	"
2:30	Notre Dame vs.	"	"	"
2:45	Indiana University	"	"	"
3:00	"	"	"	"
3:15	"	"	"	"
3:30	"	"	"	"
3:45	"	"	"	"
4:00	"	Waite Hoyt	"	"
4:15	"	Teddy Powell's Orch.	"	"
4:30	"	Blue Barron's Orch	...of Americas	be announced
4:45	"	"	"	Symphonettes
5:00	Weekend Whimsy	Mel Marvin's O...	Glenn Miller's Sunset	Benny Goodman's
5:15	Brad Reynolds	"	Serenade	Orchestra
5:30	Juliette Chauteaups	McFarland Twins	"	"
5:45	Desi Halban, songs	"	"	Sports, 5:55

EVENING PROGRAMS

Time	WEAF	WOR	WJZ	WABC
6:00	Rhythmaires; music	Uncle Don;	News; Music; Carmen	Calling Pan-America
6:15	News, Robert St. John	program preview	Cavallero's Orch.	"
6:30	Walter Van Kirk	News; F. Singiser	'Lum and Abner'	Elmer Davis, news
6:45	Frankie Frisch	Here's Morgan	Edward Tomlinson	The World Today
7:00	Defense for America:	Sports, Stan Lomax	Message of Israel:	The People's Platform:
7:15	speakers	Chester's Orch.; sports	Speaker	Lyman Bryson
7:30	Symphony in Rhythm	Confidentially Yours	Little Ol' Hollywood	Concert Orchestra:
7:45	H. V. Kaltenborn	Inside of Sports	"	Howard Barlow
8:00	Knickerbocker	'Green Hornet'	'Boy Meets Band':	Guy Lombardo's Orch.
8:15	Playhouse	"	Ted Steele	"
8:30	Truth or Consequences	'To the Victors,'	'Bishop and Gargoyle'	Hobby Lobby
8:45	Ralph Edwards	Football Quiz	"	Elmer Davis, news 8:55
9:00	National Barn Dance:	Gabriel Heatter	Spin and Win,	Your Hit Parade:
9:15	Eddie Peabody,	Red Barber, sports	Jimmy Flynn	Mark Warnow's
9:30	Lulu Belle	'America Preferred,'	Concert Orchestra,	Orchestra
9:45	"	Gregor Piatigorski	Dr. Frank Black	Battle of Boroughs
10:00	Bill Stern, Sports	Chicago Theater:	Hemisphere Revue:	"
10:15	Rex Maupin's Orch	'The Merry Widow'	Paul Laval's Orch.	Sen. D. Worth Clark
10:30	'Hot Copy,' Drama	Marion Claire,	Gordon Jenkins' Orch.	Bob Hanson, songs
10:45	"	Alan Jones	"	Mark Hawley, news
11:00	News, George Putnam	News; weather	News; Jan Garber's	Harry James' Orch.
11:15	Tune Toppers	Sports; Barrie's Orch.	Orchestra	"
11:30	Riverboat Revels	California Melodies,	Art Jarrett's Orch.	VaughnMonroe'sOrch.
11:45	"	Dave Rose's Orch	"	"

The New York *Herald Tribune* radio log for the opening date of Miller's *Sunset Serenade* series. Note the number of bands that played direct from their locations during afternoons, just to garner the valuable air exposure. WEAF (now WNBC), WJZ (now WABC) and WABC (now WCBS) continued to broadcast bands until one o'clock each morning; WOR hung around until 2:00 A.M.

Precursors of the rock-concert audiences of the sixties and seventies? Could be. What the article didn't mention was that much of the griping came from the room's waiters. The kids would pay their quarter or half a buck in savings stamps and just sit there and listen, and order nothing. And even when they did, they left practically no tips.

Nobody made out well financially. In fact, *Down Beat* magazine figured each concert cost Glenn about $1,000, because he

One of the radio-phonographs which Glenn paid for and presented each week to an armed forces services camp. In June 1942 he listed $7,000 worth of these sets among his assets.

paid out of his own pocket for all the records he sent out—"Miller buys the records from Macy's store here just like anyone else would," the publication reported—as well as for the radio-phonographs. But, as all of us close to him began to realize, Glenn was growing increasingly, almost alarmingly, concerned about the possibility of U.S. involvement in the war. And, as events were to prove a few weeks later, that concern was amply justified.

Chapter 28

The major outdoor recreation for most of the big bands was softball. Many were proud of their teams and would boast about their victories. At one time Tommy Dorsey, whose star slugger turned out to be an out-of-shape Bunny Berigan who could stretch every triple into a double or even into a single, hired as team coach the famed pitcher Grover Cleveland Alexander, who trained on the same liquids that Bunny did. The star pitcher on Count Basie's team was star tenor saxist Lester Young. Harry James pitched and hit homers for Benny Goodman's team and then, after he had organized his own band, interrupted numerous one-nighter jumps with impromptu ball games on roadside fields.

But the Miller band had little time for such fun. Rehearsals were much more important to Glenn. Perhaps, if he had let up a bit in his infernal quest for perfection, his band might have been happier and looser and more swinging.

The sad part of it was that Glenn loved athletics. He had been an outstanding end on his high school football team. Later he had taken up tennis, and finally he had become addicted to golf. He played the way he worked, always with intense fervor, as though everything in "The Game of Life"—golf, tennis, bridge, poker, ping-pong, craps and even leading a band—existed not for fun but purely for winning.

He remained an avid sports enthusiast. He loved to watch football. Dan Topping, Sonja Henie's husband, with whom

RIGHT: Softball enthusiast Harry James (right) loses to announcer Mel Allen for "last-ups."

BELOW: Ebbets Field, Brooklyn, U.S.A.

Glenn had been friendly during the *Sun Valley Serenade* days, had become part owner of the new Brooklyn Dodgers football team. To boost attendance, he hired the Miller band to play in Ebbets Field. Less than two weeks after the baseball Dodgers' Mickey Owens had dropped the famous third strike that led to a New York Yankees' World Series victory, the Miller band, in that very stadium, was regaling 12,000 Dodgers football fans from a special platform right smack on the fifty-yard line. For the sports-frustrated Miller it was a thrilling occasion. For most of the musicians it was a novelty. For a few, who'd much rather have been at Charlie's Tavern, it was just one big bore.

While at the Cafe Rouge, the band traveled down to Victor's recording studios on East Twenty-fourth Street to cut several more sides. Most famous and successful turned out to be Jerry Gray's "String of Pearls," with its marvelous Bobby Hackett solo. Naturally, Jerry was delighted with the results. "But you know what," he once told me, "I liked Benny Goodman's arrangement better than mine. I used to go over to the New Yorker where Benny was playing just to hear it."

On December 8, the day after the Japanese struck Pearl Harbor, the band recorded six more sides. One of these was another Gray original, which the band had been broadcasting under the title of "That's Where I Came In." But Glenn's patriotism changed that. Since band instrumentals seldom have lyrics (unless they become big hits, after which lyrics sometimes may be added), they can be titled just about anything. I remember once at a Bob Crosby recording session, when they didn't know what to call an original instrumental, I punningly suggested a non-sequitur, "Three Cent Stomp," as a title. And they used it, too. But Glenn pinned a *real* sequitur on Jerry's new instrumental. As a salute to the air force, which at that time he never knew he'd be joining, he retitled the number "Keep 'Em Flying."

Glenn, increasingly conscious of his broad responsibilities as the country's Number One Band Leader, assumed the chairmanship of the Dance Band Leaders' portion of the Infantile Paralysis Fund and recorded a special number, "At the President's Ball," contributing all his royalties to the fund.

Late in October of 1941, ASCAP and the radio networks finally reached an agreement, and for the first time the band could play "Chattanooga Choo Choo" on the air. On one *Sunset Serenade* show, all five service camps picked it. The listeners did too. So Glenn wound up donating radio-phonographs to all five camps. The show was becoming an expensive patriotic display.

"Chattanooga Choo Choo" became the first one-million record-seller in almost fifteen years—since Gene Austin's big hit "My Blue Heaven." (It grew so popular that Woody Herman even recorded a takeoff. He called it "Ooch Ooch Agoonattach." His train ran backward.) To commemorate Glenn's feat, RCA Victor produced and presented him with a gold record. Later the Record Industry Association of America picked up the idea and began awarding official Gold Records to artists who had sold a million copies of a recording.

The Miller career continued to flourish. Chesterfield again renewed his show. His final week at the Cafe Rouge in January netted him $3,582.63. For the fourteen-week engagement he had earned $41,750.03! Not bad for a band leader who less than three years earlier would gladly have worked the room *at a loss* just to get all that valuable air-time.

He broke records in Detroit and Toronto theaters (in Detroit he netted himself $21,693 for the week!), then returned once more to the New York Paramount, where he racked up gigantic weekly grosses of $73,000, $52,000 and $42,000.

Barry Ulanov's *Metronome* review of the Paramount show began by calling Miller "an institution on the stage of the Paramount Theatre. He devoted this show to a resume of the reasons why he is such an institution."

Then, after listing a slew of numbers the band played, Ulanov continued:

> "A String of Pearls" was certainly the musical high spot of the show. Duets between altoists Skippy Martin and Ernie Caceres and tenorists Al Klink and Tex Beneke were easy to listen to and smart showmanship. Bobby Hackett's brief cornet piece was neatly essayed and the intermittent bars of MacGregor's piano were effective.

Chesterfield announcer Paul Douglas watches as RCA Victor's Wally Early presents Glenn with a gold-plated recording of "Chattanooga Choo Choo."

Effective is the word, too, for the effervescent delivery of Marion Hutton in "Sun Valley," and the running entrances and exits of the Modernaires, who pranced around as if they were at a party of kindergarten kids. The audience ate it up.

When Glenn announced "Chattanooga Choo Choo," with a retreating train on the big back-drop, the audience roared. When it was over, and the band was dropping into the pit, the audience roared again. This deftly delivered presentation proved again what a fabulously successful formula Glenn Miller has uncovered for the care and feeding of the musical tastes of our time. A pretty gal, a suave saxophone voicing and military precision in the execution of scores, in the waving of instruments in the air, and the cueing of entrees and sorties, have combined to make this band the Rockettes of popular music.

He again won the Martin Block poll, despite the fact that his three leading competitors all had big hit records: Tommy Dorsey with "This Love of Mine" featuring Frank Sinatra and "Embraceable You" featuring Jo Stafford; Harry James with "You Made Me Love You" and "I Don't Want to Walk Without You" with the famous Helen Forrest vocal; and fourth-place Jimmy

Dorsey with all those Bob Eberly–Helen O'Connell duets on tunes like "Green Eyes," "Amapola," and "Tangerine."

Musically, he had strengthened the band by hiring powerful lead trumpeter Steve Lipkins away from Artie Shaw, with Bobby Hackett, who was not a very powerful section man, returning to his dual role of featured cornetist and unfeatured guitarist.

But, despite the sort of success that would bring serenity to almost any other leader, Glenn was growing even more restless. During the Paramount engagement he kept telling me and others that he wanted to get even more involved in the war effort. Then, just before he closed at the theater on February 15, he made a move that might have seemed merely academic: He registered for the draft with Local Board #7 in Bergen County, New Jersey. Married and too old (almost thirty-seven) to be called up, Glenn nevertheless was beginning to make plans to enter the armed services—his way.

Chapter 29

The March 1942 edition of one of the Glenn Miller fan-club bulletins stated that "the band took off for four days after closing at the Paramount with the following results: Ray Eberle spent most of his time at Glen Island with Hal McIntyre, who, by the way, did a swell job pinch-hitting for Glenn on *Sunset Serenade*. Modernaire Ralph Brewster to the dentist, ouch! Doc Goldberg to his namesake for medical attention. Marion Hutton to the dress-maker. Tex Beneke to the famous Choo Choo country and back by train and plane. Miller himself to Pinehurst, N.C., where he whacked a mighty 3 iron shot into the wind and wound up with a hole-in-one. Wow! Whatta vacation!"

The enthusiasm of those Miller fan clubs was immense. Back in February of 1940, when the Chesterfield series had just started, there were sixty-four such clubs. By 1943, 524 Glenn Miller Fan Clubs, some with over 500 members, others with just one or two, were alive and well in Arkansas, California, Connecticut, Florida, Georgia, Illinois, Indiana, Maryland, Massachusetts, Minnesota, Missouri, Nebraska, New Jersey, New Mexico, New York, Ohio, Pennsylvania, Rhode Island, Tennessee, Utah, Virginia, and Wisconsin, and even in Windsor, Ontario, and in England. They were constantly writing Glenn letters, full of gushy mush and hysterical praise, all dutifully answered by Polly Haynes and her staff of eight, most of them involved in nothing else except replying to the barrage of bobby-sox mail.

Fans at the Meadowbrook in Cedar Grove, New Jersey, and at the railroad
station in Omaha, Nebraska.

At Loew's Capitol Theatre in Washington, Glenn ran into a problem: He temporarily lost Chummy MacGregor. The band was ready to start its stage show, but, for the first time, the utterly reliable MacGregor was not around. He had said, after the previous show, that he was going out front to watch the movie, but the movie had long since ended. And so, with mock seriousness, Glenn announced that the band was missing a piano player, and he asked each of the patrons to look at the person sitting on either side of him, and, if anyone found a sleeping piano player, to please wake him up. It so happened that Chummy wasn't even in the theater. He'd gone to see a doctor instead, and anybody who's ever visited a doctor's office knows what that can do to a tight schedule elsewhere.

Glenn took an arranger from Sonny Dunham's band, saw his Chesterfield shows rescheduled, and began a big fight with his booking agency before embarking for Hollywood and another movie.

The arranger was George "The Fox" Williams, who later wrote for Gene Krupa and Jackie Gleason, and whom Glenn added as extra protection for his forthcoming picture. The new broadcast schedule substituted a Friday night show for the Tuesday night stint because the eternally popular Bob Hope had been scheduled for the same Tuesday time slot, and Chesterfield didn't feel like competing with him. A couple of months later the schedule was revamped again. Tuesday was restored, but all three shows were shifted to a much earlier time, 7:15 P.M., a move calculated to attract even more of the younger audience.

As for the booking agency fight, Glenn felt that now that he had become so firmly established, the agency's work had been greatly reduced and it no longer deserved the 15 percent commission it was getting. And so he tried to take advantage of a New York State employment agency law that limited commissions to just 5 percent. To show he meant business, he refused to remit more than 5 percent to the agency, whereupon GAC countered by holding back monies it had collected for him. The agency complained to the musicians' union, which ruled in its favor.

In another try at establishing himself as a totally independent businessman, Glenn tried to circumvent the agency by letting Don Haynes do his bookings, but here again he was thwarted by the union's ruling in GAC's favor.

On March 17 the band arrived by train in Hollywood, and six days later it began work on its second movie, *Orchestra Wives*, which again incorporated Glenn and the band right into the plot instead of merely using them for musical dressing.

The movie moguls were still on a big-band kick. One of Glenn's golfing buddies, Sammy Kaye, in Hollywood at the same time to film *Iceland*, also at Twentieth Century-Fox, never forgot the gag that Glenn pulled on him. "We had recorded our sound track and we were about to film the sequence that went with our theme song. You know how they do those things. You record first, and then you try to match your actions to the music. They give you three clicks on the sound track and then you start with the cameras. Well, the three clicks came along all right and I gave the down beat for our theme. But guess what came out of the sound track—not our theme, but Glenn's theme, 'Moonlight Serenade'! He'd gotten to the guys in the booth to switch the tracks. And you know what I did? I just kept on going. What was I supposed to do? I didn't know. It was the first time I'd even been in front of a camera."

Glenn's movie dwelt on band musicians and their wives, focusing on some bickering that almost tore the fictional band apart. George Montgomery played the trumpet-playing hero, but Johnny Best played the trumpet. Cesar Romero played the role of the band's pianist, with Chummy MacGregor providing his fingers. And Jackie Gleason mugged as the band's bass player, with audio assistance from Doc Goldberg, though "The Great One's" acting failed to draw even a single word of recognition in the all-important *Variety* review.

Ann Rutherford was the heroine, and Lynn Bari and Carole Landis also played feminine leads. Again the Nicholas Brothers danced, and again Mack Gordon and Harry Warren provided a memorable musical score that included such big Miller hits as "At Last," "Serenade in Blue," and "I've Got a Gal in Kalamazoo."

Scenes from *Orchestra Wives*: Glenn keeps Bullets Durgom from falling for Marion Hutton; Jackie Gleason mugs the way a movie director thinks all bass players mug; Lynn Bari, Glenn, George Montgomery, Cesar Romero and Gleason play a scene in front of the band.

Leaders Harry James, Glenn Miller and Sammy Kaye sandwich songwriters Mack Gordon and Harry Warren during movie-making time on the Twentieth Century–Fox lot. Note the original singularity of *Orchestra Wives*.

Though the Miller band was never torn apart by wifely bickerings, it did have its share of strong-willed spouses. The inner circle consisted of Helen Miller, Janet Eberle (who was often her bridge partner), Marguerite Beneke, Bunny Tanner, June McIntyre and Polly Haynes, by far the most easygoing, who has described herself as "the buffer in the band."

June, whose son, Hal, Jr., now leads his own orchestra, recalls that Helen Miller was just as hard-nosed as Glenn. "When the band went on the road, I often moved in with Helen. Most of the time, she and Glenn got along real well, but I do remember one running argument they had that must have gone on for ten years. And I was there the night it all came to a head and they really exploded at each other. And you know what they'd been arguing about all those years? Whether the toilet paper should drop down from the front or from the back of the roll!"

Polly Haynes has often noted how remarkable it was that two such strong-willed people as Helen and Glenn Miller did get

Three strong-willed people get together: Mattie, Glenn and Helen Miller.

along so well. "I've never known a better-adjusted couple. They both liked to have their own way, but they always supported one another, except, of course, when Glenn and I would play against Helen and Don in our regular bridge games. They wouldn't play together because, if they did, they would argue too much. But I can remember only one *big* fight they ever had and that was one night at a party in the penthouse of the Hotel New Yorker. The couple giving the party had a very little baby, and when Helen walked into the kitchen she discovered they were about to feed the baby its baby food right out of the refrigerator, without even heating it. So she went to Glenn for help, as she so often did, and asked him to please talk to the host or hostess and get them to heat the food before they gave it to the baby. When Glenn said he couldn't do that because, after all, they were guests, Helen got very angry, and finally they got into such a fight that it broke up the party and Don had to drive Helen home while Glenn drove me home.

"Helen was always caring and worrying about other people, but, you know, I think she might have had a little too much champagne that night and carried that worrying business just a bit too far."

Some of the Glenn Miller band wives, like Helen and Polly and Bunny Tanner and June McIntyre, played strong supportive roles for their husbands. Others went even further. Janet Eberle handled all of Ray's finances, especially in later years when he led his own band. Kay Finegan was constantly overseeing Bill's work, egging him on to try to meet deadlines that always seemed to be eluding him. And Marguerite Beneke took on such a domineering role in Tex's career that she actually alienated people who loved him for the wonderful guy he was and not for the gigantic success she wanted him to be.

After Marion Hutton returned to the band, Paula Kelly (Mrs. Hal Dickenson) stopped singing and concentrated on the role of an orchestra wife. Recently, on a Merv Griffin TV show, she was asked how true a picture was drawn in *Orchestra Wives*. "It was a lot of boloney!" she retorted.

It took nine weeks to finish Paula's boloney. Except for its Chesterfield shows and a few recording dates, the band did little

The *real* Orchestra Wives on the lot during the filming. Top row (left to right): Hal McIntyre's June, Johnny Best's Helen, Jack Lathrop's Barbara, Chuck Goldstein's Ruth, Tex Beneke's Marguerite, Paul Tanner's Bunny, Mickey McMickle's Dorothy. Bottom row: Charlie Grean's (he was band's music copyist) Ginny, Jimmy Priddy's Betty, romantic lead John Payne, Al Klink's Pat, Ralph Brewster's Marie.

other playing during that period. Glenn welcomed the chance to start working on the fifty-five acre ranch he had bought at 2921 Fish Canyon Road in nearby Monrovia—an investment he soon began to use as an excuse for being short of cash when hit by requests for loans from numerous "old friends" he never knew he had.

Naturally, the Palladium wanted Glenn to play there. But "The Great Unpleasantness of 1941," plus an inability to agree on terms, kept the band out of the big dance hall, except for an April 15 Military Ball for the benefit of a local army hospital that drew 7,300 customers!

The lighter schedule also gave Glenn a chance to hear some other music. Bobby Hackett reports that "when we were making *Orchestra Wives*, I used to go to hear Louis [Armstrong] every night, and usually stayed up most of the night, too. Late one night I caught Glenn coming out of a corner of the room. 'You too?' I said, and he simply said, 'That's the greatest thing that ever happened to music!' "

The band did put in a couple of appearances at Victor's West Coast studio. In April it recorded yet another patriotic piece, Jerry Gray's arrangement of "American Patrol," complete with its flag-waving sounds, and then in May it waxed three more tunes from *Orchestra Wives*: "I've Got a Gal in Kalamazoo," "At Last" and one of the loveliest of all Miller recordings, "Serenade in Blue," featuring an introduction that's one of the most gorgeous passages ever played by any band. According to Johnny Best, Bill Finegan had stayed up all night, trying to carry out Glenn's idea for an ethereal, impressionistic and rather lengthy introduction. But the hung-up Finegan couldn't come up with anything that pleased Glenn. "And so," reports Best, "Glenn turned it over to Billy May and in thirty minutes he came up with what Glenn wanted!"

Just before the band left Hollywood, on the night it had completed the picture, Glenn threw a big party for the entire cast and crew at the Beverly Wilshire Hotel. It was a wing-ding of an affair, one of the few times everyone could get together with no holds barred and all bars open.

Johnny O'Leary recalls that just about everyone had a ball—except, perhaps, Chummy MacGregor, who "idolized Glenn. He was always watching out for him and he looked after Glenn's money as if it were his own and he was convinced the party was just a waste of Glenn's money."

After the party, the grind began all over again as the band returned to the road. In Kansas City it played the biggest one-nighter in both the city's and the band's history. Glenn's take for the one night: $5,616.31. And in the first four nights on the road Glenn collected a total of nearly $14,000, more than ten times as much as he had been grossing for a full week just a little over three years ago!

Chapter 30

 It was a big secret. Not too many people even know about it today. But on June 20 Glenn Miller submitted a formal application to the commandant in the Ninth Naval District for a commission in the U.S. Naval Reserve. With it, he sent along a resume of his business and professional experience, references and an estimate of his financial worth.

One of the references came from Bing Crosby, who wrote: "It is a great privilege for me to make the recommendation for whatever it is worth, as in the many years I've known Mr. Miller, I've found him to be a very high type young man, full of resourcefulness, adequately intelligent and a suitable type to command men or assist in organization."

Glenn himself supplied his financial worth as follows:

Cash on hand	$165,000.00
U.S. Government bonds	63,000.00
California ranch	75,000.00
Automobiles and office furniture and	
fixtures (depreciated)	5,000.00
Loans receivable	11,000.00
Residence furniture (depreciated)	8,000.00
Equity in insurances	10,000.00
New radio sets in storage	7,000.00
	$344,000.00

Paid-up annuity for $75,000.00 excluded because income therefrom assigned to others.

June 22, 1942

To Whom It May Concern:

Mr. Glenn Miller advises me
that there's a possibility of his being
selected for training, with the ultimate
result a commission in the United States
Navy, and that he is desirous of securing
letters of recommendation from friends
of his that might be of some value.

It is a great privilege for
me to make this recommendation for whatever it is worth, as in the many years
I've known Mr. Miller I've found him to
be a very high type young man, full of
resourcefulness, adequately intelligent
and a suitable type to command men or
assist in organization.

Bing Crosby

BC:rc

David Mackay, after having seen these figures, recently
commented, "Glenn certainly did underestimate his worth by a
lot!" Could have been, of course, that he didn't feel like sharing
all his secrets with the navy or with the IRS.

Glenn also summarized his entire career for the navy, as shown
in the résumé on the next page.

Glenn also began to arrange for contingencies in case he
suddenly was accepted. He entered into a new employment
contract with Tex Beneke, guaranteeing him $200 a week for the
first year and $150 a week for the next two years, plus a $10,000
bonus to be paid on February 14, 1945.

Now that Glenn had made his move and applied for his
commission, all he could do was wait for others to make up their
minds. Since he was a forceful, dogmatic person who wanted

GLENN MILLER ORCHESTRA

<u>BUSINESS</u> AND PROFESSIONAL EXPERIENCE

① 1937 to PRESENT TIME

Employed By SELF AS DIRECTOR OF MY ORCHESTRA.

② 1935 to 1937

Employed By RAY NOBLE (ORCHESTRA LEADER) AS
TROMBONIST AND ARRANGER.

③ 1934 To 1935

Employed By The DORSEY BROTHERS ORCHESTRA AS
TROMBONIST AND ARRANGER.

④ 1932 To 1934

Employed By Smith Ballew (ORCHESTRA LEADER)
AS TROMBONIST, ARRANGER AND BUSINESS MANAGER.

⑤ 1930 To 1932

Employed By VARIOUS AND NUMEROUS PERSONS
To PERFORM IN A MUSICAL CAPACITY (KNOWN AS
FREE LANCE WORK)

⑥ 1929 To 1930

Employed By RED Nichol's (ORCHESTRA LEADER)
AS TROMBONIST AND ARRANGER

(OVER)

N. J. OFFICE
COTSWOLD-BYRNE LANE
TENAFLY, N. J.

N. Y. OFFICE
R K O BLDG.
NEW YORK CITY

⑦ 1928 - 1929   FREE LANCED AS MUSICIAN

⑧ 1924 - 1928

Employed By BEN Pollack (ORCHESTRA LEADER)
AS TROMBONIST AND ARRANGER.

⑨ PRIOR to 1924   FREE LANCED AS MUSICIAN AFTER LEAVING
University OF COLORADO.

Ray and Glenn before the misunderstanding.

always to be in control, the ensuing uncertainty and waiting made him more and more irritable. Maybe that's why he blew his stack so suddenly at Ray Eberle during the band's record-breaking stay in the Panther Room of Chicago's Hotel Sherman.

Circumstances surrounding Ray's departure were reported differently by different people. Glenn's version, supported by others in the band, blamed it on Ray's drinking and on a trade-paper blast that Ray levied at his boss, griping about discipline and not enough money. Ray himself recently told me, "I quit the band—I wasn't fired—because Glenn wouldn't pay me for *Orchestra Wives*. While we were in Chicago, all the guys were getting their checks for the picture. When I asked Glenn where mine was, he said I wasn't getting any because I was under contract to him and the contract didn't call for anything extra for the picture."

That Ray wasn't in the best of condition has been corroborated by others. Marion Hutton told me point-blank, "Ray was getting away with things that nobody else could do. If Glenn hadn't let him go, there would have been a revolt in the band."

Chummy MacGregor blamed the rift indirectly on Ray's behavior and directly on an incident he couldn't avoid. According to Chummy, Eberle showed up late for a Chesterfield rehearsal because a drawbridge spanning the Chicago River had stayed open too long and Ray had been caught in the traffic jam. But the legitimate excuse didn't impress Glenn. According to Chummy, he fired Eberle the minute he stepped into the studio.

Another act—this one by Glenn—helped oil the Eberle skids. Maurice Purtill remembers it. "When we were at the Panther Room, we used to do a one-hour show. There was always some big number for Ray and the Modernaires just before we went into the closing 'Bugle Call Rag.' On this particular night, Janet, Ray's wife, and her family came in to catch the show, and when it was time for Ray's big number, Glenn, for some reason or other, skipped the tune and went right into 'Bugle Call Rag.' Eberle took a burn and he had a few belts and he said he was going to kill Glenn."

Purtill doesn't think Glenn yanked the Eberle number on purpose. Yet, in retrospect, this could have been precisely Glenn's way of disciplining the young singer with whom he had been on such great terms that he once told me he'd always have a place in his band. After the firing, Glenn did relent a bit. According to Tommy Sheils, then working in the Miller office, "When Ray finally went out on his own, Glenn wouldn't take any commissions, even though he still held a personal management contract with him."

Years later, Ray, talking to me by phone from his Florida home, insisted that he had no ill feelings toward Glenn. "He was always like an older brother to me. The only way I can describe how I felt when I heard he died was the way so many of us felt when we heard John F. Kennedy was assassinated."

The years have been good to Ray. Financially he hasn't done as well as some other band singers of his time—Sinatra or Como, for example. He led his own band for a while with just slight success. Since then he has worked as a soloist in various clubs. And he has changed his habits. Better-looking than ever, with an impressive mustache added to his maturing face, he today enjoys great serenity in his nonalcoholic existence. "Now, when I get up

each morning, it's nice knowing where I am." More specifically, "I get up, step outside my house, and go fishing."

After his breakup with Glenn, Eberle joined Gene Krupa. His replacement came from the Chico Marx band, at the suggestion of Glenn's old boss Ben Pollack. Skip Nelson (real name: Scipione Mirabella), a musicianly singer who also played piano and guitar, joined just in time to record with the band on its final Victor sides. During three consecutive sessions it waxed thirteen tunes, as Glenn, harried, like many other band leaders, tried to record as much as possible before August 1, when James C. Petrillo's devastating twenty-eight-month ban against Victor and Columbia records was to go into effect.

Nelson's first recording, "Dearly Beloved," showed him off to best advantage, though "That Old Black Magic," which he sang with the Modernaires, was more popular. Biggest hit among the final thirteen sides was "Juke Box Saturday Night," which drew gripes from the coin-machine operators, who felt that their instruments should be labeled with greater dignity. Nevertheless, they were willing to retain the thousands of dollars they made from its plays. The final side, and one of the most beautiful the band ever recorded, was Bill Finegan's gorgeous arrangement of a portion of George Gershwin's *Rhapsody in Blue*, featuring a magnificent cornet solo by Bobby Hackett.

Glenn's increasing irritability could have been enhanced by the results of Martin Block's midyear poll. For the first time in several years, the Miller band did not finish first, winding up in second spot with 67,216 votes, a couple of thousand less than the winner, Harry James, accumulated. By this time Harry was really cashing in on the "Boy Misses Girl" approach, so relevant to the draft situation, with records like "He's My Guy" and "I Cried for You." Even in the *Coca-Cola Spotlight* radio series, which featured live versions of the week's most requested recordings, James had taken over the lead. (Ironically, two years later, long after Glenn had disbanded his famed civilian group, he once again finished first in Block's poll.)

A mixup in communication between members of the Philadelphia press and radio corps and Glenn and his own staff contributed more to Glenn's unhappy mood. His schedule had grown so full (six Chesterfield shows per week—three regular broadcasts and three repeats for the West Coast—plus as many as seven shows a day at the Earle Theatre) that it had become physically impossible for him to meet with everyone who wanted to interview him. (Shades of his previous confession to me!) But nobody had bothered to explain this in advance to the press, which began to lambast him, with one columnist, Sid Gathrid of *The Daily News*, writing, "If he's too busy to be grateful to people who helped make him, this column is hereafter too busy to mention his name."

Such a reaction wasn't entirely new to Glenn, especially in Philadelphia, where the critics had been notoriously thin-skinned. He tried to understand their problems, and he also expected them to understand his. His attitude was well expressed in a letter he wrote to Hal Tunis, a Philadelphia disc jockey, who had complained about what he called Glenn's "lack of cooperation" and intimated he might not play any more of his records.

Glenn's retort was terse, tart and to the point:

When I go into a town I instruct the operator to give the band manager all phone calls and not to ring my room for any purpose. The reason for doing this is that our work is very trying, what with traveling and working hard on the stand as we do. If I took all the phone calls that come in, I would be too busy answering the phone to get any rest, do any work or anything else. . . .

Regarding your attitude as to playing our records, believe you have been working on the wrong premise. A certain famous broadcaster conducting a program similar to yours is of the opinion that the bands are in no ways obligated to him, because he is deriving as much benefit by playing their records as the band is by receiving the publicity. Without the top bands' records, his program wouldn't mean too much.

Don't misunderstand me. I appreciate the time you have given us over your station. I never asked you to play any of our records and if you choose never to play them again you will hear no complaints from me.

I believe that the playing of our records over your station has done as much towards making you an institution in Philadelphia as it has to publicize us in that section. . . . The success of Glenn Miller depends partially on Hal Tunis and the success of Hal Tunis depends partially on Glenn Miller. . . .

While Glenn was busy replying to his growing list of critics, the navy had become even busier replying to its growing list of applicants for commissions. On August 1 it replied to "Mr. Alton Glenn Miller, Sherman Hotel, Chicago, Illinois," in part as follows:

You are advised that, after careful consideration, the Bureau is unable to approve your application for appointment in the U. S. Naval Reserve for the reason or reasons indicated below:

You have not established to the satisfaction of the Navy Department that your particular qualifications fit you for a mobilization billet in the Naval Reserve. . . .

Randall Jacobs
The Chief of Navy Personnel

It was a decision that the navy was soon to regret even more than the deeply disappointed Glenn did. Even a sympathetic letter to Don Haynes from Naval Lieutenant Commander Eddie Peabody, the world-famous kindly, corny, grinning banjo player, didn't help much: "Tell Glenn to keep his chin way up in the air because this happens very often and that it is no reflection on his ability or position. It's just a lack of a spot at this time. Tell him, also, that he should feel free to negotiate with his General friend, just as though nothing had happened."

The stoical Miller did continue just as though nothing had happened. The guys in the band had no idea that he had received such a rebuff. And Glenn wasn't about to let on. Instead, he had begun to formulate a letter to his "General friend," one that he hoped desperately would result in his chance to do something which to him was becoming even more important than leading the most successful band in the country.

Chapter 31

On August 12 Glenn sent the following letter to Brigadier
General Charles D. Young:

> Dear General Young:
>
> In your recent letter to me you mentioned the desirability of
> "streamlining" our present military music. This touches upon a
> subject which is close to my heart and about which I think I can
> speak with some authority.
>
> I wish you could read some of the many letters that have
> come to me during the past months from our men in military
> service expressing their appreciation of our various army camp
> appearances and our USO broadcasts. I wish you could also
> read some of the newspaper reports of interviews with our
> servicemen now in Australia and other distant places, and their
> pleas that broadcasts from home include a generous share of our
> music. These letters and reports all show that the interest of our
> boys lies definitely in modern, popular music, as played by an
> orchestra such as ours, rather than in the music to which their
> fathers listened twenty-five years ago, most of which is still
> being played by army bands just as it was in World War days.
>
> The many requests for broadcasts, records, programs, dedica-
> tions and arrangements are very pleasing to me but they leave
> me wishing that I might do something concrete in the way of
> setting up a plan that would enable our music to reach our
> servicemen here and abroad with some degree of regularity. I
> have a feeling that if this could be arranged it would help
> considerably to ease some of the difficulties of army life.

For the past three or four years my orchestra has enjoyed phenomenal popularity until we have now reached a point where our weekly gross income ranges from $15,000 to $20,000. Needless to say, this has been and is most profitable to me personally but I am wondering if it would not be more in order at this time for me to be bending my efforts toward the continuance of this income if it could be devoted to USO purposes, the Army Relief Fund or some other approved purpose. If, by means of a series of benefit performances or other approved methods, even some part of this income could be maintained and used for the improvement of army morale I would be entirely willing to forego it for the duration. At the same time, by appropriate planning, programs could be regularly broadcast to the men in service and I have an idea that such programs might put a little more spring into the feet of our marching men and a little more joy into their hearts.

With these thoughts in mind I should like to go into the army if I could be placed in charge of a modernized army band. I feel that I could really do a job for the army in the field of modern music. I am thirty-eight years of age and am in excellent physical condition. I have, of course, registered for the draft but have not been classified. Inasmuch as I have been married for twelve years, I would suppose that under the present regulations I shall ultimately be placed in Class 3A. I mention this only because I want you to know that my suggestion stems from a sincere desire to do a real job for the army and that that desire is not actuated by any personal draft problem.

I was born in Clarinda, Iowa, and raised in Colorado. Both of my parents were also American born. I am a grammar school and high school graduate and also attended the University of Colorado for two years. My connection with music is not of recent origin. I have been playing and arranging music ever since my high school days.

I hope you will feel that there is a job I can do for the army. If so, I shall be grateful if you will have the proper person contact me and instruct me as to further procedure.

With kind personal regards and appreciating your interest, I am,

Respectfully yours,
Glenn Miller

General Young's immediate and encouraging reply referred to Glenn's "willingness to make personal and patriotic sacrifice for the duration of the War." Glenn responded with a quick trip to Washington, where he filed his official application.

He took his physical exam on August 24, concerned that perhaps his poor eyesight might cause his rejection. But his "compound myopic astigmatism," though it caused 20/70 distant vision in each eye, was correctable with glasses to 20/20, and that satisfied the medics. His physical report listed a "scar over glabella area" (the smooth portion of the skin just above the nose and between the eyebrows) which I'd never noticed, attributable, according to the report, to a "trauma in childhood."

His height was 5 feet, 11½ inches; his weight 177½ pounds; his chest 39½ inches; and except for an appendectomy scar everything else was normal.

On September 10, an official telegram arrived at Glenn's office, Room 3001, RKO Building, 1270 Sixth Avenue, New York.

While all this had been going on, some of the guys had grown suspicious. Glenn had tried to keep his military activities secret, but word started leaking out, and the guys, concerned as much about their futures as Glenn's, began to ask questions. So, during one of the Chesterfield rehearsals, Glenn told Johnny O'Leary, "I want everyone out of here except the band." Once the room had been cleared of all the others, Glenn made his announcement: "Gentlemen, I am now a captain in the United States Army." And he asked the boys if they would stay with him until he went into the service. After that he hoped to arrange it so that those who wanted to could join him.

Only one man left. Steve Lipkins, who had just joined, had already received an offer from Jimmy Dorsey, and Glenn agreed to let him go, especially since Bobby Hackett's lip was now completely healed.

As soon as the word got out that Glenn was going into service, offers came pouring in to the sidemen. Eventually, all three trombones joined Charlie Spivak. Al Klink and Ernie Caceres went with Benny Goodman. Johnny Best joined Bob Crosby, and Mickey McMickle and Skippy Martin went with NBC. Billy May started arranging for Les Brown while continuing to arrange for Alvino Rey, with whom he had been moonlighting for months anyway.

Bobby Hackett formed a small jazz band. Moe Purtill soon replaced Buddy Rich in Tommy Dorsey's band. Skip Nelson returned to Chico Marx. Willie Schwartz enlisted in the navy. Doc Goldberg also entered the service. Marion Hutton, Tex Beneke and the Modernaires embarked on a theater tour of their own; they were billed as "Glenn Miller Presents the Singing Stars of His Famous Orchestra Featured in *Orchestra Wives*." Chummy MacGregor joined Glenn's Mutual Music Publishing Company.

Meanwhile, though, Glenn and the band had to act out their final roles. Anxious to clean up his affairs and spend some time at home, Miller tried to get out of a final week's booking at the Central Theatre in Passaic, New Jersey. But he had previously canceled another date there and the management wasn't about to let him bow out again. Finally they agreed to reduce the run from seven to four days.

The band's final Chesterfield show, on September 24 from the stage of the theater, held a surprise. The Miller version of "Juke Box Saturday Night" featured several takeoffs on big musical names, including a trumpet imitation of Harry James. At the end of the number Glenn told his radio listeners, "That lad that imitated Harry James really did a job. The reason: because it

Final days in the Cafe Rouge. Bobby Hackett is at far left among the trumpets;
Doc Goldberg is on bass; Skippy Martin is the saxist in the middle.

was Harry James himself. Harry, come out here and say
something." James did say something, like "Hello, everybody,"
and then Glenn continued, "Harry, naturally we're very reluc-
tant to give up our *Moonlight Serenade* after such a pleasant
association with Chesterfield for such a long time, but since I've
got a date with Uncle Sam coming up, I can sincerely say I'd
rather have you take over our regular Tuesday, Wednesday and
Thursday spots than anyone I know. You've a swell sponsor and
a great product, and with you and Helen Forrest and that band
of yours, I know you're going to do a wonderful job. Sounds like
the right combination to me. So next Tuesday, get to work,
maestro."

"Harry, I know you're going to do a wonderful job."

To this day, Harry has remained eternally grateful for Glenn's having recommended him as his replacement. Polly Haynes notes that "Glenn went to Mr. Carmichael, president of Liggett & Myers, and suggested Harry for his replacement instead of any of the bands he owned—like Spivak or Thornhill or McIntyre."

Nobody quite knew what to do about the band's final appearance. Even the guys who had griped most about the band, about its rigidity, about Glenn's discipline, were deeply affected. Quite a few fortified themselves with blasts of booze before the last stage show, while others tried to take it all in stride, as they figured the stoical Miller would be doing. Nevertheless, it turned out to be a pretty wet night—bleary, beery, and teary.

Johnny O'Leary recalls that "Don Haynes was trying to think of something to kill the gloom. I always carried a cigar but I never lit it and everybody knew that. So Don got me to walk on stage in the middle of that last show with an old Art Carney–type of hat on my head, my trousers rolled up and carrying my cigar, and I went up to Wally Brown, the comedian on the bill, and asked 'Got a light?' and Wally brought out one of those big boxes of kitchen matches and he helped me light up my cigar at last. Well, it broke up the band."

But the laughter eventually turned to tears. As the show drew closer to the end, the guys actually found it more difficult to play. *Down Beat* reported the emotional event:

> Glenn's last show at the Central Theatre in Passaic, N.J. never finished—the curtain was rung down while the band was still in the middle of its theme, with Miller and Marion Hutton no longer on the stage. Vocalist Hutton broke down in the middle of "Kalamazoo," started crying, and ran off the stage. Most of the brass section weren't doing much better on the start of the theme that followed—this was one case of the "choke-up" being no alibi. Miller, famed for his taciturnity, turned away from the band to keep from cracking up himself—only to face rows and rows of kids bawling their eyes out. "I could stand everything, all the heartache of breaking up things that had taken us years to build—but I just couldn't face those kids," Miller said.

Backstage, Johnny O'Leary stood, his ash-tipped cigar held awkwardly in his hand. "As the band was playing the final theme," he reports, "Glenn walked off stage and as he passed me in the wings he said, 'O'Leary, I hope I'm doing the right thing,' and I said, 'I think you are, Glenn.'"

PART FOUR

The Great AAF Band

Chapter 32

"School is going fine and steady and although not much music
is being discussed I am getting a lot of Army procedure, really
more than I can absorb, but am trying to learn all I can.

I know how to make an Army bed, shine my own shoes,
sweep under my bed and march in formation to the latrine with
excellent results. . . .

Sincerely,
A. Glenn Miller
Captain, A. S. C.

The A.S.C. stood for the Army Specialists Corps, to which
Glenn was immediately assigned after reporting for an October 7
induction in New York City. The quote comes from one of
numerous letters he wrote, as most lonely inductees did, to friends
back home.

He wasn't a happy officer trainee. The demotion from top dog
to just another dog-tag wearer was rough, even for someone
supposedly as calm and self-possessed as Glenn. In addition, the
months of late hours and little sleep, plus the strain of finally
making the big break and walking away from such stupendous
success, had left him physically and emotionally exhausted. Little
wonder that both his body and his mind quickly resented the
emphasis upon push-ups, rifle practice, marching formations,
and other military functions that kept interfering with his plans

321

Glenn enters the service at Whitehall Street in New York.

to contribute to the army's music and morale. In typical Glenn Miller fashion, he was raring to get things done—his way. But like a typical soldier, he was learning how to take, not give, orders.

He reported first for duty at the Seventh Service Command Headquarters in Omaha, Nebraska. Almost immediately he was transferred east to Fort Meade in Maryland for officers' training. He kept trying to be "a good soldier," but his innate impatience and intolerance kept interfering. Eventually, disgusted by the army's antiquated approach to music, he began bitching to friends. To David Mackay he complained, "All they do is to try

to teach us tempos by making us watch those godam bouncing balls on a movie screen all day long." He even allowed himself the luxury of self-pity. To band leader Sammy Kaye he wrote: "How is the Band Business—I vaguely remember being in it at one time. If you have time, drop me a note with some gossip in it. . . ."

The overall strain finally defeated him; his health matched his morale, and he wound up in the Fort Meade Hospital with a serious strep-throat infection. After ten days he returned to training, and finally, on December 4, he received his captaincy. He traveled to Omaha, only to find himself suddenly assigned to the Army Air Corps and ordered to report to Maxwell Field,

Alabama. There he received his first official assignment: Assistant Special Services Officer.

The shift into the air corps from the regular army turned out to be a major coup for the AAF, which managed to spring the celebrated captain out of the ground forces via a simple, seemingly innocuous, routine request through channels. It seems that some astute air force officer had discovered Glenn's real first name, whereupon the AAF immediately asked for the transfer of the unrecognized Alton G. Miller into its branch of the service. Several days later the regular army had lost and the air force had officially gained the services of *the* Glenn Miller.

Glenn remained at Maxwell Field for several weeks. Then at the start of 1943 he was assigned to the Army Air Forces Technical Training Command and headquartered at Knollwood Field, North Carolina.

His military training completed, and his assignment set, Glenn figured he could now go ahead and do something new and different and exciting for the AAF's music and morale. His plans centered on organizing several outstanding bands. Each would contain musicians especially selected from the draft. Each would be trained to play both inspiring marching music and outstanding dance-band music. Glenn envisioned his contribution as both a band-builder and a morale-builder. His highly developed knowledge of what the average American wanted to hear, he figured, could be of immense value to the armed services.

He would replace the stiff, stolid sounds of martial music, unchanged for more than a generation, with contemporary versions that would inspire the country's millions of young recruits. He wrote Jerry Gray, his civilian band's arranger, about his plans: "We have the authorization for a 14-man arranging staff to provide music for the Army Air Forces Technical Training Command, and it is my plan to place you in charge of this when you get one of uncle's zoot suits."

But the plan didn't work out. One after another veteran officer threw up roadblocks. Glenn hadn't counted upon the army's inbred resistance to change, nor upon the resentment of insecure career officers to anything that might remotely challenge their

WAR DEPARTMENT
The Adjutant General's Office
Washington

November 23, 1942

In Reply
Refer To AG 201 Miller, Alton Glenn
(11-23-42)PR-A

SUBJECT: Temporary Appointment.

TO: Mr. Alton Glenn Miller,
Byrne Lane,
Tenafly, New Jersey.
Temp. Add: Seventh Service Command,
Omaha, Nebraska.

A 0-505273

(Temp. Appointed Captain AUS)

1. By direction of the President you are temporarily appointed and commissioned in the Army of the United States, effective this date, in the grade and section shown in the address above. Your serial number is shown after A above.

2. This commission will continue in force during the pleasure of the President of the United States for the time being, and for the duration of the war and six months thereafter unless sooner terminated.

3. There is inclosed herewith a form for oath of office which you are requested to execute and return promptly to the agency from which it was received by you. The execution and return of the required oath of office consitute an acceptance of your appointment. No other evidence of acceptance is required.

4. This letter should be retained by you as evidence of your appointment as no commissions will be issued during the war.

By order of the Secretary of War:

Inclosure:
Form for oath of office.

CERTIFIED TRUE COPY

R E Daley

Lt. Col. R. E. Daley, AC

Major General.
The Adjutant General.

authority. Their jealousy, fear and often just plain stupidity first amazed Glenn, then enraged him. But there was very little he could do about it. The once all-powerful leader of America's music was forced to submit to the orders of what one musician-turned-soldier once described as "a horde of Mickey Mouse majors and colonels."

One project Glenn did manage to salvage was his plan to produce a super-band for the AAF. Since many of the recruits, especially those from the New York area, took their basic training in Atlantic City, New Jersey, Glenn was assigned to duty there. Knollwood Field, however, remained his headquarters, and it was there that he was eventually appointed Director of Bands Training for the Army Air Forces Technical Training Command.

Naturally, he wanted to get some of his former musicians to join him. But two of his favorites, Tex Beneke and Willie Schwartz, had already entered the navy. Glenn was disappointed, but, true to his self-imposed code, he hid his feelings. Instead, he wrote each of them half-kidding letters, the kind a salesman might write to a lost customer he thought he had all locked up. To Tex he wrote: "I was very happy to get your letter and to know that you are all set, even if you are in the Navy. Of course you know the Air Corps is going to win the war, and I had so hoped you could have been in on it."

To Schwartz, he wrote: "If you're stuck in that stinkin' Navy, I'm sorry. I haven't any more time for you. However, I'd appreciate it if you would keep writing and tell me all the dope."

He made attempts to get others to join him. Bill Finegan recalls Glenn asking him to lunch. "He said he wanted me in the Army band with him. I told him I was going to be a flyer. So he tried to talk me out of it by describing wrecked planes at fields. But he respected my wishes and he pulled no strings."

Another alumnus, trombonist Paul Tanner, reports the same sort of understanding when Glenn offered him an AAF postgraduate Miller course. "I told him I was already set at a post in Delaware; that I was working under a great conductor, Walter Heindl. Glenn realized what that meant to me and wished me luck."

However, others from the civilian band did rejoin: trombonist Jimmy Priddy, arranger Gray, trumpeter Zeke Zarchy, and bassist Trigger Alpert, who had always been one of Glenn's musical and personal favorites. In a semi-bantering, semi-bartering letter requesting Alpert's transfer into his command, Glenn wrote: "I want a man from Stout Field transferred to the TTC, and I'm willing to trade four tires (about 5,000 miles on them), a book of 'C' [gasoline] coupons and damn near anything but my wife for him." As it turned out, Alpert's command did ask for ten musicians in exchange—and got them!

Sometimes Glenn got musicians he wanted merely through official requests to other posts and commands. More often, though, he communicated directly with musicians about to be drafted. The procedure was simple: The draftee would send a letter to Glenn, giving him all the details about his induction, whereupon Glenn would request, through channels, his assignment to his command. These men would eventually report to Atlantic City for their basic training. Those he especially wanted would be reserved for the super-band he expected to organize at Yale University in New Haven. The rest would be shipped to other AAFTTC bands.

One of Glenn's most desirables was his old golfing buddy and former lead trumpeter, Zeke Zarchy, an early draftee who had wound up in a Florida camp. Brighter and more worldly than most musicians, he would, Glenn figured, make an excellent first sergeant. And so he sent for him.

April 20, 1943

Pvt. George Simon
29th AAF Band
BTC No. 7
Atlantic City, N.J.

Dear George:

Be patient.

Sincerely,

A. GLENN MILLER,
Captain, Air Corps,
Director of Bands.

AGM/mfd

ABOVE AND OPPOSITE PAGE: Typical army correspondence between a buck private wanting to know when something is going to happen and a captain who doesn't know either.

Zarchy reported to Glenn's Atlantic City headquarters at the Knights of Columbus Hotel, and, as he tells it, encountered the same "it's-not-who-you-are-but-who-you-know" set of values that influence most large organizations.

"When I walked in, after a long trip by car, I must have looked like a real sad-sack private. They treated me like dirt. When the sergeant-in-charge asked me if I knew anybody around there, and I told him, sure, I knew Glenn, he didn't believe me at all. So then he and some other guys began a big question-and-answer routine. Finally one sergeant announced triumphantly, 'Well, here he is now!' Glenn had walked in behind me, and right away we started hugging and embracing. Immediately the whole scene changed. Instead of treating me

```
        TWENTY-NINTH ARMY AIR FORCE BAND (*)
        BASIC TRAINING CENTER NUMBER SEVEN
        ARMY AIR FORCE TECHNICAL TRAINING CORPS
        ATLANTIC CITY, NEW JERSEY




Captain A. Glenn Miller
Director of Bands
Army Air Forces Technical Training Corps
Knollwood Field, North Carolina.


Dear Sir:


                O. K.


                        Respectfully yours,


                        Private George T. Simon
                        ASN. 32791159


GTS/gts



(*) Fourth Floor
```

like some dumb private, the sergeant-in-charge turned to another soldier and barked out, 'Here, Sergeant Libby, take Sergeant Zarchy's barracks bags up to his room for him.' And then Glenn and I went out and had dinner together."

It was in Atlantic City that I also caught up with Glenn again. I had been drafted early in January, and, as Glenn had told me to do when the call came in, I'd written to him, volunteering that I had recently been playing a lot of drums as training for his band, and that now I was holding tempos so well that I referred to myself as "No-Budge Simon." To which Glenn replied that he'd be delighted to have me in his outfit, and then, citing the world's number one tennis player, added, "In referring to yourself as 'No-Budge Simon' could it be that you were thinking of tennis instead of drums?"

I reported for basic training, along with some other Miller recruits, at the Ambassador Hotel in Atlantic City. Except for constantly climbing the stairs from the basement to the seventh floor of the hotel, basic training wasn't very rough. There was the usual shooting of rifles, and watching movies about not getting the clap, and learning how to march in formation. Throughout, they kept trying to instill the spirit of the Army Air Corps into each of us. I can still remember the ridiculous feeling of marching along that famous boardwalk, past the Steel Pier where so many of the musicians had worked and had been hailed as heroes, and being forced to sing songs like "Off we go into the wild blue yonder" and "Someone's in the kitchen with Dinah" and other "patriotic" arias, while some dumb drill sergeant would march along beside us, haranguing us with shouts of "Sing, goddam yez, sing!" so that any passing officers could note what a stupendous army air forces morale-building job he had been doing.

Obviously, the fact that we knew we were soon going to be playing in the Miller band and wouldn't be saddled much longer with such trifles as rifles and drill sergeants made the whole basic training bit much easier for us. However, for some reason, I was pretty gung-ho about proving myself to be a good soldier and I began to take it all so seriously that I almost blew the whole bit. Take, for example, the typing test, given presumably to see who could qualify as a company clerk or some such grandiose job. I must have been flying along at a mean 150 words a minute, trying to prove what a great typist I was, when the stupidity of the whole bit suddenly hit me. Here I was, all set to join the Miller band, but, instead of being satisfied with that, I was casting myself for some dumb clerk's job. So, for the rest of the test, I sat in front of the typewriter, one finger poised, as I kept hunting and pecking my way through the remaining sentences at a rate of something less than five words per minute!

One of my fondest memories of Atlantic City, and also one of my saddest, is meeting up with a shy but very warm young soldier who told me he was an arranger and hoped that Glenn would be using him in New Haven. He had written a few things for the bands of Claude Thornhill and Randy Brooks, but nobody really knew his work too well. We spent several evenings together, walking along the boardwalk and getting all sorts of salutes from recruits who mistook the lyres on our caps for officers' eagles. But unfortunately this nice young soldier, who I figured was just the sort of polite person Glenn would really like, never got the call to join that super-outfit in New Haven. Too bad, too, because Henry Mancini would have been a valuable asset to that great Glenn Miller AAF Band.

Chapter 33

 We didn't see very much of Glenn in those early days in New Haven. He spent most of his time down at Knollwood, trying to organize programs that would modernize military music; trying also to circumvent roadblocks erected by the majority of officers opposed to change; and, whenever possible, getting in a few rounds of his ever-loving golf. Convinced that Zarchy would make a fine first sergeant, he had sent him up to Yale to set up the barracks, which turned out to be a wooden frame house with lots of small rooms on Lake Place, practically on the college campus. The vanguard of the band arrived in March; a large contingent of us arrived in May.

By then the nucleus of the band was already functioning. So much of Yale had been turned into an air force cadet's training center that nonuniformed undergraduates looked like interlopers. During the first few months of its existence, the band's primary functions were to play as the cadets marched at morning review and evening retreat and to provide them with luncheon music in the "Glenn Miller Civilian Band Manner."

Some of the musicians took their roles very seriously. We had a drum major named Hal Winter who knew the marching routines, and some of us would march smartly, and others stupidly, behind him. Of course, when Glenn was around, which wasn't very often at first, the guys would shape up. But otherwise, like true jazz musicians, we'd often wing it. I used to carry a

The band playing for marching cadets on the New Haven Green. Drummer with just one stick (third from left) is military bands' premier cowbell player.

cowbell inside my shirt, and on the way back from retreat I'd haul it out and play Latin beats against the martial music. Somehow it worked— sometimes.

The band's most stellar shirt-stuffer, however, was a brilliant pianist named Arnold Ross, who took the army less seriously than any soldier I ever knew. The sounds emanating from inside his shirt were even more nonmilitary than mine—the muffled meows of a pet kitten that he couldn't bear to leave behind all alone in the barracks!

Ross and Trigger Alpert, pianist and string bass player, respectively, qualified for the marching band as trumpeters. They had freak lips, and delighted in astounding the rest of us by playing way high up on their horns, far beyond the accepted military range. What's more, they remained entirely uninhibited by army protocol and would, when the feeling overcame them, ad-lib their parts.

Alpert recalls, "One day there was a big review for some general, and his aide told Zeke to play the 'General's Call.' Nobody knew it, but I said I did, and I proceeded to play some hot riff for about eighteen bars until somebody grabbed the horn out of my hand. One day Glenn returned to New Haven and he spotted Arnold and me playing all those high notes and he told us right then and there to get out of the marching band."

Ross, a magnificent musician, who, according to Alpert, must have had twenty bottles of cologne in his room ("It was ridiculous when some officer would come around to inspect!"), was soon banished entirely from New Haven. Arnold could also arrange, and so when he arrived at Yale, Glenn assigned him to do some simple tune like "Honeysuckle Rose." After about six weeks and no sign of the arrangement, Glenn called him into his office to find out what was going on. "I've got the first chorus all done," Ross was supposed to have bragged. "The first chorus? One chorus in six weeks?" Miller bellowed. "What the hell have you been doing all this time?" "Quite frankly," Ross came back, "I've been so busy getting all those G.I. haircuts, I haven't had much time." A couple of days later, he was banished to St. Louis.

Ross, out of the Harry James band, was just one of many topflight musicians Glenn had garnered from the country's top bands—fine players like pianist Mel Powell, saxist Chuck Gentry, and trumpeter Steve Steck from Benny Goodman; trumpeter Bernie Privin and saxist Hank Freeman from Artie Shaw; saxists Jack Ferrier and Gabe Gelinas from Jan Savitt; bassist Marty Blitz and drummer Gene Lemen from Claude Thornhill; guitarist Carmen Mastren from Tommy Dorsey; saxist-clarinetist Peanuts Hucko from Will Bradley; lead saxist Steve Madrick from Les Brown; trumpeter Bobby Nichols from Vaughn Monroe; and Ray McKinley, trumpeter Jack Steele, trombonist Jim Harwood, pianist Lou Stein, and arranger Perry Burgett from Ray's recently formed and more recently disbanded outfit. And, of course, there were the Miller alumni: Alpert, Gray, Priddy, and Zarchy.

Zeke remained Glenn's major contact with the musicians. Throughout the band's entire career, he and Glenn retained their close personal and working relationship—or at least as close as an officer and an enlisted man could get. For Glenn, a stickler for discipline, remained removed from most of us, perhaps because of protocol, perhaps because that's the way he wanted it.

Sometimes at night he would get together with a couple of us. He lived at the Taft Hotel right in the heart of New Haven, and

Some name-band alumni on leave to the Miller band. Back row (left to right): Hank Freeman (Artie Shaw), Zeke Zarchy (Miller), Trigger Alpert (Miller), Ray McKinley (McKinley), Jerry Gray (Miller). Front row: George Ockner (NBC Symphony), Carmen Mastren (Tommy Dorsey), Johnny Desmond (Gene Krupa).

he didn't have too many officer friends. Often he would invite Zeke for a late snack at some restaurant; once in a while I'd join them. I felt sort of sorry for Glenn. His frustration was so obvious. He was getting opposition not only from some officials at headquarters but also from some of the cadets' training officers, who opposed any modernization of martial music.

As usual, he remained adamant. He believed strongly that his role was one of morale-building as well as band-building, and that he was giving the marching cadets what they wanted: exciting music, more inspiring than the usual run-of-the-mill Sousa march arrangements. But he kept on getting all sorts of flak. "Zeke," he said one evening with a mixture of contempt and frustration, "I can buy and sell any one of those goddamn idiot officers." And he was probably right. Though his base pay was only $200 a month (later it rose all the way to $275), his six months' royalty earnings from records, for the period ending February 28, 1943, exceeded $60,000! But neither his money nor his fame could help, and more than once we had to pour our frustrated captain back into his room at the Taft, New Haven's leading hotel, for which he was paying all of $3.50 per night.

When I was alone with Glenn, which was seldom, we got along reasonably well. Unlike Jimmy Priddy, who found that Glenn loosened up in the army and therefore was much easier to get along with than before, I sensed a new tenseness in our relationship. I remember one day when we were walking toward his car and I beckoned to him to get in first and he snapped at me in a very cold, impersonal way and said, "Get in. Don't you know a soldier is supposed to sit at the left of an officer!" How different, I thought, from the early days when we used to kid about entering revolving doors, wondering who worked harder, the guy who went in first or last, and finally deciding that the real parasite was the member of a trio who entered second.

Still, we did work well together on an impersonal organizational level. I reassumed the role I had played when he first started his civilian band back in 1937, this time helping him locate and secure just the right musicians for his AAF outfit. My recruiting consisted mostly of correspondence with individual players and also with headquarters at Knollwood, making occasional phone calls on his behalf—like the one to Johnny Desmond at his father's grocery store in Detroit to ask Johnny if he'd like to join the band.

Of course, I also played in the marching band—right next to Ray McKinley, my onetime idol—and as I had when Glenn first organized his civilian band, I sat in a couple of times with the big dance band. But things were different this time. Maybe Glenn didn't need me as much as he did in 1937. Maybe my drumming had deteriorated drastically. In any case, he began giving me some of those "What-the-hell-are-you-doing-anyway" glares. And for the first time I could empathize with some of those musicians who used to complain so bitterly about Glenn's intolerance. I never again suggested sitting in, and he never again asked me. Nor did he ask me to play with the large orchestra, complete with strings and singers, which he was readying for a series of radio broadcasts. Obviously, he was more thrilled with my organizational and writing talents—I proceeded to send out press releases about the band through the post's public relations office—than with my drumming. And, frankly, I couldn't blame him too much—maybe just a little—but not too much.

On the other hand, I proceeded to get some thrills of my own playing alongside Ray McKinley in the marching band. Ray wasn't too enamored of my drumming either, and at first would mumble sarcastic critiques whenever I messed up, even slightly. Eventually I got bugged at him, too, and after a particularly unpleasant march I snapped back at him, emphasizing that I was doing the best I could and why the hell didn't he keep his big mouth shut! And from then on he did, which proved to me that he was more tolerant than our captain.

That big military band was an inspiration, the loosest, most swinging marching band we'd ever heard, and the appreciative grins the cadets managed to sneak us as they passed by us in review made us realize we were playing for more than our own kicks. Glenn and his arrangers had instilled some swinging syncopations into the trite old marches. The horns played with zest and freedom, occasionally bending some notes and anticipating others, the way true jazz musicians do so well. And McKinley had created some imaginative drum beats that the section, despite some paraprofessionals like me, knocked off with fire and precision.

The imaginative McKinley contributed a lot to the band. One day when he and arranger Perry Burgett, who had worked in Ray's civilian band, were sitting outside the house on Lake Place, Mac came up with a revolutionary idea. "How about taking some blues and giving them a marching beat? You know, take a tune like 'St. Louis Blues' and get the drums doing something under that opening call and let's see if we can make the whole thing swing." And he hummed the opening bars of "St. Louis Blues" and at the end of the phrase he added the drum part, "darum-da-dum, darum-da-dum, da-rum-de-de-de-de-de-dum-da-dum," and told Burgett to take it from there. Then, as McKinley tells it, "Perry wrote it out sort of like a trumpet call and we played it and everybody liked it. So Glenn had Jerry Gray write up a full band arrangement of the thing." And that's how the AAF band's most famous arrangement and recording were conceived.

A tolerant Ray McKinley, a lovable Trigger Alpert and a struggling drummer-author in the Yale Bowl. The spectator turnout in the stands reflects McKinley's and Alpert's opinion.

The idea of creating swinging march arrangements of jazz tunes knocked us all out—Glenn included—and soon we were playing jumping martial versions of "Blues in the Night" and "Jersey Bounce." The cadets' grins grew wider and wider, their strides more bouncy than ever.

But some of those officers dedicated to reliving their good old West Point marching days rebelled against breaking with the Sousa tradition. Out-of-step with the cadets' generation, they preferred to retire to the-world-that-was and they cringed at anything new and different, especially when it came not from one of them, but from one of those newly created officers they sneeringly referred to as "instant captains."

And so the commandant of cadets lodged a strong complaint against the newfangled sounds with the post commander, demanding a showdown. His attack upon Miller combined reverence for tradition with sarcastic contempt for anything not purely military. "Look, Captain Miller," he groused, "We played those Sousa marches straight in the last war and we did all right, didn't we?" To which Glenn retorted with equal contempt: "You certainly did, Major. But tell me one thing: Are you still flying the same planes you flew in the last war, too?"

The band continued to play its swinging blues marches.

Other annoyances nettled Glenn. "The golf here stinks too," he wrote a friend, "and I've considered using a black ball to show up on the white snow." Even some of his own hand-picked musicians were bugging him, especially a few nonconformists circa 1944, for whom army tradition was pure anathema. Trumpeter Bernie Privin, once a star in Artie Shaw's band, admits he was one who opposed Glenn's strict discipline. Other chief rebels, according to him, included pianist Mel Powell, bassist Joe Shulman, clarinetist Peanuts Hucko, who, no matter how hard he tried (and as his roommate I knew how hard he tried) could never quite make formations on time, and a brilliant French horn player named Addison Collins, Jr.

These five, especially, seemed to resent, as some musicians in his civilian band had, Glenn's seeming preoccupation with discipline merely for discipline's sake. Usually most of the other musicians adopted a "Let's-make-the-best-of-it" attitude. But every one of us reacted bitterly when Glenn, in a move nobody could understand, suddenly ordered all musicians with mustaches to shave them off. For some, who had nursed their growths for years, it became a traumatic experience. And for others, like some brass players, whose very blowing of their instruments had become dependent upon those mustaches, the loss was indeed serious. Of all the moves that Glenn ever made, this always seemed to me to have been the most senseless and least sensitive.

"The only explanation he ever gave us," Privin, who looked naked without his mustache, recently told me, "was that he thought we looked too much like gangsters!"

The band, as a whole, happened to look rather clean-cut, except perhaps for the pale-faced string players, some of whom struck me as looking more like worn-out pinochle players than like soldiers.

Probably the best-looking soldier of the lot was Tony Martin. Before coming into our outfit, he had already achieved fame in movies and on radio and records. Musicians often resented such star-status-singers. But the guys in the Miller band loved Tony, who tried hard to be one of the boys. For example, as a celebrity, he was asked to numerous parties; almost always he made sure that some of the other soldiers in our outfit would be invited to come along with him.

Glenn was also fond of Tony and spent some of his off-duty time with him. He was aware that Tony had come into the army under a cloud of suspicion because of a navy commission that he was supposed to have received through what some claimed were irregular channels. And so when Tony, possibly to vindicate himself, applied for AAF Officer Candidate School, Glenn supported his move wholeheartedly. Later, when Tony, after having completed his OCS course with very high grades, was refused his commission at the very last moment because of what seemed to be pure vindictiveness on the part of the brass, Glenn really rallied to his support, pleading Tony's cause with several top officers.

In Glenn's personal files rests a five-page handwritten letter to him from Martin, apparently penned shortly after Tony had been notified of his non-appointment. Parts of it are quite revelatory:

> Well, no use talking about the past. I'm taking it from here on. After all, there is a war on and my set-back is just an atom compared to the realities that are taking place all over. Please thank the many officers and friends for sticking their necks out for me. . . . No, Captain, I'm not beaten down; just want those guys way up high to 'let me up,' to quote Mel Powell. . . .
> You've really been wonderful to me for which I will always

Glenn beams at Tony Martin (directly below second-from-left trombone player's slide) during a Yale Bowl appearance.

be grateful, and, as the days go on into years, here's one guy who will extol the goodness of one Glenn Miller.

Glenn's capacity for kindness and understanding is reflected in another letter in his files. This one came from Sol Meyer, a writer in the radio unit, whose wife had died and whom Glenn, in a very quiet way, had helped obtain a hardship discharge. Sol, a very sensitive soul, who like almost everyone else in the outfit had never been able to penetrate Glenn's emotional defenses, later wrote:

> We never had much to do in the off-the-record department, unfortunately, for there were many times when I'm sure a couple of casual minutes would have brought about a better understanding and closer affinity in our work. But that's all water long since passed under an old bridge.

I'm leaving for California in a few weeks and don't know when our ways will cross again. I just wanted you to know that I was a very proud guy to work for you and any time there is anything I can do for you, I'll consider it an honest to God pleasure to knock myself out.

I'm very sincere about this, Glenn; you did more for me than anyone else in the army, especially when I needed understanding sympathy—and there is nothing in my power that isn't at your disposal. Good luck, and God bless you.

Why did it take a death to lower Glenn's emotional guard? It had happened before in his civilian band; now it happened again. Unfortunately, military protocol, which drove such a cleavage between officers and enlisted men, continued to give Glenn an extra excuse to continue to hide his feelings. Stoicism seldom lost a bout to Glenn Miller's emotions.

When Martin left for OCS, Glenn needed another singer for the emerging radio series. He had Bob Houston and Bob Carroll in the outfit already, but apparently he didn't feel either one would fill the bill. So he sloughed them off—rather cruelly, I thought—and reached out into the AAF hinterlands to bring in Johnny Desmond.

To be more precise, at Glenn's request I reached for a phone one afternoon and called Johnny at his father's grocery store in Detroit, where he had been spending his ten-day furlough. It seems Glenn felt it wasn't proper protocol for an *officer* to phone an enlisted man to ask him to join his band.

Johnny, who later became a movie and Broadway stage actor, had contacted Glenn months before then. "I was stationed in Enid, Oklahoma, and I'd read in *Down Beat* that Glenn was looking for guys from the big bands. When I had been on the road with Gene Krupa, I used to hear Glenn's band, and I kept wishing I could sing with it some day. I had met Glenn briefly in Chicago, so, after I saw the *Down Beat* article, I decided to write him and ask him if he could use me. Ruth, my wife, and the guys in the band in Enid thought I was nuts. But I figured I had nothing to lose. For a long time it looked like they were right. Then finally a letter came from Glenn. He was interested."

There followed a whole series of typical army snafus, with lost orders and lots of ineffectual correspondence. Finally Johnny was transferred to Chanute Field, outside of Chicago, where he eventually gave up hope—until that fateful phone call to his father's grocery.

"Like almost everyone else," Johnny went on, "I was scared stiff of Glenn. Sometimes he could be very nice and at other times he'd be cold as ice. He made me feel like one of those kids whose father doesn't love him, or at least never shows that he does.

"I must say, though, that he always looked out for my best interests, even though I didn't always appreciate what he was doing at the time. I remember right after I joined the band and we got into that G.I. haircut business. When he had seen me during a visit to Chanute Field, I had had a crew-cut, but by the time I got to New Haven it had grown in again. He didn't like my hair long, so he told me to get a haircut. I got one, but it wasn't short enough for him, so he told me to go right back and get another one. The barber must have thought I was nuts. But he cut off some more. And guess what. Again Glenn said it wasn't short enough. *Then* he told me to get a *real short crew*. Well, you can imagine what that barber must have been thinking when I went back for the third time inside of two hours! Later Glenn explained his reasoning: The band had to act and look more disciplined than any other outfit because we were musicians and all those officers were just looking for something, like hair that was too long, to pin on him and on us."

Desmond's singing debut with the band was most inauspicious. Before he ever opened his mouth, he was hospitalized with what everyone thought was acute appendicitis. But tests proved negative, and so he returned to duty. Came the next chance to sing, and along came another attack. Back to the hospital. This time the diagnosis was acute gastritis. "I didn't realize it then," Johnny recalls, "but now I can see it was all just a case of nerves!"

Eventually Desmond made his debut with the band. He thought he was doing just great, and so when Glenn told him after the third weekly radio show that he wanted to talk with him, Johnny was filled with rosy confidence. Then the ax fell.

"Tell me, Desmond," Glenn said, "whom are you going to sing like next week?" Johnny didn't know what Glenn was driving at. So Glenn explained: "Look, the first week, you sounded like Bing Crosby. The next week it was Tony Martin. Last week you sounded like Frank Sinatra. Now, if I wanted Martin that much, I'd have kept him. If I wanted Bing, I'd have kept Bob Houston, who sounds just like him. And if I want Sinatra, I can get him because I understand he's about to be drafted." Sinatra, who had been reported going into service, a few days later was rejected because of a perforated eardrum. "Your trouble," Glenn went on, "is that you're not singing like Johnny Desmond. I sent for you because I want *you*, not a carbon of somebody *else*. Remember this: As long as the *real* thing is around, people will never buy an imitation." From then on, Johnny Desmond proceeded to sing like Johnny Desmond.

By this time, the role of band singer had become an important one in the Miller AAF organization. In mid-1943 Glenn had finally inaugurated the weekly radio series. Titled *I Sustain the Wings*, it combined the music of the full orchestra, which now included strings and vocalists, with dramatic episodes glamorizing the activities of the Army Air Forces Technical Training Command. Its purpose: to entice volunteers into that branch of the service.

In June Glenn had tested the program with a few local shows emanating directly from Yale and beamed into the Boston area over station WEEI. By mid-July it was ready for nationwide consumption.

At first the show was broadcast over the CBS network, but after seven or eight weeks it was switched over to NBC, where it remained for eleven months. By this time Glenn had assembled an entire radio production staff that included several writers, an announcer, Lieutenant Donald Briggs, who had been a radio actor and who later became the unit's executive officer, and a producer-director, George Voutsas, who for several years had been producing and directing strictly longhair classical-music shows for NBC.

Having been associated with many of the world's leading conductors of so-called serious music, Voutsas had every right to

ABOVE: Three-fourths of the rhythm section—guitarist Carmen Mastren, pianist Mel Powell and drummer Ray McKinley—dig Phil Cogliano's hot fiddle, as arranger Jerry Gray casually smokes and drummer Frank Ippolito looks over Powell's shoulder.

BELOW: The Crew Chiefs and Ray McKinley: (left to right) Gene Steck, Murray Kane, Steve Steck, Artie Malvin, Lynn Allison and McKinley. Steve Steck also played trumpet; Malvin clashed cymbals in the marching band.

be skeptical of Glenn's conducting ability. But once he saw Glenn in action, that skepticism turned to admiration. George, who returned to NBC after the war and became a fixture as a producer of *Monitor*, recently told me, "I would put Glenn on a par with the great symphony conductors of our times. He had a tremendous ability to get the most out of his men and the arrangements. In his conducting, he was especially good at producing just the right shadings. He would study every score very carefully until he knew just what he wanted from it and then he would go out and get it. Even the arrangers themselves, who wrote the scores, couldn't come close to him."

Of course, Glenn had a magnificent group under him. The string section contained top musicians from the NBC, Cleveland and other leading symphonies. The brass was powerful, clean and accurate with two fine, experienced section leaders, trumpeter Zeke Zarchy and trombonist Jimmy Priddy. (Captain Miller, true to protocol, seldom played with the enlisted men.) The strong sax team was led by Hank Freeman and featured some brilliant clarinet playing by Peanuts Hucko. Bernie Privin and Bobby Nichols took the jazz trumpet solos. And the full band was carried along by the propulsive drive of a rhythm section of Ray McKinley on drums, Trigger Alpert on bass, Carmen Mastren on guitar and Mel Powell at the piano. In addition, the unit had a brilliant French horn player named Addison Collins, Jr., and a fine vocal quartet called the Crew Chiefs.

Until he left for OCS, Martin had been the featured singer. Most colorful and best known among the actors was big, brawny Broderick Crawford, already a famous movie star. Well equipped to handle his booze, he was known to spend hours at a time with the Captain when both felt like falling into less military moods. In fact, Crawford became so dedicated to Glenn and his radio series that, even though he broke his arm and could have put in for an army discharge, he elected to stay on.

Glenn appreciated Brod's loyalty and made sure that the upper brass in the Pentagon heard about it. He wrote them a letter dated July 31, 1943, in which he stated, "Although his arm is almost certainly permanently disabled [It wasn't.], he takes the attitude he can be of assistance to us in the business we are in and isn't going to attempt to be discharged."

The omnipresent top brass postponed the July 10 start of the radio series. The trouble: script clearance, the kind of interference usually reserved for sponsors of commercial radio shows. How Glenn must have longed for Chesterfield and "the smoke that satisfies"! The series did debut a week later. But throughout its eleven months' run it could never escape the threat of instant interference from a jittery Pentagon.

In October there was talk of shifting the show to New Haven. One of the reasons, according to a letter from AAFTC headquarters: "Everyone would be very happy if the trip to New York could be eliminated. If anything should happen to one of the trucks en route to New York it would make very good pickings for [Westbrook] Pegler and Uncle Walter [Winchell]." Even some advertising agencies showed more guts.

Eventually the air force began appreciating the public relations value of the radio series so much that it decided to relieve Glenn of his duties as band director of the AAFTC so that he could concentrate completely on the radio unit. Glenn, who was still bucking a bunch of tone-deaf brass, minded not one bit. In a November 5 letter to Mary Dillon, his former secretary at Knollwood Field, he announced, "I'm not connected with the stinking music program in the AAFTC. It is really G.I. now."

But his troubles continued. Top brass officers kept up a nit-picking attack, second- and third-guessing Glenn and his radio series. Three days after his letter to Mary Dillon, Glenn fired a bitter barrage to Lieutenant Colonel Richard E. Daley at Command Headquarters. It ran the emotional gamut from threats to self-pity:

> The point I'm trying to make is that if we are persistently heckled by various higher authorities for trying to do the job as best we know, my own personal desire would be to forget about the whole thing and to get into some routine military function where this opposition wouldn't be ever present.
>
> The higher authorities do not realize that in the radio business that channels would delay action on important matters to such an extent that the scheduled radio time would probably

be long gone before an answer was obtained from Fort Worth through Greensboro and this Headquarters.

As you know, I have no personal ambitions for publicity or anything else in attempting to make this unit successful. I don't intend to have a band after the war so there is no use of plugging me or anything like that. I only figured to do a public relations job for the Air Forces, and the best one I could. I don't understand why so many people want to make it so difficult.

Chapter 34

The heckling continued. But Glenn obviously had no intentions of carrying out his threat "to get into some routine military function." Instead, he forged ahead with even more innovations.

The most dramatic occurred on July 28 in the Yale Bowl. There, in the midst of a giant war-bond rally, Glenn unveiled his modernized military band. Instead of the usual dozen or more marching snare and bass drummers, just two percussionists, complete with the complex drum kits used in big swing bands, and two string bass players, never before heard in a military band, provided all the rhythm. And instead of marching along with the rest of the soldiers, they rode on top of two jeeps that rolled along with the marching band.

The sight and the sound electrified the large crowd. Cheers went up as the swinging band marched by. The cadets strutted as they had never strutted before. Military music in general, and the Sousa marches in particular, had never had it so good.

But, as *Time* magazine reported, "Oldtime, long-haired U.S. Army bandmasters had the horrors." Commenting on Glenn's attempt to swing some of the Sousa marches with such *Time*-styled descriptions as "military rug-cutting," "the U.S. Army swinging its hips instead of its feet," and "there was an Afro-Saxon in the woodpile," the article quoted Glenn: "There hasn't been a successful army band in the country. . . . We've got to keep pace with the soldiers. . . . Why, there's no question about it—anybody can improve on Sousa."

The new, modern Glenn Miller marching band, complete with two jeeps carrying drums and string basses, debuts in the Yale Bowl.

Deprecating Sousa in those war years was like insisting your local Boy Scout troop smoked pot. Though he vehemently denied having made such a statement, Glenn was lambasted, especially by Sousa's successor, Edwin Franko Goldman. In a wire to *Time* demanding a retraction, Glenn supplied what he insisted was his correct quote: "There has not been a successful military-type band in civilian life for the past five or six years. I feel modern harmony would greatly improve the inspiring melodies of the Sousa marches."

Glenn did enlist one strong supporter from the American Musical Establishment. Marshall Bartholomew, the highly respected director of the Yale Glee Club, noted in a long letter to *Time* that he was "well aware that much could be done to improve the status of military band music in the U.S., but the trouble lies in Washington, not in New Haven. My hat is off to young men like Capt. Glenn Miller who can put aside the glamour and the big money of topflight professional careers and enter upon the unexciting routine of an army band on army pay and throw into this new task such energy, enthusiasm, and skill

To William Johnson
Time Magazine
Time and Life Bldg.
New York City.

Statements attributed to me by
Times Reporter inaccurately quoted in
Time 8 Sept 1943. Correct statement
Follows Quote There Has not
Been a successful military type
Band in civilian life for
the past 5 or 6 yearsstp I
feel Modern Harmony would
greatly improve the inspiring
melodies of the Sousa Marches
Unquote. Suggest you advise your
readers of correct quotation.
Glenn Miller
Captain AC

The original draft of Glenn's reply to *Time* magazine.

as to quicken the pulse and lighten the heart of everyone within
hearing distance."

As might be expected, the *Time* story encouraged more
grousing and nit-picking from the traditionalists. Headquarters
command sent up a lieutenant in charge of band training to
review the Miller marching band. We never could understand
why Glenn didn't break up and laugh right in the guy's face
when, after having watched the band march by in review, he
cornered Glenn and told him, amidst lisps, "Captain Miller, I
think your muthic ith thenthathional! But I mutht tell you I

notithed thomething lacking. It dothn't have enough thowman-thip. When the men in the front—the tromboneth—were marching, they weren't alwayth together. One man had hith trombone thlide here; another had it here, and another had it way out here. Why can't they move their thlideth in the thame way at the thame time?"

If Glenn was becoming paranoid by this time, who could blame him? "I have some authentic information regarding a condition that irks the Jesus out of me," he wrote his friend Colonel Daley in February 1944, and proceeded to inform him of what appeared to be a plot to limit his recording of V Discs, the twelve-inch vinyl platters that were being sent directly to the troops. "Don't record any more V Discs by the 2nd AAFTC Radio Unit because we do not want to build up Miller," he insisted a colonel had ordered. "This seems to me like a hell of a good way to win the war," Glenn added sarcastically. "I am perfectly willing to make V Discs *without* my name appearing on them. However, Major Dunstetter's name is on the Santa Ana discs and all civilians that make V Discs have their names on them. . . . I would like to see the 'Plastic Surgeon's big britches' pinned on this Lt. Colonel who is so magnanimous and open-minded in setting up his personal music policies."

In his earlier letter to Colonel Daley, Glenn had claimed that he didn't intend to have a band after the war. Surely this must have been a ploy merely to strengthen his position. None of us ever believed that he didn't intend to continue his career. In fact, Billy May claims that Glenn once told him, "I'm going into this war and coming out some kind of a hero."

Certainly, if he hadn't intended to have a band after the war, he wouldn't have become so upset by the threat of his name being left off V Discs. Because the musician's union had stopped bands from recording for commercial companies, these records had become important to any leader who wanted to keep his name and music before his fans. And Glenn obviously wanted to do just that.

Further evidence: In a letter to music publisher Jack Robbins, written early in 1944, Glenn, after expressing pride in the music of his new, enlarged orchestra, explicitly announced: "Come post war, I plan to carry on in a vein similar to this."

Maybe Glenn had begun to develop some masochistic streak, because, despite constant hammering from above, he did continue to come up with revolutionary suggestions for the utilization of his music. He volunteered his services to the Office of War Information (OWI), proposing that his band make propaganda transcriptions, beamed into foreign countries along with announcements in the local languages. He offered to create and produce a WAC-recruiting radio series, enhanced with romantic music by his lush strings and by singer Johnny Desmond, and, according to his letter of proposal, "with female celebrities like Kate Smith, Helen Hayes, Margaret Sullavan, Katherine Cornell, or Gertrude Lawrence plugging the WAC's and their activities in some very interesting dramatic skits." And he also proposed cutting into his regular weekly shows with live segments from London to create an ever-greater feeling of immediacy with the combat zone.

Clearly, Glenn was completely devoted to the war effort. Unfortunately, few of his superiors seemed to sympathize with his modern, imaginative approaches. His suggestions went unheeded; his frustrations kept growing and growing.

His biggest ambition of all was to take his band to Europe to play for the troops there in person. Time after time, he had contacted the War Department heads, even going to Washington to plead his case in person. Time after time he had been rejected. Sometimes, according to his friend Jerry Gray, "he would come back feeling so dejected that he'd say things like, 'Jerry, I guess I'm all through.' "

What Glenn might not have realized, or at least admitted to himself, was that he was doing such a stupendous job raising money playing for war-bond drives that the Pentagon might have felt he was more valuable as a fund-raiser than as a potential overseas morale-booster. Certainly his grosses were exceedingly impressive. At one rally in Garden City, New York, he raised $2,300,000 in pledges. A few weeks later, at two rallies in Chicago and St. Louis, he helped to bring in more than $4,000,000 per night.

Bond buyers.

And yet, despite all his gung-ho enthusiasm for playing in person for the troops, Glenn must still have had some reservations. For after so many years of hoping, he and Helen had, in the spring of 1943, finally achieved their greatest ambition: a child of their own.

What nature couldn't produce for them the Cradle Society of Evanston, Illinois, did. They had filed their adoption application two years earlier. Finally, after many interviews and much waiting, they were awarded their Stevie.

To some grownups Glenn Miller was strictly a cold, emotionless fish. But not to his Stevie. The affection gushed forth. Nothing like it had ever happened to him before. He truly

Glenn with Stevie and Helen
outside their Tenafly home
shortly before the band shipped
overseas.

popped his emotional cork. Whenever he had free time, he would
go home to Tenafly to see his new son—to play with him; to hold
him; to love him.

Chicago, Illinois
I Sustain The Wings
Service Men's Center

June 10, 1944
Saturday
NBC-5:00 P.M.

I SUSTAIN THE WINGS
(Capt. Glenn Miller-J. C. MacGregor-Pvt. Sol Meyer-M/Sgt. Norman Leyden)
          Lt. Don Briggs: I Sustain The Wings.---I Sustain The Wings. The Army
               Air Forces present the Band of the Training Command under the directi
               of Captain Glenn Miller. And now Captain Glenn Miller.
Captain Glenn Miller: Thank you, Lieutenant Don Briggs and good evening everybod
     It's been a big week for our side. Over on the beaches of Normandy our boys
     have fired the opening guns of the long awaited drive to liberate the world.
     And over here the folks who are backing up those boys are staging another big
     push of their own, the Fifth War Loan Drive. To lend a hand with the band we'r
     swinging around the countryside ourselves to do what we can to keep those
     invasion dollars moving over to the fighting front where they're needed in the
     shape of guns, tanks and planes. And tonight we're at the Service Men's Center
     here in Chicago where already over twelve million service men and women have
     been guests of the city of Chicago. Now to get a little music here are the boy
     with their rocket gun version of Flying Home.
FLYING HOME
(From "Swinging A Dream")
(DeLange-Benny Goodman-Lionel Hampton)
Captain Glenn Miller: Now here's Sergeant Johnny Desmond.
LONG AGO AND FAR AWAY
(From the film "Cover Girl")
(Jerome Kern-Ira Gershwin)(Norman Leyden arrangment)
          Vocal refrain by Sergeant Johnny Desmond
AIR FORCE COMMERCIAL---INCIDENTAL MUSIC AND SOUND EFFECTS

I SUSTAIN THE WINGS   AM. POP. MUSIC END-390-1176   Victor SPA-7-17
(Capt. Glenn Miller-J. C. MacGregor-Pvt. Sol Meyer-M/Sgt. Norman Leyden)
          Captain Glenn Miller: This is Captain Glenn Miller saying so long
               for all our gang. Next week I Sustain The Wings will be brought to
               you by another band of the Training Command of the Army Air Forces
               with Captain Bob Jennings the C.O. and the music under the direction
               of Sergeant Harry Bluestone. We've enjoyed playing for you and we
               hope you've enjoyed listening to us.

Opening and closing remarks
by Glenn during his final U.S.
radio show.

     And like almost any father who could afford to, Glenn kept
buying toys and more toys for his new boy. Tom Sheils, who was
handling much of Glenn's business while Glenn was in service,
reports that when Glenn came into New York each Saturday for

the radio show, "there would always be a present in the trunk of his car for our Tommy—and exactly the same thing for his Stevie. Glenn was very careful what he bought, too. There would be things like leather blocks—always toys that couldn't possibly hurt the kids."

By the time Stevie had reached his first birthday, Helen and Glenn became convinced that parenthood was for them. And so they applied again to the Cradle Society—this time for a sister for Stevie. And again they proceeded to wait.

But then, waiting had become the name of the game for Glenn. Finally, after all that badgering of the War Department to permit him to take his band to Europe, hopeful news did begin to trickle through, but so very slowly. Early in May Glenn traveled once more to Washington. This time he went to talk with Colonel Ed Kirby, a highly influential officer on the Washington scene. Kirby loved the band's music and he appreciated Glenn's talents and ideas. Even more importantly, the hip colonel had direct ties to General Eisenhower, in charge of all European forces. That meant he could, if necessary, bypass all the AAF brass—those who had been thwarting Glenn's ambitious plans—even top air force general "Hap" Arnold himself. Suddenly the military wheels began creaking a little less.

Extra support came from another important officer, General Walter Weaver, the commanding general of the Army Air Forces Technical Training Command, who had been primarily instrumental in setting up the Radio Production Unit. On May 9, in a letter of appreciation for past kindnesses, Glenn informed the general: "We have a deal going at the present time which looks pretty much as though we will be sent overseas shortly. As you know, this has been our goal for a long, long time, and one of the happiest things I could report to you is that we have received favorable answer to our request for overseas service."

Not all of us in New Haven would go overseas. Some months earlier, when the second AAFTC Radio Unit had been set up, Glenn had selected those soldiers he considered best equipped to carry out his morale-building plans. Their major duties centered on the radio series. Included in the unit were musicians, arrangers, singers, script writers, radio actors and directors, and even an instrument-repair man. Later, on April 30, 1944, so that Glenn could wield even greater control over his personnel, the outfit became the 2001st Base Unit (Radio Production), with all of the men assigned directly to Glenn's group instead of, as previously, to the Headquarters Detachment at Yale.

With the unit now firmly under his own control, Glenn proceeded to firm up its personnel prior to the overseas trek. In a letter to Colonel Kirby, Glenn listed the names and the duties of all the sixty-two men he wanted to take with him. He also requested two more soldiers he thought would be very valuable: Vicente Gomez, the famed Spanish guitarist, and "Almost-Second-Lieutenant" Tony Martin. He got neither.

As usual, in his planning Glenn overlooked no details. In his letter to Kirby he requested "that priority be given the shipment of such equipment as is necessary to enable the unit to function properly. This would take care of the quite bulky library and also allow the men to bring their own instruments. Each man owns his own instrument and many of them are extremely valuable. Most of the string section have three- or four-thousand-dollar instruments. My thought was that should a group of soldiers walk into a POE with bundles of instruments under their arms and music etc., they would be ordered to leave them here unless authority be granted in their transportation request."

Late in May, the news that some of us were bound for overseas trickled into New Haven. I had for a long time known about Glenn's tremendous desire to go where the action was. I had told him that I wanted to go along, and, even though I hadn't been assigned to the radio unit, I had hoped Glenn would, when the time came, use me as a writer—as a reporter and in public relations—and as a substitute drummer. When, following a news leak on columnist Jimmy Fidler's radio show, the news was finally confirmed, and I didn't find my name on the list of those going, I asked Glenn why. But I could never get a direct answer from him. Someone—I think it was Don Haynes—gave me some sort of a story that Glenn was so fond of me personally that he figured I'd be safer back in the States. I never did buy that explanation. All I knew for sure was that my relationship with

Glenn had lost much of its intimacy and mutual trust. I didn't know exactly why. And I guess I never will.

Don Haynes, who had been so close to Glenn in civilian life, both as a friend and as a personal manager, had been drafted later than most of us. After much urging from Glenn, he had finally gone through Officer Candidate School, and, after getting his commission, had been assigned to the unit in New Haven as its administrative officer.

His was one of the most difficult of all jobs. Planted right in the midst of a pack of musicians—many of whom wanted to know from nothing when it came to discipline—he was made responsible for their toeing their military marks. He was primarily a businessman, so that on a creative level he had very little in common with his enlisted men. What's more, businessmen too often are looked upon with suspicion and mistrust by musicians. So Don really had to prove himself.

To me, Don was always a very decent and warm gentleman—an opinion not shared by some of the guys in the band who knew him only as an administrator and disciplinarian, and one that I myself questioned one morning when Don came around to inspect our quarters. For some reason or other, he decided to reach up inside my closet and run his finger along, of all places, the top of the door casement. Sure enough, he found some dust. "Better get that clean," he snapped with a deadly serious look, and left me wondering whether he really had gone completely G.I., as some of the guys claimed, or if he were putting me on.

In any case, the incident didn't ruin our friendship. During the New Haven days I didn't see very much of him because he spent most of his time with Glenn and the radio unit. But after the band went overseas, he and I corresponded quite a bit, and then, after it returned, we saw a good deal more of each other.

Shortly before he died in June of 1971, he and his wife, Polly, and I spent a beautiful evening together. We reminisced about the old days, about the happy days with Glenn and Helen, and Don filled me in on more details about Glenn and the band's European jaunt. I learned that he had kept a diary of his and Glenn's and the group's overseas activities. When I saw Polly again about a year later, she very kindly offered to make me a

Don Haynes (second from right) with Mel Powell, Zeke Zarchy and Bernie Privin, looking very naked without his mustache.

copy of that diary, and to let me quote from it in this book. Naturally, I accepted her generous offer. And so you, my reader, as well as I, are indebted to Don and to Polly Haynes for many of the details in the pages that follow.

Chapter 35

"Next to a letter from home, Captain Miller, your organization is the greatest morale builder in the ETO," General Jimmy Doolittle told Glenn at the end of one of the seventy-one concerts that the band played during its five and a half months' stay in England.

Glenn didn't disagree, either. He was proud of his contributions to the war effort. In a letter to me he mentioned that "we came here to bring a much-needed touch of home to some lads who have been here a couple of years. These lads are doing a hell of a job—they have been starved for real, live American music." He then went on to describe his own reactions to the response of the G.I.'s, calling it "the most important sound that can possibly come out of such concerts—the sound of thousands of G.I.'s reacting with an ear-splitting, almost hysterical happy yell after each number."

Glenn had flown to London ahead of the band. He left on June 18, ten days after the final *I Sustain the Wings* broadcast, attended at his insistence by his mother and sister, who arrived from Colorado, and just five days after Germany had begun to blitz the English capital with V-1 buzz bombs that were to kill close to five thousand people.

On June 19 the entire radio unit departed from New Haven for Camp Kilmer in New Jersey for a long series of shots and a lot of indoctrination. Its travel orders, shrouded in mystery,

1 July 1944

SPECIAL ORDERS)
          :
NUMBER   125)   E X T R A C T

  *   *   *   *   *

  26. VOSC, Captain ALTON G. MILLER, 0505273, AC, Hq Comd, WPGV to Bedford,
England, o/a 2 July 1944 to carry out the instructions of the Supreme Commander.
TCNT. Reimbursement for quarters and rations is authorized in accordance with
Circular 63, Hq ETOUSA, 5 June 1944, for such times as government quarters and
messing facilities are not available. TDN. 60-136-P 432-02 A 212/50425.

  27. VOSC, 1 July 1944, the following named enlisted men are attached unassigned to Hq Co, Hq Comd:

M/Sgt Norman F. Leyden, 20126112	M/Sgt Rubin Zarchy, 14083172
T/Sgt Paul Dudley, 32967492	T/Sgt Generoso Graziano, 31354534
T/Sgt Raymond F. McKinley, 38430383	T/Sgt John W. Sanderson, 20126109
S/Sgt Herman T. Alpert, 35161800	S/Sgt Henry Freeman, 20126120
S/Sgt Harry Katzman, 14083156	S/Sgt George Ockner, 32413903
S/Sgt Mel Powell, 32801024	S/Sgt James R. Priddy, 35652920
S/Sgt Carl E. Swanson, 11056322	S/Sgt George Voutsas, 36367412
S/Sgt Ralph N. Wilkinson, 32903779	Sgt Vincent H. Carbone, 32868252
Sgt William R. Crawford, 39267223	Sgt Johnny A. Desemone, 18094162
Sgt John R. Halliburton, 34546410	Sgt Harry Hartwick, 12092497
Sgt David D. Herman, 32907667	Sgt Michael A. Hucko, 32287826
Sgt James B. Jackson, 32861212	Sgt Carmen N. Mastandrea, 32863218
Sgt Robert J. Nichols, 32886031	Sgt Bernard Privin, 32967251
Sgt David Sackson, 32230674	Sgt David Schwartz, 35301352
Sgt Stephen Steck, Jr., 33462453	Sgt William E. Thomas, 34172407
Sgt Emanuel Wishnow, 18121658	Cpl Eugene Bergen, 14084522
Cpl Morris P. Bialkin, 32684329	Cpl Henry Brynan, 31248742
Cpl Philip A. Cogliano, 31360218	Cpl Addison S. Collins, Jr., 18126025
Cpl Earl R. Cornwell, 18102660	Cpl Paul A. Dubov, 32889468
Cpl Milton A. Edelson, 36642741	Cpl John M. Ferrier, 32886327
Cpl Frederick G. Guerra, 31311614	Cpl Stanley Harris, 14084447
Cpl Murray Kane, 32962615	Cpl Nathan Kaproff, 14083236
Cpl Ernest S. Kardos, 35266657	Cpl Arthur S. Malvin, 32785992
Cpl Richard M. Motvlinski, 14084526	Cpl Robert L. Ripley, 14084517
Cpl Joseph Shulman, 32792640	Cpl Julius Zifferblatt, 32900168
Pfc James L. Allison, 36661310	Pfc Thomas P. Cochran, 13141822
Pfc Lawrence Hall, 32719514	Pfc Francis J. Ippolito, 34546411
Pfc Joseph J. Kowalewski, 31335483	Pfc Fredy Ostrovsky, 32626828
Pfc Veto S. Pascucci, 36813244	Pfc Nathan Peck, 32907040
Pfc Jack M. Rusin, 32792603	Pfc Eugene Steck, 33603187
Pfc James J. Steele, 35090229	Pfc Mannie Thaler, 32812461

  28. VOSC the following named Enlisted men, attached unassigned, Hq Co, Hq
Comd, WPGV to Bedford, England, o/a 2 July 1944 to carry out the instructions of
the Supreme Commander. TCNT. Reimbursement for rations is authorized in accordance with Circular 63, Hq ETOUSA, 5 June 1944, for such times as government messing
facilities are not available.

- 1 -
R E S T R I C T E D

instructed the band to proceed to the European Theater of
Operations "via NY 8245," whatever that might have been.
They finally left Kilmer just before midnight of June 21, arrived
at a siding in Jersey City an hour later alongside a ferry and
boarded the ferry, which sailed up the Hudson River directly to a
large ocean liner moored at pier 90. At 1:15 A.M. the guys began
climbing what amounted to five flights of stairs of "NY 8245":
the gigantic *Queen Elizabeth.*

As Don Haynes recalled in his diary: "A sight I will long
remember was those fine musicians, who for the last ten days had
had very little rest, with sore arms from countless inoculations
(with more to come aboard ship), carrying, dragging, pushing

Helen and Glenn in front of a car with an "A" gas ration sticker.

their barracks and duffle bags, instrument cases, overcoats, and their carbine rifles strapped to their shoulders, pointing every direction, as they climbed those stairs and across the gangplank onto NY 8245."

The six-day Atlantic crossing ran into rough seas. Consequently, many band members divided their time between playing for the 17,000 troops on board and retiring to staterooms or to rails to attend to fits of seasickness. "We must have played seven or eight shows in one day," Ray McKinley recalls. "Just as soon as one group left that main ballroom, another would come in. I don't know how the brass players' lips took it."

When the ship finally dropped anchor in Scotland's Firth of Clyde, the band was greeted by a tired-looking Glenn, who immediately started to impress the men with the seriousness of the terrible blitzing that the Nazis had recently begun inflicting upon London. He pointed out that he had been sleeping sporadically in a bomb shelter beneath the BBC (the British Broadcasting Company) studios because it had been totally unsafe to sleep above ground.

The guys in the band found out for themselves precisely what

Glenn was talking about. Almost as soon as they arrived in London, they were greeted by a buzz-bomb alert and eyewitnessed the devastating results of a hit only about half a mile away.

The band's quarters turned out to be a house at 25 Sloane Court, which it shared with numerous M.P.'s. Reportedly, 90 percent of all buzz bombs traveled over this area, which had been nicknamed "Buzz Bomb Alley." The situation disturbed Glenn greatly. Intensely concerned with the welfare of his men, many of whom he had recruited himself, Glenn immediately started to find ways of getting them out of the "Alley" and into a safer spot.

But the guys were just as concerned. On opening night, the constant barrage of buzz bombs, every quarter-hour or less, had convinced all but four to desert 25 Sloane Court and to join the rest of the soldiers and regular citizenry in their already crowded bomb shelters. When the guys had first arrived, some had gone to the roof of the building to get a closer look at the bombs. "I had the crazy feeling that as long as I could see a bomb, it couldn't hurt me," Johnny Desmond rationalized. But almost all the others, after having seen the bomb's awesome power, faced up to reality and ducked down as far below ground as they could go.

But not sergeants Desmond, Zeke Zarchy, and Paul Dudley, and Corporal Tommy Cochran. Claiming they couldn't take the foul, dank air of the shelter, they decided to spend the night in their assigned quarters. Don Haynes, who returned the next morning with Glenn, reported that "we found the Fearless Four huddled together in a corner of the room on the first floor. They made *Lost Weekend* look like a company picnic.

"Glenn was more determined than ever to get the boys out of there, but fast. So we went to SHAEF [Supreme Headquarters of the Allied Expeditionary Forces], and after phone calls to a dozen or more U.S. Air Bases, we finally secured two busses to move the outfit from Sloane Court to Bedford two days later."

Two days later fell on a Sunday and some of the musicians griped at having to give up their day off to repack all their belongings onto trucks and to be driven away from London,

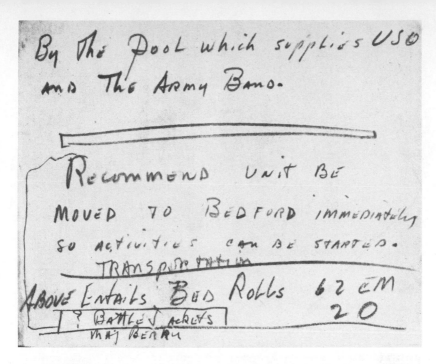

The move to Bedford was initiated when Glenn scribbled this recommendation.

which they wanted to see, to a remote village fifty miles north. But the majority did recognize the risk of remaining. Besides, few, if any, had yet caught up with a decent night's sleep.

That all happened on Sunday, July 2. On the next day in Bedford, the entire band began transforming what had once been a pottery factory (it is now a social club called Co-Partners Hall, owned by the local Gas Board) and then, during the German blitz, a temporary studio for the BBC, into a studio suitable for music. This meant deadening the sound that bounced off the brick walls, to get the tight, closed-in feeling that characterized the recordings and broadcasts of the early forties. And so the guys got hold of dozens upon dozens of burlap bags, and, using these plus their shelter halves and extra blankets, spent a couple of days lining the brick walls.

Fortunately, the direct line into the BBC recording and broadcasting studios back in London had already been hooked up, so that within a couple of days the band could start broadcasting. The guys christened their new studio "8-H" in honor of the huge NBC studio back in New York from which

ABOVE: Co-Partners Hall as it looks today in Bedford. It is currently being used as a local social club.

BELOW: 25 Sloane Court right after the buzz-bombing.

Arturo Toscanini and the NBC Symphony used to broadcast and Benny Goodman had aired his famed Saturday night *Let's Dance* programs.

Meanwhile, early the next morning, back at Sloane Court, one of Hitler's best-directed buzz bombs had burst just a few feet from the front of No. 25. According to the Haynes diary, "The entire front of the building was blown in and the place was a shambles." Twenty-five M.P.'s were killed and seventy-eight others were dug out of buildings on Sloane Court. Thanks to Glenn's foresight and determination, none were Miller bandsmen.

Glenn was both shocked and grateful. For a couple of years he and Don had had a thing going about what he always called "The Miller Luck." It had been holding out beautifully all through their association, and Glenn used to tell Don, "As long as it stays with us, we have nothing to worry about." The Sloane Court escape fortified Glenn's current optimism.

Obviously, some members of the ETO brass were impressed with having the band under their jurisdiction. Within a week after its arrival it had officially been renamed "Captain Glenn Miller and his American Band of the Supreme Allied Command."

Exactly one week after its arrival in Bedford, the band had completed the radio studio and was broadcasting its first program over two large networks: the Allied Expeditionary Forces Network, beamed at the troops in England and on the Continent, and the BBC, England's only radio network, government-owned, and the sole source of all programming for the British citizens.

With his keen commercial sense and his great organizational ability, Glenn had created a whole series of programs—thirteen, in all, per week. The schedule included broadcasts by the entire concert orchestra, complete with the large string section and the various singers; a series called *Swing Shift* that featured a seventeen-piece dance band led by Ray McKinley, which played many of the Miller favorites of civilian days plus some arrangements that McKinley's civilian band used to play; and another series called *Uptown Hall* by a seven-piece jazz group led by pianist Mel Powell, and featuring Peanuts Hucko on clarinet and Bernie Privin on trumpet. Singer Johnny Desmond and a few strings, plus Addison Collins on French horn and Jackie Russin on the piano, also had a regular program called *A Soldier and a Song*. And finally there was a series called *Strings with Wings*, featuring the entire string section led by George Ockner, with its

Glenn huddles with Ray McKinley and Mel Powell, leaders of the big and small jazz bands respectively.

many symphony musicians. This series of programs created such glorious sounds that, according to Privin, "the rest of the band would get around the radio every Saturday morning just to listen."

The broadcasts over the AEF network lasted throughout the five and a half months that the band was stationed in England. The broadcasts over the BBC lasted one week.

On the evening of July 13 Glenn received a call to report to Broadcast House, the BBC's headquarters, at eleven o'clock the next morning. When he arrived with Don Haynes, they were ushered into the office of Maurice Gorham, in charge of relations between the BBC and the American Forces. Surrounded by several other BBC executives, Gorham, who seemed to be almost a caricature of "the typically British executive," and who buried many of his vowels and consonants in a walrus mustache, informed Glenn that the BBC had heard from listeners in fringe reception areas, remote from the nearest transmitter, complaining that they could hear only the band's louder passages. There were times, during the orchestra's softer music, he explained, when listeners thought the BBC had gone off the air. "And so, Captain Miller," Gorham stated, "I must insist that you keep your volume constant at all times!"

Glenn, never a tact master with critics, looked at Gorham in seeming disbelief, then asked him to repeat what he had said.

Gorham did. "I thought I heard you right the first time," Glenn said. He then proceeded to try to explain the importance of dynamics in his music; that contrasts in sound were an integral part of his band's style; that much of the music was soft for a definite purpose. And the more he tried to explain to the executive, who obviously was totally unfamiliar with the Miller music and the reasons for its tremendous popularity, the more frustrated and angry Glenn grew. Finally he looked at Gorham coldly, and very slowly and very emphatically suggested "a solution. Our mission over here is to broadcast to the troops over the AEF network and not to the civilians over the BBC. Therefore, you can do us and yourselves a favor by canceling all broadcasts over the BBC." And with that, he turned around and walked out. And the band went off the BBC.

Reactions came swiftly. One of the band's missions had been to foster even better Anglo-American relations. Glenn's exasperated exit tossed that portion of the mission into the "unaccomplished" heap. English listeners, thrilled for just a few days by live broadcasts by the band they considered the greatest in the world, bombarded the BBC for its actions. Newspaper editorials strongly condemned the move. But Glenn and the BBC wouldn't give one farthing. Finally, according to Haynes, one of the BBC diehards, in a final fit of futile frustration, excoriated not merely the Miller band but most American troops with, "You're over-paid; you're over-fed; you're over-sexed—and you're over here!"

"Over there" the band most certainly was—all over the place over there. Soon, in addition to its broadcasts, it began flying to bases throughout the British Isles to entertain the troops in person. According to statistics compiled by Sergeant George Voutsas, director of the band's radio shows who doubled as keeper of the daily activity reports, during its stay in England the band played seventy-one live concerts before a grand total of 247,500 ultra-enthusiastic listeners! And each week the band would also play a live broadcast before a gathering of townsfolk in a large meeting hall in Bedford called the Corn Exchange, still standing and still so named, which the bandsmen immediately rechristened Lombardo Hall, in honor of the band leader most commonly associated with that particular grain of music.

TOP: On the way to somewhere.

BOTTOM: Glenn and the band appear at an air base aboard a flat-bed truck.

Some of the appearances at the air bases produced some dramatic overtones. Bernie Privin recollects that often while the guys were waiting to play, they and their audiences would be scanning the skies for the return of planes. Then, when one of them would arrive, it would be greeted by spontaneous cheers.

Sometimes at those open-air concerts soldiers would lean on their carbines with their chins. "One guy accidentally shot himself that way," reports Privin.

On its trips, the band would take off from Thurleigh Air Base, six miles from Bedford, and return to Twinwood Farm, the airstrip three miles from their quarters—the same field from which Glenn would take off in December on his dramatic flight to Paris.

Much to Glenn's chagrin, such air travel became an important and often time-consuming way of life. Zeke Zarchy, the band's first sergeant, estimates that the band must have spent around six hundred hours flying to and from the various air bases. Sometimes, returning after dark, some of the inexperienced pilots assigned to the band had difficulty finding the field, and the men would be flown around for some scary hours before landing. Zarchy recalls one especially frightening descent: "We were just about to land when suddenly a bright red flare cut directly in front of us. Somehow or other we just missed barging into an entire squadron that was just taking off!"

Everywhere the band went, it was greeted with immense enthusiasm. The G.I.'s reacted to its appearances with just the sort of wild cheering and yelling that Glenn had expected. Starved for real live music and "the touch of home" that Glenn kept talking about, they stomped their feet and clapped their hands and let out long, loud yells wherever they gathered—often in huge airplane hangars in which they had built makeshift stages, many out of large crates piled high on top of one another, so that as many G.I.'s as possible could see the band. And Glenn and the guys really put out, blowing their brilliant sounds with never-failing enthusiasm, embellished by the bits of horn-blowing showmanship that had become an integral part of the civilian band's performances.

The enthusiasm infected not only the servicemen, whom it reminded of home, but also some new British converts, including some whose rich, royal blood flowed faster to the Miller band's provocative sounds.

One day in Bedford, Don Haynes was introduced to the queen of England, who had been inspecting the local Red Cross facilities. To quote from Don's diary: "The Queen extended her

ABOVE: Inside the band's traveling C-47 air bus.

BELOW: Outside the band's traveling C-47 air bus. Back row (left to right): Glenn, Hank Freeman, Milton Edelson, Paul Dudley, Carl Swanson, Whitey Thomas, Jack Ferrier, Murray Kane, Vince Carbone, David Saxon, Johnny Halliburton, Bob Ripley, Bobby Nichols, Lynn Allison, Jack Steele, Julius Zifferblatt, Larry Hall, Dave Schwartz, Morris Bialkin, Trigger Alpert, Phil Cogliano, Addison Collins, Jack Sanderson, Gene Bergen, Bernie Privin. Second row: Henry Brynan, Mannie Thaler, Jimmy Priddy, Joseph Kowelewski, Jimmy Jackson, Freddy Guerra, Dave Herman, George Ockner, Stan Harris, Carmen Mastren, Earl Cornwell. Third row: Johnny Desmond, Manny Wishnow, Freddy Ostrowski, Ernie Kardos, Harry Katzman, Dick Motolinski, Frank Ippolito, Nat Peck, Artie Malvin. Lying in front: Zeke Zarchy, Peanuts Hucko, Nat Kaproff, Ray McKinley, Mel Powell.

Cockney comedian Hal Monty (left) and Scottish comedian Peter Sinclair gang up on Glenn on the *Variety Band Box* program broadcast from the Queensberry All Services Club.

right hand and shook my hand warmly, and smiling all the while said, 'Leftenant 'Aynes, let me commend you, Captain Miller, and the members of your fine organization for the wonderful morale work you are doing. The Princesses Elizabeth and Margaret Rose are avid fans of the Glenn Miller Band and listen to your nightly broadcasts over the wireless regularly.' "

Another big fan turned out to be General Dwight D. Eisenhower, then heading the entire Allied Expeditionary Forces in Europe. According to Haynes, at the conclusion of an appearance by the band which Ike had requested, he made a point of going up to Glenn and personally thanking him for the band's immense contributions to the morale of his troops.

This sort of recognition obviously pleased Glenn tremendously. He was finally doing precisely what he had set out to do when he had written that letter back in the summer of '42, offering his services to the War Department. Little wonder, then, that when a gent named John Harding, managing director of a military entertainment center called the Queensberry All Services Club, suggested to Glenn that he bring the band into London for weekly concerts for the troops in the bomb-ridden city, Glenn jumped at the opportunity.

The late Sergeant Paul Dudley (soon to become Warrant Officer Paul Dudley), former producer of the *Coca-Cola Bandstand* radio series before the war and a new member of Glenn's group, reported that on July 30, two thousand uniformed youngsters filled the auditorium for the first show. Another two thousand waited hopefully outside, even though told that there would not be a second show. Midway in the program the sounds of a buzz-bomb alert filled the air. Harding rushed outside, trying desperately to disperse the crowd. "But," according to Dudley's report, "the Tommies and the G.I.'s, the WREN's and the WAC's still stood their ground, wearing those hopeful but determined looks." When Glenn heard about this, he immediately offered to play another show for those brave and dedicated fans, and from then on the band often put on repeat performances whenever enough uniformed servicemen and women were turned away from the first one because of lack of room.

Despite his aversion to planes, Glenn almost always flew with the band—to AAF and RAF camps and occasionally to hospitals, where he would divide the group into smaller units that could roam around and play in the various wards. Don Haynes reports that Glenn would go through every ward, "signing autographs and doing his best to cheer 'em up. These boys were so appreciative. The ones who couldn't applaud or yell showed by the expressions on their faces how much they enjoyed the entertainment."

But Glenn began to curtail his air travel after a particularly hairy incident at Hendon Airdrome near London. The Haynes diary reveals that "as we were heading in for a landing, red flares shot up on both sides of our plane and just about scared the pants off us! They were signaling for us not to land, so the pilot revved the motors, pulled up the flaps, and the plane shook, shimmied and stuttered across the field about a hundred feet off the ground, then finally gained altitude. We all thought we'd had it. Had we continued our landing pattern, we'd have landed right on top of the B-17 taking off directly in front of us!"

The Miller luck continued to hold out.

Still, the constant flying and occasional close calls began to have their effect upon Glenn. He began to act more irritated and to be annoyed by little things. As Haynes explained, much of his restlessness was aggravated by trouble he was having with his ears. Planes were not pressurized then, and Glenn would suffer

Somewhere along the southern coast of England, Glenn points skyward for Ray McKinley, Don Haynes and Tommy Corcoran.

from ringing in his ears for sometimes as long as twenty-four hours after a trip.

During the band's flights, Glenn, as leader, had the right to sit in the copilot's seat. But he seldom stayed there. According to Haynes, "He was just too nervous to sit still. He wanted to walk around and to stand up. He really suffered terribly on those trips.

"What used to bother him especially was the condition of some of the planes we flew in. He was, of course, just as conscious of the safety of his men as he was of his own, and he could never understand how they could assign us some of those war-weary crates. 'How can you risk the lives of all those musicians,' he used to ask some of the AAF officers. 'Aren't they more important than some of the bombs you carry on the *good* planes?' "

Several times, when Glenn could avoid traveling with the band, he and George Voutsas, who was directing the radio shows and wasn't needed for personal appearances, would sit and talk together back in Bedford.

"I finally got to know what Glenn was really like during some of those sessions," Voutsas recently told me. "It was just the two of us. I found him to be extremely warm, except that he still had that 'Don't-come-too-close-to-me' protective shell.

"Of all the officers and G.I.'s, I don't know of anyone who was as homesick as Glenn. [Ray McKinley reports that during a concert for General Eisenhower, Glenn sidled up to him in the middle of a long drum solo and called out softly, "Play it good, Mac. Maybe they'll send us home!"] When we were sitting in front of the fireplace, he would love to talk about his wife and his kids back home, even though he still hadn't set eyes on his little daughter. And he would also go into details about his plans for the future. 'When the war is over,' he once told me, 'I will guarantee all the guys, whether they like me or not—he knew he wasn't the most popular person in the world with some of his men—a professional career with my band. If they don't like it, I will replace them with other guys who have been in the service.' And then he told me how he would help finance them with loans and down payments on their homes.

"He told me about the plans he had for his own career. [Don Haynes reported that in addition to his music Glenn expected to take over a tri-state Coca-Cola distributorship and to invest in a string of motels.] The band would broadcast and record regularly for six months out of the year. And it would make movies and play theaters. And it would also play concerts. There is where he was thinking so far ahead—those concerts—because bands like his hardly ever played them. But of course, as you know, later on that's exactly where most of the money turned out to be for the bands.

"He also had a model house for his ranch Carl Swanson [a member of the string section] and Gene Steck [a member of the Crew Chiefs] helped him build. It was a very impressive thing, and he loved to look at it.

"One night, during one of these talks, he was feeling particularly low and homesick. He again had been talking about what he would do after the war. Then suddenly he looked up and said with about as much emotion as I'd ever seen him show: 'Christ, I don't know why I spend my time making plans like this.' I asked him why he said that, and he said, 'You know, George, I have an awful feeling you guys are going to go home without me, and I'm going to get mine in some goddamn beat-up old plane!' "

The model of "Tuxedo Junction," the California home that Glenn had
intended to build and live in. Bernie Privin, at right, also could dream a little.

Chapter 36

From back in the States, I had been sending the band newsletters, which Don Haynes used to tack up on the bulletin board at Bedford. Up at Yale a Captain Fiveash, a friend of Glenn and the band during their stay there, let me in on some news that had just appeared on the official orders: Effective August 17, 1944, Glenn had officially been promoted to major.

Naturally, I thought Glenn would be one of the first to hear, but that wasn't always the way the army worked. I included some congratulatory remarks in a newsletter that went out a few days later, and, much to my surprise, discovered that the first Glenn knew of his promotion, which had been in the works for quite some time, was when my newsletter got tacked up on that bulletin board. So my being left at home did pay off for him in one small way at least. And it paid off even more for me.

Captain Bob Vincent, in charge of V Discs, the twelve-inch, vinyl, 78-rpm records that went directly to the troops, had been having personal troubles with the sergeant handling most of the recording sessions. A mutual friend told Vincent about me, and a few months later I was transferred out of New Haven and into New York where my primary army duty was to record anyone I wanted to wherever I wanted to—provided, of course, I could get them to record for the troops for free. Fortunately, I had made many friends during my *Metronome* days (a fact that Vincent hadn't overlooked), so, combining my contacts with the preva-

RIGHT: Captain John Woolnough congratulates Glenn for having "made Major." They are inside an officers' club latrine, "the only place where we could find enough privacy to take a picture," noted Woolnough.

BELOW: Dinah and Glenn.

lent patriotic feeling, I had little difficulty lining up such recording stars as Benny Goodman, Louis Armstrong, Harry James, Ella Fitzgerald, the Dorseys, Lionel Hampton and many more.

In addition, various radio shows let us record dress rehearsals and actual broadcasts. Fortunately, before I arrived on the scene, someone had had the good sense to request almost all of the Miller band's *I Sustain the Wings* broadcasts and/or rehearsals, which is why so much of that orchestra's marvelous music was first made available on V Discs, and later on a big five-record set which RCA culled from the same sources.

Because of the metal shortage in England, however, few of the band's programs were recorded, and those that were had to be scrapped so that the metal discs could be recoated for future shows. Therefore, very little of the music the band played in England has been preserved. This includes one memorable session on August 30, during which the band was joined by Bing Crosby, who was then traveling through Europe for the USO, and another with Dinah Shore on September 16, who had flown over for the same purpose.

Crosby was completely knocked out by the band, and, after the session was over, took off a beautiful hand-painted tie and autographed it to "Glenn Miller's AAF Band—the Greatest Thing Since the Invention of Cup Mutes!"

Trumpeter Bernie Privin was immensely impressed with Crosby's total lack of formality, especially the way it contrasted with the Miller disciplinary attitude that he and the other rebels resented so deeply. "I remember Glenn came in and immediately said, 'OK, fellers, let's go.' But Bing stepped in and said, 'Hey, wait a minute. This is a freebee for the guys, isn't it?' And he brought out bottles of Scotch and whiskey for all of us. I got to tell you, that day we recorded some of the best stuff the band ever played!"

The band members' fond memories of Crosby match those that Bing still holds for Glenn. Aware of their sometimes-close relationship, I recently wrote Bing and asked him if he would like to contribute a few reminiscences to this book. He replied:

> We had several amusing incidents happen in England. One night, we were dining in a restaurant in Soho after the conclusion of a concert—he and I and Brod Crawford—and a great crowd gathered in the square below, demanding a song.

Bing with Jerry Gray and Glenn.

I came to the window and agreed to sing if they would disperse, because there was a law in effect then that because of the bombing no groups were allowed to assemble in the streets.

I asked them if I sang a song, if they would disperse, and they said they would. I sang "Pennies From Heaven," and they quickly dispersed. I don't know if it was a form of criticism or not.

A fog came in that night, I remember, and we had to crawl back to our hotel about a mile distant from the restaurant, on our hands and knees, feeling the curb as we moved along.

I was going over to France in a day or so, and Glenn offered to send Jack Russin, his pianist, over to expand my accompaniment. He left on a later plane, and though he got to France, we never did get together. I think Jack had a marvelous time, touring around France, looking for me, and visiting the various pubs and military installations.

All best wishes,
[signed] Bing Crosby

The longer the band remained in England, the greater its popularity grew. The result: Ever-increasing demands from various posts for personal appearances. It also meant that, in order to be able to fulfill those engagements, the band was forced to double up on its broadcast schedules, often recording shows in advance to be aired on dates when it would be out on the road entertaining the troops. The entire routine turned out to be much like the civilian band's when, back in the winter of 1940, the stiff schedule of the Paramount, the Hotel Pennsylvania, the regular Chesterfield shows and the regular recording dates almost created a complete collapse of the entire personnel and eventually did send Glenn into the hospital.

During the first two weeks of September the guys busted their backs trying to create enough advance programs so that they could continue with their personal appearances. During one period of six days they completed a total of twenty broadcasts while also playing at two more camps. In another two-day period they recorded a total of ten broadcasts!

To make matters worse, cold weather was setting in, but personal appearances were still being scheduled for outdoors. On one occasion, there was nothing the band could do—it was so cold in the hangar at Hardwicke right off the North Sea that the guys had to wear gloves to protect their fingers, and more than one brass player must have had some fears about his mouthpiece freezing to his lips!

Finally it all caught up with Glenn again. The heavy schedule and the raw, damp climate laid him low. Suffering from a bad sinus infection and running a high fever, he decided to cancel all activities, and directly following a recording session with Dinah Shore on September 16, he gave the band a four-day vacation, the first such rest period since the guys' arrival in England.

I had been hearing reports back in the States about Glenn's increasing irritability. Yet I was totally unprepared for his September 25 letter to me, written right after he had read a review of the band in *Metronome*. Filed from England by one of our correspondents, Private First Class David Bittan, it included the following excerpts:

At an 8th Air Force Station in England Glenn Miller unveiled the 20-piece edition of his famous band and showed that he could whip a bunch of GIs into a smart, clean-sounding band. But it doesn't come up to the Miller band of old. . . . There is little doubt that Miller's is the most popular band among boys in the service, and their enthusiasm showed Glenn he hasn't lost any of his popularity.

The outfit started off with the inevitable "In the Mood" featuring two mediocre tenor men, one a character named Carbone who sounded like Georgie Auld on a bad kick, and the other, Jack Ferrier, who played fourth tenor for [Jan] Savitt and a lot of other bands but seldom took any solos. The band showed right off the bat that something was missing.

That started it off, and arrangement after arrangement followed, through "Choo Choo" and "Black Magic," right up to "Anvil Chorus." The rhythm section with Mel Powell, Trigger Alpert, Carmen Mastren and Ray McKinley kicked off a good beat, but Mel was plagued by an inefficient p.a. system which drowned him out. . . .

The kick of the evening was Peanuts Hucko, out of the Bradley-McKinley combo, taking a back seat to the unoriginal

Carbone on tenor. Peanuts was playing alto! He surprised with a fine clarinet solo on "Stealin' Apples" which featured him all the way through. But that still didn't make up for the lack of his tenor work. . . .

Powell, McKinley, Alpert, Privin and Hucko are a kick. And the GIs in England and France are getting a lot of pleasure out of Glenn's being over here. But this reviewer thinks that with the personnel Glenn has at his disposal the band could be a lot better. No doubt it is one of the best service bands ever, but here is one lad who is eagerly awaiting a chance to hear a second service band now in England, the Navy Band led by Sam Donahue. Then he hopes to get some real musical kicks instead of a repetition of arrangements that have been played and replayed, all in the same precise, spiritless manner that has characterized Miller bands since he first attained commercial success.

I didn't happen to agree with everything that Bittan wrote, though I thought he had made some good points. And, besides, it had always been the magazine's policy to permit reputable critics to air their opinions without editorial interference.

Obviously, Glenn didn't agree with our policy. And he disagreed even more vociferously with Bittan's opinions. His response certainly does reveal some lack of skin depth. But it also reveals a man intensely concerned with and proud of a job that he and his men were doing. Here is his letter in its entirety:

Dear George: I've been intending to write you for a long time but we have been awfully busy since arriving here. During the month of August we played at thirty-five different bases and during our "spare time" did forty-four broadcasts. It damned near killed the guys but the reaction to the band's appearances is so great that the boys eat it up despite the ruggedness.

We get occasional reports from Yale via The Beaver [the post's weekly newspaper] and some of the boys hear from friends there.

I couldn't write this letter without bringing to your attention an article that appeared in Metronome. You know my feelings about being criticized by people who do not have any technical knowledge of music. Well, this little item tops everything. We, the band, didn't come here to set any fashions in music or to

Drummer McKinley, bassist Alpert and clarinetist Hucko all provided kicks for reviewer Pfc. Bittan.

create any new swing styles—we came merely to bring a much-needed touch of home to some lads who have been here a couple of years. These lads are doing a hell of a job—they have been starved for real, live American music and they know and appreciate only the tunes that were popular before they left the States. For their sake, we play only the old tunes. You know enough about musicians to know that *we* would certainly enjoy playing new tunes and plenty of them. I expect the "critic" who wrote the article expected to hear mainly new arrangements featuring a bunch of guys taking choruses à la a Town Hall Concert.

We played, as usual, in a hangar atop two fifty foot crash trucks and this stupid observer even criticized our P.A. set. Anything resembling an efficient P.A. set in this E.T.O. is locked in a safe every night and is for use where it will do the most good—on military frontline operations. Our critic's peeve about Hucko not playing tenor is great. If Hucko didn't, I wonder who WOULD play lead clarinet? Or if he would double where he would get the tenor upon which to play.

This lad missed the boat completely on the conditions and the purpose for our being here. I'm surprised that the Metronome editorial staff printed the thing because they should realize the needs over here, even though the "hot soldier" over here doesn't seem to. While he listened for things which he opined were musically "wrong," he failed to hear the most important sound that can possibly come out of such concerts— the sound of thousands of G.I.'s reacting with an ear-splitting, almost hysterical happy yell after each number. That's for us, Brother, even if it doesn't happen to be for Metronome.

The net result of all this is a determination on my part to never spend another dime with Metronome magazine. What they print about any civilian band of mine is O.K. with me and they are certainly entitled to print anything they like without me taking any action to defend my position. But when they take cracks at a wonderful bunch of G.I. musicians who are doing a great job here, that's too much.

I am so firmly convinced that these boys over here ARE great that, should I have a band after the war, and should any of them desire a job, I would gladly give it to him regardless of his musical proficiencies.

Glenn, the band and the GI's for whom they came to play, and to hell with the critics!

At least, George, you know my feelings on the subject. Drop me a social note if you have time—don't speak for Metronome as I'm not interested.

Sincerely,
[signed] GM

Chapter 37

Playing and living grew even more intense for Glenn and the
band during October. The Germans had extended the range of
their buzz bombs and Bedford no longer remained a remote
target. Though no bombs actually hit inside the town, they did
drop near enough to shatter a number of its windows.

The band's fame continued to grow. Up till now its personal
appearances outside Bedford had been limited to playing for
service personnel only. But the public's demand for an "in-per-
son" concert mounted so high that the band was finally booked
for a Jazz Jamboree, open to the public, at the Stall Theatre in
the Kingsway section of London, with all proceeds from admissions going to charity. The concert was a complete sellout.

Throughout the entire European Theater the band continued
to gain more and more recognition, not merely for its contributions to morale but also for the quality of its music. And when the
musically illiterate but propaganda-wise Pentagon heard that its
official U.S. Army Band had been pretty badly cut in competition with the service bands from other countries, a keenly
disappointed General George C. Marshall, head of everything
military back in Washington, decided something had to be done
to recapture some of our lost prestige. So, having heard about the
success of the Miller band, he ordered Lieutenant General
Walter Bedell "Beetle" Smith, Eisenhower's chief of staff, to
contact Glenn.

Glenn with admiring British musicians. Top: Glenn congratulates
"boy-drummer" Victor Feldman as comedian-drummer Max Bacon looks on.
Feldman later migrated to America and developed into one of the West Coast's
top jazz musicians. Bottom: Band leader Vic Lewis lights his cigarette as
another maestro, Jack Parnells, watches.

Lieutenant General Walter "Beetle" Smith.

When Glenn received his orders to fly to Versailles to see General Smith, he hadn't the slightest notion why he was being summoned. He'd known about Smith, of course, though, in the light of what took place between the two officers, it's unlikely that Smith had ever heard of "In the Mood" or "Moonlight Serenade" or "American Patrol," or perhaps even the Glenn Miller band.

Upon his arrival in Smith's office, Glenn tossed the general a long salute, holding it for about half a chorus, until Smith, a short, wiry man, noted for his curtness and toughness, looked up and signaled him to segue into "at ease." The interview lasted little longer than the salute.

"How would you like to direct the U.S. Army Band?" Smith asked.

"I wouldn't, sir," replied Glenn quickly.

"Why not, Major?"

"I don't understand that kind of music, sir."

"Thank you. That's all, Miller." And the interview was over.

Later, a somewhat perplexed General Smith paid Glenn a

backhanded compliment. "At least that son-of-a-bitch Miller knows what he wants," he reportedly said. Amazing, isn't it, what an accurate impression Glenn had made in just fifteen seconds!

Glenn's curtness was no surprise to those who had been close to him. Just as in New Haven he had become increasingly frustrated by not being able to get his men overseas, so in England he had begun chafing at the bit to get the band over to Paris where it could play directly for the front-line troops. He kept pushing his musicians as far as their lips could blow. He even inaugurated a new radio series, strictly for propaganda purposes. Beamed directly into Germany, it contained all of the band's magnificent instrumental sounds with one extra added attraction: The words, including Glenn's announcements and Johnny Desmond's creamy vocals, were in German.

Desmond had emerged as a real star. His singing had improved greatly, which in turn bred a new self-assurance that projected the handsome sergeant beyond the "just-another-boy-band-vocalist." He had been dubbed "the Creamer," which some naively attributed to the smooth, flowing quality of his voice. Many of the band members, however, realized the sobriquet had not an *udder* but an *other* implication, more tactile than lacteal.

Johnny recalls Glenn's increasing irritability. "One thing that would bug him especially was when some general or colonel would come up to him and make some flip crack like, 'I bet you're getting real tired of having to play "In the Mood" all the time.' Glenn used to tell them, 'I just hope some day you'll find something as good to you as "In the Mood" has been to me.'

"After a while we didn't see too much of Glenn. He was living at the Mount Royal Hotel in London and spending a lot of time there. He just didn't seem happy at all."

When he wasn't at the Mount Royal, Glenn would be spending a good deal of time at the Langham Hotel, directly across the street from BBC's Broadcast House. There, on the fifth floor, he and Paul Dudley shared an office right next to one occupied by Cecil Madden, England's most respected radio producer, who had been put in charge of all shows using the BBC's facilities.

The Creamer.

Now retired, after an illustrious career in television, Madden holds fond memories of "the Major. He was a very sweet man—marvelous—charming. We became quite friendly. I still treasure a copy of a book of cartoons by George Price called *It's Funny to Be People* that he gave me."

Miller and Madden were thrown together in their work and sometimes in other circumstances. During air raids, they would often find themselves side by side in the basement concert hall of the BBC, one of the safest air-raid shelters in all of London. Madden, with whom I recently talked in London [I also examined the BBC building and found it to be one of the most solid edifices I'd ever seen in my life], reports, "Sometimes we would have as many as three hundred bodies down there. People would have to step over one another. Once in a while there would be a well-known singer there with us, and he or she would entertain those three hundred bodies!"

One well-known entertainment celebrity often in attendance was David Niven, who represented the RAF in a supervisory quartet that included Madden, the BBC's Maurice Gorham, and the AEF's Ed Kirby. "We had three excellent musical organizations—Miller's and the Canadian Air Forces unit conducted by Captain Robert Farnon [today Farnon is one of the world's most admired arranger-conductors], and the British AEF outfit conducted by Regimental Sergeant Major George Melachrino."

The caliber of the music must have been magnificent. But nothing impressed Madden as much as the night the Miller band, the U.S. Navy dance band directed by Sam Donahue, and an English dance band headed by Geraldo combined forces to blow a scorching version of Count Basie's "One O'Clock Jump," one of the great musical sights and sounds of World War II. According to Bernie Privin, "The Donahue band really cut us that night. Glenn knew it, too, and he kept trying to get a rematch. But we never got it. That really was *some* band!"

Glenn, in his quieter moments, also impressed Madden as "a most regular chap. I can still see him in his draped uniform, standing in the queue of a fish-and-chips shop just like everyone else, and then out there in the street, eating them. He loved them, you know."

But Madden's most poignant Miller memory concerns the last talk they ever had together—a couple of nights before he set out on his fateful journey. "I tried so very hard to stop him from flying over to Paris, but he kept telling me that he had given his word to attend a reception over there, and he wasn't going to break his word. It really was so bloody silly of him to go."

Glenn with some of his musicians (foreground) and some of Sam Donahue's (background).

Chapter 38

 Early in November the marquis of Queensberry, at whose club the band had been playing at least once a week, gave a party for all the musicians. It was a gala affair, and, after it was over, Jack Hylton, the famous English band leader, invited Glenn and Don Haynes and several others to his flat for a series of late drinks. Hylton traveled in the highest circles. Included among his guests that night was A. V. Alexander, the first lord of the admiralty, equivalent in rank and importance to the United States secretary of the navy.

After some music, during which Alexander sang and played piano, everyone's inhibitions became pretty neatly dissolved in the booze, whereupon Alexander proceeded to recite some astonishing statistics regarding the horrendous damage inflicted upon London and Londoners by the new German buzz bombs. And then the first lord of the admiralty dropped his own bomb into the conversation: The United States was developing a new weapon called the atom bomb, and its potential devastation simply staggered the imagination! (The rest of the world would not hear of the bomb's existence and horrifying power until eight months later when it would be dropped on Hiroshima.)

Such growing magnitude of the war's horrors must have depressed the ever-growing-lonelier major even more. To Haynes and others, Glenn began to look more and more tired and drawn. English cooking didn't appeal to him, and so he ate poorly. He

liked Italian food most of all (the Villanova Restaurant in New York had been his favorite), but England had little or none to offer. He also liked steaks and roast beef, but not the way the English cooked them. He had always been a very fussy eater anyway. If he ordered chicken, for example, he insisted that it be perfectly clean. And he liked to drink between ten and twelve glasses of ice water—very difficult to get in England—with each meal.

Haynes noted, too, that "Glenn's health wasn't any better than his appetite. He had several of those bad sinus attacks, and he lost a lot of weight, and after a while those military gabardine blouses which he had had tailored for him at Saks Fifth Avenue didn't fit him well at all. They merely hung on him.

"You could tell how nervous and restless he had become by the way he walked. Just to keep up with him, you'd find yourself going at a very fast clip—like he was in a big hurry and had many things to do, but not enough time in which to do them."

Two nights after he first heard about the atom bomb, Glenn and Don became embroiled in a hot poker game at the Officers' Club. According to Haynes, "He nearly almost always won—in poker, with the dice, even picking hit tunes. Everything that he touched, it seems, had a gold or silver lining."

But that evening, for the first time in Haynes' memory, the

usual Miller luck which helped sustain Glenn through so many hard times, really deserted him. He couldn't seem to draw any good cards at all, and by the end of the evening he had dropped eighteen pounds. It was the worst beating Don had ever seen him take. On their way back from the Officers' Club, Glenn began talking in a fatalistic way that Haynes had never heard before. "Don," he said, "I have a strong feeling that I'll never see Helen and Stevie again. I know that sounds odd, but I've had that feeling for some time now. You know the Miller luck has been phenomenal for the last five years, and I don't want to be around when it changes." Then he elaborated: "I've had a feeling for a long time now that one of those buzz bombs has my name on it."

A week later Glenn's premonition almost came true. He and Don were sitting in his room at the Mount Royal when suddenly a new kind of buzz bomb, the faster-than-sound V-2 rocket, whose actual impact explosion preceded the noise it made coming through the air (the way lightning is followed by thunder), hit dangerously close and shook the entire hotel.

On November 15 Glenn was again summoned to SHAEF headquarters at Versailles. Nearby Paris, liberated ten weeks earlier, was now being filled with troops on leave from the front lines. Their morale needed boosting. "How would you like to bring your band over here next month and stay for six weeks and entertain the G.I.'s and the guys in the hospitals?" Glenn was asked.

He loved the idea. It was exactly what he had been wanting to do for months. But he knew that the trip was out unless he and his men could record enough broadcasts in advance so that there would be no break in their series of radio shows to the troops throughout the area. Since the various units were now doing seventeen shows per week, this meant that during the next six weeks the guys would have to complete a horrendous schedule of recording six additional sets of seventeen programs, or 102 extra shows—all in addition to their already existing schedule of live broadcasts!

Upon his return from Versailles, Glenn presented his musicians with the challenge. To a man, they accepted it.

However, one major obstacle remained. Whenever the band

had left Bedford on trips to bases in England, it had recorded a few programs ahead of time, using a direct line from its studios into the BBC's recording facilities in London, where the music was then etched into acetate discs. But, like so many other products during the war, these discs were in short supply, and so, when Glenn told the BBC about the monster recording schedule, Maurice Gorham, the walrus-mustachioed executive with whom Glenn had tiffed back in July, remonstrated: The BBC had no way of coming up with such a large number of discs!

Once again Miller, the doer, went into action. He immediately put in a phone call to an old friend, Oliver Nicoll, director of production for the American Broadcasting Station in Europe. "Ollie," he said, "I need five hundred discs in a hurry. Can I have them? . . . Good . . . Just send them to the BBC, care of Maurice Gorham. He knows what to do with them."

And so the next day it began—the most lip-busting, callous-raising series of sessions ever experienced by any set of musicians, in or out of the service. There was so much to record that on some days the guys would get up early in the morning and wouldn't stop playing until 2 A.M. of the following day.

George Voutsas, who directed from the control room, points out that the uneven qualities of the wartime discs posed an extra burden on the musicians. "Just when we thought we had a program all finished, we'd get a call from the recording engineer in London saying, 'Sorry, chaps, faulty disc,' and we'd have to start all over again from the top of the show."

Compared with the recording output of artists of the seventies, those performances of the Miller bandsmen shape up as monumental. For a rock band to complete one long-playing record usually takes weeks and sometimes months. On the other hand, the superbly trained and disciplined Miller band, bulging with truly professional musicians, during an eighteen-day period beginning November 25 recorded a total of eighty-five half-hour shows, equivalent in time to approximately eighty-five long-playing records. And all that in addition to its regularly scheduled live broadcasts!

After the recordings had been completed, Glenn notified Gorham of the BBC. "That's good," Gorham reportedly replied.

The band records. Brass in rear: Nat Peck, Johnny Halliburton, Jimmy Priddy, Larry Hall, Whitey Thomas, Bobby Nichols, Jack Steele, Bernie Privin. Saxes: Mannie Thaler, Freddy Guerra, Vince Carbone, Hank Freeman, Peanuts Hucko, Jack Ferrier. Addison Collins is the French horn player; Steve Steck stands behind him; Frank Ippolito is seated. Trigger Alpert is the bassist; Ray McKinley and Gene Steck are against the right wall; Mel Powell is at the piano. Back to the left: Jerry Gray stands behind the conducting maestro. Carmen Mastren is on guitar. The strings (inside row, left to right): Stan Harris, Dave Schwartz, George Ockner, Harry Katzman, David Sackson, Phil Cogliano; (second row) Morris Bialkin, Bob Ripley, Manny Wishnow, Milton Edelson, Carl Swanson, Dick Motolinski, Ernie Kardos, Gene Bergen, Earl Cornwell, Nat Kaproff, Joseph Kowelewski. At far right: Freddy Ostrowski.

"Now see to it that you get over there and back here in one piece. We don't want to lose you, you know." To which Glenn retorted tartly, "*You* should worry. *You've* got the recordings!"

Glenn's downward emotional spiral continued, and, despite his attempted stoicism, it kept cropping out more and more. David Mackay, still his lawyer but also a colonel with close Pentagon associations, had written a letter in mid-August to Don Haynes, in which he stated, "I shall be very interested to hear some of the tall tales you are preparing to tell upon your return, which, you may be sure, will not be too long delayed—Glenn's pessimism to the contrary notwithstanding."

On November 26 Glenn unleashed his anxieties directly to Mackay. He concluded a letter about his tax situation with an almost pitiful plea: "Just let me come home and give the government all the money—I don't care."

Finally, early one morning, Glenn's almost total unhappiness erupted. He called a meeting of the entire band for eight o'clock and almost immediately began to unleash a devastating verbal buzz-bomb attack of his own. Almost nobody escaped his pent-up emotions. Ray McKinley, one of the unmolested few, recalls, "He really let some of the guys have it—but good! I remember how he tore into poor Mel Powell—it was really something!"

According to Bernie Privin, "He threatened to send those who didn't shape up into the infantry." And George Voutsas remembers, "What made it seem so bad was that he called out each guy, one by one, and evaluated his conduct and attitude and contributions right in front of the rest of us."

Undoubtedly, the pressures of all those recordings were taking their toll on Glenn, and on many of the guys as well. But Glenn had withstood pressures just as great before without showing strains of cracking. Of course, then he had always had Helen around him, and buzz bombs weren't bursting outside his London hotel room, and he wasn't constantly being faced with the terrible dread of flying and perhaps beginning to doubt himself—maybe even to hate himself—for what surely must have seemed like a character defect to this puritanical, stoical, forthright, upright midwesterner, so conditioned by his upbringing never to reveal any of his emotions, and certainly not the most "despicable" of them all, fear itself.

Chapter 39

 Late in November Don Haynes flew to Paris. His mission: to locate suitable quarters for the band. These he found in the heart of the colorful Montmartre district at 22 Square Clignancourt. The Hôtel des Olympiades was a small, narrow, five-story hotel with not very modern facilities, but still quite adequate for a group of enlisted men.

While in Paris he ran into a lieutenant colonel with whom both he and Glenn had become friendly. This was Norman F. Baesell, the executive officer at the nearby Milton Ernest post, with whom the band had worked out a deal: In exchange for the band's playing concerts on some of its off-days for Milton Ernest officers and enlisted men, the post would regularly feed all the musicians. Baesell liked music and he appeared to like a good time, though he wasn't especially well liked by some of the guys in the band. Johnny Desmond recalls him as "the kind of a pain-in-the-ass who puts lampshades on his head at parties and wants to take over the drums."

Baesell, who had often flown to Paris, had made good contacts with "the right people." He showed Don a great time: visits to various leading perfume shops, where he seemed to be well known; lunch at the very swank Raphael Hotel; dinner at another excellent restaurant, the Crillon; a show at the Casino de Paris with its semi-nude show girls; and a round of nightcaps at Fred Paine's Bar, off the Rue de la Paix.

In the morning, Baesell again took Haynes on a round of perfume shops. "Schiaparelli's, with padded velvet walls and ceiling and five-inch-deep carpet on the floor, and with a scent that wouldn't quit, was the most outstanding shop I have ever seen," reported Don. Following that tour, Baesell again took Don to lunch at the swank Raphael. "Nothing but the best!" Don wrote in his diary. Obviously, Baesell knew how to entertain, how to have a ball, and how to get the money to do so. No wonder he flew to Paris so often! No wonder, too, that so many G.I.'s, struggling on their meager pay and fed such consistently mediocre chow, learned to resent some officers so vehemently!

Meanwhile, during those eighteen days and nights, the band remained closeted in its Bedford studios, recording those dozens upon dozens of extra radio shows. Sometimes Glenn would be there to supervise the sessions, but he spent even more of his time in his London office and at his hotel. Just a week before he was to go to Paris, one of the new German V-2 rockets scored a hit just two blocks away from the Mount Royal. Some civilians were blown into such tiny pieces that their bodies couldn't even be identified. The horrors of war were closing in even further on Glenn.

On the morning of December 12 the band finished its last recording. That evening, after its final concert at the Queensberry Club, the marquis gave the group a farewell dinner. From then, until their departure several days later, the guys concentrated on packing their own belongings and the more than five thousand pounds of equipment they would need in Paris.

A "Shipment Packing" list uncovered in Glenn's files contains thirty-six different entries for boxes, cases and trunks, including such items as drums, cymbals, music and instrument stands, recording equipment, sound equipment, two music libraries (Miller's and McKinley's), manuscript paper, radio-show scripts, administration records and instrument-repair kits.

The last set of items, the repair kits—further examples of Glenn's farsightedness and penchant for details—had proved to be a boon to the band. Not only were musical-instrument parts rarities overseas but so were specialists who knew how to use them. Glenn had recruited two of these. One of them, Julie

Zifferblatt, had been making routine repairs for the band long before it left the States. The other, Vito Pascucci, taken on at the last minute, performed more like a jazz musician: He was a near-genius at improvising repairs for reed and brass instruments. For example, on one of the plane trips Bernie Privin's trumpet slipped into a well and was crushed by falling baggage. Within twenty-four hours—and nobody still knows how he did it—Pascucci had straightened out the horn so magnificently that Privin insisted it played better than when it was new! Pascucci's talents eventually paid off for him, too. Today he is the highly respected, well-paid president of one of the world's largest musical instrument manufacturing firms.

On December 12, two days before Glenn was scheduled to fly to France, the BBC's Maurice Gorham sent Glenn a bon-voyage letter.

> Just a line to wish you luck on your trip to Paris. I am sure you will do a great job there. I hear you have done wonders here in the way of pre-recording, but I shall still look forward to getting some shows from you in Paris to freshen up the schedule. As you know, the thing I really want most is the Christmas Day live broadcast, and I hope we shall also be able to arrange a live broadcast on New Year's Eve.
>
> I hope to see you over there before very long; so meanwhile good wishes.

From the duke of York's headquarters came a letter that expressed a good deal better the sentiment of those Glenn was leaving in England. Written on the same day, it read:

> Dear Major: Happily to-day is merely au revoir and not good-bye, but it is an opportunity for me to send a brief note of gratitude to you for the immense enjoyment you have given to the troops in my administrative area over the last few months. What they have thought of it all is fully evidenced by the regular football struggle there was every time to get in the doors, and then by the rapturous applause with which the lucky ones always greeted you. [An ironic twist: The last two letters of "greeted" were then crossed out in pen.]
>
> It is a great job and on their behalf I do thank you and every member of your organisation most sincerely.

The final photo—Paul Dudley, Glenn
and Don Haynes—taken on
December 12, 1944.

For my own part, you know I am a complete fan, and there
will be no one who will miss you more.

The best of luck to you in your new journeys—I hope all goes
well and I look forward to your safe return at not too distant a
date.

Glenn's official orders, calling for him to depart on or about
December 14, 1944, by military aircraft (ATC) "and upon
completion thereof to return to present station," were issued "By
command of General Eisenhower."

Orders to go to Paris ahead of the band had originally been
issued to Don Haynes, but at the last minute a growingly
impatient Miller had decided he wanted to go instead, and so
Don's orders had been canceled and new ones issued to Glenn.

Glenn decided to fly from London to Paris on the day
following the farewell party. So Don remained in London
overnight to see Glenn off on the morrow. But the weather on
December 13 turned out to be so bad that no military aircraft
were flying, and so, after giving Glenn all the details about whom
to see in Paris, including the owner-manager of the hotel where
the band would be billeted, Haynes started to drive back to
Bedford. "The fog was now so thick," he wrote in his diary, "that
the conductors of the big double-deck buses were walking three

feet in front of the buses with a torch (flashlight) pointed back toward the bus driver so that he wouldn't run up over the curbing, or smash into another vehicle! I'd seen fog before, but nothing like this. It took me four hours to get to Bedford—ordinarily an hour-and-fifteen-minute trip."

At lunch the next day, December 14, at the Officers' Club, Don ran into Colonel Baesell, who said he was flying to Paris on the following day in General Goodrich's private plane. He invited Don to join him, perhaps for some more good times. Don explained that he had to stick around to take the band over on Saturday, but that Glenn wanted to fly over. So Baesell suggested calling Glenn in London and making arrangements for him to fly over with him on the following day. What followed is revealed most explicitly in these excerpts from Don's own diary:

> We called Glenn and, sure enough, he was grounded and had little hopes of getting out tomorrow as there had been no SHAEF SHUTTLE to Paris for the past five days, and he was outranked even if flying weather prevailed tomorrow. So he welcomed the Colonel's invitation and asked me to drive in and get him.
>
> Left for London right after lunch, arriving at the Mount Royal at four o'clock. Glenn was all packed and ready to go, so back to Bedford in time for dinner with Colonel Baesell at the Officers' Club. After a few hands of poker with the Colonel, Major Koch and WO Earlywine, Glenn and I left for the ARC [American Red Cross] Officers' Club to get a good night's sleep, as the Colonel would be calling early, as soon as he got weather clearance.
>
> Glenn and I sat in front of the fireplace at the Club until three-thirty A.M. He was in a talking mood, and though he had said earlier that he wanted to get a good night's sleep, he seemed restless and not at all tired. So we sat and talked and planned.
>
> We talked about the post-war band, taxes, etc., and came to the conclusion that we'd work not more than six months a year. The other six months we'd play golf, buy a trailer and go up into the Northwest and do some salmon fishing in the Columbia River, raise oranges at "Tuxedo Junction," Glenn's ranch in Monrovia, California, do an occasional recording date, and the

balance of the time we'd just loaf! And, of course, devote some time to our families.

It was Glenn's plan to deed a piece of "Tuxedo Junction" to Polly and myself, and we'd build a home there, and Glenn and I would be partners in the post-war band, he having reiterated several times that with taxes as they are, one can net only so much money, and in view of the fact that he already had a nest-egg socked away, he wanted me to be set up the same way financially.

We even discussed who would be in the post-war band, and our first engagement after getting out of uniform would be for Bob Weitman at the Paramount Theatre, New York City. Glenn and I had an agreement with Weitman that the Paramount would be the first engagement for six weeks with an option of two more at $15,000 weekly, which was more money than had ever been paid for a band.

So, these were the plans we discussed into the 'wee sma' hours of this cold and rainy 14th of December, 1944. We both took a hot shower and went to bed.

On the next morning I was awakened by a phone call from Colonel Baesell at nine A.M. The weather was still bad; couldn't get clearance this A.M. but it showed signs of clearing by early afternoon, so he suggested that Glenn and I come out to the Club for lunch and bring Glenn's luggage, 'cause if the weather cleared they'd go to Paris this afternoon. Glenn was awake when I returned from the lobby telephone, and though I had intended climbing back into the sack for a few winks, he wanted to get up. So we got dressed, and, after first getting an egg apiece out of the foot-locker, we went to the dining room and into the kitchen where they boiled our eggs, and we ordered waffles and tea. . . .

We read the morning papers, loafed around the lounge for a couple of hours. Glenn rechecked his bag, and we went by the EM's billet and found everything in readiness for our move to Paris on the morrow. Then out to the VIIIth Air Force Headquarters and the Officers' Club.

Colonel Baesell was packing his bag when we entered his room. The Colonel said he had just talked with Flight Officer Morgan at Station #595, a base one hundred miles to the north, and Morgan said the weather was improving and he'd know shortly after noon whether or not he'd get clearance for the flight to Paris. While at lunch, the Colonel was called to the phone. He returned, smiling, and said Morgan had just received clearance and would pick them up at Twinwood Farm within the hour.

Major Bill Koch and Warrant Officer Earlywine strolled out to the staff car with the Colonel, Glenn and myself, and after a few slaps on the back and a warning to look out for those Mademoiselles on the Rue de la Paix, Glenn and the Colonel closed the door and I drove to General Goodrich's chateau, which was in the general direction of Twinwood Farm, as the Colonel wished to see the bed-ridden General for any last-minute instructions.

Glenn and I sat in the staff car while the Colonel ran into the General's chateau, and it started to rain again. Dark clouds, the low-hanging variety, were now much in evidence, and Glenn expressed doubt that F. O. Morgan would be able to even find Twinwood Farm to pick them up. The Colonel came running out, and ten minutes later we drove up to the Flight Control Tower at Twinwood Farm, shut off the motor and sat in the car awaiting the arrival of F. O. Morgan.

The hard rain had now levelled off to a steady drizzle, and, looking skyward, the ceiling was not more than two hundred feet. I also began to doubt that Morgan could locate the field. He was now overdue, and we had sat smoking and talking for more than half an hour. The Colonel bundled his trench coat up around his neck, and got out of the car and climbed the ladder leading to the Control Tower. Ten minutes later he came back down and, having talked to Station #595, was told that Morgan took off from there in a C-64 fifty-five minutes ago, so was due here any minute.

Glenn, visibly nervous, couldn't sit in the staff car any longer, opened up the door and got out, peered skyward, and as a result his glasses became blurred from the drizzle. He was wiping them off with his handkerchief when the Colonel and I decided that the smoke-filled air in the staff car was getting pretty "ripe." So we got out and joined Glenn on the concrete strip. It was cold, and, walking over to the Tower, I took a look at the thermometer alongside the ladder. It registered 34 degrees.

As I walked back, adjusting my trench coat to prevent the saturating drizzle from going down the back of my neck, Glenn said, "Morgan will never find this field. Even the blankety-

SUPREME HEADQUARTERS
ALLIED EXPEDITIONARY FORCE
REAR HEADQUARTERS
APO 413

AG 201-ASP-Miller, Alton G. (Off)   12 December 1944.

SUBJECT: Orders.

TO   : Major ALTON G. MILLER, O505271, AC, G-1 Division, SHAEFF REAR.

1. You will proceed by military aircraft (ATC) on or about 14 December 1944 from present station to SUPREME HQ ASF MAIN on the Continent to carry out the instructions of the A.C. of S., G-1, SUPREME HQ ASF, and upon completion thereof return to present station.

2. Travel by military aircraft is directed. Baggage allowance is limited to sixty-five (65) pounds.

By command of General EISENHOWER:

B. C. CHAPPELL,
Lt. Col., AGD,
Asst. Adjutant General.

DISTRIBUTION:
Maj Miller...... 6
G-1 Div Secr.... 1
ATC............. 1
Trans Off, Hq
  Comd Rear.... 1
SUB Rear........ 1
ASP............
AGR.............

---

blank birds are grounded today" (He might have been right, 'cause there wasn't a bird in sight, nor was there *anyone* or *anything* in sight.) when we heard the steady drone of an airplane motor. It seemed to be in a northerly direction, and it was getting louder when the Colonel said, "That's Morgan, all right. A single-engined plane and the motor sounds like a flock of outboard motor boats."

The engine noise was getting louder now, and it sounded as though the plane was directly over the field and not too high, though we couldn't see it on account of the poor visibility and low ceiling of the cloud layer which couldn't have been more than two hundred feet.

Now the motor noise was diminishing as it was apparently past the field and heading south. "What'd I tell you, Colonel. In this muck he couldn't even find the field," said Glenn. "He missed it."

"Don't bet on it, Glenn," said the Colonel. "Morgan's a helluva pilot. He flew thirty-two missions in B-24's, and he's used to weather like this. My money says he'll be on this airstrip within ten minutes."

As the Colonel talked, the sound of the motor over the far end of the field indicated the plane was in a turn, and a couple of minutes later it came through the heavy overcast directly over the center of the field, circled the field once. Evidently,

The runway at Twinwood Farm—probably Glenn's last view of the earth. (This photo was taken by the author in 1973 from inside a car racing down the runway.)

Morgan had taken a look at the windsock on the control tower and came down into the wind which was blowing from west to east and driving the drizzle in an easterly direction.

We climbed back into the staff car and drove out to the end of the airstrip, and Morgan taxied down the strip and turned around alongside the car. Leaving the motor running, he opened the door of this small, nine-place cabin job and greeted us with a wave, "Hi." He said, "Sorry I'm late—ran into some heavy squalls, but the weather is supposed to be clearing over the continent."

The Colonel handed his bag to Morgan and went back to the car for the case of empty champagne bottles he was taking to Paris. (Bottles are scarce in Paris and unless you have the empties they won't sell anyone a case of champagne to take out.) I shook hands with Morgan as I tossed Glenn's B-4 bag through the open cabin door. Glenn and the Colonel climbed aboard. The Colonel seated himself in the co-pilot's seat and Glenn sat in a bucket seat directly back of the Colonel facing the side of the ship. Morgan climbed into the pilot's seat, and, as they all fastened their seat belts, I waved a goodbye. "Happy Landings and Good Luck. I'll see you in Paris tomorrow," I said, as Glenn replied, "Thanks, Haynsie. We may need it!" *

* Though the Haynes diary doesn't report it, it was at this point that Glenn asked, "Hey, where the hell are the parachutes?" and Baesell replied, "What's the matter, Miller, do

you want to live forever?'' Johnny Desmond also told me that when Glenn's apprehension increased because the plane had only one motor, Baesell reportedly retorted, "What the hell, Lindbergh had only one motor and he flew clear across the Atlantic! We're only flying to Paris."

I closed the door, secured the catch and stepped away from the plane to get away from the prop wash as Morgan waved and revved up the motor. He released the brakes and they started down the runway, gaining speed, and were soon airborne. In less than a minute they climbed into the overcast and were out of sight. I got in the car and drove back to Bedford.

Chapter 40

The guys in the band arrived in France three days later. "Our trip was uneventful," Don Haynes later wrote me, "but not his," referring, of course, to Glenn's.

Actually, nobody in the band had any inkling that anything had happened to Glenn. They presumed that he had landed and probably would be waiting for them when they arrived.

First Sergeant Zeke Zarchy relates the events: "On the morning after Glenn took off, the band drove approximately fifty miles to the Air Transport Command at Bovingdon, where three C-47's were to take us to Paris. But the weather was very bad, and so, after hanging around for several hours, we turned around and went back to Bedford. The next morning it was an exact repeat of the same scene. On the following day the sun came out and the sky was clear. It was a gorgeous day. No clouds. We took off and landed at Orly Field in France, clear at the end in a lot of mud.

"I guess we should have had an inkling that something was wrong when there was nobody and no transportation to meet us. Don Haynes got off and said he would call the Major (Glenn) and get transportation for us. We must have waited for at least two hours. Finally, two civilian-type French buses arrived with Don in the first one. We all got in. Someone asked, 'Where's the Major?' But there was no panic—yet.

Zeke and Peanuts Hucko in Paris.

"We went to a little hotel on the northern outskirts of town. It was just big enough to hold us. Don explained that there was a curfew because the Germans were making a last-ditch stand. Then he said, 'I'll get hold of the Major,' and he left.

"The next day Don came back. 'I don't want anyone to write home about this,' he told us, 'and there's no cause for alarm, but they can't locate the Major. They are checking various places.' And he repeated the same thing to us for several days."

Meanwhile, Haynes had been doing some intensive checking with headquarters. He found that all flights out of England had been grounded for the past week; that there was a report of only one flight having left for France, a single-engine plane, but that it hadn't been heard from since.

After getting the bandsmen billeted at their hotel and calling places like the Ritz Hotel and the Raphael Restaurant, where Baesell was well known, but finding no trace of him or Glenn, Don went directly to SHAEF headquarters. There he suggested to General Barker, head of personnel, that a call be placed directly to Baesell's commanding officer, General Goodrich, back in England. Barker told Don to listen in on the conversation.

From Don's diary: "Barker asked if Colonel Baesell was there, and with that Goodrich let out a blast to the effect that Baesell flew to Paris on Friday and was due back yesterday, and the so-and-so hadn't returned and he hadn't heard from him. Barker then brought Goodrich up-to-date on what was going on. He was furious when I told him they had flown a C-64, which he said had no de-icing equipment, because icing conditions were prevalent. (It was 34 degrees at Twinwood Farm, and over the Channel it was eight to ten degrees colder.) Goodrich expressed great disappointment with F. O. Morgan, his personal pilot, for flying a C-64 over the Channel in that kind of weather. General Goodrich said he'd have a search instituted as of daybreak tomorrow, but that it appeared they had iced up and gone into the Channel!

"General Barker hung up the telephone and, turning to me, said, 'It looks very bad, Lieutenant. I'm afraid Major Miller has had it!' "

Knowing the facts wasn't hard. But accepting them was—and still apparently is! Perverted reports about "what really happened," invariably either third- or fourth- or perhaps even sixteenth-handed, have never contained anything even remotely resembling authentic documentation. Rumors that "the plane was shot down and Glenn is now a basket case somewhere, too ashamed to face his public"; that "Glenn was killed in a brawl in a brothel"; that "Colonel Baesell was implicated in the black market and shot Glenn and the pilot on the way over to France, then landed the plane himself"; and other similar concoctions of fictional crap continue to circulate even today. Why should it be so difficult to accept the most obvious: that Glenn was simply the victim of some terribly bad judgment on the part of a colonel, too anxious for his own good to get to Paris, and a pilot, too adventuresome for his or anybody else's good.

The realization that Glenn would not be joining them permeated the band through a period of days. Each time that Haynes would return from headquarters with one of those "We're still looking and hoping" reports, the guys realized more and more that hope was slowly fading. Gradually they reconciled themselves to the inevitable.

Not so, though, for Helen Miller back home. For eight days after Glenn had disappeared, she had had no inkling that anything had gone wrong. Breaking the news to her became one of Don's chief concerns. He kept hoping that Glenn might still show up, and that Helen could be spared that devastating telegram from the War Department. Therefore, Haynes kept pleading with the authorities to postpone the notification.

But by December 23, they could wait no longer. The telegram, with its two stars, arrived at the Miller home in Tenafly, followed shortly thereafter by a personal phone call from General "Hap" Arnold, head of the entire AAF. Tom Sheils, who was still handling Glenn's business affairs, dropped in to visit Helen shortly after the telegram arrived. "She was very stoical. And you know something ironic: Five days after Glenn had been reported missing, a beautiful console radio-phonograph arrived for Helen. Glenn had arranged for it as a surprise Christmas present to her."

Nothing exemplifies more accurately Helen's constant concern for the feelings of others—a concern that helped her and Glenn so tremendously during their various times of stress—than her attitude during her terrible ordeal. Soon after receiving the fateful telegram, she cabled Don as follows: "POLLY WITH ME I'M FINE JUST WAITING FOR GOOD NEWS OF GLENN." And on Christmas Day, just two days after she heard the news, she wrote this letter to Don:

> Dear Don—Polly has been here with me since day before yesterday when I got my terrible wire from the War Dept. It was such a horrible shock to me but after I thought it all over it will take more than a "Missing in Flight" message to get me down. Believe Glenn will turn up sometime—maybe not for months, maybe real soon—but if you hear from him first tell him I'm fine and just waiting for him.
>
> Last night we trimmed a Xmas tree and you should have seen Steven early this A.M. His eyes popped out of his head with the tree, toys, etc. I've been telling him about Santa Claus and he was so excited and has had a glorious time all day. We heard the Xmas Day program from Paris and it's so good to know you are there.
>
> Polly has been such a real comfort to me and we're sensible and hoping for good news. Write me soon. Love, Helen.
>
> Polly says she will write later.

The Christmas Day program to which Helen referred was a five-minute greeting from the guys in the band to the folks back at home. It opened with the orchestra playing "Moonlight Serenade" and was followed by a reading of the names of the men in the organization, a subtle but certain way of informing the families of the musicians that the men were alive and hadn't gone down in the plane with Glenn. Carmen Mastren, the band's guitarist, reports that some of the wives had already heard from Joy Hodges, the movie star who had been contacted by her husband, Warrant Officer Paul Dudley, and who had then phoned various wives to assure them that only Glenn was missing.

Helen continued to hope. On Glenn's forty-first birthday she again wrote to Don Haynes:

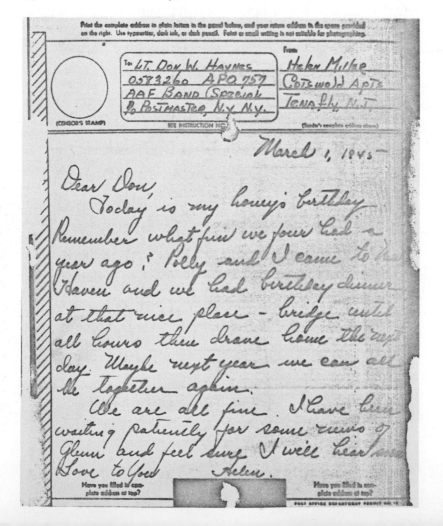

With Miller gone, some of the top brass had second thoughts about the future of the band. Almost as soon as the band had arrived in Paris, the Battle of the Bulge had begun. "We were allowed to go out at nights only in groups," recalls Zeke Zarchy, "because guys were having their throats cut by infiltrators." To stem the fearsome drive, the Allied forces began pouring every bit of available manpower into the battle. Rumor had it that the band would be deactivated, and that the musicians would be reactivated as stretcher bearers, ambulance drivers, and serving in other capacities up at the front.

But the band's first public appearance saved it. On December 21, with top brass in attendance, it played a concert at the Palais de Glace for combat troops on forty-eight-hour leave from the front. The reaction was fantastic. The troops screamed and yelled for more. Right then and there General Barker recognized the importance of such an event to the troops' morale. The next day he assured Haynes, "If you can continue the schedule originally set up for your appearances here on the Continent and can control this fine aggregation of men, you will receive our complete cooperation and assistance."

Haynes *was* able to control the aggregation, the general kept his word, and all talk about the men being activated for duty on the front lines disappeared. Instead, they embarked on an intensive tour of personal appearances—at theaters like the Olympia and the Marignan; at the huge sports palace, the Palais de Glace; at various Red Cross Clubs and Enlisted Men's Clubs; and often within hospitals. The entire orchestra recorded weekly for broadcasts, as did the *Strings with Wings* unit and the *Swing Shift*. It was a full schedule all right, but, according to Ray McKinley, "Compared with England, it was a snap!"

McKinley was especially respected by many of the musicians. The only member of the outfit with previous experience as a name leader, he knew how to run a band. In England he had been leading the big dance band. In France he continued to do so, but at times he would also take over as more or less morale-leader of the entire unit.

Bassist Trigger Alpert once told me a story of McKinley being cornered at some function by some general and being asked how

New leader McKinley and his men.

everything was going. Instead of "sir-ing" the officer in accepted enlisted men's fashion, Mac told him things were going pretty terribly so far as living conditions were concerned. More specifically, he pointed out that the heating situation was so bad at the hotel that some of the men feared having some of their more vital organs going into a deep freeze. Nobody knows for sure whether it was merely coincidental or whether Ray's words had some effect. In any case, fuel for heat did arrive at the hotel within the next few days.

McKinley, a man of wit, imagination and integrity, recently told me he doesn't recall too clearly just what did happen that night. "I do know the general in question was General Spatz, who, as you know, was a big wheel. But I also know that a lot of booze was flowing that night, so I might have said some things I wouldn't ordinarily have said. Maybe I did talk up. Or maybe Trigger is just giving me too much credit."

What McKinley and Alpert and Zarchy and others whom I have interviewed all do agree upon is that Glenn had done such a magnificent job in organizing and routining the band and its activities that even without his presence everything could run very smoothly. Glenn's penchant for discipline and formulas made it possible for the band to continue to function without any

The six Miller alumni in Paris: (left to right) Trigger Alpert, Bill Conway (a member of the Modernaires who joined the group in France after months of infantry service and attempts to catch up with the outfit), Zeke Zarchy, new Commanding Officer Haynes, Jimmy Priddy and Jerry Gray.

hitches—as a unit, and as several units within a unit—for the eight months that it was to spend on the Continent.

As the group's new commanding officer, Haynes did what he could. But he was in a peculiar position. He had always been strictly an administrator, following the plans laid down for him and the group by Glenn. He had little knowledge of music, so that he could assume none of Glenn's directional leadership. Yet he remained constantly aware of the tremendous personal responsibility that he had suddenly inherited under the most trying of circumstances, and he knew that he was the primary link between the sixty-two members of the unit and the AAF headquarters upon which their future depended. Though some of the men resented his spending as much time as he did away from the band, others began to recognize the necessity for him to function as liaison between them and headquarters.

Don was faced with another difficult job—winding up Glenn's

personal affairs. Aside from the emotional wrench it presented, the task required a great deal of digging, though here again Glenn's penchant for details helped out.

Most service bands were supplied with materials requisitioned through channels. But the Miller band's music was so unique—so distinctly Glenn's—that practically everything it used, except the men's personal instruments, had been supplied by Glenn himself. Don's report to headquarters listed a huge array of personal property which the missing major had contributed to the war effort, to wit:

  2 trombones
  2 trombone cases
 62 mutes
 24 music stands
  2 music stand cases
  2 music trunks
  1 mute box
 30 music cases
 12 music hats (for the brass players)
  8 trombone stands
  1 foot locker containing Glenn's wearing apparel
  5 reams of manuscript paper
950 musical arrangements

While Haynes took over many of Glenn's administrative leadership functions, others pitched in to fill the musical void. Jerry Gray conducted the full orchestra on its radio shows and on personal appearances. McKinley continued to lead the dance band.

Norman Leyden, along with Zarchy one of the outfit's two master sergeants, also jumped into the breech. He had been top sergeant to many of us way back in Atlantic City, where he had helped whip us into shape. Then, after Glenn had begun to take a more active part in our musical and military lives, Norm had receded into the background. A tall, quiet man—and a helluva fine arranger, by the way—he gently but positively reassumed some of his leadership roles.

Paul Dudley, who had recently been appointed a warrant

officer, also blossomed. More gregarious, more accessible and more attuned to music than Haynes, he found it easier to relate to the men and their musical and personal problems. Consequently they would often turn to him for advice and confessions and even companionship, and also to intercede, if necessary, between them and Haynes.

However, except for one incident, few disciplinary problems arose. But that one incident was a dilly!

Head of the USO in the European Theater of Operations was Will Roland, formerly Benny Goodman's manager and before then leader of his own dance band in Pittsburgh. Some of the men had known him back in the States, and, even though he now had become an important person in France, he still related to them on the same friendly basis as before.

Bernie Privin's wife, Ethel, had been Will's secretary back in the States when Bernie had been playing in the Goodman band. So one day, as Privin relates it, "Will told me he was going back to America for a few days and said that if I wanted to get a note to Ethel, he'd deliver it for me. So I wrote something very innocuous and gave it to him. I told some of the other rebels, like Mel Powell and Peanuts Hucko and Junior Collins and Joe Shulman, and so they decided to write letters and give them to Will to mail when he got back to America. This way they could say what they wanted to without passing through the censors."

The plan would have worked neatly if Will, before boarding the plane, hadn't been asked to declare what he had with him. He surrendered the letters, some of which apparently had some unpleasant things to say about Haynes. In addition, Hucko had written to his wife, "The code is working," referring to some sort of system whereby he had been able to get censorable material through to her.

Naturally, when Haynes heard about this through official channels, he was forced to take some action. He summoned the men and gave them their choices of court-martials or demotions in rank. All chose the latter. But the situation, not of Haynes' choosing, and which would have been handled, I suspect, exactly the same way by Glenn, created a schism between Don and some members of the band that was never fully breached.

Except for the intense cold, not only in many of the large halls in which they played but also in their hotel, the guys didn't fare too badly in Paris. They did work terribly hard and seldom had a day off, but the pressures were never as intense as they had been in England, and, of course, when V-E Day arrived on May 8, the entire atmosphere became more relaxed.

Just before then, the band had enjoyed its first vacation—five days in Nice and Cannes on the French Riviera—the only such period of complete freedom during all those fourteen months away from home.

In mid-May the orchestra played at a memorable luncheon in Bad Wildungen, Germany, where top American officers, headed by General Omar Bradley, hosted a large contingent of Russian officers, headed by Marshal Ivan Stepanovich Koniev. The impact of the band upon the Russians was tremendous, though Haynes had been warned that it shouldn't play its famed version of "Volga Boatmen" for fear of creating an international incident!

The whole latter part of June was also spent in Germany, culminating on July 1—the one-year anniversary of the band's start of activities in England—in a magnificent concert before 40,000 Allied troops in the famous Nuremberg Stadium, the same stadium in which Hitler, who had labeled jazz a decadent form of music, had so many times exhorted his rabid followers into hysterical anti-American outbursts.

More concerts throughout July, culminating in a spectacular appearance before more than 10,000 SHAEF personnel who had come to pay their respects to the band. The group was presented with a beautiful plaque, and Haynes was awarded the Bronze Star for its contributions.

And what tremendous contributions they were, too! In just a little over a year, the band had entertained servicemen overseas via more than 800 separate musical activities. That came to a bit over two per day! Included in this grand total were approximately 500 radio broadcasts—some live and some transcribed—that reached millions of our troops. In addition, the bandsmen performed in person more than 300 times—at concerts, at dances, and in hospitals—to a total attendance of more than 600,000 men! No civilian band has ever even remotely approached such astounding statistics.

19 May, 1945.

Dear Sergeant McKinley,

Although Marshal Koniev called it jazz rather than swing, he was as delighted as the rest of us in the grand performance of your band during our reception on May 17. While beating time to your West Point football song arrangement, we also took a great American pride in the distinctiveness of your music.

Will you thank the members of your band and tell them how pleased we were to have them with us and how grateful we are for their good works among our troops.

Sincerely,

O. N. BRADLEY,
General, U. S. Army.

Sergeant Ray McKinley,
    Care of Special Service Section,
        Headquarters ETOUSA,
            APO 887, U. S. Army.

Most of the men figured that with the war in Europe concluded, they would be going home, there to be discharged. But rumors kept filtering through that, though the band would return to the States, it might stay there for just a short while. Then it might be reshipped to the Pacific to repeat its morale-building job for the troops in that part of the world.

Before July ended, orders for the return to the States did appear. After the usual deprocessing routine, spread over several days, the men finally embarked from Le Havre on the S.S. *Santa Rosa.* Feelings were mixed. Certainly, getting home for a while would be a ball. But that trip to the Pacific . . . !

Then, on August 7, over the ship's p.a. system, came the news that the atom bomb had been dropped on Hiroshima. The next day came further news: Russia had declared war on Japan. The chances for an end to hostilities in the Orient before the band could be redeployed suddenly looked very bright.

And they looked even brighter when on August 11 the p.a. system announced that Japan's unconditional surrender seemed imminent. On August 12 the band landed in New York. Fifteen days later Japan did surrender.

The band was greeted upon its arrival with tenders and harbor boats blowing their horns, plus a bunch of signs like "Welcome Home, Glenn Miller AAF Band" and "Well Done!" and various other enthusiastic greetings—and, of course, by their wives, girl friends, parents, brothers, and sisters, plus a host of other loving admirers.

Still uncertain of their military futures, the guys were assigned and transported to nearby Camp Shanks. "I was there at the camp to greet the band when it arrived," recalls singer Marion Hutton, "and I sang with them that night. It was so tremendous —and so moving—even to the rest of the G.I.'s. There weren't many dry eyes. The feeling just kept growing and growing. It was almost like electricity—and we were all plugged in together. Joe Louis was there, and when I had finished, he lifted me up and carried me across the mud—and they were all singing—and so was I!"

The band was almost immediately given a thirty-day furlough.

TOP: New York arrival. Missing, one leader and one *n* of his name.

BOTTOM: A joyous, disembarking Ray McKinley gets blasted by Broderick Crawford.

A few men received their discharges, but after their furlough, those remaining reassembled and broadcast several *I Sustain the Wings* programs on Saturday nights over NBC—exactly like the ones they had been playing two years earlier, only this time without their leader.

The final personal appearance of the Glenn Miller Army Air Forces Band took place at the National Press Club in Washington, D.C., before a distinguished gathering headed by President Harry S. Truman and Generals Dwight D. Eisenhower and "Hap" Arnold. Singer Joy Hodges and comedians Joe E. Lewis and Eddie Cantor also performed that evening. But the star, closing spot was reserved for the Miller band.

It was an important event for all the men, though none knew why until the very close of the evening. Then, after the band had finished playing, General Eisenhower went over to talk with the musicians. He thanked them for the tremendous job they had done overseas. The guys appreciated those words, but not nearly so much as those that immediately followed: ". . . and now, gentlemen, that you are getting out of the army. . . . "!

It was the first official announcement that all the guys were being released—that any plans for shipment to Japan were out. And what could be more official than coming directly from the lips of their top general!

But it took the commander-in-chief of *all* the armed forces, the president of the United States, to supply the most significant and memorable moment of the evening. It had been presaged by a very warm and emotional speech from Eddie Cantor. The exact words of his introduction of the Glenn Miller band have not been preserved, but they have been paraphrased for me by some of those who were there as follows:

Glenn Miller was a very wonderful man who led a very wonderful band. As a civilian, he led an orchestra that for three and a half years was the Number-One band in America.

Now, Glenn could have stayed here in America. He could have stayed and made himself a lot more money, and then, if he had wanted to, he could have retired, an independently wealthy man.

Generals Dwight D. Eisenhower and "Hap" Arnold express their thanks for a job-well-done.

But he chose not to. He was an extremely patriotic man, and he felt an intense obligation to serve his country that had gone to war. So he disbanded his great orchestra, and he formed an even greater one. Still, he could have remained here in America. But again he chose not to.

Instead, he chose to take himself and his orchestra overseas, to where he felt he could do the most good for our fighting men. And what a tremendous morale-building job he and his men did over there!

And now this great band is back here with us this evening— but without its most important member, Major Glenn Miller himself. For, as we know all too well, he made the supreme sacrifice for his country.

But he will never be forgotten, for always we will have the

CODA

Not only President Truman and Generals Eisenhower and Arnold remembered Glenn Miller after he was lost. Millions of other Americans did and still do.

On June 6, 1945, less than six months after Glenn had disappeared, theaters throughout the land honored him via a series of special, star-studded, war-bond-selling evenings. At New York's Paramount Theatre, where Glenn had planned to play after his return from the war, Miller enthusiasts and fellow-enter-tainers responded with an extraordinary show of music and war-bond sales. Milton Berle emceed. The bands of Count Basie, Benny Goodman, Louis Prima, Charlie Spivak and Fred Waring played. Eddie Cantor, Perry Como, Morton Downey and Kate Smith sang. But the most moving moments during the long evening that raised a fantastic total of $4,775,000 in war bonds (what a tribute to Glenn!) came when two of his own singers, Marion Hutton and Tex Beneke, appeared on stage and reprised some of the tunes they'd sung so often with Glenn.

The Miller sounds continued—on radio, on records, and in person. For a while NBC reactivated the *I Sustain the Wings* radio series with Jerry Gray conducting a large contingent composed mostly of Miller AAF and civilian band alumni. But the public began clamoring for the band to appear in person. So Don Haynes and Helen Miller and David Mackay decided to do

431

what they figured Glenn would have done: to continue the band on a permanent basis.

Gray was a good conductor. But for personal appearances, the band needed a more colorful front-man. The logical choice was Ray McKinley, but he wasn't interested. Months earlier, back in England, Glenn and Ray had been discussing postwar innovations. "He told me," Ray recently stated, "that he felt he had gone as far as he could with the reed sound and asked me for some suggestions. I kept thinking and wound up with what I thought were some pretty good ideas. On the way back on the boat, Don had asked me if I would be interested in leading the band when we got back—that maybe he could work things out. But when I told him some of the ideas I had in mind for changing the style, I guess I scared him away."

Meanwhile, Tex Beneke, long a personal favorite of Glenn's, Helen's, Don's, Polly's and just about everyone ever connected with the Miller band, had received his naval discharge. Certainly, no sideman was more closely identified with the Miller civilian band than Tex. So Don contacted him, and soon consummated a deal: Tex would lead the band and Don would run the business.

Helen Miller remained discreetly in the background. One of her few appearances took place in February of 1945, when Glenn was awarded, posthumously, the Bronze Star.

She asked me to stand with her that afternoon in the Miller band office on West Fifty-seventh Street. There, in one of the most simple ceremonies on record, she accepted the award from Colonel F. R. Kerr, who read this citation:

> For meritorious service in connection with military operations as Commander of the Army Air Force Band (Special), from 9 July 1944 to 15 December 1944. Major Miller, through excellent judgment and professional skill, conspicuously blended the abilities of the outstanding musicians, comprising the group, into a harmonious orchestra whose noteworthy contribution to the morale of the armed forces has been little less than sensational. Major Miller constantly sought to increase the services rendered by his organization, and it was through him that the band was ordered to give this excellent

Helen holds Glenn's Bronze Star after having received it from General F. R. Kerr (second from left). Others (left to right) are Lieutenant Colonel Howard C. Bronson, Polly Haynes, Tom Sheils, Major John Shubert and Sergeant George T. Simon.

entertainment to as many troops as possible. His superior accomplishments are highly commendable and reflect the highest credit upon himself and the armed forces of the United States.

It was a most moving, though brief, ceremony. Helen—stoical, kind, warm and gracious as ever—accepted the award, believing then, as she did for a long time thereafter, and as Colonel Kerr tried to reassure her then and there, that her husband would come back some day to accept the award himself.

For the remaining twenty years of her life, Glenn's widow lived quietly on the West Coast, seldom appearing in public. She sold the big, fifty-five-acre ranch and bought herself a small but comfortable home in a built-up neighborhood in San Marino,

California, where she devoted almost all her time to raising her two children.

I had the good fortune of seeing her once more in the early sixties during a trip to the West Coast. I phoned her from my hotel, knowing that she cherished privacy and wondering whether she'd want to see me. Her warm greeting dispelled my doubts. "When can you come out?" she asked. And so it was that we did spend one final evening together, one of the nicest, most relaxed, warmest times I have ever spent with anyone.

I had heard that she was still hoping for the miracle of Glenn's return. But she never mentioned it. For her, the old band was now relegated to the past. Her current thoughts and plans centered almost exclusively around her two children.

Years later, in mid-1973, seven years after Helen's death from a blood clot, I was to meet those two "children," both, of course, by now thoroughly grown-up. They held extremely fond memories of their mother. But neither held any memories at all of their father. Steve hadn't seen him since early infancy; Jonnie had never seen him at all.

Both have led their own private lives, far removed from the operation of the current Miller band. This they have turned over to David Mackay, the soft-spoken, self-effacing, superbly efficient executor of the estate, who, in addition to his role as financial and often personal confidant, serves as trustee for Steve and Jonnie.

Steve, who has become quite adept as a gunsmith, worked for several years as a policeman, then turned to selling and servicing firearms. Father of two children by his first wife, and since remarried, he lives in southern California. A very reserved man of thirty, he reminded me at the start of our dinner-meeting of the way his father would react to inquiring strangers. His responses to my questions were direct but curt, and for a time almost chilly. Gradually, though, after we had been talking for a couple of hours, that typical Glenn Miller reserved warmth began to seep through.

He had never had any show-business ambitions, he told me. "Mother always insisted that I not go into the entertainment field. She used to say, 'It's no way to live a life.'" Helen Miller's

Steve (at right) with wife Lona and Gil Rodin, who almost half a century earlier had brought Steve's father into the Ben Pollack band.

deep and admirable concern for her children's welfare may have been overprotective. "She was very strict with us. For years she wouldn't let Jonnie wear any make-up."

Jonnie has emerged as a reticent but charming young lady, seemingly full of love. She admits to being bothered by never having known her father, and by not ever even having been seen by him.

"I was the child my father never returned to see," she once wrote me. "But he knew of my existence, and he chose my name." When I met her, she was expecting her second child (her second son arrived in September 1973) and living in a suburb of Los Angeles next to neighbors who hadn't the slightest clue that she was the daughter of such a famous man. "It's better that way," she told me. "Now we can just be ourselves."

She remembered her mother as "an inspiration. She had a quiet kind of strength, not the kind which need tell you outright how to carry on, but that exemplified a subtle kind of courage and fortitude. . . . She was the type of person who always thought first of other people and their feelings."

We discussed her father, too. Here I did just about all the

Jonnie with her older boy.

talking. She seemed tremendously appreciative that someone who had known him so well was telling her first-hand what he was like, and eventually she responded by opening a trunk from which she drew hundreds of photos and other memorabilia which we perused together, some of which appear in this book. And when I told her that I recognized some of her mother's qualities in her, her often-sad face just beamed.

Steve also wanted to hear about his father. So I invited Gil Rodin, who had originally brought Glenn into the Ben Pollack band and had remained his friend forever after, to join Steve, his wife, Lona, and me. Together Gil and I told Steve what we knew. "What I'm very anxious to do," he kept saying, "is to establish some sort of a repository where we can gather everything about Dad. A couple of universities have already called me about doing just that."

He also filled us in a little more about his mother. The story we had heard—that she kept Glenn's bed made for many years—was, he said, true. "I have accepted the fact that he is dead," she used to tell Steve, "but I can't let go of the feeling that one of these days he may come walking in that door."

Helen had never revealed her sublimated hopes during that evening in the early sixties that we spent together. She had the perfect setting, too: The television set near us was showing a weird, science-fiction play about a plane that had crashed in the African desert and with the spirits of some of its occupants still living twenty years later. But she never referred to the eerie coincidence, and, of course, neither did I.

On January 17, 1946, "The Glenn Miller Orchestra under the direction of Tex Beneke," stocked with a cast of close to forty musicians and singers, approximately two-thirds AAF band alumni, debuted at New York's Capitol Theatre. But Haynes, who handled the band's business affairs, soon discovered that not many places could afford to pay for so many musicians, and so the dozen strings were dropped. The personnel kept changing (Henry Mancini played piano and arranged for a long time) because some of the ex-soldiers kept deciding they'd rather stay at home, others got bored playing the same old tunes over and over again, and still others didn't like the way the band was being run.

Moe Purtill, the band's civilian drummer who had returned, recalls that the atmosphere was pretty G.I. "One night Haynes called a meeting after the last show at the Capitol Theatre in New York. It meant that I'd have to miss my last train home to Huntington out on Long Island, so I asked Don if the meeting

Tex leads the Miller band.

was that important. He told me 'Yes.' And do you know why he called the meeting? Because all of us were supposed to wear our service discharge buttons and a few of the guys hadn't been doing it. So I asked Don, 'How does it sound? Does it sound better with the discharge buttons?' Soon after that I quit."

Haynes and Beneke didn't get along too well, either. Tex, goaded on by his wife, Marguerite, who seemed to resent her husband's working merely as an employee of the Glenn Miller Estate rather than as a leader of his own band, kept wanting him to establish his own identity. Larry Bruff, who had worked so closely with the band on its Chesterfield broadcasts, points out that "Beneke would even set wrong tempos so as not to sound too much like Glenn."

Arrangers Norm Leyden and Perry Burgett, out of the Miller AAF band, as well as Tex, wanted to modernize the band's style somewhat. "Glenn never would have stood still," Tex kept arguing. And, referring especially to Haynes and Eli Oberstein, the highly commercial recording chief who had returned to RCA Victor, the harnessed progressives complained, "They all scream that we have to stick to the old Miller style. Even the ballroom operators kick if we don't have the trumpets playing 'boo-wah, boo-wah' all the time. They keep reminding us that we've got to make money and that we can't afford to try to be progressive or anything like that and that there are too many people in our organization for us to take chances."

The identity battle lasted a couple of years, during which the billing of the band changed from the original "Glenn Miller Orchestra under the direction of Tex Beneke" to "Tex Beneke and the Glenn Miller Orchestra" to "Tex Beneke and his Music in the Miller Manner" and finally simply to "Tex Beneke and his Orchestra."

Haynes, with additional support from Helen Miller and David Mackay, continued to fight even harder for retention of the Miller musical style. Tex grew even more adamant. The final showdown just could not be averted.

It occurred in December of 1950. Mackay, acting on behalf of Helen Miller, who still owned the library, reports that he drove with Haynes to Groton, Connecticut, where the band was playing a one-nighter. "I walked into the dressing room and told Tex I had come to collect the library. Apparently he was expecting me, because he simply asked when I wanted it, and when I told him, 'Right now!' he let me take it. I picked up what I figured was the bulk of the library, but since I wasn't a musician, I really didn't know exactly what to look for.

"But Tex had gotten wind of what was up, and he later admitted that he had already had most of the important parts recopied, so that he still could play some of the Miller music."

Other bands were playing a lot of the Miller music during 1950—which was one reason why Haynes had kept after Beneke to concentrate even more on Glenn's sound. In fact, a whole Miller boom burst at that time, instigated by the current success of Ralph Flanagan's band, created in, and for a long time limited to, the studios of RCA Victor Records.

The success of Flanagan had infuriated Haynes, who couldn't understand why the company would permit such a counterfeit group to compete on the same label with the genuine article. Head of recording for Victor at the time was an astute, imaginative entrepreneur named Herb Hendler, who had once issued "A Salute to Glenn Miller" on his defunct Cosmo Records label. The album had sold well, and so, when Hendler took over

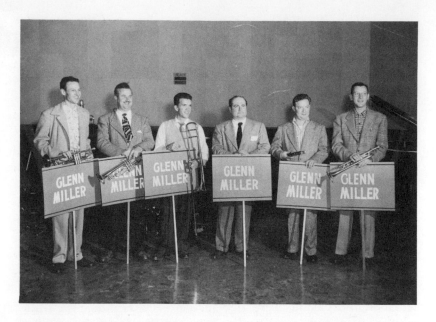

Five Miller alumni joined Jerry Gray in the fifties to re-create the Miller sounds. Left to right: Mickey McMickle, Johnny Best, Jimmy Priddy, Jerry Gray, Willie Schwartz, Zeke Zarchy.

at Victor, he contacted Flanagan, who had conducted the Cosmo album, and asked· him to create some more Miller sounds for Victor. (Eventually, Hendler left Victor to become Flanagan's partner.)

A highly believable though never officially confirmed report indicates that some of the executives at Victor thought the new band had close Miller ties. "After all, wasn't Ralph Flanagan one of Glenn's most important arrangers?" He wasn't, of course. He had never written a note for the band. But Bill Finegan— whose name could be, and apparently was, easily confused with Flanagan's—had. Only, Bill had nothing at all to do with the new band. Years later he recalled a phone call from Flanagan. "He asked me certain things about the Miller voicings and I told him what I knew." What he didn't know was what Ralph would eventually be doing with the information.

The sudden success of Flanagan's records spurred Miller alumni into action. Beneke once again began emphasizing Glenn's original sounds. Ray Anthony switched from his semi–

jazz-band style to the clarinet-led reeds and the ooh-wah brass sounds. And in the Hollywood studios, where he had been conducting a regular radio show, Jerry Gray assembled the best-sounding of all the Miller-styled bands, staffed by a number of Glenn's alumni and featuring Willie Schwartz's unique lead clarinet.

Much of the public loved the Miller revival sounds. But some questioned the morality of cashing in on the creativity of a dead man. I recall one evening sitting in the New Yorker Hotel with Teddy Powell, one of the most thoroughly dedicated if not the most literate of band leaders. His band was not doing especially well, but the thought of trying to jump on the Miller bandwagon just to make some extra bucks repelled him. "If Glenn Miller were alive today," he insisted, "he'd be turning over in his grave!" And he was undoubtedly correct.

Good as the bands were, none could quite duplicate the Miller sound and mood. According to Johnny Desmond, who heard all the imitators, "What all of them never found was Glenn's use of dynamics. I can still hear him shouting at his musicians, 'Observe the markings! Observe the markings!' "

The renewed interest in the Glenn Miller sound naturally attracted the moguls of the entertainment field. Though the popularity of the imitative bands decreased after a couple of years, they had sparked a renewed interest in the genuine article.

RCA Victor responded in October 1953 with the release of a sleek, deluxe, five-record album containing many of Glenn's original recordings, interspersed with numerous never-before-re-leased selections taken from his radio programs. And Mackay got Universal Pictures into the act with *The Glenn Miller Story*, a part-factual, part-fictional biography starring Jimmy Stewart and June Allyson and highlighting some superbly played and recorded samples of the band's biggest hits. Even though Glenn's mother insisted that Stewart "wasn't as good-looking as my son," and the picture contained numerous inaccuracies, it was ex-tremely well received. It has turned out to be easily the most popular of all big-band movies and a long-running staple on late afternoon and late night television shows.

The successes of the big album and the big picture spurred the

ABOVE: Jimmy Stewart, Universal Pictures' "Glenn Miller."

BELOW: Real music makers join Stewart on the lot. Back row (left to right): Ben Pollack, Gene Krupa, Louis Armstrong, Stewart, Joe Yukl, who played while Stewart posed, pianist Marty Napoleon. In front: trombonist Trummy Young, drummer Cosy Cole, clarinetist Barney Bigard, bassist Arvell Shaw.

June Allyson and Stewart, who hands Stevie Miller his trombone mouthpiece as Jonnie and Helen look on.

release of more and more Miller records, including two additional mammoth collections by Victor, one composed entirely of the civilian band's air shots, the other a collection of the AAF band's magnificent performances, taken from rehearsals and actual broadcasts of the *I Sustain the Wings* series.

When, by 1956, the Miller interest still hadn't abated, Mackay decided it was about time to reorganize the official Glenn Miller Orchestra for personal appearances. "I called Helen and said, 'Let's get the band together again.' And all she said was, 'How much trouble do you want in one lifetime?' " But Mackay prevailed.

By this time, Ray McKinley had seemingly completed his own big-band-leading career. He had fronted one of the most musical outfits ever assembled. But he hadn't made much money with it. Haynes had departed from the Miller scene, after disagreements with Mackay and Helen, and so Mackay contacted Willard Alexander, the veteran booker who had helped launch the bands of Benny Goodman, Count Basie, Vaughn Monroe, and others, and who had remained dedicated to the big bands. Willard had

The Miller band in the late fifties. McKinley is second from right, down front.
Standing at far left is David Mackay, executor of the Miller Estate.

also handled McKinley, and when he suggested Ray as the new
leader, Mackay relayed the idea to Helen. She loved it. She had
known Ray all the way back from the Dorsey Brothers days, and,
like so many others close to him, admired his imagination,
intelligence, integrity, and, of course, his musicianship.

So Glenn's complete music library came out of storage, and on
April 6, 1956, McKinley and the revived Glenn Miller Orchestra
played their first engagement. The band has been working
steadily ever since then. Mac remained at its helm for three
months less than ten years, during which the band toured not
only the United States but also many European countries and
even Japan. And when Ray packed it in after all those years of
traveling to return to his family, Buddy DeFranco, one of the
world's greatest jazz clarinetists, took over.

The thinking of some of us who backed the choice of DeFranco
was that a clarinetist, leading both the reed section and the full
orchestra, was a natural. "But I never had the right sound to lead
the reeds," he recently told me. And so he has featured himself as
a jazz-clarinet soloist only and never as leader of the reed section.

With musical tastes changing and new songs never associated
with the Miller music becoming hits, Buddy faced a dilemma.

Leader De Franco with the Miller band during its 1973 gig in New York's St. Regis Hotel. Peanuts Hucko has since replaced Buddy.

Like many who knew Glenn well, DeFranco realized that musically Miller would never have stood still. And so now and then he struck out in new directions, not merely extending the Miller style to current songs, many of them arranged by Bill Finegan, but also using new voicings and modern rhythms that bear little resemblance to the familiar Miller sounds.

Some of his listeners, notably musicians, and especially some in his band, have appreciated his desire and efforts to get out of what they look down on as a musical rut. But they have not been nearly as vociferous in their opinions as the dyed-in-the-wool Miller band fans, many of whom, even at this late date, will brook nothing except the original sound.

DeFranco reports that no matter where the band is playing—even as far away as Japan—he is inundated by constant requests for the big Miller hits. "In the Mood" heads the list, followed in order by "Little Brown Jug," revived by its prominence in *The Glenn Miller Story;* "String of Pearls," and "Serenade in Blue." But Buddy also gets some unusual requests. "Many of today's kids in the high school and college age brackets have taken a real interest in the Miller music and some have even researched it. And instead of asking for all the obvious tunes, they'll request some that most people don't even remember—like 'Boulder Buff,' for example."

DeFranco is constantly surprised and amazed by the number of people who tell him "confidentially" what really happened to Glenn. "If I were to believe all those stories, there would have been about twelve thousand four hundred and fifty-eight people there at the field in England seeing him off on that last flight!"

The fanaticism of the Glenn Miller stalwarts sometimes extends beyond anything resembling reality or logic. One of the leaders of several Miller fan clubs recently bombarded me with a whole series of claims that he truly seemed to believe. Among them: (1) "When Glenn died, the whole industry fell apart. He was the pace-setter; he was the whole big-band industry"; (2) "They were going to change the name of Twentieth Century-Fox movie company to 'Twentieth Century-Miller' "; (3) "The Miller band's broadcasts into Germany were breaking down the Morale Structure of the Hitler regime. Miller was one of the main reasons for the downfall of Germany!"

Much more in touch with reality have been the members of the Glenn Miller Society, which headquarters in England. Founded in 1950, it has about a thousand active members, many of whom meet regularly to play records and tapes, look at photos, and talk about their long-lost leader and the members of his band. They publish a well-written monthly newsletter, complete with interesting photos, that keeps members *au courant* of the band's activities and also digs up interesting historical data.

When my wife and I were in England in the spring of 1973, Doug LeVicki and Roland Taylor, two of the society's leaders, drove us to Bedford. It turned out to be quite a moving trip, especially when we sped in a car down the very runway from which Glenn had taken off on his final flight.

The attention to minutiae has been exemplified by a lengthy series contributed by an American, Al Timpson, that traces the complete history of the band via reports taken from the April 7, 1937, through the December 20, 1950, issues of *Variety*. Timpson is one of several dedicated Millerians with a fantastic collection of photos and information about Glenn. Another is a Canadian, Warren Reid, who specializes in early Miller and has an amazing array of pictures of that era. A third is another American, Ed Polic, who focuses on the Miller civilian band at its height and also upon the AAF outfit. All three are extremely knowledgeable and sane; they are also very kind gentlemen, anxious to share their lore with all interested parties, who extended me some mammoth cooperation in the preparation of this book.

But the most exhaustive report of the original band's activities appears in a 554-page discography that lists each of the civilian band's appearances, recordings, and broadcasts, complete with the names of participants. Prepared by John Flower of Toronto, with notable assistance from Polic, and published by Arlington House, *Moonlight Serenade* reflects better than anything I have ever come across the deep dedication of the true Glenn Miller devotee.

And the normal rate of human attrition apparently hasn't significantly depleted the ranks of those millions of Miller fans. As Buddy DeFranco pointed out, members of today's younger generation are replacing those who have departed. And they pop up all over the world, wherever the authorized Miller band happens to be booked. "We work forty-eight weeks out of every year," reports David Mackay. "And we could work fifty-two, but the guys need a few weeks off just to replenish themselves."

In January 1974, Peanuts Hucko, clarinet star of the AAF band, became leader of the official Glenn Miller orchestra. Travel-weary DeFranco returned to the jazz scene.

Live Miller music isn't restricted to the "Official Glenn Miller Orchestra," as Mackay has tabbed the band. Music played in the Miller manner has been performed throughout the United States by Tex Beneke and a smaller unit, and by Ray Eberle and a group called the Modernaires, that contains none of the original members. But far and away the most musically impressive of the imitative outfits has been Syd Lawrence's Orchestra in England, whose leader has freely admitted copying the most famous Miller arrangements. The band's precision and sound are remarkably close to those of the original, and many of its concerts

How they look today: (upper left) Ray Eberle; (upper right) Marion Hutton;
(lower left) Tex Beneke and Paul Tanner.

How they look today: (upper left) Jimmy Priddy with granddaughter, Shanyan, and one of two of Glenn's trombones given to Priddy; (upper right) Trigger Alpert; (below) on a recording date, left to right: Tex Beneke, Rolly Bundock, Billy May, Willie Schwartz, Johnny Best.

are sellouts. In November 1969, for example, all tickets for the 3,200 seats in London's Royal Festival Hall were sold within twenty-four hours. Cecil Madden attended a Lawrence band concert in November of 1972. "The whole hall was packed. But," he noted wistfully, "of all the people in the place, I was the only one who really knew Glenn."

But in terms of reaching people, nothing can compare in authenticity and in the number of ears reached with the sounds coming out of the grooves of the reissues of the original band's recordings. RCA Records still retains a goodly number of albums in its catalog, many more than those by any other name band.

To meet the combined demands for the original Miller music, as well as for modern stereo sound reproduction, the official Miller band, under DeFranco, recently recorded thirty tunes featuring many alumni, including Ray Eberle, Bobby Hackett and a slew of the original civilian-band sidemen, plus Ray McKinley and Johnny Desmond of the AAF band.

It was Desmond who was called upon to deliver the sales pitch on a series of television commercials for these recordings. One evening, while editing the final pages of this book, I happened to catch one of those commercials. There was Johnny, suave and debonair, extolling the virtues of the Miller band that was supposed to be relegated to the background. But the more I listened, the less I heard Johnny's voice and the more the Miller sound seemed to emerge into the foreground. My initial reaction was that the sound mixer had really goofed. And then I began to wonder—had he really, or was this the way it was supposed to be? And the more I thought about it, the more I began to realize that the cause really didn't matter. What did matter was the effect. And perhaps the effect was justified after all. For here I was, not listening so much to one member of the Miller organization, but rather hearing once again the rich, full sonorities of the entire Miller sound itself!

. . . Which, I realized once again, is precisely the way Glenn always wanted it to be.

RECORDINGS
BY GLENN MILLER
AND HIS ORCHESTRAS

For those readers who'd like to hear what they have been reading about, there are many long-playing recordings by Glenn Miller and his orchestras available. Most appear on the RCA Victor and RCA Camden labels.

Most come from his studio recording sessions and from Chesterfield and on-location broadcasts. The former usually have better recorded sound, but the latter often reveal more of the band's spirit.

For the uninitiated, I would recommend a couple of two-record sets as starters. To hear what the civilian band sounded like, listen to *Glenn Miller—A Memorial (1944–1969)*, which contains just about every one of his big hits among its thirty selections. And to get an idea of how great his AAF band was, listen to *This Is Glenn Miller and the Army Air Force Band*, the only available collection, unfortunately, of the splendid aggregation's music, taken from a previously issued, limited-edition, five-record set, *Glenn Miller Army Air Force Band* (LPT-6702), which is truly worth looking everywhere for.

RCA Victor also had previously issued two other five-record sets. Both are titled *Glenn Miller and His Orchestra*, and both also claim to be limited editions. Neither contains the most famous Miller selections, but each will give you a broad sampling of how the Miller band sounded on its radio broadcasts—if you can find copies of them, that is!

By far the best recorded of the civilian band's performances appear on the sound-track recordings from *Sun Valley Serenade* and *Orchestra Wives*, issued by 20th Century Records and also available on the Reader's Digest's six-record set, *The Unforgettable Glenn Miller*.

Speaking of good sound, Columbia House, a division of Columbia

Records, recently issued three records, a two-record set called *The Best of the Glenn Miller Orchestra* and a single record titled *The Voices of Glenn Miller.* Though not by the original Miller band, they do feature some of its stars and sidemen along with the official band of 1972 vintage conducted by Buddy DeFranco.

The postwar band, under the various directions of Tex Beneke, Ray McKinley and De Franco, recorded for different labels—RCA, Epic, ABC-Command, in addition to Columbia House—and though the sides contain elements of interest, they can hardly be considered as Glenn's own performances.

You can also find one or more authentic Miller band selections among various big-band anthologies released by RCA Records, Reader's Digest and Columbia Records (for some of the early Brunswick dates) and on England's Ace of Hearts label and the Longines Symphonette Recordings (for some of those initial Decca sides).

As of early 1974, the following albums by Glenn Miller and His Orchestra were listed as being available:

Glenn Miller—A Memorial (1944–1969) (RCA Victor, VPM-6019)
Moonlight Serenade; Sunrise Serenade; Little Brown Jug; To You; Stairway to the Stars; In the Mood; My Prayer; Johnson Rag; Indian Summer; Stardust; Tuxedo Junction; Danny Boy; Pennsylvania 6-5000; Anvil Chorus; Song of the Volga Boatmen; Perfidia; Chattanooga Choo Choo; Adios; Elmer's Tune; A String of Pearls; Moonlight Cocktail; Skylark; Don't Sit Under the Apple Tree; American Patrol; At Last; I've Got a Gal in Kalamazoo; Serenade in Blue; Juke Box Saturday Night; That Old Black Magic; St. Louis Blues March.

This Is Glenn Miller and the Army Air Force Band (RCA, VPM-6080)
Flying Home; Holiday for Strings; Sun Valley Jump; Farewell Blues; Everybody Loves My Baby; St. Louis Blues March; A Lovely Way to Spend an Evening; Anvil Chorus; I Love You; Begin the Beguine; Stardust; Tuxedo Junction; Blues in My Heart; Song of the Volga Boatmen; Stormy Weather; Juke Box Saturday Night; In the Mood; Poinciana; Mission to Moscow; Tail-End Charlie.

The Best of Glenn Miller, Vol. 1 (RCA Victor, LSP-3377)
In the Mood; Along the Santa Fe Trail; Johnson Rag; Chattanooga Choo Choo; Sunrise Serenade; Anvil Chorus; St. Louis Blues March; Don't Sit Under the Apple Tree; Tuxedo Junction; Stairway to the Stars; Juke Box Saturday Night; Song of the Volga Boatmen.

The Best of Glenn Miller, Vol. 2 (RCA Victor, LSP-3564)
Moonlight Serenade; Elmer's Tune; A String of Pearls; The Lamplighter's Serenade; Who's Sorry Now?; I've Got a Gal in Kalamazoo; Moonlight Cocktail; By the Waters of Minnetonka; Serenade in Blue; Glen Island Special; Take the "A" Train; American Patrol.

The Best of Glenn Miller, Vol. 3 (RCA, LSP-4125)
Little Brown Jug; Falling Leaves; Sliphorn Jive; A Nightingale Sang in Berkeley Square; Sweeter Than the Sweetest; Moonlight Sonata; Perfidia; Indian Summer; Say "Si Si"; Delilah; Skylark; At Last.

Glenn Miller on the Air, Vol. 1 (RCA, LSP-2767)
Slumber Song; Yes, My Darling Daughter; I Don't Want to Set the World on Fire; Song of the Bayou; A Nightingale Sang in Berkeley Square; On the Sentimental Side; Mutiny in the Nursery; The Lamp Is Low; Don't Wake Up My Heart; I'm Not Much on Looks; My Best Wishes; Moonshine over Kentucky; The Gentleman Needs a Shave; Slumber Song.

Glenn Miller on the Air, Vol. 2 (RCA, LSP-2768)
Beat Me, Daddy, Eight to the Bar; A Handful of Stars; I Know That You Know; There I Go; You've Got Me This Way; I Guess I'll Have to Dream the Rest; Back to Back; Dreamsville, Ohio; Oh, Baby; Do You Care; When Paw Was Courtin' Maw; This Time the Dream's on Me; Light's Out! Hold Me Tight!

Glenn Miller on the Air, Vol. 3 (RCA, LSP-2769)
Moonlight Serenade; Why Do I Love You; Can't Help Lovin' Dat Man; Make Believe; Ol' Man River; Papa Niccolini; The Moon Is a Silver Dollar; Don't Worry 'Bout Me; Hold Tight; The Masquerade Is Over; Our Love; Pinball Paul; Sometime; Beer Barrel Polka; Starlit Hour.

The Chesterfield Broadcasts, Vol. 1 (RCA, LSP-3873)
Chicken Reel; Blue Champagne; Poor Butterfly; The Sky Fell Down; I'm Gettin' Sentimental over You; Black and Blue; Booglie Wooglie Piggy; Something to Remember You By; Long Time No See Baby; High on a Windy Hill; Yours Is My Heart Alone; Skylark; Outside of That I Love You; Harlem Chapel Bells.

Glenn Miller Plays Selections from The Glenn Miller Story *and Other Hits* (RCA, LSP-1192)

Moonlight Serenade; American Patrol; Pennsylvania 6-5000; In the Mood; I've Got a Gal in Kalamazoo; Tuxedo Junction; St. Louis Blues; String of Pearls; Little Brown Jug; Farewell Blues; King Porter Stomp.

The Great Glenn Miller and His Orchestra (RCA Camden, CAS-751)
Juke Box Saturday Night; Moon Love; Humpty Dumpty Heart; April Played the Fiddle; That Old Black Magic; Moonlight Becomes You; The Man in the Moon; The Chestnut Tree; So Many Times; The Cowboy Serenade.

The Original Recordings by Glenn Miller and his Orchestra (RCA Camden, CAS-829)
Sunrise Serenade; My Reverie; Pagan Love Song; To You; And the Angels Sing; Elmer's Tune; Ciribiribin; Runnin' Wild; Blue Evening; Melancholy Lullaby.

"The Nearness of You" and Others (RCA Camden, CAS-2128)
The Nearness of You; April Played the Fiddle; A Nightingale Sang in Berkeley Square; Fools Rush In; Missouri Waltz; My Blue Heaven; My Melancholy Baby; Alice Blue Gown; Faithful Forever; Old Black Joe.

The One and Only Glenn Miller (RCA Camden, CAS-2267)
The Man with the Mandolin; The White Cliffs of Dover; Says Who? Says You, Says I!; Dearly Beloved; Three Little Fishes; Under Blue Canadian Skies; I'm Old-Fashioned; Starlight and Music; Good-bye, Little Darlin', Good-bye.

Sunrise Serenade (RCA Camden, CXS-9004)
Sunrise Serenade; The White Cliffs of Dover; I'm Old-Fashioned; Fools Rush In; Moonlight Becomes You; A Nightingale Sang in Berkeley Square; Dearly Beloved; To You; Moon Love; Juke Box Saturday Night; Elmer's Tune; Three Little Fishes; The Chestnut Tree; And the Angels Sing; Pagan Love Song; My Reverie; Humpty Dumpty Heart; The Man in the Moon.

String of Pearls (RCA Camden, ADL2-0168)
String of Pearls; Don't Sit Under the Apple Tree; Under a Blanket of Blue; At Last; Serenade in Blue; Chattanooga Choo Choo; Sweet Eloise; Imagination; The Lamplighter's Serenade; Johnson Rag; Bugle

Call Rag; King Porter Stomp; Little Brown Jug; Blues in the Night; American Patrol; Anvil Chorus; Five O'Clock Whistle; I Want to Be Happy.

Remember Glenn: Selections from the Sound Tracks of Sun Valley Serenade *and* Orchestra Wives (20th Century, T-904)
In the Mood; Moonlight Sonata; Serenade in Blue; Moonlight Serenade; At Last; American Patrol; I've Got a Gal in Kalamazoo; Sun Valley Jump; Chattanooga Choo Choo (long version); Bugle Call Rag; It Happened in Sun Valley; The Spirit Is Willing; People Like You and Me; I Know Why; Boom Shot; That's Sabotage; You Say the Sweetest Things, Baby; Measure for Measure.

The Unforgettable Glenn Miller (Reader's Digest, RD-4-64): Moonlight Serenade; Make-Believe Ballroom Time; Stardust; I Want to Be Happy; Stairway to the Stars; Anvil Chorus; A Handful of Stars; Farewell Blues; I Cried for You; This Changing World; Marie; Blue Skies; Five O'Clock Whistle; Yours Is My Heart Alone; Slumber Song; Ida!, Sweet as Apple Cider; Fools Rush In; St. Louis Blues March; Our Love Affair; My Blue Heaven; Alice Blue Gown; The Lady's in Love with You; Londonderry Air; Song of the Volga Boatmen; You Stepped Out of a Dream; When Johnny Comes Marching Home; Frenesi; The Story of a Starry Night; Rug Cutter's Swing; Falling Leaves; Who's Sorry Now?; Boulder Buff; Along the Santa Fe Trail; The Spirit Is Willing; Elmer's Tune; The Angels Came Through; Goodnight, Sweetheart; I'm Stepping Out with a Memory; When My Baby Smiles at Me; A Blues Serenade; It Happened in Sun Valley; In the Mood; At Last; Sun Valley Jump; I Know Why (and So Do You); Chattanooga Choo Choo; Serenade in Blue; American Patrol; Moonlight Sonata; I've Got a Gal in Kalamazoo; People Like You and Me; Bugle Call Rag; Rhapsody in Blue; Sweeter Than the Sweetest; Pavanne; Moon Love; Adios; Glen Island Special; Sunrise Serenade; Shake Down the Stars; Baby Me; The Lamplighter's Serenade; Slow Freight; Dreamsville, Ohio; Caribbean Clipper; Oh! You Crazy Moon; Booglie Wooglie Piggy; Deep Purple; Yes, My Darling Daughter; The Nearness of You; I'm Old-fashioned; I Got Rhythm; Polka Dots and Moonbeams; Crosstown; My Devotion; Limehouse Blues.

The Best of the Glenn Miller Orchestra—Featuring Bobby Hackett, Al Klink, Ray McKinley, Hank Freeman, Peanuts Hucko, Bernie Privin, Willie Schwartz with other alumni, plus the 1972 edition of the Miller

Orchestra conducted by Buddy DeFranco (Columbia House, P2S-5718)
In The Mood; Sunrise Serenade; A String of Pearls; Rhapsody In Blue; The American Patrol; Little Brown Jug; Alice Blue Gown; Tuxedo Junction; Adios; My Sentiment; St. Louis Blues March; Song of the Volga Boatmen; Everybody Loves My Baby; Pennsylvania 6-5000; Sun Valley Jump; Anvil Chorus; Caribbean Clipper; Swing Low, Sweet Chariot; Now Is the Hour; Moonlight Serenade.

The Voices of Glenn Miller—Featuring Ray Eberle, Johnny Desmond, Ray McKinley, with Dorothy Claire, Chuck Goldstein, Ralph Brewster and Gene Steck (Columbia House, DS-922)
Chattanooga Choo Choo; Moonlight Cocktail; Don't Sit Under the Apple Tree; Serenade in Blue; Along the Santa Fe Trail; Elmer's Tune; At Last; Perfidia; The Lamplighter's Serenade; I've Got a Gal in Kalamazoo.

ILLUSTRATION CREDITS

The publisher wishes to thank the following for providing illustrations: page ii, Jonnie Miller; 3, Ed Polic; 10, Bob Altshuler; 11, Roc Hillman; 12, *Metronome*; 14, *Metronome*; 15 (upper left), Harry James; 15 (upper right, below), *Metronome*; 22 (above), Alan Timpson (photo by Duncan P. Scheidt); 22 (lower left), Ed Polic; 22 (lower right), Warren Reid; 23 (upper left), Jonnie Miller; 23 (upper right), Ed Hilliard; 23 (below), Jonnie Miller; 26, Jonnie Miller; 28 (upper left, upper right), Jonnie Miller; 28 (lower right), Alan Timpson; 29, Jonnie Miller; 32, Julius Kingdom; 33 (above), Miller Estate; 33 (below), Alan Cass, University of Colorado, Julius Kingdom; 34 (above), Alan Timpson; 34 (below), Alan Timpson, John Baker; 35, 39, Jonnie Miller; 46, *Metronome*; 48, 50, 52, Jonnie Miller; 55, Miller Estate; 57, 60, Jonnie Miller; 66, Roc Hillman; 67, *Metronome*; 71, Ed Polic; 72, George T. Simon; 75, John Simon; 85, *Metronome*; 89, Jerry Jerome; 89, *Metronome* (photo by Arsene Studio); 92, 93, Jerry Jerome; 97, 101, *Metronome*; 110, John Flower Collection; 112, Miller Estate (photo by Arsene Studio); 117, *Metronome*; 122, Ed Polic; 125, *Metronome*; 126, Tex Beneke; 127, *Down Beat*; 129, *Metronome*; 136, Stan Aronson; 140, *Metronome*; 141 (above), Alan Timpson and CBS; 141 (below), Alan Timpson; 155, Alan Timpson; 158, Miller Estate (photo by Arsene Studio); 162, George T. Simon; 165, Johnny O'Leary; 167, 169, RCA Records; 173, Miller Estate; 175, *Metronome*; 176, George T. Simon; 178, Ed Polic; 181, RCA Records; 183, *Down Beat*; 185, Miller Estate (photo by Arsene Studio); 187, George T. Simon; 190, *Metronome*; 194, Polly Haynes; 196, Jonnie Miller; 198 (above), Ed Polic; 198 (below), John Flower Collection; 199, Alan Timpson; 203 (above), Miller Estate; 203 (below), 204,

George T. Simon; 207, Miller Estate; 208 (above), Miller Estate; 208 (below), *Metronome*; 212, Miller Estate; 213, Ed Polic; 216, *Down Beat*; 221, Trigger Alpert; 225, Polly Haynes; 228, John Flower Collection; 230, Miller Estate; 231, *Metronome*; 233, Miller Estate (photo by Arsene Studio); 237, Johnny O'Leary; 240, 244, Alan Timpson; 246, Miller Estate (photo by Arsene Studio); 249, Ed Polic; 251, *Metronome*; 254 (above), Alan Timpson and CBS; 254 (below), Johnny O'Leary; 255, *Metronome*; 257, Ed Polic; 259, Miller Estate; 261, John Flower Collection; 264, Jonnie Miller; 265, Miller Estate; 266, 268 (above), Ed Polic; 268 (below), John Flower Collection; 274 (above), RCA Records; 274 (below), Alan Timpson and CBS; 276, John Flower Collection; 278, Wide World Photos; 280, Polly Haynes; 282, Ed Polic; 284, Miller Estate; 285, RCA Records; 287 (above), *Metronome*; 287 (below), Ed Polic and John Flower Collection (photo by Arsene Studio); 290, Miller Estate; 293 (above), Charles Peterson; 293 (below), Johnny O'Leary; 296 (above), Jonnie Miller; 296 (middle), Ed Polic; 296 (below), Johnny O'Leary; 297, 298, Jonnie Miller; 300, Jimmy Priddy; 303, 304, Miller Estate; 305, Alan Timpson and CBS; 307, Ed Polic; 313, Miller Estate; 315, Arnold Dean; 316, Alan Timpson and RCA Records; 322, Miller Estate; 323, Polly Haynes; 325, Miller Estate; 326, RCA Records; 328, 329, Miller Estate; 333, Zinn Arthur; 335, *Down Beat*; 338, *Metronome*; 341, Alan Timpson; 345 (above), Miller Estate; 345 (below), Jonnie Miller; 350, *Metronome*; 351, 354, Miller Estate; 355, Jonnie Miller; 360, Alan Timpson; 362, Miller Estate; 363, Jonnie Miller; 365, Miller Estate; 366 (above), George T. Simon; 366 (below), Polly Haynes; 368, *Metronome*; 370 (above), Frank Ippolito; 370 (below), Polly Haynes; 372 (above), Vince Carbone; 372 (below), Zeke Zarchy; 373, Jonnie Miller; 375, Polly Haynes; 377, Miller Estate; 379 (above), John Woolnough; 379 (below), *Metronome*; 383, Polly Haynes; 385 (above), *Metronome*; 385 (below), Miller Estate; 387, *Metronome*; 390, Jonnie Miller; 391, Ted Bergmann; 393, RCA Records; 395, 397, Miller Estate; 400, RCA Records; 405, George T. Simon; 410, George T. Simon; 411, Jonnie Miller; 414, Zeke Zarchy; 419, Miller Estate; 420, Air Force Museum and Alan Timpson; 424, Ray McKinley; 426 (above), *Down Beat*; 426 (below), Ray McKinley; 428, Polly Haynes; 429, Jonnie Miller; 433, Jonnie Miller; 435, 436, George T. Simon; 438, 440, *Metronome*; 442, RCA Records; 443, Jonnie Miller; 444, *Metronome*; 445, Marvin Drager (photo by Ed Sullivan); 448 (upper left), Tom Sheils; 448 (upper right), George T. Simon; 448 (below), Tex Beneke; 449 (upper left), Jimmy Priddy; 449 (upper right), Trigger Alpert; 449 (below), Capitol Records.

INDEX